TOXICSUCCESS

How to Stop Striving and Start Thriving

TOXICSUCCESS

How to Stop Striving and Start Thriving

Getting What You *Want*
Without Losing What You *Need*

Paul Pearsall, Ph.D.

INNER
OCEAN

Inner Ocean Publishing, Inc.
P.O. Box 1239
Makawao, Maui, HI 96768-1239

Printed in Canada

Publisher Cataloging-in-Publication Data

Pearsall, Paul.

Toxic success : how to stop striving and start thriving / Paul Pearsall. -- Makawao, HI : Inner Ocean, 2004, c2002.

p. ; cm.

Originally published in hardcover: Inner Ocean, 2002.
ISBN: 1-930722-33-8 (pbk.)

1. Success. 2. Life Skills. 3. Simplicity. 4. Stress (Psychology) I. Title.

BF637.S8 P43 2004
158.1 --dc22   0405

For our son Scott, who makes my wife, Celest, and me feel like the most successful parents in the world. Our prayer is that the insensitivity of so many to those with impairments will someday end, allowing Scott and others like him to know the true joy of sweet success.

**I'm terrified that I'm going to die
without having ever really lived.**

*—38-year-old multimillionaire
diagnosed with lung cancer*

There are two kinds of success. One leaves you and those who live and work with you feeling constantly pressured, overwhelmed, and with too little time to share the enjoyment of the simple but profound things in life. The other results in feelings of shared contentment, calmness, and loving connection with all that really matters in life. This is the difference between toxic and sweet success.

It is a tragedy of our turn to live on planet paradise that millions of us are too busy, too distracted, and too self-absorbed to realize that we already have the success we are so desperately seeking.

CONTENTS

Dedication   v

Foreword   xi

Preface   xvii

Acknowledgments   xxiii

Introduction
The Most Successful Person in the World   1

PART ONE
The Causes of Toxic Success   23

Chapter One
The Curse of Success   25

Chapter Two
Coming to Your Attention   49

Chapter Three
Being Normal Can Drive You Nuts   65

Chapter Four
The Meaning of Monday   85

PART TWO
The High Cost of Success   107

Chapter Five
Overcoming Competition Obsession   109

Chapter Six
A Measure of Success   133

Chapter Seven
Too Busy to Love, Too Tired to Care   155

Chapter Eight
The Sciences of Sweet Success   177

PART THREE
Coming Back to Life:
A Detoxification Program
for the Toxically Successful   199

Chapter Nine
Secrets of Success from Paradise   201

Chapter Ten
Being Content: Knowing When Enough Is Enough   229

Chapter Eleven
Calming Down: Knowing How to Be Still   247

Chapter Twelve
Connecting Always: Remembering "And"   273

A Beginning
It's Just a Matter of Time   297

Notes   311

Glossary   329

Bibliography   337

Index   347

FOREWORD

Thriving for Success
By Matt Biondi, Olympic Gold Medalist

I was never unhappier than the moment when I finally attained the level of success I had devoted my life to achieve. I had become only the second swimmer in history to win seven medals in one olympiad. I had earned a total of eleven medals in three olympiads, and a total of eight Gold Medals overall. Yet I noticed that each time another Olympic medal was draped around my neck, a strange thought flashed through my mind: that success as I had thought of it all my life was an illusion.

The book you are about to read exposes that illusion and, if you are willing to stop striving long enough to give your full attention to it, it can save you from the futility of pursuing a life of "toxic success."

During the most intense moments of those medal ceremonies, even as I felt the weight of my Gold Medals against my chest, I feared that the director of this drama would rush in any minute to holler, "Cut! Get this kid out of here and send him home where he belongs!" I remember flashbacks of falling, scraping my chin, and running like a frightened child to be comforted by my mother. I recalled what it felt like to show my vulnerability freely rather than to appear invincible and above it all. I didn't want to be heroic—I wanted to show my ordinary needs like anyone else. I wanted to be free to share in a full and meaningful life with people I loved, to relish the feeling of being a good brother, a loving son, and someday a husband and father soothing my own children and sharing all the wonderfully ordinary chaos of life with someone who loved me not because of, but despite, my success.

In my new role as an Olympic hero my life became more complicated, confusing, and less my own. Like most people in our modern culture, I had believed that striving to achieve the highest level of personal success would change everything in my life for the better. I had sought success because, like many, I assumed it would somehow elevate me above all others, and that I would feel on top of the world. But with the success I craved came the realization that being on top of the world made me feel less a part of the real world—instead, I felt lost within it.

I had assumed that success would make me somehow immune to daily stress. In fact, my constant striving did not result in any sense of thriving. I had assumed success would give me the freedom to enjoy a life of privilege and prestige. Instead, success enslaved me, because once I seemed to have it, it ended up having me.

I now understand that with awareness of toxic success comes the realization that all the money and prestige in the world cannot buy the real life that is the ultimate base of true success. I have learned that the joy of leading an ordinary life is priceless. It cannot be bought or won. As Dr. Pearsall says, it must be attended to.

Dr. Paul Pearsall's fascinating, original, and highly important book has confirmed my own sense that success as our culture defines it has become a seductive and potentially lethal illusion, a temptation away from a truly meaningful and enjoyable life. Consumed, as I was, by striving for a result, we can lose sight of the joys that come from allowing ourselves to be immersed in the process of an ordinary life and its simple pleasures.

Make no mistake. Each time I stood on the podium with the crowd cheering, I felt the thrill of excitement and elation that come with winning. High-level success is a powerful emotional rush, and the efforts and sacrifices we make for it seem, at least for that moment, more than well worthwhile. The sign that we have been giving too much is the sense of immense relief that eventually equals or overwhelms the elation. "The thrill of victory" is much more than a catchphrase, but that emotion is only temporary and is inevitably followed by a letdown, by sadness, and sometimes by the clinical "cyclothymia" that Dr. Pearsall describes, and which he shows has become so widespread in our culture. I myself experienced how the exhilaration that comes with high-level success is soon followed by a sense of "Is that all there is?" and "Now what?" Dr. Pearsall observes that, too often, highly successful people learn that in their striving to get somewhere they have forgotten to pay attention to where they are. He rightly warns us that sweet success depends on reclaiming our attention and investing it now and intensely where our heart needs it to be, on the process of living and loving in this moment, rather than striving for the illusion of better moments in the future.

This is emphatically not a book about not trying hard, cutting back, or giving up. Dr. Pearsall emphasizes that there is nothing toxic about having high goals, trying our best, and working very hard. But he shows us the danger of assuming that the success we seek will somehow render us psychologically immune to the natural chaos of life, and that, in fact, it is our full absorption in and attention to that chaos that is the ultimate success. The toxic view of success teaches that, when we finally "arrive," we will be on easy street. Dr. Pearsall warns that none of us will ever feel that we have finally arrived, because life is a process, not a result. "Life is a journey and not a destination" may be a cliche, but I have found it to be nonetheless true. As Dr. Pearsall points out, if success happens to you because of your full joyful engagement in and attention to activities that cause you to feel content, calm, and connected even as you work hard, you will experience and share sweet success.

With my wife, Kirsten, I have found these qualities in my life. She loves me not because of what I have accomplished but because of who I am and how we are together. I met her when we trained at the UC Berkeley swimming pool. She herself was a highly skilled swimmer who understood the joy of swimming and winning. She understood, better than most, the significance and meaning of my accomplishments, but somehow those achievements were not of major consequence to her. She was interested in how I wanted to live and share my life, not the results of my life to that time. The shine of my medals never blinded Kirsten. She seemed to be able to look behind the glare directly into my heart. She saw me as I so badly needed to be seen, as an ordinary person with ordinary needs. I think it likely that it will be those like Kirsten, who love the toxically successful, who will give this book to them in hopes of getting their attention. If someone you love gave you this book, please honor that gift by reading and reflecting long and hard about its messages. Your true success depends on it.

Kirsten and I now share a sweetly successful life together with our son, Nate, on the Big Island of Hawai'i. I teach at the Parker School, where I try to help instill in my students the idea of healthy success that Dr. Pearsall describes in these pages. I could have coached swimming at a university, but I wanted to experience a different kind of success in a different arena. I wanted to help young people learn the value of leading a good life with and for others and not just how to be winners over others.

As Dr. Pearsall emphasizes, sweet or meaningful success happens not because you have accomplished something that makes you *stand out*. It happens because you have lived so that you are able to easily and happily *stand with* everyone else. It happens when the same people who applaud your extraordinary accomplishments are able to distinguish *who you are* from *what you did* and see you as one of them and not a star separate from them. It happens when you can feel totally absorbed in a family dinner without hearing whispers about the "Gold Medal winner over there." It happens when you don't have to endure the unintentional insensitivity of those who diminish and explain away your accomplishments as due to your good luck of being born to grow to six-foot-seven-inches tall and therefore only doing what comes naturally. I've learned that you feel sweetly successful when, as the subtitle of this book suggests, you feel you have finally learned to stop striving and start thriving.

Dr. Pearsall presents a detox program for the toxically successful. Unlike many self-help programs, his approach is based on the Hawaiian model of success and excellence called *po'okela*, what he calls the "oceanic" way of thinking about success. As a swimmer, I appreciate his references to "water logic" as opposed to "rock logic," and I applaud his creativity and courage in bringing this much-needed message to the world.

As Dr. Pearsall describes it, *po'okela* means excellence through shared values rather than personal objectives, and I could have used his advice when I was in the midst of my Olympic-sized toxic success. I had no "success consultant" then, and I hope corporations, schools, and any organizations concerned with healthy success will consider providing this book for those looking for a safer and more enjoyable path to success.

There have been many books about how to be successful, but this is the first book to teach us how to survive it. We rightly try to help those who do not seem to be experiencing success, but we pay less attention to helping those who are. We assume they need no further help or counseling because they seem to "have it all" and to be doing just fine on their own. Dr. Pearsall warns us that, in a society in which wealth and the other symbols of what we consider success are so unevenly distributed, we assume that those who have those things must be the happiest, be the most successful, and have what we think will make us feel successful. But this book shows us how wrong we have been. We offer an endless number of seminars on how to be successful, but few on how to survive success or love someone in the throes of its toxicity. This book suggests that high-level success can be a unique kind of failure, involving an "attention deficit disorder" that is also in need of support, counseling, guidance, and direction.

I have one reservation about Dr. Pearsall's book. I am afraid that those who need it most will not read it. They may consider themselves too busy or may feel that their own success and its pursuit are not toxic, simply realistic and necessary in a dog-eat-dog world. I am concerned that they may reject it without reading its clearly presented proof that success can be so terribly toxic, and that they will wrongly assume that it is a book about being more laid-back, relaxed, easygoing, or about seeking a balanced life. I wonder if, as consumed as they are in their striving, they will think that this book may present an unrealistic view of what it really takes to be successful. I am concerned that, because they feel they have so little attention left to pay and believe that "time is money," they will think that time spent not making money is time wasted. I assure them that they are dangerously wrong.

I have known the highest level of athletic success and what it feels like to be seen as extraordinary, and for many I was a role model of high-level success. I fear that I myself might not have been willing to read this book when I was so toxically involved in the striving phase of my life. I hope you will take the advice of someone who has known the pinnacle of "success," and that you will read this book before it is too late—and before it takes more than a book to save your marriage, your family, your health, or even your life.

Those who speak of success often urge us to "look to the stars." They usually mean to set our goals high and keep our focus on a future goal. In the spirit of the sweet success offered in these pages, I regularly experience another way of looking at the stars. Sometimes, late at night, when there is no moon to brighten the pitch-black Hawaiian sky, I look up at the infinite clusters of stars. I allow myself to pay my full attention to where, with whom, and why I am. I feel the contentment, calmness, and connection of *po'okela* and my ordinary life in paradise, the kind of life this book offers as the way to sweet and healthy success. At that moment, I feel I am not a single outstanding star but one among the billions of stars. It is at these moments that I feel thankful that I am thriving and that I have finally become successful.

After reading this book, I believe you will also know what that kind of sweet success feels like in your own life.

PREFACE

('Ōlelo ha'i mua)

Strive: 1 a: To struggle in opposition or contention: carrying on a conflict b: to contend for dominance, mastery, or superiority: conduct war; fight c: to compete as a rival;

Thrive: 1: to grow vigorously: become increasingly larger and healthier; 2: to prosper outstandingly: advance successfully; 3: to achieve growth or progress toward one's own goal.

—*Webster's Third New International Dictionary* (Unabridged)

"What's wrong with striving?" I heard this question when I was young whenever I asked my teachers why they said that hard striving was the sure path to success. I heard it again when I began my research on toxic success, and I still hear it when the *hālau* (dancers) and I present our *'aha mele* (lecture concerts) about sweet success to the strivers coming to corporate meetings in Hawai'i to celebrate their success. You might have asked this same question when you read the subtitle of this book, "How to Stop Striving and Start Thriving," but I hope when you finish your reading, you will have abandoned forever striving as a way to healthy, meaningful, shared, joyful success.

I have never been a striver. It would make a dramatic story if I claimed to be a recovering toxic succeeder converted from striving to thriving by some sudden epiphany, but I have always lived among thrivers who expected the same of me. My parents, grandparents, and my Hawaiian *'ohana* (family), though working intensely hard, have always seemed very contented, calm, attentive to the simple joys of daily living, and, most of all, profoundly connected with life and with others. Unlike striving toxic succeeders, their *attention* has always seemed to be totally their own to place where and how their hearts desired. I was raised with the idea of sweet shared success and that we work not to win, obtain, or attain but to share, grow, and become.

Webster's Third New International Dictionary defines thriving as growing vigorously, becoming healthier and happier, and flourishing despite or because of circumstances, and that has always been my family's view of the path to sweet success. I grew up in Michigan. Like most of our neighbors, we were very poor. My father and mother worked almost twenty hours a day, and financial security was never ours. Despite this, we were rich in *aloha* (love) and being at home was being at peace. I almost died at birth and have suffered many serious illnesses throughout my life. Although our family doctor told my parents I was intellectually gifted and they should seek special programs for me, finances would not allow it. I attended public schools and though my grades were high, we didn't have enough money for me to go away to a university. While working full-time as a musician in a rock band, I attended community college. I saved as much money as I could and finally managed to attend the University of Michigan. I earned my teacher's certification and taught elementary school to make money to attend graduate school. Eight years after my high-school graduation, I earned my doctorate in both clinical and educational psychology.

Immediately after earning my Ph.D., I became a neuropsychologist at Sinai Hospital. Working with very sick patients, I often saw the devastation of toxic success and the deadly toll it took on the body, mind, spirit, and family of those suffering from and usually denying it. I decided to design a clinic that offered help for toxic success syndrome (TSS). To distinguish it from the traditional pathology model of medicine, I called it the Problems of Daily Living Clinic. It was a section within the Department of Psychiatry at Sinai Hospital in Detroit, and people came as clients, not patients, from around the world to detoxify their success. The International Psychiatry Association presented the clinic with its Rush Gold Medal Award for achievements in preventive psychiatry, but we were really a place for life enhancement. While serving as director and chief of the clinic, I also taught full-time at Henry Ford Community College and was in private practice with several psychiatrists. I did extensive post-graduate training and wrote professional articles and books. When the toxically successful strivers I meet today say that I do not understand what it means to work hard to be successful or that, because I live in Hawai'i I must not appreciate the "real world of hard work," they are wrong. I have worked as hard as most, but my attention has always been mine to give to my wife, my children, my family, and my soul.

Through all my years of working very hard, my wife and I also thrived together through the tough times. We faced the challenge of raising two impaired sons who were repeatedly discriminated against in their education and personal lives. In a short time span, three of four of our parents died suddenly and unexpectedly and I was diagnosed with what was supposed to be terminal cancer. We know what hard work and stress is, but through it all, we thrived. It is my *pule* (prayer) that the following pages will show you how to give up striving for thriving.

In 1973, I was invited to address the International Psychiatric Association's meeting in Honolulu, Hawai'i. It was our first trip to Hawai'i, and we immediately connected with the people and the culture. Hawaiians I had never met snuck in to hear my talk about thriving and the dangers of the Western toxic view of success. Many of them met with me after my talk and said, "You must be Hawaiian." My family's lineage includes possible Hawaiian connections, but our records are not clear. We knew right away, however, that we had come home. We connected with the nonstriving culture of *aloha* and with hardworking people who thrived despite discrimination and adversity and the taking and using of their home by those who often disrespected it and failed to understand its sacredness. We decided then that Hawai'i was where our hearts lived.

Clinical and family responsibilities on the mainland prevented us from moving immediately to Hawai'i, but until we moved to Maui in 1987, we immersed ourselves in the Hawaiian culture. We read and learned as much as we could about *po'okela*, the Hawaiian-style success based on shared values rather than personal objectives that is presented as a success-detoxifying program in this book. It was on Maui that I met Kawaikapuokalani and his *hālau*. Kawai is a *kahuna*, a healer, and I had just been diagnosed with cancer. He and his *hālau* embraced us into their *'ohana* and assisted in my healing. Today, we teach together as *'ohana* about the wisdom of *po'okela* and other Hawaiian concepts that have important relevance to an increasingly hectic world.

Hawaiians are *mana* (spiritual energy) sensitive. Their attention is not on what you say, or have, or the status you have attained. It is on your *pu'uwai* (heart) and what you do and how you share. They are not yet numbed by the Western way of selfish striving, and they know if you are thriving your way through life with *aloha* or are distracted from life. They sense when you sincerely show humble respect for the true spirit of Hawai'i, and my family and I have committed ourselves to continuing to learn forever about the wise culture that gave birth to *po'okela* and a life of sweet success and *aloha*.

To this day, we continue to learn from our extended Hawaiian *'ohana*. This book is written by me, but it was really created by them and their ancestors. We are honored that we were taken in as part of Kawaikapuokalani's *'ohana*, an *'ohana* that grows every day with the mission of perpetuating the wise culture of Hawai'i. We take their loving acceptance as a sacred trust and a responsibility to continue to learn from them and to share their knowledge with those willing to abandon striving and start paying attention again to what matters most in life.

My Hawaiian name, *Ka'ikena*, means "person of vision." It was given to me by Tutu Mama Elizabeth Nalani Ellis, a 98-year-old Hawaiian woman whose *'ohana* we are also proud to be a part of. When she gave me my name, she said, "Like all names, with your name comes an awesome responsibility. You must continue to learn and you must share what you learn with those who wish to live with *aloha*. You must teach them to pay attention to their lives and those they love. You must teach them about a gentler, more sharing and joyful meaning of success. You must tell them before it is too late."

Now, as my parents' and grandparents' homes did, our Hawaiian home resonates with *aloha*. We are not distracted by the need for individual success. Instead, our attention is on sharing the splendor of rainbows, ocean, clouds, and the wind. We all continue to work hard. All of us work at several jobs just to make ends meet. We sing, dance, teach, suffer, complain, swim, fish, boat, laugh, eat, cry, grieve, hope, and pray together. There is no such thing as individual success for us, and there is not solo happiness, and sadness. We are always one together in all that life offers us and what we try to offer back. Our success is made sweet by our sharing of all that life

offers and by paying attention together everyday to what matters to us—
aloha for our family, our ancestors, the land, and the Higher Power who gave
us our gift of life. That, for us, is sweet success. That is *po'okela*. That is
what our lives and this book are about.

Paul Ka'ikena Pearsall, Ph.D.
Honolulu, Hawai'i
February 2002

ACKNOWLEDGMENTS

(*'Ōlelo Ho'omaika'i*)

My family is my life. They are the reason for all of my books and for me being alive. I will never be able to fully express my loving appreciation to my wife, Celest, and my sons, Roger and Scott, for the healing love that makes my life so sweetly successful. My mother, Carol, my brother, Dennis, and the memory of my father, Frank, provide continuing loving support in all that I do. My Hawaiian family, Kuhai Hālau O Kawaikapuokalani Pā 'Ōlapa Kahiko, honors me with their *aloha*, wisdom, and daily lessons in profound sharing. Kumu Kawaikapuokalani, Mapuana Ringler, Carmen Kanei, Nalani Badua, Pat Gooch, and Michelle Kaulu Amaral from the Big Island travel the world with me sharing the lessons of *po'okela*. Aunty Betty Kawohiokalani Jenkins and her husband, Jack, have taught me much about the meaning of excellence. This one, big, loving *'ohana* (family) is the inspiration for all that I do.

The scientists and researchers whose work I quote throughout this book are the behind-the-scenes heroes who provide the foundation for what I have written. There are too many of them to thank by name here, but I am particularly indebted to the pioneering work of David McClelland. His brilliant insights and careful research revolutionized psychology's understanding of the relationship between working, loving, stress, and our physical, mental, and spiritual well-being. His genius will be missed, but his work will inspire all of us forever. A special *mahalo* (thank you) to Larry Dossey, James Gleick, David Myers, Steven Bertman, Joel and Michelle Levey, Martin E. P. Seligman, and Susanne Ouellette Kobasa. Their ideas will be found throughout this book, and the credit goes to them for their originality. I hope they will all forgive any errors or misinterpretations I may have made in my eagerness to address the issue of the unhealthy pursuit of a toxic kind of success.

My very special *mahalo nui loa* (many thanks) to Inner Ocean Publishing. As you will read in this book, they had faith in me and my ideas about toxic success when so many other publishers did not. They had the sensitivity to the issue of toxic success that allowed them to publish this book, knowing that those who need it the most might reject it. We can only hope that those who love the toxically successful will give this book to them. Despite their own high levels of success, they all understood the difference between striving and thriving. *Mahalo* to Inner Ocean Publishing's *po'okela*-style publisher, John Elder, and CEO, Chip McClelland, who always models *aloha* even in the competitive business of publishing. *Mahalo* to Bill Greaves for his brilliantly creative and sensitive cover design, to the tireless John Nelson for always doing so many jobs so very well while still retaining his creativity, kindness, and humor, and to Barbara Drew for her superb copy editing of this book. *Mahalo* to all of the support staff at IOP for putting up with all of us and helping us do what we say we will do and remember what we said. And finally, a very special *mahalo* to my former agent, Hawaiian neighbor, new editor, and now lifelong friend Roger Jellinek. Without his unwavering faith in and patience with me, this book would never have seen that light of day.

Mahalo to all of you. May your lives be blessed with sweet success and *aloha*.

INTRODUCTION

The Most Successful Person in the World

Spend the afternoon. You can't take it with you.

—Annie Dillard

I met the most successful person in the world. He was sitting on the lawn under a sprawling monkeypod tree. His body was dotted with spots of bright Hawaiian sunlight filtering through the leaves, and he seemed to be swaying with the movement of the branches rustling in the gentle trade wind. He was watching his son play soccer in a special event being held on the island of Oʻahu, Hawaiʻi. Children of all ages had come to Hawaiʻi from the mainland, and while their proud parents circled the field, many of the adults seemed to be distracted from the game. Aside from a few mothers and fathers screaming at their children to try harder or at the referees for not trying hard enough, most were not watching the game at all. They were squinting to read messages that scrawled across their pagers, poking away at palm-sized computers, reading the *Wall Street Journal*, or talking into their cell phones. Some had fallen asleep. Even those who seemed to be watching the game were looking down and pacing as if mentally distracted and planning for their next obligation. Sitting with his book-sized computer on his lap and cell phone at his side, one father bragged, "Even way over here, I'm still totally connected." My wife and I laughed as we wondered if he realized the irony of his statement.

Among the crowd of distracted parents, one man stood out in his total

1

but quiet attention on his son. While some parents would occasionally stop what they were doing to urge their children to give it all they had, this man seemed to be calmly but intently giving all he had to his son. Leaning against the tree with his hands comfortably grasped around his knees to pull them to his chest, he was smiling and nodding his approval. He joked with a passing referee, laughed when his son missed the ball, and occasionally let go of his legs to give a two-thumbs sign that his son flashed back. The peaceful, joyful, almost reverent look on the man's face indicated that he was totally absorbed, not in the game but with this special moment with his son. The man had control of his own attention, and he was giving it fully to make this onetime opportunity a memory that would last his son and himself a lifetime.

The Hero of the Year

I recognized this contented and connected man from one of my presentations to a sales-incentive meeting that had been held on the neighbor island of Maui. He had been singled out at that meeting of one thousand of the company's "top performers" as "performer of the year." He had also won "the most successful man in the world" award for outearning the entire international sales force by more than a million dollars in sales.

For the combination of these accomplishments, he had been given yet another accolade, called "the hero of the year" award. That one came with the keys to a new car. With the flare and ceremony befitting a coronation, he was featured in a long testimonial. A professionally produced videotape was shown on a giant screen as the inspiring song "Eye of the Tiger" from the movie *Rocky* played loudly in the background. The tape showed him running through airports, jogging, lifting weights in the gym, golfing, gesturing to sales charts, and holding an array of various trophies hugged to his body. One short scene showed him with his family. They were all screaming as they white-water rafted on one of what the tape narrator called "their power vacations."

I remembered this man for another reason. In that large group of hurried, assertive, and tense-looking men and women, he seemed no more or less pressured than the rest. He did, however, convey an eerie vacancy of spirit. His eyes seemed tired and glazed over as if looking but not seeing. Despite his tight-lipped smile and constant handshaking with his admiring colleagues, there was a sad emptiness about him that I had come to recognize as characteristic of those suffering from what I call "toxic success syndrome," or TSS. But on this sunny Hawaiian day, his eyes glistened with energy as he looked out at his son.

When I first met him, this winner among winners had said all the polite words of greeting. Yet despite his social graces, he still seemed distant, detached, and distracted. He had slipped into the front of a line of people waiting to speak with me after my lecture about toxic success, its symptoms, and its cures. He seemed unaware of the other people waiting to talk to me and oblivious of the fact that he was interrupting a woman who was on the verge of tears. She was telling me of her concerns for her husband and their family and sharing her feelings related to the points I had just made about toxic success. Even in this most simple act of talking with the presenter at the meeting, his inattentiveness typified the conduct of those who suffer from TSS.

Driven to Distraction

Like most of the highly successful people I interviewed in preparation to write this book and despite his assertive and confident manner, he seemed to be on an unrelenting mission to make up for something still missing in his life. As if driven by a strong need to compensate for some personal deficiency, he seemed as pushed as he was pushy. He showed the one consistent characteristic I now know from my research distinguishes the toxically from the sweetly successful: Despite the rewards and recognition he was receiving for his record accomplishments and high-level success, he seemed distracted. In the words of the spouse of one of the winners I interviewed, "For him, enough is never enough. His attention is always on doing better, getting more, and winning."

This man reminded me of many of the highly successful people I have met over the several years of collecting information about success, how it is achieved, and its impact on our life. His ascent to the pinnacle of his profession seemed to be giving him everything he had always wanted, but it was leaving him feeling, during his rare reflective moments, that he lacked what he really needed. His relentless striving had not resulted in a sense that he was really *thriving* in his life. He had become a slave to modern society's ideology of success. He felt compelled to keep working to protect his hard-earned reputation and to act with the confidence and self-assertiveness expected of highly successful people. Yet, something inside him seemed to be telling him that the more individual success he experienced, the more self-doubt, personal deficiency, detachment, disappointment, and even depression he felt. His energetic demeanor masked the postsuccess depression characteristic of TSS.

Sweet Success

Sweet success is being able to pay full and undivided attention to what matters most in our life. It results in a state of consistent and adaptive satisfaction and delight with one's blend of love, work, and play. Rather than being consumed by earning a living, it results in feeling totally alive.

Success feels sweetest when it is experienced as a fulfilled and calm spirit, free of the need to compare ourselves with what we see as the happiness and success of others. It is characterized by an unhurried daily life led without the burden of the drive for victory over others or to get more status and "stuff." It is being able to regularly share with those we love a persistent sense of glee in the simple pleasures that derive from being alive and well at this moment in time.

One of the key differences between sweet and toxic success is that sweet success "ensues." It seems to just happen to those who are available to receiving it. It is a result of their intense attention to sharing their life with the people they love. Toxic success is a state we "pursue," a goal for which we seem pushed to work. It is a means of enhancing our individual selfish life and operating by the accepted self-interest norm (SIN) of Western cultures. Sweet success results from finding joy with someone else in the good life in the *present*. In contrast, toxic success results from looking to the *future* for success, a reason perhaps that so many TSS sufferers speak of moving forward.

Put simply, toxic success is constant distraction caused by pressure to do and have more; sweet success is attending fully to the now with the confident contentment that enough is finally enough. Overcoming toxic success syndrome is not a matter of giving up the good life, it is a matter of getting it back by freeing ourselves from the short-term illusion that so many of us now call "success." It is recovering from the social virus author John de Graaf calls "affluenza . . . a painful, contagious, socially transmitted condition of overload, debt, anxiety, and waste resulting from the dogged pursuit of more."[1]

Winning and Dying

I learned about sweet success from the people I interviewed for this book. One group I called "the mortals." The other I called "the one hundred winners." The winners were a highly occupationally and financially successful group of men and women selected from my patients and various lecture audiences around the world. Their peers had acknowledged them as having "won" their success. They were seen as able to outdo or outthink competitors and present tangible credentials of their achievements through their effective mastery of the capitalist system.

The mortals were my fellow patients who, like me, had been near death on various cancer units. A few of us on the bone-marrow-transplant unit had called ourselves "the midnight mortals" because we all felt so keenly aware of our fragile hold on life. Like the man quoted on the first page of this book, we often experienced the despair of missed opportunities to cherish life before it seemed that we were losing it. We grieved for our failure to realize how successful our lives would have been if only we had paid more attention to them. We would wheel our chairs together just after midnight to talk about how we might live differently if we were given the chance to come back to life.

While I am not sure what happened to all of the members of our mortals group, I do know that nine of them died before I wrote this book. Because of my own reflections about the meaning of a successful life during my several bouts with cancer, I thought the mortals group might offer a unique perspective on the differences between sweet and toxic success.

I asked each member of the mortals group one question about success. It is a form of the "if you had your life to live over" question. I asked, "If you died and came back to life, what one thing would you do differently?" This question was a way of asking those fearing losing their life what they thought constituted a successful life. I wrote their answers in a journal more than ten years ago. I hope the dying words presented throughout this book will help you reflect on what you would consider a successful life.

One of the mortals, a 32-year-old woman suffering through her last days with breast cancer, offered her view of success. Unable to lift her head and shaking so badly that the rubbing sound of the sheet made it difficult to hear her failing voice, she whispered, "If I could come back to life, I would pay attention to just being alive. I would pay attention to the chance to be with my husband and our kids. It seems like I spent too much of my life giving my time for money. Now, I would give all my money for just a little more time to be with my family." She began to cry and, as I reached from my wheelchair to try to dry her eyes with a tissue, she grabbed my hand and looked into my eyes. Her voice became stronger as she said, "If you make it, write about it. You're an author, so tell them. You must tell them to pay attention. Tell them to forget what they think they want and pay more attention to what they need."

Do You Feel Pushed or Pulled?

My interviews with the winners and mortals revealed that the toxically successful feel "pushed" through life—something inside seems to be driving them on toward the illusive better life. Those who seem more sweetly successful act as if they are "pulled" through life. They are "flow-ers" rather than "fighters." They are able to allow themselves to "go with the flow" and be drawn deeply, profoundly, and joyfully into their working, loving, parenting, and playing. They are responsive rather than "driven." They feel in charge of their daily life rather than obligated by its constant demands. They are more likely to lose all sense of time than be dominated by it. They appear highly attentive to what the world offers them and free of automatic reactions. They stand out as more fully and energetically alive than many others. Most of all, they seem to be paying much more attention.

The difference between the "push" of toxic success and the "pull" of sweet success is subtle.[2] Ask yourself if you feel "pulled" into your day by the wonders and joys that await you or "pushed" out of bed by the sense that you have to get going. People who can attend fully to the simple pleasures of daily life tend to be attracted or "pulled in" by them. As fifteenth-century philosopher Marsilio Ficino described, they turn toward the opportunities of the day as the sunflower turns toward the sun. The toxically successful tend to leave bed feeling "pushed" from the inside out. They feel compelled to get going, keep doing, and "get on with it" before a competitor passes them from behind.

Toxically successful people have another characteristic. Despite their achievements, they seem nagged by self-doubt. No matter how successful society says they are, they seem driven to make up for some vague but insatiable deficiency. The result is the kind of detachment described by one of the winners group. He said, "The further I climb up the ladder of success, the more out there and alone I feel. Something keeps pushing me up and up and makes me keep climbing. It's like something is nagging at me to keep going. Whenever I stop and think for a while, I feel very alone. The more alone I feel, the more it seems I have to keep climbing."

Is Being Normal Healthy?

Toxic success has become so "normal" that you may not notice anything unusual about those who suffer from it. In a world of driven and competitive people operating in "push" mode, those who allow themselves to be pulled in by simple, seemingly nonproductive and no-money-earning things can seem like failed jerks.

One of the winners group lived down the street from me when I lived in Michigan. He described one of our neighbors this way. "There's this guy on my block. He lies in his hammock on his front porch. He just looks out at his front lawn and his trees. It's like he's watching the grass grow. He just looks and looks. Then, all of a sudden, he pops up, walks out under a tree, looks up, and stands there staring at a bird or something. I'd feel like a jerk if someone saw me doing that. The guy seems to have no drive. He must be a real weirdo."

The man he was describing was a family physician with a very successful practice. He had been one of the survivors from the "mortals" group. I knew him to be very busy yet fully attuned to his family and the simple joys of life. He spent time on his porch in his hammock so he could, in his words, "just let life come to me. I spent months lying there dying, so now I want to lie there living. After staring at the walls of intensive care, I'm always on the lookout for things to pay attention to."

The wife of a toxic success sufferer pointed out how "normal" the drive of the toxically successful can seem to the capitalistic world that so highly rewards them. She said, "He's a well-adjusted robot. You have to live with these guys to see it. You have to sleep with them, go on vacation with them, raise kids with them, and try to eat a peaceful dinner with them to know that they have TSS (toxic success syndrome). It feels like I have a virtual husband, not a real one. He can't stop trying to prove something, but I don't know what he's trying to prove. I have to practically shout to get his attention. Everybody else thinks he's just fine and the perfect husband. He pays lots of attention to people at parties and work. They think he's given us everything, but the sad thing is that we still don't have him."

The toxically successful are the heroes of our society, the Joneses with whom we wish we could keep up. They are the celebrities we admire for their accomplishments and mastery of the system. This book is an invitation to look more closely at our success heroes and to ask if success as society now defines it is coming at too high a price. As you will learn, that price includes serious health risks, disruption of our intimate relationships, and a relentlessly consumerist society. We are acting more like owners than guests on planet Earth, viewing success in terms of how much of the planet or its bounty we think we can possess. We have made almost every aspect of life into a commodity.

If you look into the private lives of the toxically successful, you will see that no amount of success has been able to calm them down. Being "driven" is seen as normal and "lack of drive" a sign of laziness. The toxically successful are constantly climbing up the ladder of success, but those who love and live with them sense that they are really trying to climb out of a life they cannot seem to embrace, celebrate, and share.

Success Informants

Despite the Maui man's evident tangible success and his upbeat and energetic manner, it seemed at that meeting that some dark force was behind his success. He appeared hounded by a vague lifelong grievance for some thwarted aspiration or desire for which no amount of his and society's version of success could free him. His broad smile seemed to be a mask and, like his laugh, more self-advertisement than genuine delight.

"Good talk," he had said speaking right past the tearful woman he had interrupted. He shook my hand firmly while already beginning to move away. "I want to take you to lunch. I've got a seminar to teach now, and then a golf tee time with a potential client for a quick nine holes, so I've got to rush. See you in about three hours in the lobby?" While stated as a question, it was clearly a command. He was used to getting his way, and without waiting for my response, he hurried away high-fiving several success groupies to whom he was an idol.

"That's the number one producer in the company," said the woman he had interrupted as she dried her eyes. "I do hope you will talk to him because he's the poster child for what you just described about toxic success. He is actually a very sad and lonely man, but I don't think he knows it. I do. I'm his wife." There were too many people around to allow me to respond to this woman's distress. In the hope that I could refer her for help, I gave her my card and told her to call my office. Her report was not atypical and, like the many others I heard, is the reason I tried to interview as many spouses of TSS sufferers as I could.

The hero's wife's words are reflective of the fact that those who live with the toxically successful have the clearest view of its ravages. They are the ones who feel the alienation first. They sense the lack of attention and feel left out by their spouse's constant effort for a better life. They are the ones who live day to day with the agitation and disconnection of TSS that leads to more sadness for everyone than an often envious outside world would ever imagine.

In addition to each of my one hundred interviews of the winners group, I interviewed as many spouses, family members, or close friends of the winners as I could. These informants were of help to me and eventually to the winners themselves. They were able to recognize and give examples of the degree to which TSS was spoiling the lives of their winners and their families. Where possible, I tried to have the informants take the tests you will be reading about with their winner.

Unless a comment revealed an interviewee's identity, all the quotes from my interviews are presented without editing. To protect their privacy, I have not included names, but the job descriptions and other details are accurate. From this data, I learned that the best way to assess the level of severity of

9

TSS is to ask his or her spouse or someone trying to live with and love someone who seems to suffer from it. Before you read much further and based on the limited information in this introduction, I suggest you ask someone who loves you if your success and how you are going after it seems toxic to you or to him or her.

A Powerful Lunch

When it came time to meet the most successful man in the world, I waited for nearly an hour in the lobby. I enjoyed passing the time talking with several of my Hawaiian friends who worked at the hotel. Then seemingly out of nowhere, the sweaty and breathless man appeared. "All set?" he asked. He was rubbing his hands as if trying to cleanse himself of what he had been doing to get ready for the next challenge. "Ready to do our power lunch?"

My Hawaiian friends smiled knowingly and seemed to understand why I would not try to introduce the man to those to whom he seemed oblivious. They had seen the signs of toxic success many times before in visitors to our islands, and we often talked about how so many come to paradise but are never truly in it. We often asked one another, "Why don't they pay attention to where they are and the opportunity they have to enjoy paradise?" This is a key question that I hope to encourage anyone suffering from TSS to ask him or herself.

"Well, I don't know if I'm up to *doing* a lunch, but I'm ready to *share* lunch with you," I answered in a feeble attempt to joke my way into connecting with this highly driven person. He looked puzzled and answered, "Yeah, right," then put his hand on my back and piloted me toward the restaurant. I could see he was well practiced in not paying attention.

As we approached our table, he pointed out where he wanted me to sit. "Have a seat," he said in the typically pleasant but controlling tone of the toxically successful. As we sat down, he told the waitress, without looking at her and with the typical "nonquestion" of the self-absorbed, "We're kind of in a hurry, sweetie, so can you get us two menus right away?" Having worked for years in the upscale resort, the waitress seemed used to this kind of treatment and hurried off.

While looking down at his menu, he asked me, "So, Dr. Pearsall, tell me, if I move here, will I get rid of my toxic success? If I move to Hawai'i, will I find paradise?" I remember the details of our conversation and almost every word because it was one of the events that led to my writing this book. I remember answering, "I notice you said 'I.' Would you be moving here alone or with your wife?" The man seemed confused and slightly aggravated by my response. "Of course I mean me and my family," he had answered. "I mean, would we find paradise here?"

"Paradise is kind of like your luggage," I answered. "If you don't bring it, you aren't likely to find it." The man closed his menu, pushed his chair away from the table, took a deep breath, sighed out loud, and said, "I guess that's why I asked you to lunch."

For the next two hours and over an only partially eaten lunch, we "talked story" about the various causes and cures of toxic success about which you will read in these pages. We spoke of his feeling of having it all but still sensing no true, deep, shared, and enduring sense of contentment. We talked about his experienced "push" of toxic success that was overwhelming the "pull" of his heart. We discussed how sweetening success would not require "doing" more or less or a set of steps and life plans. We talked about learning to *be* by paying more attention to whom and what we already have in our life. I asked him if he had seen his wife talking to me. He seemed startled and answered, "My God, no." As our meeting ended, we both felt our "lunch" had been more powerful than we could have imagined.

Giving It Everything You Have

Our lunch became a guide for the interviews I would conduct later for this book. As a clinical neuropsychologist, I had long been interested in and written about the influences of stress on our body. I had worked with hundreds of successful people and noted the failure of their success to result in the joy and bliss they needed. As a student of the Hawaiian culture, I wondered why it seemed that so many of my Hawaiian friends and family who seemed so unsuccessful in Western capitalistic terms were remarkably successful in spiritual and loving terms. I wondered why the most successful society in history has, since the early 1960s, seen the divorce rate double, teen suicide triple, violent crime quadruple, the prison population quintuple, and depression soar to more than ten times the pre-World War II level.[3] I wondered, if we're so successful, why aren't we happier and healthier?

My discussion with the man in Maui helped me focus my exploration of the issues of deficiency, doubt, and detachment that lead to the underlying disappointment and, finally, clinical depression experienced by the toxically successful and their families. We spoke of his feelings of self-doubt seldom relieved by even the most acknowledged and highly rewarded of his accomplishments. We talked about his constant sense of deficiency in life that seemed unsatisfied by any amount of money, praise, status, security, or material goods. We discussed the fact that no amount of assurances from his wife and children that all they wanted was *him* could penetrate his insecurity. Perhaps most difficult for him, we spoke of his feeling of being detached from his family and from life in general. Apparently unaware of or in denial about his wife's already deep despair at his isolation, he said he feared that his family might eventually become detached from him. When I told him about his wife's tearful sharing with me, his eyes moistened. He looked down and whispered, "I guess you could say I have given them everything they could have wanted except *me*."

By the end of our meeting, the man had wiped away tears and blown his nose vigorously several times. He had begun to talk more slowly and softly. He seemed to feel he was sharing a deep secret that none of his competing colleagues could ever understand. However, he was wrong: TSS seems to be becoming an epidemic.

As a clinician and scientist, I always keep careful notes. I know that one case is an anecdote, but I also think that many validated cases become data. I would use the notes of my conversation with this man to construct many of the tests I would use with the winners group, in my clinical work with the toxically successful and their families, and as a guide in my interviews. I had developed my theory of TSS during my decades of clinical work, but this man's story guided me in gathering further information about its causes and effects.

The Danger of Getting There

As we moved toward the end of what had become a lunchtime therapy session for him and a learning experience for me, he and I discussed a paradox of success. It seems that we are often weakest and most vulnerable when we think we have finally achieved the level of success for which we have been striving most of our life. It is when we think we have finally arrived that we recognize that we have ended up in the wrong place. As one winner would later say, "I think when you begin to look at yourself as having made it, you'd better look at what you've lost." We have become so used to striving that when we finally achieve our goals, we go into success-protection mode. Instead of reflecting on what we may have missed along the way to our success, we may get busy trying to stay successful. We fail to thrive because we keep striving harder in order to get more success assurance.

High-level success is a dangerous place to be. It is the time in our life when we are likely to let down our guard. We begin to take life for granted and become bored. We may emotionally crash and become depressed or seek to restimulate ourselves by striving even harder. We may have an affair, turn to drugs or alcohol, engage in stimulating reckless behaviors, or commit "sofa suicide" by lying on the couch and gorging ourselves on junk food.

Highly successful persons often either crash or run. They feel there's little left to live for or keep running faster to see if there might not be something still out there that might make them feel content. Instead of finally allowing themselves to thrive by focusing their attention on what they really need, they remain convinced that they must keep striving to be successful enough to never want.

Postsuccess shock can result from the sudden decline in stress hormone levels that happens when we drop out of the rat race. We feel disoriented and don't know what to do with ourselves. "I couldn't retire," said one of the winners. "My wife couldn't stand having me around the house. I drove her nuts. I didn't know what to do with myself, so I just hung around and got in her way. She said she got tired of looking at me just sitting there and waiting for something to happen."

If our quest for a life that is better causes us to fail to pay attention to what makes life good, we feel lost when we finally have what we thought we wanted. We have become skilled at searching for where to go but poor at paying attention to where we are. When we think or someone tells us we have arrived, it feels that there is no there there. No matter how successful others say or we think we are, something still seems to be missing. As one of the winners group pointed out, "It seems that just when I think I have finally made it, it feels like I've lost it. Instead of feeling on top of the world, I feel strangely sad. I don't know where I thought I was going, but I know I'm not happy where I've ended up. Even worse, I feel like I've missed out on enjoying the trip."

During our "learning" lunch (a sweet success alternative to the "power" lunch), we talked at length about the idea that it is precisely when things seem to be going very well and when we feel most individually successful that we might be wise to look more deeply at our living and loving. It may be that just when it seems we don't have to pay as much attention to what we're doing, we would be wise to realize that we haven't been paying enough attention to what matters. The hero and I talked about success signaling a spiritual alarm rather than a time to celebrate. One of the winners group described this danger when she said, "The higher up on the ladder of success you climb, the further away you end up being from what grounds you—things like your family and your religion."

What's Your Life's Song?

As my lunch partner man wiped away more tears, he told me that listening to my preliminary findings about toxic success had somehow diminished his "most successful man in the world" and "the hero of the year" awards. He said I had "set something off inside him." Sitting through the company video after my talk had made him sad and angry rather than proud. He said, "Your talk on toxic success ruined the video for me. I wrote on the speaker evaluation that the company should not have you speak to us again because you upset us. I wrote that we were there to celebrate our success and to be motivated, not to think about what success means. I don't feel good about writing that now, and I sure didn't feel proud watching that tape. I felt guilty and tired just from looking at my life summed up in a five-minute video. I thought, *This is what I have worked for all my life?* It all seemed like a tragedy unfolding on film. I felt like a fraud because I really didn't deserve the hero award. I felt like a failure and I was embarrassed."

As you prepare to read the following chapters, I suggest you sit back a moment before continuing. Imagine how a five-minute video summary of your living and working would look. What would it say about your values, your success as a spouse and parent, and how you have chosen to spend the years of your life? What theme song would play while your tape was showing? Would it be a rousing song like the theme from the movie *Rocky* titled

"Eye of the Tiger?" Would it be a more calming and reflective song about valuing every moment with those people you love, such as Mike and the Mechanics' "The Living Years" or Cat Stevens's "Cat's in a Cradle"?

The Importance of Not Making Big Changes

As our conversation ended, he promised that he would be making some big changes in his life. He promised to try to be less "type A," work less, put in more quality time with his wife and family, take more vacations, meditate, and try to get more balance in his life. In the typical selective listening of the toxically successful, he had not heard a key part of my lecture. I had pointed out that all of these strategies would likely fail. I told him that the search for life balance is another symptom of toxic success, a kind of popular psychology "BS," or "balance stress," that only creates a sense of more obligation and guilt. I warned him that the real challenge was to get at the root of his toxic success, the "five Ds" of TSS: deficiency, doubt, detachment, disappointment, and eventual depression. I promised him that my years of clinical work with the toxically successful indicated that it was possible to detoxify TSS and "sweeten it up" by changing our mind and taking back our attention. I told him that many toxically successful people had learned to reclaim their attention and invest it more fruitfully in those things their hearts told them they needed.

Sweetening success requires putting your mind where your memories are. Our fondest memories are usually not about how many deals we've closed, how many stock options we've earned, or how we made the honor roll at school. They are most often about special moments shared with Mom, Dad, our grandparents, and our children. They are typically focused on a special summer vacation with our family, a joyful Christmas morning, or just sitting talking with someone we love. Since our most cherished memories are made of these things, they are what should demand our attention. Sweet success is memory making. Cluttering our mind with the flotsam and jetsam of a hurried and demanding view of what constitutes success robs us of making the memories that are the measure of a life well lived.

As you will also be learning more about in the chapters that follow, I told the man that research shows that being type A can be good for your health. While the idea of type A makes for a popular social concept, it is based on

15

poor research. This is the same research that shows there is a need to work smarter, not less. I told my top performer that he might not be working hard enough at paying attention to what matters most. I warned that trying to spend "quality time" would mean that he would end up dividing his life into high- and low-quality times. I told him that trying to "cut back" or be a DOMO—a downwardly mobile person—would only become yet another goal to be achieved. He was falling into the toxic success trap of trying to "do" his way out of his problems rather than "be" his way to coming back to life.

"Don't try to make big changes," I counseled. "That's the style of those suffering from toxic success. They try to do everything big and fast and solve problems before they fully understand their causes. You can still have what you really want just so long as you pay more attention to what you truly need. You have to change your mind, not just your behaviors. Stress isn't killing you—you are. Work pressures aren't causing your suffering—you are. You aren't bringing your work problems home—*you're* the problem!

"My *kumu* (Hawaiian teacher) once told me," I continued, "that the only difference between a diamond and a lump of coal is that the diamond has had a lot more pressure put on it. Being under pressure isn't what is doing you in—it's how you are thinking about life that's the problem. You have already begun your quest for sweet success because you're thinking differently about success. Don't try to do big things. Just try to pay more attention to the little things that mean a lot to you. Do some small things, but do them with big love.

"It will be much more difficult for you to change your mind than your schedule," I went on. "Begin by focusing on the very first thing that comes to your mind when you awaken in the morning. If it isn't your mother or father, a dearest friend, your wife, your children, or just the simple joy of being alive, try to refocus your attention the next morning. Try to get your own attention back and put it on whom and what you really need instead of what you think you have to do to get what society tells you to want. If you're not sure you can tell what you need from what you think you want, ask your wife and family about what they love most about you and what they need most from you now. These are the same things you need. If you pay attention to them, they will define success for you."

My words to the man are the same invitations I extend to you as you begin to read this book. Try to be a little more alert to your automatic competitive mental default state. Notice how you seem to automatically compete with others for a better life rather than connect with the good life you have right now. Notice how your competitiveness has become so automatic that it kicks in when you drive or stand in a line, or makes everything a contest rather than an opportunity. Ask, "Am I content with a good life?" Wake up. Pay attention. Focus on what a good life you could be sharing right now. Toxic success can be a form of living death. If you learn to pay attention, you can come back to life.

A Readers Guide to Sweet Success

Throughout this book you will read about the "five Ds" of the sickness of toxic success I discussed with this man: deficiency, doubt, detachment, disappointment, and depression. In part 1, you will read about the various meanings of success and the most powerful of all human abilities, our capacity to choose where we focus our attention. You will learn about the danger of being "normal" in a world of chronic strivers, many of whom are suffering from mass attention deficit disorder and going mad from the side effects of an aggressively competitive definition of success, and you will discover that you do not have to succumb to that path to success.

In part 2, you will read more about the deadly consequences of competition and why it isn't necessary to compete to win. You will be offered a test to assess your own level of toxic success syndrome and read about the side effects of that syndrome. You will learn that the keys to success we have been given open doors to very dangerous places and about scientific research that offers new keys to a sweeter kind of success for you and your family.

In part 3, you are offered the thriver's way to success, a detoxification program for TSS. It is based on one of the oldest approaches to successful working, living, loving, and playing in the world, the Hawaiian model of excellence called *po'okela* (po-oh-kay-la), meaning success through shared values rather than personal objectives. I discovered *po'okela* almost twenty years ago. It was taught to me by my Hawaiian friends and *'ohana* (family) in Maui and continues to be taught to me today at my home on the island of O'ahu.

Like many indigenous beliefs, Hawaiian *po'okela* derives from a "collectivist" culture that does not value the individualistic self-interest norm (SIN) of the Western world as the way to a successful life. It is a view of success given birth to by voyagers, not conquerors, and because it comes from an island society, it is based on the value of having fewer over more choices. This path to success is likely to be unfamiliar to most people, who see Hawai'i as a nice place to visit but may not know that its host culture offers a profoundly wise way to succeed in life.

Books offering ideas about personal well-being are influenced by their authors' cultural backgrounds. You are probably used to books with a Western cultural bias or, more recently, Eastern cultural concepts. Part 3's program for healthier success is based on my Hawaiian cultural background, but it also applies the lessons learned by the emerging new science of success, including the fields of psychoneuroimmunology, energy cardiology, and neurotheology. It presents Hawaiian-style "how to think its" rather than just "how to do its." It is in the form of "invitations" rather than steps.

I will provide you with some things to "do," but these suggestions are made only in an attempt to get you to change your mind. Even though popular psychology asserts that we behave as we feel, psychological research shows that you can also "do it to feel it." You do not see a bear and then run because you are frightened. You see a bear and then feel and think fearful thoughts because you are running for your life. Your emotions and thoughts react to your body as much as your body reacts to how you feel and think. Because you can come to feel and think as you behave, I offer things to do. The objective, however, is to help you change your mind about the meaning of success. To assist you in this process, you will be reading about ancient ways of thinking that can result in healthier success.

Three Ways to Know Your Success Is Detoxified

"But how will I know if I'm curing my toxic success?" the most successful man in the world asked me at the end of our lunch. He said, "I wrote down the three *po'okela* principles you mentioned in your lecture (contentment, calmness, connection), but I always write things down. That doesn't mean I'll do them."

I cautioned again, "Sweet success is an outlook on life, not a series of steps. You'll get some idea if you are achieving a less toxic success if you try to remember and check for three things that are indicators of *po ʻokela*-style success. If you're reducing toxic success, you will find yourself laughing harder and longer every day. You will cry more easily, often, and openly. Most of all, you will find yourself taking much more time to reflect more deeply and longer about the meaning of life with those who matter in your life. You will find yourself paying much more attention to where you want to attend."

As you read this book, I hope you will remember these three indicators of sweet success—to laugh, to cry, and to reflect. You will have to practice silencing your Western brain's bias against slow and contemplative thinking. Like a patient parent, you will have to encourage it to take a chance on trying the oceanic way of attending to the world. Your continental brain will not always be willing to cooperate, but give *po ʻokela* a chance to work its magic. It just takes time.

When I try to get you to reclaim your own attention by teasing and coaxing you into a different, slower, more reflective and connective daily consciousness, your hard-driving know-it-all brain will be sure it is right. It will resist and even mock what you read. It will not comply easily with the detoxification program in part 2.

I do not promise that curing TSS is easy. If you picked this book up to see if it offered a quick fix, it is even more important that you do not put it down. It was your toxically thinking brain that may have been fooled into selecting this book as another strategy-for-success approach. If so, it is in dire need of a new outlook on success. You will be asked to rethink your definition of success and what you have come to accept as the only way to achieve it. The rewards for your change of mind can be immense. The memories you will begin to create and share can be wonderful and last you a lifetime.

I have tried to include just enough science and referenced theoretical material to support my thesis without overwhelming or distracting readers of all ages and backgrounds. I have used many letter codes and phrases to help you remember some of the ideas of sweet success. I hope you will not mistake my attempts to simplify the concepts presented here for a lack of seriousness. Toxic success is indeed killing us and ruining our families.

This is a book for anyone trying to succeed in life. Toxic success is an equal-opportunity condition that is not exclusive to those we tend to see as highly successful adults such as business executives, athletes, movie stars, doctors, and others in high-profile and high-pay positions. It has also permeated the daily lives of most of our children and adolescents as they compete to be the best child for their parents, be the best soccer player for their team, earn the best grades in their class, or be the most popular person in their group. It has become a way of life, the internal combustion of baby boomers that have quested so long and hard for a better life. Our senior citizens also suffer from toxic success as they feel the pressure to "never really retire" and have demanding second careers. Because of this range of toxic success victims, I have tried to make a very serious problem as simple and clear and the solutions as accessible as possible.

If you feel overwhelmed with stress in school or at work, if your marriage seems at serious risk, if you have a set of daily stress symptoms such as headaches, stomach problems, high blood pressure, constant fatigue, and abuse of food or other substances, you may want to enter part 3's toxic success rehabilitation program before reading parts 1 and 2. It offers ways you can begin to change your mind and open your heart *now*. Then be sure to return to Parts 1 and 2 so you can fully understand the reasons why and how you developed your own toxic success syndrome. Unless you learn to recognize its causes and symptoms, you will not be able to prevent its recurrence or know how to help others avoid it in their lives. But be forewarned: The toxically successful tend to be a busy, distracted, hurried bunch who seek quick and easy steps out of most problems. Part 2's program offers difficult changes in how you think about life that will take time to take effect.

Bringing Paradise to Hawai'i

As I watched the man enjoying making memories with his son and reflected on the time we had spent together on Maui, I decided to risk disturbing what seemed to be his most enjoyable state of mind. My wife, my son, and I approached him as quietly as we could. He saw us out of the corner of his eye, smiled, and then held up his hand as if to say, "Just a moment." He gave another thumbs up to his son, then stood up and gave me a hard and most surprising hug.

"You're the toxic success guy," he said laughing. "I forgot you live here on O'ahu. I've been meaning to write to you." Talking as quickly as he did when I first met him but now with more humor and sincerity, he added, "I will never forget your lecture and our lunch. Do you remember what you said when I asked if I would find paradise if I came to Hawai'i? Well, we're here, and this time we brought it with us."

The man apologized for not immediately acknowledging my wife and son and introduced himself to them. We apologized for disturbing him, and began to move away. The pushed and pushy man of years ago gently touched my shoulder and softly said in a calm voice, "Do you all have just one more minute, please?" He reached into his pocket and pulled out his cell phone and wallet. He slipped a laminated card from his wallet and showed it to me. In large bold letters, it said, "Be content, calm down, connect always."

"I carry this card with me," he said. "If you don't mind, I want you to say hello to my wife. She is with my daughter at the hotel getting ready for a surprise birthday party for my boy out there. Could you all say *aloha* to them?" As he dialed his phone, my son asked him, "Is your son's team winning?"

"I have no idea. I just know we're having a blast being together," he laughed. "We're just enjoying being in paradise together."

As I spoke briefly on the phone with the surprised wife, she shared her gratitude for what she described as the "safe return" of her husband. "You really got his attention. He's not a new man, but that's not what we wanted. We wanted *our* man," she said laughing. "He works as hard as ever, but he is back with us mentally and emotionally. He seems so much more content and fun to be with. He can still be a severe pain in the ass and still works until he drops, but he is just much more with us when he's with us. He's more of a joy to be around. He seems more content with life. We almost lost him, he almost lost us, but he's back."

As we prepared to leave, the man gave us each a hug. "Remember the award I won? I won it again this year, but this time I feel we really deserve it. I said *we* because I wish you could see the video this year. It's me doing things with my family, and the song this time is "The Living Years" by Mike and the Mechanics. The whole crowd cried when they saw it, and so did we. At this time in my life, I feel like I really am the most successful man in the world."

PART ONE

The Causes of Toxic Success

That millions share
the same forms of mental pathology
does not make those people sane.

—*Erich Fromm*

CHAPTER ONE

The Curse of Success

Show me a hero and I'll write you a tragedy.

—F. Scott Fitzgerald

There is an ancient Chinese saying that states, "May you have an interesting life." While this may seem to be a nice wish for someone, it was actually a form of curse intended to warn of the dangers inherent in not being careful what we wish for. Wishing for a very interesting life may not only bring great excitement and joy but also terrible suffering. Your interesting life might require your constant attention to an endless series of obligations and crises—a most interesting but not a very happy life.

In the modern world, the new version of that Chinese curse might be, "May you have a successful life." Success as it is defined and pursued today can result not only in the joy that comes with having many choices and things, but is also increasingly a source of disappointment and lonely despair for those who experience it and those who love them. It too often comes at the price of the toxic success syndrome (TSS), a chronic sense of deficiency, doubt, disconnection, disappointment, and eventually depression that ruins our health, destroys our marriages, and leaves our children suffering from our emotional neglect.

Stuff Rich, Spirit Poor

"If you want to talk about an interesting life, look at mine. I could not have dreamed of what I've been able to achieve and all the experiences I've been able to have," said a 26-year-old professional basketball player. She played in the National Women's Basketball Association, drove a car worth more than many houses, was building her own massive dream home, and had jewelry on her wrists and fingers worth thousands of dollars.

"I'm at the top of my game but I feel like I'm at the bottom of my life," she continued. "I cry every night when I'm alone. I gave my whole young life to get here, and now I wonder if it was really worth it. Sometimes, I hide in the corner of the training room and just cry and cry. Everyone thinks I'm upbeat, but I put up a good front. My dad died before he ever saw me play in the NWBA, and I never got close to him. I think that's what got me thinking about your lecture on toxic success. Now my mom is very sick, but I don't have time to help her and still be successful at basketball. I don't think I'll ever have kids because every relationship I've had has been a disaster. I just don't have the time or energy to put in to making a relationship, and I think my success scares most men away.

"My coach says I'm a great physical specimen, and if I was half as happy as I am healthy, I'd feel great," she went on. "I have to work out for hours every day just to stay in good enough shape to keep up with the younger players. They're getting faster and faster, and they're willing to give up anything to take my place. We practice for hours on end, and no one dares to complain about it because it may look like you're not giving your full attention to the success of the team. We're supposed to 'leave it all on the court' and we do, so of course we don't have anything left for off the court. I play golf and tennis to relax, but even they become a battle. It's a thing with me. I just seem to always need to win. I feel guilty when I relax, like I should be doing something more to get that extra edge. I'm afraid to pay attention to what really matters in my life because it only makes me sad. I guess you'd say I'm a great example of your toxic success syndrome. I'm stuff rich and spirit poor."

This woman is a member of the group of one hundred highly successful men and women I interviewed for this book, the group I call the "winners." Her words are presented exactly as they were recorded on tape. While she gave me permission to use her name, I will protect her identity as I have with everyone in the winners group. It seems that admitting to toxic success can result in rejection and isolation at work and attract success predators ready and willing to take your place at the top of the heap.

26

The Winners and the Mortals

I selected the winners from two groups. One group was composed of patients who volunteered from those who had come to my psychiatric outpatient clinic at Sinai Hospital of Detroit called The Problems of Daily Living Clinic. These were upper-middle-class men and women coming for help with varying degrees of depression, marital and sexual problems, and family distress and conflict. The rest of the group was made up of audience members who had attended my early lectures on my ideas about toxic success syndrome. They each volunteered to be interviewed after hearing my description of the symptoms of TSS. A third source of interviews was from the "mortals group," cancer patients with whom I had shared months on a bone-marrow-transplant unit when I was treated for stage-four lymphoma more than ten years ago.

The winners group seemed to take comfort in the fact that they were not alone in their toxic success and that there was something that could be done to cure it. They seemed relieved to be affirmed in what they had suspected all along: that success as it is seen in our modern world is not all its cracked up to be. They gained comfort from learning that their depression and dysfunctional family lives were symptoms they shared with thousands of other people whose success had resulted in feelings of failure.

While the mortals group came from a wide range of economic backgrounds, each member of the winners group had attained high-level financial rewards, were acknowledged as successful by their respective peers, and would be envied by most people for their outstanding achievements and the status it had brought. Fifty men and fifty women made up the one hundred winners, and twenty of my fellow cancer patients composed the mortals group.

Over almost ten years, I conducted taped interviews with each of the hundred winners. I asked them to take the tests I had been using with my patients for years and that are contained in this book. When possible, I interviewed the spouse or close friend or family member of the winner and in some cases was able to meet with the entire family. While this group does not constitute a random research sample, the consistency of the content of their reports offers insight into the impact of our current view of success and how to achieve it.

The mortals group contained twelve men and eight women cancer patients who were dying with me when I had cancer. I had met these people more than ten years previously when I was being treated for a cancer that was eating away my bones. Early in the morning just after midnight, the corridors were eerily quiet except for the occasional moan of pain. Those of us who were able to, would wheel our chairs to the various rooms of those who were bedridden. We would talk about many things, but most often about whether or not we felt we had led successful lives.

I kept a journal containing the words from what we called our midnight mortals meetings, and I was not sure how or when I should share these special reports. As I worked on this book and began to edit and rewrite it, I decided the time had come. It seemed that there were few people in the world who have given more thought to the meaning of a successful life than those who were in the process of losing theirs. I treasure the words of my fellow mortals group members. I hope that along with the hundred winners, this special group's spiritual retrospective on success will encourage you to reflect on your own definition of success.

The Symptoms of Toxic Success

As derived from my interviews, here are fifteen symptoms of toxic success syndrome. This is a long list, so the toxically successful may lose patience after reading the first few symptoms. For those in a hurry and suffering from an attention deficit disorder common to TSS, I offer first a short test that measures the symptoms of TSS.

A SHORT TEST OF TSS FOR THE ATTENTION IMPAIRED

Would the people who know you the best say that
1. Your success is coming at the price of being insensitive and even oblivious to the needs of others?
2. You have given in to the stressful pace of the modern world and see it as an inescapable requirement for success?
3. You vacillate from morning to night from high energy to total crashing?
4. You are critical and intolerant of other people?
5. You are grumpy and don't laugh easily?
6. They are afraid to bother you when you're busy?

7. You're usually doing several things at once?
8. They have trouble getting and keeping your attention?
9. You often seem tired or "just beat"?
10. You think of time as money?
11. You don't touch and hug much?
12. You don't talk much about spiritual things?
13. You're a controlling person?
14. You have your own personal health and self-help program that does not involve them?
15. Because of how you are pursuing success, you're at risk of serious illness such as heart disease or cancer?

_____TOTAL NUMBER OF "YES" ANSWERS

The more "yes" answers to the above questions, the more likely it is that you are suffering from TSS. The average number of "yes" answers by the one hundred winners group was ten. Throughout this book I will be using my Hawaiian friends and family as a "control" group to compare to those I interviewed. As you will be reading, they tend to operate from a different view of success from the Western Euro-American world. This group of fifty friends and family of all ages who share my life in Hawai'i had an average of two "yes" answers.

I encourage you now to slow down, pay attention, relax, and reflect in more depth on the degree to which the following symptoms of TSS apply to you. If you're not sure, ask someone who loves you to go over the list with you. As is the case for those dealing with alcoholism and other addictions, you may need a sponsor to help you detoxify your success, someone who will help draw your attention to the fact that you are not paying enough attention to what matters most. I have included a sample report from my interviews that illustrates each symptom.

THE TOXIC SUCCESS SYNDROME

1. **Self-sightedness**: Constant distraction and self-focus resulting in what psychologists call "inattentive blindness" to the most important things and people in our life.

The spouse of a winner said, "He doesn't even see me. It's like I'm a ghost that cries out and startles him once in a while. He's one of the most experienced pilots at [a major airline] so I assume he's pretty observant at work. But at home, he just doesn't seem to have either the interest or the energy to pay attention to me unless I demand his attention. If he does pay attention, it's usually to me and the kids together and not just to me as the one he married. For him, it seems that his 'wife and kids' are becoming just another obligation that it's easier just not to see unless he absolutely has to."

2. **Stress surrender**: An "external locus of control" indicated by feeling that one has no choice but to behave and react to "the way the world is."

A 62-year-old male architect said, "You can talk all you want about toxic success, but you have to get real, man. It's just the way it is out there. It's kill or be killed. You're either a winner or a loser. Unless you just drop out completely and go to a monastery or something, you have to get out there and deal with reality. All that New Age stuff about going with the flow, life balance, and meditation might sound good, but we're all products of the system. Anybody who is truly doing something with their life and has become really successful does not have time to watch Oprah Winfrey and her psycho-gurus talking about their emotional pain, loving themselves, and finding their inner child. Anybody with a life is leading it. They're out there busy being successful."

3. **The "ups and downs" and "ins and outs"**: Vacillating between anxious nervous energy and depressive withdrawal and between total attention at work and inattentiveness at home.

A 20-year-old leukemia patient from the mortals group said, "I can't imagine why I was so moody. I felt like the burden of the world was on my shoulders. I would either get really up to deal with the stress or really down that it wasn't worth the effort. Every test in college was such a damn big deal. When I got an A, I was high and the family was happy. When I didn't do well, everything crashed. We were always up and down. I could see that I would bring my family with me on these ups and downs, and I really feel terrible about that now.

"I was sort of 'in and out' of my family most of the time, and now I just want to be with them totally, always. I think success is being with your family and being the reason your family is a happy place. It's being a blessing and not a burden to them. Now I really have something to deal with and I really need them, but I feel I don't deserve them and that I'm using them again."

4. **Chronic cynicism**: Unrelenting distrust, cynicism, and hostility for other people and their ideas.

   A spouse of a male physician from the winners group said, "I don't think I hardly ever hear a good word come from his mouth. Watching TV, listening to a lecturer, going to the movies, on the tennis court, driving . . . no matter what we do, he has something bad to say about whatever it is. When he drives, he does this angry narration of how stupid other drivers are. He seems to think he is a genius living in a world populated by jerks and inferior people who, if they are successful, don't deserve it nearly as much as he does."

5. **Grouchiness**: Anhedonia, the loss of the ability, willingness, or taking the time to relish the small things and to smile and laugh easily at oneself and with others.

   The sister of an 18-year-old top academic high school student who had received national attention for starting a successful software company while in high school said, "He's brilliant, but he's a pain in the ass. All he thinks about is about being the best and at the top of every class he's in. He takes everything, including mostly himself, way too seriously. He sees anyone who jokes around as not really all that smart. He even says that the world is divided into winners and losers. We seldom see a smile on his face and, when we do, it's only a little crack and his eyes and the rest of his face don't join in."

6. **Feeling pestered**: Feeling "annoyed" and "bothered" when so many people and things seem to be constantly demanding attention.

   The 11-year-old daughter of a computer software developer said,

"We're all afraid to go near him sometimes. Everybody thinks because our dad works at home it's great for us, but we don't see him much. If you walk in quietly to talk to him, you can scare him and he jumps when he sees you. He is so into his thoughts and staring at the computer that if we bother him, he sighs and rolls his eyes and says real sarcastic-like, "Yes, what is it?" It's like we're a distraction or something, but when he's ready to be with us, we'd better be ready, too. Mommy says he's just working hard for all of us, but I wish he wouldn't work so hard and just be around us more. Now, he just wants us around when he wants us."

7. **Polyphasia ("multitasking")**: Feeling that doing only one thing at a time is a "waste of time."

   A 44-year-old sales executive said, "For me, doing one thing at a time is the biggest waste of time. I can easily be thinking one thing and doing another. I can talk on my cellular phone, read something important, and plan for my next meeting all at the same time. Really. Anyone who is very successful has to do that. If you're not a multitasker, you just can't compete any more. You have to be able to spread your attention around."

8. **Psychological absenteeism**: Racing mind; thinking "back" to what wasn't done (resulting in depression) and/or "ahead" to what remains to be done (resulting in anxiety). Being mentally "at work" when home and "at home" when working.

   A 47-year-old leukemia patient from our mortals group said, "What I regret most is never really being in the present moment. You talk a lot about getting your own attention. Well, nothing gets your attention like cancer. It forces you to be here right now. Pain isn't back there or ahead, it's now. Right now. That's probably one of the great ironies about pain. You're never more alive that when you're in agony and never more in the present moment than when you are soaking your bed with pain sweat. There's no hiding from the pain that slams you right into the now.

   "Before I got sick, I was always regretting what I didn't do or worrying about what I should do. I feel like I missed out on life. I

pray every night that I will get another chance to live in the present. I want to be with my wife and kids—really with them. When they visit me, I want to drink them in, hold them, and never let them go. Why didn't I do that when I was healthy? You want to know what success is, it's that. It's waking up in time to the people who matter most. It's paying all your attention to them right now in the now instead of thinking about how you can make their life better later."

9. **Weariness**: Unrelenting fatigue, disrupted sleep patterns, and dozing off when sitting quietly.

    A 59-year-old female dentist and single mother said, "I don't remember not being tired. In fact, if I wasn't tired, I'd be sure I had failed to do something I should have done or wasn't working hard enough. If I go to town to a play or try to read at night, I fall asleep right away. Forget meditation. If I try it, I'm gone; I go right to sleep. In fact, I'm starting to feel sleepy right now as I sit here talking to you. Sitting is a real strong sedative to me. It's like, if I pay hard attention to one thing, I become hypnotized."

10. **Chrono-currency**: Viewing time as money and any time not spent productively earning money as a waste of time.

    A 49-year-old optician said, "Of course time is money. Any time you spend not making money is wasted time. You can afford to waste a little time, but not much. It drives me nuts when someone wastes my time or I am forced to waste it by someone or some situation. I can't stand slow talkers and slow drivers. In effect, they are life thieves. They are robbing me and my family of our money."

11. **Relationship exploitation**: Neglect, usery, and abuse of our most intimate relationships by taking them for granted, using them only as safe havens from stress, a quick intimacy fix, or a stress-reduction technique.

    The spouse of a 44-year-old gynecologist said, "You'd think a guy who spent his entire day looking at naked women might want to look at his own naked wife once in awhile, but he doesn't. When we have sex, it's like a sleeping pill for him. It's a form of stress relief. I know when he wants sex because I see the stress. He expects me to be there for him, but he never seems to be there for me. I'm trading sex for just a few minutes of postcoital cuddling."

12. **Spiritual deficit disorder (SDD)**: A sense of spiritual emptiness and meaninglessness often accompanied by periods of spiritual longing and questioning the "meaning of it all."

A 77-year-old retired entrepreneur said, "I have left my spiritual account empty. I have made millions investing, but I'm afraid I didn't put much into my soul. I used to mock the spiritual stuff and the way I'm talking to you right now. I've always been an atheist. Frankly, I saw people who talked about spiritual stuff as not too smart. Now, I can see that I didn't invest any of my attention into the meaning of life and death.

"I'm starting to think about these things more and more now, just like my wife told me I would. God, I miss her. When she died, I saw it just as more evidence that there is no fairness, no God, no meaning in life. She always wanted to talk about that stuff, but my attention was totally on what I called the real *world. Now, I wonder what real means. I wish she were here now to help me with all this. She was such a spiritual person, and I hate myself now for mocking her for it. I am not so concerned now about whether I believe in God, but I do hope some higher power believes in me enough to help me find some meaning in all of this."*

13. **Inhibited power motive (IPM)**: A high need for power, frustration with not having enough power and control, and a decreasing awareness and neglect of the need for affiliation and connection.

The wife of a top executive of an international investment and insurance firm said, "He's constantly frustrated because he says he has so much responsibility and very little power or control. He craves power. I think he compensates by taking total control of everything in our family life or at least sitting back and criticizing how the home is run. He plans and controls our vacations, our family finances, the kids' schooling, even our lovemaking. He plans it, but he isn't really a part of it.

"He's more like our family's CEO. He runs us, but he doesn't really connect with us. He would much sooner be in control than let us take care of him and do things for him. It seems that he thinks no one can do anything as well as he can, so we feel we are always disappointing him and not living up to his expectations. He is brilliant, but his need for control exhausts all of us and, even if he doesn't know it, probably him, too."

14. **Self health and help**: Selfish focus on exercise, diet, "self help" seminars and books, and various quick and easy stress-reduction techniques to "manage" rather than "address" stress.

    The spouse of a 34-year-old wireless phone company executive said, "He's in perfect health. He jogs every day, works out with weights three times a week, and has self-motivation quotes pasted everywhere in the house. The kids and I are usually home waiting for him to finish jogging, but then he says he has to meditate and do what he calls his affirmations. He's really into some 'self-power' tape program and the guy who sells it is his guru. He does all this, but he's still under stress. He has all the gimmick phrases, writes his mission and vision statements, and has steps to follow for this and steps to follow for that. Sometimes I think it would be better for him to stop jogging and meditating and just sit quietly with us and watch some stupid TV show. I personally think his stress-management program is causing him stress. If you ask me, I think he should stop trying to manage stress and do something about it."

15. **Success sickness**: A whole set of the diseases of modern civilization ranging from asthma and chronic infections to cancer and heart disease that we now know can be side effects of toxic success syndrome, and the way of living, loving, and working indicated by the above list of symptoms.[1]

    The wife of one of the mortals group members said, "I know it's silly to say you know what caused his cancer. Nobody really knows. But I do think his constant striving for success played some role. You just can't live that way every day without it taking a toll on you. He was so much into growth. I'm into reading psychology and health

*books, and I think too much growth can be like a cancer. I think all
the cancer and heart disease we see is not just diet, genetics, or the
environment. I think a lot is the result of the way we have come to
live every day and what we think makes for a successful life."*

You can overcome the curse of toxic success syndrome as indicated by
the fifteen symptoms you have just read. Success becomes toxic when it
ends up costing too much in terms of what we say we truly value in our life.
Success fails us when we give up the gift that we use to give our life meaning: our personal attention. Success poisons our life when we begin slipping
from a sense of ample opportunity to fully enjoy life into a nagging sense of
constant obligations to seek a better life. Detoxifying success is primarily a
matter of reclaiming your own attention and placing it on what and whom
you need to feel that you are living fully, loving totally, and letting go completely. It is freeing yourself from our hyper society's grip on your attention.

Success Is a Warm Cup of Coffee

Most of my clinical career has been spent helping the toxically successful survive their success. It may seem that those who appear to have so much
are only the unappreciative, worried, well-off who deserve very little sympathy. The so-called "sudden wealth syndrome" suffered by those who are
depressed by their prosperity elicits little sympathy from those who feel they
would know exactly how to enjoy great success. My experience with society's
success role models teaches that few things seem to fail as much as high-
level success. Those who attain it often seem more miserable than those who
have much less and many fewer choices. As pointed out by author Ken
Hubbard, "It's pretty hard to tell what does bring happiness. Poverty and
wealth have both failed." [2]

With the exception of abject poverty, surveys of happiness reveal that
there is no relationship between level of income and general satisfaction
with one's life.[3] As you will be reading throughout this book, objective life
circumstances have very little to do with how happy a person feels. What
matters is the quality of the images we elect to put in our own mind and
being able to regularly recognize and celebrate our freedom to attend to what
we know in our heart matters most to us.

Most of the very successful persons I have met are either still looking for something more or fearfully consumed by trying to sustain and protect their success. My research indicates that the "something more" is being able to focus their attention when, where, and how they choose. One of the mortals group emphasized this point by saying, "What I've learned about a successful life is that it is first and foremost a selfless life. A funny thing happens when you really focus on the people and things you love. You lose all sense of your self. When you're dying, you really pay attention to your family, to the trees, to the smell of a hot cup of coffee. Smell this—I drank coffee every morning of my life and never enjoyed the smell as much as I do now. When you face death, you realize you could have been paying attention to all these things and millions more like them every day if you had only put your mind to it. If you want a definition of success, mine is short and sweet: Wake up and smell the coffee."

Sweet success is experienced when we take back our life to determine what will constitute its daily tone and rhythm and with whom we will spend it. It is writing and singing our own song rather than dancing to the accelerating tune of our hyper culture. We find sweet success when we regain our own attention and intentionally put our mind on what we need to feel fully content, calm, and connected. By doing so, we experience the subtle awe of a blurring of the boundaries of the self that allows a total immersion in the simple pleasures of life. The toxically successful gulp down a cup of coffee to give them energy. The sweetly successful calmly see, smell, taste, and feel the coffee. They become aware that they can choose what they will be aware of. This is the kind of experience the winners and mortals felt they needed for a sweeter kind of success.

A Formula for Toxic Success

Based on what I have learned from my work with the toxically successful, I have derived a formula for toxic success. Many books have been written and seminars offered that present formulas for success, but the formula for toxic success is an equally important equation:

$$\textbf{TOXIC SUCCESS: De + Dh + Df + Ds = D}$$

In this formula, **De** is a chronic sense of **D**eficiency and feeling that enough is never enough. **Dh** represents an agitated state of self-**D**oubt accompanied by the compensatory **h**urry to use every minute to make up for perceived inadequacy. **Df** stands for distracted **D**etachment usually sensed first by a spouse, close friend, or family members. **Ds** means persistent **D**isappointment and sadness that eventually leads to the fifth **D**, depression.

As indicated by the sum signs in this formula, my clinical work and interviews reveal that these five Ds of toxic success are cumulative. This means that even if one of the D factors is very low, the others or even just one factor could still add up to a high degree of toxic success.

Here are examples from the winners group of each of the five components of the formula for toxic success:

De = Deficiency. A 40-year-old sales executive said, "No matter what I've accomplished, it never seems enough. Maybe it's because, when I was a kid, nothing I ever did seemed enough to impress my dad. He would say I did well, but I never felt he really meant it. It always feels that whatever I've done, I could have done more. Even before our new home was finished, I was thinking about another house and ideas. I don't know whom I think I'm trying to impress. But, then again, I guess I just told you."

Dh = Doubt. A 31-year old woman executive said, "If I don't keep going, I feel like I'll fall behind. No matter how many people tell me how wonderfully successful I am, I feel I have to go faster, talk faster, and go at top speed to be as good as they think I am. It's like going fast helps me avoid how insecure I really am."

Df = Detachment. The spouse of the woman executive above said, "She's in perpetual motion. No matter how much we ask her to slow down and just be with us for a while, she seems to think *doing more for us* is the same as *being more with us*. It's not. She's not usually connecting with much even when she is home with us. We really miss her and sometimes wish it were like it was before when she wasn't such a big success. The kids really feel it, too. They're always asking, 'When's Mommy coming home?' What really scared me the other day is that she was home when they asked."

Ds = Disappointment. A 48-year-old national politician said, "Well, I've done it all and none of it makes me feel like I thought I would feel. Instead of relishing my success, I feel disappointed that I have it. I miss the old days on the campaign trail. My family was with me and it was hectic but great. Now, dozens of aides I hardly know have replaced my family. It's like getting the gift you really wanted for Christmas, being happy you have it, but sort of missing how your attention was always on it. It's like you had it more when you didn't actually get it, if you know what I mean."

D = Depression. The politician above reported, "I never would have imagined that I would end up on antidepressants. It drives my wife nuts. She says I have it all and everything any man could want, and she's right. But like you said in your lecture about the difference between getting what you think you always wanted and what deep down inside you know, and your family knows, you really and truly need, I just don't feel I have what I need from life. I never thought I, of all people, would consider suicide, but I am more and more." He paused and then joked, "If it wouldn't give the Democrats a majority in the house, I think I'd do it."

It may seem that the accounts offered by the winners group all reflect sadness and a negative personal assessment of their lives. They also shared many happy stories and descriptions of the tangible benefits of their success, but my lengthy interviews requiring them to pay more attention to their lives and the various tests related to TSS that they took usually resulted in their awareness of the failure of their success.

To make my points, I have chosen the strongest TSS examples. Some winners showed less profound degrees of TSS, but in general when these very successful people took time to focus their attention on the quality of their everyday life, they saw their world as disappointing and often at the root of a lingering clinical depression. The good news is that most of these people were able to turn their lives around and find sweet success. They examined the causes of their failed success and employed the various aspects of the detoxification program offered in part 2 of this book to, as one winner put it, become a "success survivor."

The Making of a Toxic Succeeder

The D factors of toxic success manifest differently in different individuals, but my interviews indicated that there were various combinations of several developmental factors common to proneness to toxic success. One factor revealed in the winners' histories was a childhood during which the person felt that no amount of success seemed good enough to win unqualified parental approval.

This factor was compounded when the person grew up in the presence of a highly successful mother or father who, knowingly or not, had become a competitor instead of a nurturer and more a judge than an unconditionally loving parent. When I asked, "Did your parents let you know they were very proud of you?" most of the winners did not respond quickly and positively. Instead, they would offer a defense of their parents with phrases such as, "I think my dad was proud of me, but he wasn't big on showing it" or "They weren't the demonstrative type." Sometimes, one or both parents themselves seemed to have felt like a failure and were seeking "a life do-over" through their own children. These parental factors often contributed to the self-doubt of the toxically successful.

A second developmental factor was the unquestioning internalization of society's stress-inducing comparative and competitive values. The TSS sufferer had often internalized the value of trying to be all one can be, better than anyone else, and able to accomplish anything if one "puts his or her mind to it." They had become used to a life of a frenetic pace and seemed lost and uncertain about what to do with themselves when not living at top speed. They were used to having things demand their attention and were unaccustomed to focusing their attention on where, when, and how they chose. The result of this kind of attention disorder is the detachment aspect of TSS.

A third developmental factor related to TSS was the sufferer's complete and unquestioning acceptance of the modern "self-interest norm," what the winners group called their major "SIN." Modern society stresses a "me" over "us" way of thinking, and when the boundaries of the self are firmly established, rigid, and defended, the detachment of TSS can be the result.

The fourth TSS-causing factor was exposure through childhood and adolescence to what might be called a "tyranny of freedom."[4] The toxically successful were often overwhelmed as children by their indulgent parents who provided an array of options and possibilities. Others felt that they had been deprived of the abundant choices they saw their peers enjoying and felt they had to compensate now by providing themselves and their families with an endless menu of choices. Either way, their view seemed to be that their level of success was reflected to others by the number of choices available to their family. As a result, those suffering from TSS were constantly anxious, insecure, and engaged in incessant second-guessing of the choices they did make. They were never certain that they had seen all of their choices or were doing enough to present them to their family. Because they could never have enough choices or be certain they had considered them all, they were bothered by a sense of deficiency difficult to understand by those who have much more limited life choices.

Many TSS sufferers came from high-income homes. They had seldom experienced deficiency until finding their own success. When they did achieve high-level success and could have almost anything they wanted, they discovered that they didn't feel they really needed anything. Having been given almost everything, they were inexperienced in need identification. No matter how many expensive things or fantastic experiences they purchased for themselves and their families, the feeling of contentment eluded them. As one winner put it, "If you never really felt you needed anything because you had everything, you never got practice in developing the sense of what you need. You just keep trying to get more stuff, but it never works."

In contrast to the overindulged winners described above, there were a few winners who were raised with very little in terms of tangible things in their lives. They knew well from experience the sense of deficiency and seemed compulsively driven to do all they could to, as one winner put it, "Never but never be in need of anything again and to see that my wife and kids never have a need that is not met." One set of winners didn't know how to need and the other was doing all it could to never need again.

Needing to Need

There is a common mental error made by the toxically successful. They are unaware of the fact that a state of needing can serve to invigorate and energize life. We are biologically engineered to be in need. We thrive on the change motivated by needing. Toxic success is working hard to achieve a predictable, stable life. Sweet success is not only accepting but even relishing what a constantly changing mess life can be.

Research in psychology shows that when it comes to happiness, what matters is that things are changing. It doesn't matter if things are changing for better or worse, only that they are changing.[5] Better than having a big income is experiencing a rising one. Better than moving into our dream home is planning and struggling with someone else to build a house.

Sweet success is the selfless sharing of the joy of constant life change. We may be numbed by having so much that we lose sight of our needs or work tirelessly to never need again. Sweet success is embracing and knowing what we need without becoming slave to it and being able to relish the joy of change. No matter how successful we become in the eyes of the modern world, sweet success is realizing that happiness is a moment-to-moment thing that ebbs and flows with the natural chaos of life.

We were made to be adapters, not final achievers. If we become all we can be and get everything we think we need, that is all we will ever be and all we will ever have. As psychologist David Myers writes, "Our very human tendency to adapt to new circumstances explains why, despite the elation of triumph and the anguish of tragedy, even million-dollar lottery winners and paraplegics eventually return to variations on moment-to-moment happiness."[6]

Damned by Great Praise

Another developmental factor contributing to TSS is the overly indulgent parent who gives his or her child constant positive feedback about how unconditionally wonderful and perfect the child is. Child rearing in modern America has become another test of success. Children are often seen as representatives of our success, and the schools they attend and the contests they win are viewed as symbols of successful parenthood. Even the act of having children has become a skill to be mastered and an experience to be had if one is to have had a fully successful life. Advances in reproductive biology make parenthood possible at almost any age and, regardless of the availability of a loving partner, an option to round out one's life. If they are to be successful, we believe that our children must have their self-esteem constantly stroked and nurtured at all costs.

Dr. Spock preached it and modern childcare experts still extol it. Make your children feel wonderful about themselves; tell them how great they are even if they aren't. However, while positive self-esteem is important, the result of this unqualified continual praise and glory throughout one's childhood begins to ring hollow, particularly when it comes from parents who seldom seem to have the time to be home enjoying life in the company of these extraordinary beings.

The result of constant praise can be suspicion and self-doubt on the part of children who know they are nowhere near as perfect as their parents keep telling them they are. They either become used to praise, and feel pressured to live up to a false image of perfection or come to suspect and dismiss almost all compliments as insincere or manipulative. As a result, no degree of high success and its accolades seem to mean anything. The consequence is an unrelenting search for validation of an elevated self-concept few could live up to and to be the person their parents seem to think they are or wish them to be. One winner joked about his self-concept and the pressure of toxic success striving by stating, "I have a weird self-image. I fall somewhere between what my mother thinks I am and what my father thinks I should be. I'm working hard to confirm my mother's ideas and impress my father. I don't think I'll ever get there."

Old Wisdom, New Science, Healthy Success

As common and socially ingrained as the features of toxic success are, part 2 of this book offers new hope for sufferers of TSS. It presents the detoxification program I have been using for years to help the toxically successful. It is based on a combination of the research from three of the newest sciences with one of the longest-tested models of excellence and success, the Hawaiian concept called *po'okela* (po-oh-kay-la), meaning achieving success through shared values rather than individual objectives.

The new science of sweet success borrows from three relatively new fields of study. The first is psychoneuroimmunology (PNI), the study of how our attitudes and beliefs affect our immune system. The second field is energy cardiology, the field that studies the heart as a thinking organ with its own unique form of energy and intuition. The third is the field of neurotheology, the study of the neurobiology of spiritual experience and how the brain experiences a sense of the sacred when it pays full and total attention to the sources of simple pleasure. All of these fields deal in their respective ways with the issue of healthy success. They show how regaining control of our attention can improve the emotional, physical, and spiritual quality of our life.

Po'okela is an ancient model of success, literally translated as meaning "leading an excellent life." It is a different way of thinking about what constitutes a successful life and how to attain it. It directly addresses the deficiency, doubt, detachment, disappointment, and depression of TSS by offering a way of attending to life based on contentment, calmness, and connection.

A Formula for Sweet Success

Based on the latest of modern science and the oldest of ancient Hawaiian wisdom about which you will be reading in the following chapters, here is a formula for a sweeter and gentler kind of success. As learned by my patients and many members of the winners group, this equation offers ways to take back our attention and become more absorbed in those aspects of life we value most:

$$\text{SWEET SUCCESS} = C_s \times C_c \times C_l = C_a$$

In this equation, C_s represents Contentment that is shared with another person. C_c is Calmness born of confidence in one's worth and acceptance of one's weaknesses. C_l stands for Connection characterized by loving caring. The product of these factors is C_a: Consciousness constructed by and composed of the process of elective attention to those people and things we most need to have on our mind and in our heart.

The modern image of a highly successful person is someone who is quick thinking, assertive, competitive, powerful, striving, confident to the point of arrogance, and in control. The Hawaiian *po'okela*-style successful person is a contemplative and reflective thinker who seems comfortable, contented, modest, patient, and concerned more with connecting than controlling. The view of success in the modern world, what I am calling toxic success, is behavioral more than mental. It is primarily focused on what an individual has managed to accomplish for him- or herself and then shared by those who live with that person. In contrast, the measure of success in the *po'okela* model is based on how people show they are thinking about the world and everyone and everything in it. It is reflected in their *mana,* or spiritual energy, as shown in their degree of contentment, calmness, and connected way of daily living. The new sciences you will read about confirm that success *po'okela* style is the sweetest, healthiest success.

Where's Daddy, Where's Mommy?

To see the devastation of toxic success, we need only to look at our youngest children. They are asking the questions we ourselves should be asking about the curse of success. They are not yet numbed to the homesickness that is unconsciously tugging at the hearts of their busy and distracted parents. Until their own toxic success overcomes them, their childish awareness of our spiritual absenteeism saddens them and may cause them to act out in order to get the attention they feel is lacking. We seem to be working harder and longer to give our children everything, but too often we fail to give them the gift of our own full attention and signs of our own contentment as a model for their own living and working. We are teaching them how to compete, but not how to be content.

I ask my success-suffering patients six questions about toxic success that get at this point of childhood attention neglect. I ask them, if you were your own children and being parented by you,

- Would you want to live and feel just like your parents?

- Would you say that your parents are content with their lives right now?

- Would you say that your parents value and really enjoy being with you and doing everyday things with you more than they enjoy working?

- Would you say that your parents are content with who and how you are?

- Would you say that your parents pay a lot of attention to you and seem calm and content when they are with you?

• Would you say that your parents love one another and take plenty of time to show it?

Putting yourself in your child's place, have you answered an unqualified yes to each of the above questions? If so, chances are you are more sweetly than toxically successful. Our children are still toxic success sensitive, so look at your success and how you are seeking it through their eyes. They are aware that no one is home waiting for them, and not really and fully "there" when they are at home. They sense our hurried quest for success driven by our underlying discontent with what we have, our eagerness to have more, and our expectations that they should do and want this same kind of life. They are the ones wandering through the big houses that sit empty most of the day for want of spiritual homemakers—calm, contented, loving adults committed to *being with* more than just *doing for* their families.

Family Outsourcing

Perhaps the ultimate test for the presence of toxic success syndrome is summed up in the childhood lament "Where's Daddy?" or "Where's Mommy?" As parents head off on the quest for success, they have chosen to "outsource" their family's lives. They leave their children's development during the most crucial years in the hired hands of strangers by providing them with purchased "daycare." The term itself implies that they have decided that they must buy hours of caring for their children. The assumption seems to be that a little night care will be good enough and that no matter how tired they are from their day, they will have enough loving energy left for the few hours before their child sleeps.

While outstanding daycare centers can be wonderful for those who can afford them, most parents are working longer and harder than they have to just to pay for daycare that is not nearly as beneficial for their children as their own regular presence.[7] Whether or not daycare is used, the key issue related to toxic success is "where your attention is" most of the day and when you are with your children. Is it with them or still on your striving for success?

In a kind of "deprivation domino effect," we have become accustomed to the idea that our older children will go off to school not only to learn but essentially to be babysat by teachers who themselves may be sufferers of TSS who have sent their own children off to other professional babysitters. The message at school is also often one of toxic success, including competition, winning, and striving hard to constantly be better than someone else. Those children who do not adapt to this toxic system or cannot comply with its code of competitive social and academic conduct may drop out or withdraw into an angry depression. They may turn to substance abuse to provide a temporary buzz of pharmacological success, the feeling of what a successful life might feel like, or the pharmacologically induced sense of contentment for which they have no role model and with which they have so little experience at home.

Sometimes the frustration of toxic success in our children can manifest itself in the form of violent acting out against "the system" of toxic success itself. If no one will pay attention to them or if the only attention they get is mockery, they may try to get attention through drastic actions that stick out so obviously that everyone has to pay attention.

The "fits," those who have strongly internalized and bought into the toxic success path yet feel they have somehow fallen short in their own success or failed in their parents' or "the system's" eyes, sometimes consider or commit suicide. Those who externalize toxic success and feel excluded or rejected from a cruel success system are often the "misfits" who are killing other students and teachers. Most children fall somewhere in between fitting and being misfits and struggling with how to be content in a world that keeps telling them to never be content and to keep going onward and upward over and beyond others.

The very ones we say we are working so hard to be successful *for* are often those being left longing to just be *with* us. Like all of us, they crave the attention that is invested elsewhere by their distracted and tired parents. American children today spend more than twice as much time in institutions as in their families.[8] These abandoned children sense that what we have come to call success is really socially sanctioned separation, an adult version of running away from home. A drive through any suburban area will reveal row upon row of large, beautifully landscaped but empty homes from which those who should be inside are constantly away working hard to pay for them.

Perhaps one of the most troubling aspects of all of this unconscious homesickness is that so many of our children seem to have stopped asking where we are. They seem to have accepted our physical and emotional absenteeism. Perhaps they are too distracted to miss us anymore. After all, if you want to be a success in this world and buy your own empty castle, you had better start early.

CHAPTER TWO

Coming to Your Attention

The choice of where we put our attention is
ultimately our most powerful freedom.

—*Jane Katra and Russell Targ*

"**W**ake up. The horizon's falling." It's a reminder my wife and I share every morning as we prepare to take our daily walk. What most people call a sunrise is really the planet tilting downward as we fall into another day. What is called a sunset is the horizon rising as we ride upward into a new night. Tomorrow morning and tomorrow night, direct your attention to the experience of "planet riding." Attend to the experience of being carried around and down toward the sun for a new day and around and up again into another night. How you attend to the beginning and ending of your day will change how you experience these most predictable natural events. It will provide evidence of the power of your most precious resource, your ability to make up the content of your consciousness and the quality of your life by how you focus your attention.

Attention is a filter between us and the outside world. Whether we experience the sun as revolving around us or ourselves rotating toward and away from it is up to us. Whether the world is the constantly stressful, demanding, time-pressured place in which the toxically successful live or a gentle and joyful carousel ride on planet Earth depends more on how and where we focus our attention than what is actually happening to us.

It All Depends on How You Look at It

One of the three new sciences of sweet success, psychoneuroimmunology (PNI) studies the influence of attention on our biology. It has proven that not only the quality of our mental experience but the quantity and effectiveness of our immune cells are influenced by the content of our consciousness as determined by the focus of our attention. It is not just what happens to us but what we make of what happens that affects our health, the kind of day we have, and ultimately the kind of life we will experience.

Another of the new sciences of sweet success is called energy cardiology. It has shown that our heart has its own way of thinking and its own unique energy to which we refer when we say, "I know it in my heart." Just like our brain, our heart is full of neurons and hormones. It can beat outside our body because it has a memory, and it reacts to other hearts because it senses their energy. Rather than just reacting to the brain's stimuli, it sends messages to the brain based on its own data.

One way to experience the effects of altering your attention is to try to listen to what your heart has to say. Sit down, quiet down, and try to tune in to the gentle, quiet, subtle messages from your heart that are telling you what you really need. The messages are likely to come in the form of vague feelings rather than clear thoughts or ideas. The brain tends to tell you what to do to get where you're going, but the heart tells you what and whom you need, so you can recognize it when you are already there. By listening to your heart's subtle wisdom, you may discover that you don't have to strive so hard anymore.

Just as the earth is not the center of the universe, neither does the brain have to be the center of our consciousness. Whether we suffer from TSS or enjoy sweet success depends on how we choose to pay attention to our life. If we feel like we are riding through it rather than passively waiting for the sun to come and go, and if we listen to our heart and other hearts and not just to our selfish and demanding brain, success takes on a whole new perspective.

Beyond Our Monkey Mind

Our brain has a remarkable and almost limitless capacity for awareness. It is capable of perceiving and processing billions of bits of information.

Toxic success results less from not being aware than from being aware of far too much for our own good. Even our children seem in a state of pre-TSS. They have become so overwhelmed by the amount of information bombarding their awareness that they can't seem to pay sufficient attention. Use of Ritalin, the strong stimulant chemical most commonly used to increase attention and treat what is called attention deficit disorder (ADD) is nine times what it was just ten years ago.[1]

Awareness comes before attention. It takes very little effort to be aware because our senses are doing that for us all day long. The function of attention isn't perceiving but filtering. Attention is selecting what we will allow to become part of our consciousness, including messages coming from our "other brain"—our heart.

Through awareness, we respond and gather immense amounts of information. In our information-overloaded world, that amount of information long ago passed overwhelming. Attention is our last line of defense against the info-anxiety of TSS. Through attention, we decide what information will have meaning in our life and what we will have "on our mind."

Psychologist Ellen Langer used the word *mindful* to describe our unique human resource of being able to pay attention by filtering out what we don't want on our mind.[2] Buddhism and other meditative traditions refer to the "monkey mind" as attention, which involuntarily reacts to whatever information is presented to it. Sufferers of TSS tend to have "monkey minds." About five million years ago, humans and chimpanzees ended their ancestral relationship, but we still share 98 percent of our genetic code with our monkey distant cousins. Our crucial 2 percent evolutionary advantage rests largely with our capacity to be free of our reactive monkey mind and to pay attention to that which we want on our mind and in our consciousness.

The root word of attention is the Latin *attendere,* meaning to tend to or take care of something. When we experience TSS, we are not taking care of the business of our own life. We are failing to tend to and care for that which is most precious to us. If we are constantly distracted by the outside world, we can't pay attention to our *inside* world where the wisdom of the heart resonates. TSS is a chronic form of attention deficit disorder through which we surrender to our monkey mind and go through most of our day trying to attend to everything but not being fully mindful of anything.

No matter how strong, "natural," or "necessary" we feel our drive is toward the kind of toxic success described in this book, we do not have to accept it. We don't have to be involved in monkey business. We can select for our consciousness what we want to be our business.

Our 2 percent advantage over our primate relatives provides us with one of the most unique and profound of all natural gifts: the freedom of where we will put our attention. What we are, who we are, and what we can become depend, in large measure, on those fleeting moments when we decide where we will invest our attention. TSS sufferers surrender that choice. They allow themselves to be overwhelmed by the busyness of life. In contrast, because they can pay attention when and how they choose, the sweetly successful feel they are minding their own business.

Consider the deluge of the objects competing for our attention. The Internet is doubling in content every hundred days. The Sunday edition of the *New York Times* now contains more information than all the written information available in the fifteenth century. There are more than three hundred thousand books and four hundred thousand scholarly journals published every year. Twenty years before Columbus discovered America, the largest library in the world was at the Queen's College in Cambridge. It contained only 199 books, a number usually exceeded by the personal library of most Americans. Fifteen billion catalogs arrive at our homes every year, usually piled in with more than seven billion pieces of direct mail delivered a month. We are certainly aware of this information bombardment, but no amount of Ritalin can help us pay attention to all of it.

The cost of high-level success and the expansion of information that fuels it are driving us out of our minds. The result is a serious cultural attention deficit. The business world is learning that the new capitalism is one in which, as scholars Thomas Davenport and John Beck point out in their groundbreaking book *The Attention Economy*, attention has become the new currency.[3] If we are to avoid TSS and becoming a planet of the apes, we have to stop monkeying around and reclaim our attention. We have to invest it wisely and carefully and guard it as our most precious resource.

The Myth of Multitasking

The demands on our attention that come from those we love cannot be quantified, but they too are extensive. In what economists call the "200-message-a-day economy," the needs of those we love must constantly compete for our attention from within a sea of stimulation.[4] We may call ourselves consumers, but we in fact are consumed by the information we ourselves generate. As one spouse of a winner reported, "When you lectured about the monkey mind, I thought right away that you were talking about my husband. I feel as if I should call his secretary and make an appointment if I want to get his attention. His attention wanders constantly from this task to that task and he brags about being a multitasker, but that's just another word for lack of attention to me. Now I'm going to call him monkey mind."

Anyone who brags of being a multitasker is confessing to being a sufferer of TSS. Research indicates that multitasking is another name for attention deficit disorder and lack of productivity and effectiveness. More than fifty years ago, studies conducted in British textile mills showed conclusively that trying to attend to several tasks at once leads to reduced productivity, mistakes, accidents, and worker dissatisfaction.[5] When we try to multitask, we may increase our awareness but not our attention. Attention is filtering things out to focus on one thing, not trying to be aware of and deal with many things.

Once we "pay" a little of our attention, it is gone forever. By deciding to attend to this book, you are not attending to something else that probably begs for your attention. Nobel prize-winning economist Herbert Simon points out the costs of the increasing demands on our attention. He writes, "What information consumes is rather obvious: it consumes the attention of its recipients. Hence a wealth of information creates a poverty of attention."[6] A poverty of attention is another definition of toxic success.

The World Hasn't Changed—We Have

When I present my ideas about toxic success to business audiences, I often hear the protest, "You're being unrealistic—the world has changed." I am told that we have very little choice but to go with the wave of the future. But it is not the world that has changed; it is how we have come to see the world. We bemoan what computers are doing to us, forgetting that we gave birth to these ever-demanding monsters. We are the ones who raised them and taught them how to think. If our creations are not user friendly, it's because *we* aren't.

We created the click-and-delete technology. We taught our computers the commands of quick escape, cancel, and cut at the click of a mouse. One winner said, "I get so used to interrupting that lady's voice on voice mail that I have started to interrupt live people. I'm so used to deleting all day long that I think I've started to delete people in my mind. My brain is starting to work like a mouse, almost unconsciously cutting, pasting, and saving. The world is beginning to look like a computer menu to me."

We delude ourselves if we think that the modern world has changed so much that we now work much harder and longer than our great-grandparents. They worked hard and long, too, and without the many so-called time-saving devices we now have that seem to demand so much of our time. The problem is not that we have busy bodies but that we have developed incessantly busy brains that squander our attention resource. It is not a new world that is causing toxic success—it's our insanely and incessantly busy brains. As Mahatma Gandhi pointed out, "The only devils in the world are those running around in our own hearts. That is where the battles should be fought."[7]

It is not life that is distracting and driving us so hard—we are. We can be extremely busy and still have a calm mind, but we have internalized the buzz and pace of the outside world and made it our brain's default mode. It is our consciousness, not our computers, that is at the root of the problem of toxic success.

Because toxic success includes an addiction to doing rather than being, those who suffer from it try to solve problems by trying to do something differently rather than learning to think differently. It is much easier for the brain to try to change behaviors than its own mind. It is easier to attend brief "spiritual retreats" or take "quality-time vacations" than to change our mind about what we will filter out of our consciousness.

Learning to manage our attention resource is the key to sweet success. It is important to understand, however, that attention management and time management are not the same thing. The field of time management began in the early 1960s and flourishes today in the form of hundreds of books and time-management daily-planning systems. Time is a convenient illusion and artificial measure we impose upon our lives. If you have ever attended a long lecture, you will have experienced the reality that you can spend a lot of clock time without paying much attention. You can also invest a huge amount of attention in a small amount of time, but first you have to stop monkeying around and accept the idea that your attention is yours to spend as you will and not a reactive impulse.

One winner, the mother of four children, discussed the impact of taking back her own attention and investing it as she chose. "I was big into time management. I had my schedule planned to the minute, including trying to fit in more and more 'quality time' with my kids. Then I saw what you meant about the difference between time and attention management.

"I was rocking my 5-year-old daughter. I just had a few minutes before I had to go to work. I wasn't counting this as 'quality time,' just as spending a few moments with her. For some reason, I was really focused on her. I told her how much I loved her and how much she meant to me. I looked into her eyes and saw her more intensely than I could remember. I saw her light up and smile. That one brief moment of full attention was worth days of what I used to call quality time when I would be so busy doing things with her that I never really saw her."

Destined for Busyness

We were made to be busy. Our body craves activity and accomplishment and we feel most alive when we are highly involved in life and working hard. A sweetly successful life is not one of sitting in the garden plucking at a harp. It is a happy, shared, highly active and involved life that constantly hums with activity, much as a forest sings with the hustle and bustle of the very hard work of daily survival. It is also a life characterized by our own control of where, how, when, and for how long we will focus our attention. It is having sufficient control of what is on our mind and how we react so that we are able to feel that we are leading our life, rather than life is leading us.

Toxic success is feeling that we are too often not in control of our senses and that our attention and interest are taken from us, scattered about, and lost.[8] It is creating a culture where the droning of an unwatched television has replaced the singing of birds and viewing the dancing images on a computer monitor's screen saver has taken the place of watching the horizon rising.

My *kumu* (Hawaiian teacher) often reminds me, "Do you hear the birds in the morning? They are saying, 'Wake up. Pay attention.' Before you can feel a sense of control of your life, you must wake up and give your undivided attention to it. Nature is offering wake-up calls all the time, from the rainbows to the shooting stars. Wake up. Pay attention. Take back control."

I extend this same invitation to you. Whenever you hear birds singing, think of their song as a spiritual alarm clock. Instead of "getting up," lie back down, slow down, and practice paying attention to being alive and able to love.

Toxic success is less a state of being busy than of being constantly distracted. Like when we brag of our multitasking ability, it is divided attention. Sweet success is really undivided attention free of our chronically busy and hyperreactive brain. It is paying full attention to the fact that we are already successful because we are alive to enjoy every day.

When our attention divides, it gets spread too thin. We become mentally exhausted from competing and pursuing what the brain thinks is success. As a result, we tend to shut down and fall asleep when we are not busy. You can be sitting quietly and still feel stressed and pressured by the insistence of a brain still consumed by thoughts of what is left to do, so just taking a break won't help. We don't need a nap; we need our attention.

One winner, a 38-year-old man who managed several fast-food restaurants, said, "I don't mind being busy. What gets to me is that in my mind I am always busy, even when I'm not. I can't seem to pay attention to anything for very long. I'll be sitting in church and my mind will still be racing. My brain is stuck on fast-forward. I even pray fast."

Stay Tuned

As you read these words, your own toxically successful brain may already be trying to reject this challenge to its idea of success and how to achieve it. It may be urging you to put this book down and "get busy" or to "just skip ahead" or "speed-read." It may be making you feel tired so you will put the book down and go to sleep. If you are going to deal with your TSS, you will have to stay tuned in despite your brain's resistance.

The brain can mistake calmness and contentment for loss of control and even the threat of nonexistence. As with a nervous child, frightened as you try to turn off the light at bedtime, you have to offer the brain assurance and comfort. As you would an impulsive child, I suggest you tell your brain out loud to "calm down and be patient." Tell it you are not going to hurt it, only try to settle it down and comfort it a little by making life a little less of what it considers interesting for a while.

Toxic success is becoming hard-hearted, not working hard. It is the brain in a lethal alliance with its body without the intervention of a calming heart. As you have read, energy cardiology shows that the heart has its own subtle way of thinking and its own calming energy. It literally thinks, but not as fast and competitively as the brain. When we surrender our attention to the ever-striving brain focused constantly on ways to get what it wants, we can't pay attention to what the heart is trying gently to remind us: that we need to thrive. The brain is concerned with what has to be done to be successful, but the heart is more concerned with paying attention to what it knows we need to feel fulfilled. To stay tuned in to the points raised in this book, you will have to be willing to go a little out of your mind and more into your heart.

Umbrella Woman and Gorilla Man

A woman carrying an opened umbrella walks through the middle of a basketball game and no one notices. A man wearing a gorilla suit walks into the same game, stops, faces the camera, thumps his chest, and walks off the court, and again no one notices. This is exactly what happened in psychological experiments conducted on a central component of TSS called "inattentional blindness."[9]

Researchers showed a film of two teams playing a game of basketball. They instructed observers to count how many times a basketball passed between members of one of the teams while ignoring the other team. When a woman carrying an open umbrella walked across the court for several seconds, most of those watching the film were "blind" to her.[10] In a later replication of this study, half those watching failed to see a man in a gorilla suit thumping his chest for nine seconds at center court. One of the researchers, Dr. Arien Mack, stated, "I came away from our studies [on inattentional blindness] convinced that there's no conscious perception without attention."[11]

Toxic success results from this "inattentional blindness," our failure to take control of how and where we pay attention.

"It seems impossible to me," said the brother of a female executive from the winners group. "She can look right through me like I'm not even there. I can stand right in front of her talking, and she is blind to me. Her mind is almost always somewhere else. We can be looking at the same beautiful picture, but I can tell she just doesn't see it. She's looking at it, but she's not really seeing it." This example of a toxic state of mind illustrates that TSS is a form of blindness to the grandeur of life and love all around us, the very sources of sweet success and what we and those we love know in our hearts we really need to feel that life has been a success.

Do You Have "Insight" or "Outsight"?

Another difference between toxic and sweet success is a matter of your point of view. Research in psychoneuroimmunology has shown that stress-related diseases are associated with where people tend to fall on a continuum between an "external" or "internal" locus (center) of control. For purposes of my interviews, I called these "outsight" or "insight."[12]

TSS sufferers tend to be monkey minded, so they are usually "outsighters" who feel helplessly reactive to an "external locus of control." They are directed, dictated, and often disrupted in their living, working, and loving by whatever current obligation enters their awareness. Their attention filter is weak, so they try to process almost every bit of information. If they do happen to think about how they think (and they usually don't), they consider what they are doing and feeling to be an automatic, necessary, and only "normal" reaction to the outside world. They operate from the point of view that whatever happens to them is essentially unrelated to their own thoughts and behaviors.

Outsighters are frustrating to live with because they externalize almost everything. Things tend to be "just how they are." They engage in the attribution error illustrated by one of the winners who says, "If I'm upset, it's his fault. If he's upset, it's the situation."

On the other hand, "insighters" have an inner locus of control. Their attention filters work well, so they select what will be on their minds. They feel that they can choose what to think and for how long. They consider themselves free to attend to what, whom, and where they like. They tend to have a more laserlike attention that picks through all the incoming information and focuses on what it needs to. As a result, the insighters are much more likely to see umbrella woman and gorilla man because they are in charge of where they place their attention. They may choose to ignore them, but they are not inattentionally blind to them. While their "insightfulness" can sometimes lead to painful reflection and exaggerated self-accountability in too many situations, they are also free to determine the nature of their life experience and the content of their consciousness.

One of the one hundred winners I interviewed for this book showed her "outsight" point of view. When I challenged her outsightedness, she responded angrily, "That's absurd. It's the real world—what choice do I have? My husband and I both have to work because the world demands it. We have to be aware of hundreds of things at once. We have no choice but to get up, drive three kids to different schools and daycare, talk on the cell phone while were doing it, and check our e-mail from our laptop as soon as we can. You multitask or you fail in this world.

"What do you expect of us?" she went on. "Do you think we want to live and feel like this all the time or that we don't want to be home with our kids? We're like anyone else who wants to be successful nowadays. We have to live and work in the real world whether we like it or not. If we are going to be successful and offer a successful life to our kids, this is how it has to be."

One of the "insightful" winners argued back with the woman above. She said, "It's my life, and I make it what it is. I have choices and they influence what happens to my family and me. I'm not going to buy in to what the world tells me is the way to live and be successful. I'm a single mother with two kids. I have to work. But I choose what's on my mind. I decided to find a job where I could work at home and be with the kids. I looked inside and saw that I was spending almost as much or more money on daycare as I was making at work outside the home. The choice became my money or my kids.

"When the kids go to school," she continued, "I'll have time to go back outside the home to work if I want. We probably don't have all the stuff you guys have, and I probably won't be as successful, but at least we have our sanity. I'm still really, really busy, but I now can pay much more attention to my kids. It's not that I cut back. I just learned to filter out a lot of the stuff I don't want to deal with. I've just tuned in much more."

Psychologist Phillip Rice summarized the "outsighter and insighter" difference in consciousnesses when he wrote, "If the theme song for the external [locus of control] is 'Cast Your Fate to the Wind,' the theme song for the internal [locus of control] is 'I Did It My Way.'"[13] Sweet success is associated not with simply casting our fate to the whims of the cosmos but with realizing that the quality of our life depends in large measure on the quality of what we elect to put on our mind. It is taking back control of our attention so that, unless we choose not to see her, umbrella woman doesn't walk right past us.

One of my winners group member's spouses said, "I wish my husband was as interesting as his life." A highly successful businessman, he had apparently become a victim of the Chinese curse mentioned at the beginning of this chapter. He had made an interesting life for himself, but it now seemed to be pushing him away from the person he loved. As his wife said, "He doesn't have a life, it has him. I sure don't." In contrast, if you feel that your attention is on the people, places, and things you want to hold in your heart and use as memory makers, you are well on the road to sweet success.

The idea of the importance of our sense of control in our lives and how we think about living, loving, and working began to be studied several decades ago.[14] It was then that it began to become clear that our point of view— "I must" or "I choose"—has profound influence on all aspects of life. As psychologists and researchers use the term, *control* does not mean being in command of events or people. It refers to the deep-seated belief that we can impact a situation and what a situation does to us by how we choose to look at the problem.[15] It refers to the fact that, unlike most other animals, we can choose how we will decide to focus our attention. This choice of an "inner locus of control" and self-responsibility for the mental and spiritual quality of our lives is fundamental in moving from toxic to sweet success.

Sweet Success at Grandma's and Grandpa's House

My grandparents were models of the calm and contented inner sense of control associated with sweet success. Their attention filter seemed to work beautifully. Our visits to their home were some of the most joyous times in my life. In the early 1930s, my grandfather worked long hours at an automobile assembly plant in Detroit, Michigan. Times were difficult, but unlike so many other adults I saw around me, he always seemed in calm control. His hands were scarred by years of cuts from heavy machinery, and my grandmother was bent over from years of caring for my disabled aunt whom she had to feed, move, and lift every day for more than fifty years. They had both worked hard from morning to night throughout their lives and continued to volunteer in various church and community efforts well into their nineties. I never heard a rushed or impatient word from either of them and when they spoke to us, we felt almost nervous that they paid such rapt attention to our every word and gesture. No matter how hard life became, nothing ever seemed to take their attention away from aspects of their family life.

When we visited our grandparents' house, we would all sit around engaging in an activity that might seem frustrating for sufferers of TSS. We simply sat together and waited for something to which we chose to attend. What ended up in our minds always seemed to be wonderfully and blissfully calming. We engaged in what the busy brain would consider "doing nothing," but at those family times it seemed like everything. We seemed to become of one mind and a group, where SIN, the self-interest norm, was inconceivable. Sitting with people who know how to pay attention and filter out distractions seems to bring out a heightened attention in everyone around.

I can still hear the tick of the old clock that seemed to set the pace for my grandparents' life. I try to focus on that ticking when I become too toxically involved in my own pursuit of success. We would all circle around the radio or record player to listen to music, but it was the sitting together and not the sounds that set the stage for the shared feeling of contentment I call sweet success. We would listen, look around the circle, and nod from time to time at one another when we particularly enjoyed a song or passage or seemed to have an association that others sensed beyond words.

Our dinners were prepared and brought to the table by all of us, and cleanup was a family event and opportunity for good gossip. A prayer preceded every meal, a practice that often seemed to irritate some of our toxically successful visitors and cause them to sneak a peek at their watches. The meal proceeded at a slow pace that also seemed to bother some of our visitors. Some guests would lose patience and suddenly reach across the table to grab a dish of potatoes from the hands of a family member neglecting the task of potato passing due to being totally engrossed in the telling of a story. There was as much talking as eating, and the only loudness was the laughter that seemed essential to our digestion.

No one left the table during a meal, no one answered the phone if it should ring, and when the meal ended, we all remained to talk about fun times we had shared together. From time to time, one of us would sample another piece of food intentionally left sitting on a dish. Popping the food in our mouth, we would say, "Just to keep my taste." Everyone would laugh—a shared ritualistic acknowledgment that there was really no need to hurry off.

If it seems to you that the above description sounds just too good to be true and a romanticized version of life that is totally unrealistic in today's world, you probably lean toward being an "outsighter." You believe that the world demands that attention be paid in a particular way and manner, and you have to comply. Sweet success says otherwise. Life in my parents' home was much the same as at my grandparents' house, and they also worked hard and long and suffered through many very serious crises of their own. My father often worked three jobs, and my mother took the bus daily to work long hours in a law office. There were layoffs, severe financial stresses, and a series of health problems, but somehow my parents always seemed in calm control. I always felt that when I needed their full attention, I received it. My dad would say, "The problems come in, but you don't have to swallow them whole. You chew them up, take in what you need, and spit out the rest. The world is what you make it."

Hawaiian Style

Today, my own home in Hawai'i is still much like my childhood home. It resonates with the laughter of my Hawaiian *'ohana* (family). *'Ohana* refers to an extended group of friends, work colleagues, children, siblings, mothers, fathers, and grandparents from many biological families. The Hawaiian *'ohana* includes attention to the presence of the *'aumakua*, the ancestors, who are just as much family now as they were when they were alive. The common link is an irrationally deep, profound, and demonstrated unconditional concern for one another's welfare.

Over the decades of my life in Hawai'i, I have been embraced by Hawaiians. It seems that my upbringing, research, clinical work, and writing has resonated with their values. They have, through a process called *hanai*, taken my wife and me as family in every sense of that word as used by most Westerners.

Symbolic of being *hānai* to my *'ohana*, I was given my Hawaiian name, *Ka'ikena*, as a family responsibility. *Ka'ikena* means, "person of vision with the responsibility to share that vision." The name was given me by Tutu Mana Ellis, the oldest living member of our *'ohana*. My wife was given the name *Kalālani,* meaning "light from the heavens," and her healing strength gives testimony to the appropriateness of that name.

The *'ohana* bond is one of *aloha* (love) and not blood, and one is expected to focus attention on *'ohana* in all aspects of daily life and work. Most importantly, *hānai* is forever. All of what you will read in this book about *po'okela*, the Hawaiian version of success, I learned from my Hawaiian *'ohana*. In our *'ohana*, we spend much of our time singing, dancing, and just "talking story," meaning sharing our feelings and thoughts about the simple things of daily life. Sometimes after a busy workday, we watch a horizon rising. When we are together, it is considered rude and disrespectful to be distracted by issues of work. Ukuleles and guitars have replaced the "phonograph," but we also have our computers and cell phones. All of our schedules are hectic and busy and many us have two or more jobs, but we still attend fully to making our world what we need it to be.

If for some reason we cannot find time to be together on a given day, we still try to keep our homes at the center of our consciousness and our attention. The slow ticking of my grandparents' old clock is still the pulse of our daily life. It resonates in our home and hearts. It serves as a gentle rhythmic reminder of a loving memory that the outside world does not have to control how we are inside or the rhythm of our consciousness.

Wishing Well

The modern version of the Chinese curse for an interesting life might be replaced by a wiser and healthier wish. We could hope for a sweeter kind of shared success based on learning to be content and even delighted with a simpler life with plenty of time to love. We could wish that no matter how busy we are, we can still pay our fullest attention to what we know and sense in our heart matters most.

As pointed out by ecopsychology researcher Alan Thein Durning, we could choose to wish for the sweet success that comes from what all of the data indicates are the two primary sources of a feeling of true happiness in life—social relations and enjoyable leisure.[16] As Durning suggests, we could wish to feel that "clotheslines, window shades, and bicycles have a functional elegance that clothes dryers, air conditioners, and automobiles lack."[17] We could choose to wish for a healthy shared success as measured not by striving to meet our brain's insatiable wants but by the amount of daily life we spend thriving because we are attending to what we know in our heart matters most to us. We could wish for the calm contentment of fewer choices and the wisdom to find contentment with what we have chosen. To do so, however, we will have to be willing to develop a level of insight that will make us seem abnormal to all the toxically successful people around us.

CHAPTER THREE

Being Normal Can Drive You Nuts

Trying to be normal almost killed me. The only way to survive in this crazy world is to be willing to be weird enough not to fit in to it.

—Cancer Patient

Mrs. Horgan patrolled our eighth-grade classroom with a wooden yardstick in hand. She would sneak up behind us and, if we seemed the slightest bit distracted, would smack it loudly on our desk and yell, "Mind on your work!" She called her approach the "success shock treatment," and we learned to at least look like we were working hard. She had placed a large sign over the chalkboard that read, "Quiet. Winners at Work." One day after catching me daydreaming again, she sent me home with a note to my mother. I have a framed copy of that note that I've kept as a reminder of success Mrs. Horgan style and how it relates to the toxic success syndrome. It says:

> *I am very sorry to inform you that your son Paul is an underachiever who refuses to work as hard as he is able. He lacks a winning attitude and is perfectly content with a B when he could be earning all As. He should be at the top of his class, but he shows no concern for that at all. He is not self-motivated, lacks independence, and often stops focusing on his own work to help the slower students with theirs. His attention is focused on irrelevant things. He shows a most annoying tendency to waste time by just sitting and thinking but not doing anything. He pays more attention to the tree outside the window than to being the winner we all want him to be. He is setting a very bad example for the rest of the students.*

When I returned home with the note, my mother greeted me with her usual after-school question: "Did you enjoy school today?" I answered that I had but that Mrs. Horgan had not seemed to enjoy me. I handed my mother the note and she read it out loud. She laughed as she read, hugged me, and said, "You're not normal, and I'm proud of you." When she got to the last sentence, I saw deep concern and sadness in her eyes. She read, "Paul is not at all like my other successful students, but I will work tirelessly all this school year to see that he is." My mother rose from her chair, took out paper and pen, and read out loud as she wrote her response. It said, "Dear Mrs. Horgan: If your aspirations for my son are that he seek success the way your other successful children in your class do, I fear that your aspirations for my son are far too low."

My mother had constantly warned me of the dangers of being "normal." Every time a new fad emerged and true success in my adolescent life seemed at stake if I could only do what all the other highly successful and popular kids were doing, my mother issued her warning. She would say, "Just because everyone else is doing it doesn't make it right. If everyone ran off a cliff, would you follow them?" So strong was the pressure to succeed in the socially prescribed manner and to keep up with my peers that I wanted to answer yes.

My mother's philosophy was one grounded in the value of a noncompetitive, joyful, altruistic approach to a successful life. When she'd ask, "What do you want to be when you grow up?" and my brother and I would answer, "Doctor, soldier, cowboy, fireman, or pilot," she would follow with the question "How would that make you and everyone else very happy?" She seemed more proud of us when we seemed content than when we were competitive and when we expressed more concern for others than for ourselves. Even though we were more interested then in the image than the realities of our careers-of-the-day, her question still resonated within us and influenced our definition of success.

When we grew older and became immersed in the same hectic pace toward success that all the other "normal" people were following, she would say, "There is much more to life than being successful." And as we went through college, my brother and I thought that she might be suffering from a form of success senility or perhaps indulging in the luxury of philosophizing allowed only to those who already had their piece of the pie and had forgotten what it took to get it. However, based on my personal experience and the research presented in this book, I know now that my mother was right all along. Success and the way contemporary society defines it and says we should achieve it is a risk to our well-being. When it comes to a successful life, our modern version of "normal" is nuts.

The Pathology of the Norm

My mother's warning speaks to the essence of this book. As psychologist Erich Fromm pointed out in his quote on the title page of part 1, just because millions of people seem to share the same forms of pathology it does not make them sane.[1] The following are some examples of modern behaviors that have become the norm. They are related to living and working in the competitive, self-focused, hectic-pace orientation of toxic success mode that, as one of my Hawaiian friends put it, "mistakes intensity, newness, and having a lot of stuff with having a lot of soul":

- **Eating too much and exercising too little**. Three of every four Americans eat too much, carry at least ten too many pounds, and fail to get enough exercise. As a result of this statistically "normal" behavior, an estimated 300,000 Americans die each year from the combination of poor diet and chronic inactivity.[2]

- **Going shopping instead of parenting**. Most Americans spend, on average, six hours a week shopping and only forty minutes playing with their kids. The amount of time parents are spending with their children has diminished by forty percent in the past generation.[3]

- **Getting away "to" it all**. Thirty-four percent of Americans say their favorite activity is shopping, while only 17 percent say they enjoy communing with nature. The number-one rated "scenic drive" in America is now the Las Vegas Strip.

- **Paving paradise**. Every sixty minutes, forty-six acres of prime American farmland are lost to the development of malls and the building of larger and larger homes to hold what they sell. Highways and parking lots cover more land every day, and two-thirds of the land area of Los Angeles is now paved over.[4]

- **"Stuffing" instead of learning**. Americans spend more on jewelry and watches (about $80 billion a year) than on higher education (about $65 billion). We have more than twice as many shopping centers as high schools.

- **Building bigger empty homes**. Our homes are hundreds of square feet bigger than several years ago and keep growing in size as we work harder to pay for them. Our cars have houses (garages) that are, on average, 200 square feet bigger than the average home built in the early 1950s. Comedian George Carlin said that our home has become "just a pile of stuff with a cover on it."

- **Delighting in debt**. Americans carry an average of almost $8,000 in credit card debt and continue to pay the minimum amount required each month. Because of the high interest rate on credit cards, they end up paying more than double the original cost.[5]

- **"Spaving."** Despite the fuzzy math involved, Americans seem to think that spending money is a way to save it. "I am a professional spaver," said one of the winner's spouses, proudly holding up two stuffed shopping bags. "I spent almost $1,000 this morning at the mall and I spaved us at least $200." As authors John de Graaf, David Wann, and Thomas H. Naylor point out, "The road to bankruptcy is *spaved* with good intentions."[6] My study of TSS indicates that the bankruptcy is not only financial but spiritual.

- **Relationship neglect**. More marriages fail than survive. The divorce rate is more than double what it was in the 1950s, and most new marriages won't last longer than seven years. Even when couples stay together, they spend, on average, less than twelve minutes a day talking with each other.

- **Cyber-intimacy**. Millions leave their family members alone, go to their chat room, and "communicate" with people they don't know. Millions of people spend hours in online sexual talk with persons they have never met, the kind of behavior psychologist Erich Fromm referred to as "simultaneous but not shared pleasure."[7]

Eating too much, exercising too little, consuming at levels that boggle the mind, and increased disconnection from people and nature have become the normal or usual ways of the successful American way of life, but are these behaviors healthy for our planet and us? Does going along with this way of living and view of success really result in the sweet success we long for, or is it a form of commonly accepted cultural pathology that is polluting our planet and poisoning our souls?

What we have come to define as success and the normal way to achieve it in all areas of our lives is a destructively limiting one. Normal now seems more diagnosis than definition. Columnist Ellen Goodman writes, "Normal is getting dressed in clothes that you buy for work, driving through traffic in a car that you are still paying for, in order to get to the job that you need so you can pay for the clothes, the car, and the house that you leave empty all day in order to afford to live in it."[8]

The "normal" drive for success we are all supposed to have and the sacrifices we are expected to be willing to make to achieve it are toxic not only to our own health but to the well-being of those we love. While it may seem a gross exaggeration, you will read that our current definition of success and the prescribed paths for attaining it lead to a dead end, the cliff my mother warned about. They stem from the same materialism, consumerism, attention deficit, and SIN (self-interest norm) that has plagued the so many highly successful civilizations before us.[9]

While I never had the courage to actually answer yes to my mother's question about following others off a cliff, I remember thinking then that I might indeed consider it. I thought it might be worth it to be spared the dreaded label of being "weird" or left behind as a social failure. However, I owe much of the happiness and healthy success in my life to my mother's warning about the inherent dangers in trying to be what is seen as normal and moving with the pace of the current fast lane to success.

Is Greed Really Fear?

When the main character played by Michael Douglas in the film *Wall Street* says, "Greed is good," he elicits both our shock at his selfishness and perhaps unconsciously our feeling that he might be right. Even if by surrender to what is considered normal and necessary in today's world, the character's arrogant self-certainty and interest and his unrelenting competitiveness are often role models for those seeking success. As one observer of the film stated, "He's the hero you hate to love." To the degree we admire this toxically successful man and surrender to his "normal" ways of success, this view of a necessary way to seek success is a risk to our well-being and the health of our families.

As tolerated and accepted as the motive of greed seems to have become, my interviews of the highly successful indicate that it is driven by an underlying and deeply personal fear of not being seen as successful in the eyes of others. It is based on an image-protecting surrender to the self-interest norm which eventually results in the unrelenting sense of deficiency, over-compensation for self-doubt, and detachment from loving relationships that made the Michael Douglas character such a horrific example of toxic success.

Because the film *Wall Street* seemed to be a good example of the psychological ecology that has resulted from capitalism, free enterprise, and a money-focused society that makes a commodity out of almost everything, I asked some of the winners group if they had seen the film. Most of them had. When I asked them what they thought about the Michael Douglas character, all of them found him to be a self-absorbed, obnoxious, and unlikable person. All but seven of this group, however, admitted to at least some level of admiration and envy. One winner said, "I wouldn't want to go on a cruise with the guy, but I wouldn't mind having his power and confidence. You can't deny that he had achieved a huge amount of success. He was really at the center of where the action was. He was ruthless, but you have to kind of admire his ruthlessness in a way. You can't say he didn't attain a very high level of success and the perks that come with it."

Dying for Attention

Our greed is not just for money and the things money can buy. It is also a craving for attention. For the winners I spoke with, it didn't seem enough to be or feel successful, they had to be sure their success showed and other people easily saw it. Sociologist Charles Derber suggests that the greed illustrated by the character in *Wall Street* relates to an inordinate desire for individual attention. Derber writes that we increasingly fail to engage in true give-and-take conversations because we are so eager to talk about ourselves.[10]

Our greed is for personal recognition and to "stand out" more than to "fit in."

The self-interest norm and its "what's in this for me" emphasis have become so normal in our society that we have forgotten another of my mother's classic warnings. She told me, "Everybody wants attention. Remember that you only get attention by giving it. If you want someone's attention, you have to really pay a lot of attention to them." A mistake made by TSS sufferers is that in their eagerness to be the center of attention, they forget this give-to-get rule. The result is the ultimate detachment of toxic success.

How Normal Are You?

Psychologist Abraham Maslow wrote, "Certainly it seems more and more clear that what we call 'normal' in psychology is really a psychopathology of the average, so undramatic and so widely spread that we don't even notice it."[11] Toxic success has become the modern, widely accepted, and celebrated psychopathology of the above-average, the "usual" way to view and seek success.

Are you a success? Do you think others think you are successful? If so, you are probably well adjusted to what has become an increasingly crazy world. If you think you are relatively successful and normal in terms of how life is led today, you probably will answer yes to many of the following questions. You have probably been turned "inside out" and succumbed to what society says success is and how it should be pursued.

I gave the "normalcy test" presented below to the winners group. All of them had received honors and awards as winners in their respective lines of work, saw themselves as very successful, and would be seen by most Americans as highly successful people to be envied for their accomplishments and the life that they had achieved for themselves. Take the test yourself to see how "well adjusted" you have become.

Warning to TSS suffers: *This will not be an easy test to take.* Its length frustrated and even angered the winners group. They felt that the short survey for the toxically rushed as offered in chapter 1 was "good enough." Their attention deficit disorders caused them to want to give up before they had answered even half of the items. Now is the time to practice learning to pay attention. As taught in most Eastern meditative traditions, try to catch your mind wanting to wander away as you work through the test. Think of yourself as an expert dog trainer and your mind a rambunctious puppy. When you notice your mind wandering, stop a moment and wait. We are not only blessed as humans to be able to place our attention where we want it; we can also train it.

By tolerating your impatient brain's tendency to wander off like an undisciplined puppy and remembering that yelling at or scolding the dog would only be counterproductive and even cause it to run away, you can learn to wait until your attention returns. In fact, thousands of years of experience with various meditative and contemplative practices indicate that the more times you patiently allow your wandering attention to return, the more you are learning how to take back your attention.

The only tool you will need to negotiate through the intentionally long test ahead is attention. When a Zen teacher was asked, "What tools do we need?" the teacher answered "Only one. We've all heard of it, yet we use it very seldom. It's called attention."[12]

ARE YOU NORMAL?

Using the following scale, score yourself on each of the items below.

0 = No   1= Yes   2 = That's for sure!

1._____ Are you divorced, in a chaotic or unfulfilling relationship, or unable to find someone with whom you are willing to spend a loving life or who is willing to share one with you?

2._____ Do you feel that your time is not your own, there is too much to do in too little time, that time is money, and that there is never enough time in the day to do all you want or need to?

3._____ Do you make well-intended but unkept promises that you are going to cut back, take it easy, get your life back in balance, put in more quality time, get away for a while, make it up to those you feel you have been neglecting, or will make some big changes as soon as you "have enough"?

4._____ Do you say to yourself and others, "The world has gone crazy," yet feel unable to extract yourself from the madness?

5._____ Do you compare your life and its successes with others' achievements, feel competitive, jealous, and sometimes resentful of others' good fortune?

6._____ Do you feel tangled in the Internet, always one step behind in the electronic race, and that you cannot seem to keep up with the very latest in computers, cellular phones, and other so-called interactive devices?

7._____ Do you feel that even though you have a lot of time saving gadgets, you seem to have ended up with less and less time to call your own?

8._____ Have you begged of, yelled at, and even hit your computer or thrown a temper tantrum when some electronic glitch erased hours of work?

9._____ Have you talked on your cellular phone while those you are with sit waiting, or engaged in a "cellular circle" of people talking to people who are not present?

10._____ Has your cellular phone or beeper gone off in a movie theater, religious service, or other social event?

11._____ Have you ever felt that you have just too many choices and can never be sure you've considered them all or you're confidently content with the choice you've made?

12._____ Have you been annoyed by someone talking loudly on his or her cellular phone?

13._____ Have you ever become a human antenna by wandering around with your cellular phone in search of a "good reception" area?

14._____ Have you reflexively and suddenly turned away from someone in a "cellular spasm" to search frantically for your phone or beeper before it stops ringing?

15._____ Have you became frustrated to the point of near rage at hearing the fake sincerity of the message "Your call is very important to us" or by an endless menu of number options, none of which seem to relate to your needs?

16._____ Do you complain that it seems that people are becoming more and more selfish, insensitive, dishonest, and uncaring, and that you have to be even stronger and more clever than others to be sure you get and protect your piece of the pie?

17._____Have you felt nagged by your spouse or family that you are ignoring them and pressured by what you see as even more demands by them on your already insufficient time?

18._____Have you ever lied to avoid a phone call or to explain a missed appointment?

19._____Have you ever lied to those you love in order to avoid disclosing that you have put your work before them?

20._____Have you become so accustomed to feeling stressed that you feel disoriented and don't know what to do with yourself when you are not under stress?

Are you still with me? Is your attention wandering away? Wait a moment. Notice how it feels to have your attention leave. Try to focus back on the test and wait for your attention to return. Don't be impatient with yourself and, most of all, don't try to be a success at your attention training. Even puppies know when the trainer is losing patience and, when they sense it, are likely to try to run away from their trainer. Your brain may be a narcissist, but it is very sensitive and can have its feelings hurt easily. When that happens, it tends to give up or sulk. Just by trying to train your attention, you are already making progress in detoxifying your success and quieting your monkey mind.

21._____Do you defend your competitive reflex by saying that you are really only competing with yourself?

22._____Have you felt a "stress rush" with your blood pressure seeming to go up, your face warming, and your heartbeat starting to race?

23._____Do you have several little "stress seizures" in the form of anger tantrums?

24._____Have you become much more cynical than you used to be?

25._____If you stop now to think about it, do you notice that you are not laughing and crying as much as you used to?

26._____Do you feel that you don't have enough time to just sit and think and to "get your wits about you"?

27._____Do you feel spurred on by a chronic impatience, drive over the speed limit, coast through stop signs, try to get a running start before the light turns green, or speed up to squeeze ahead at a "merge to one lane" area?

28._____Have you sworn or gestured angrily at other drivers?

29._____Do you feel constantly competitive with others and frustrated by long and slow-moving lines?

30._____Does it seem to you that all of the really dumb and sluggish people in the world have somehow gotten ahold of your daily schedule and conspired together just to get in your way?

31._____Have you angrily glared at someone who was slowing you down?

32._____Do you sigh in frustrated disgust with someone who seems hopelessly inept, inefficient, and slow?

33._____Have you tried and failed at several diets or felt "health guilt" for weighing too much, eating the wrong food, and not exercising enough?

34._____Do you take a lot of vitamins, herbs, and other supplements in an attempt to compensate for your rushed living style and poor diet?

35._____Do you know your cholesterol number and weight, worry about it, but do not seem to have the time to do much about it?

Congratulations! If you made it this far, you are beginning to reduce your attention deficit disorder. Take a deep breath, wait for your attention to return, and continue. There are only two hundred items left to go. Did you panic when you read that number? There are actually only fifteen items left, but the winners group was really struggling by number 35. Let the attention panic attack pass, allow your focus to return, and remember how it felt to lose and regain your focus. It's that feeling that will eventually help you reclaim your own attention.

36._____Do you feel you are not getting enough sleep or brag that you don't need much sleep?

37._____Do you tend to feel sleepy or doze off when you are in a situation where you have to sit down and be quiet?

38._____Do you have more stress than sex in your life and feel that you are not getting enough enjoyable and fulfilling sensual contact?

39._____Do you have the "dash and crash" syndrome characterized by vacillating during the day from feelings of boundless energy to feeling totally drained?

40._____Would those who know you best say you are moody to the point that they are sometimes afraid to bother you?

41._____Do you feel at least mildly depressed much of the time and sometimes to the point of wanting to "junk it all" and "run away"?

42._____Have you promised that "things are going to change" and that you are going to get more control of your life?

43._____Do you feel you are living at an unhealthy pace but feel helpless to do anything about it?

44._____Do you long for a simpler, slower life but feel unable to achieve it?

45._____Does the slightest little hassle seem to "set you off" more than it should?

46._____Are you a "multitasker" who does several things at once and never really feels completely finished with any one task?

47._____Despite all of your electronic devices, do you feel unorganized?

48._____Do you feel that time seems to be running out?

49._____Does it seem that you are "just going through the motions" and not really fully enjoying your life?

50._____Do you feel you have more responsibility and accountability than you do power and control?

_____ TOTAL POINTS

Well done! You made it. Remember the "ins and outs" of your attention and how you allowed it to return. This lesson will come in handy when you try the detoxification program in part 3 of this book.

The higher your total score, the more "normal" and "well adjusted" you have become to our toxically successful way of life. Based on my interviews and clinical work, a score over 20 indicates that you may be well adjusted to the modern world but not at all "well" in terms of your physical, emotional, spiritual, and love life.

Accustomed to Craziness

If you scored "normal" on the test above, you have become an outpatient in a psychiatric community of pressured, alienated persons rushing right past their one and only opportunity to enjoy the gift of being fully alive. You have probably achieved a good measure of what this crazy community calls success and have learned how to be well adjusted to a way of life to which no one in their right mind should be adjusting. Unless we become aware that what we see as normal is really sick, the all consuming epidemic of "affluenza" described by author John de Graaf, our "normal" way of living will lead us to the same fate of every fallen, highly successful culture before us.[13]

Research indicates that many of the behaviors and ways of thinking that have become prerequisites for success are in fact pathological—an emotional condition called *cyclothymia*.[14] Cyclothymia is sometimes referred to as manic-depression or bipolar disorder, but these are clinical conditions often helped with medications. I use the term cyclothymia because it seems to carry less clinical baggage. Those who want to address this component of TSS more easily accept it and its symptoms as listed below.

Cyclothymia is characterized by moodiness, impatience, and bouts of unhappiness that persist despite the highest level of success. William Blake, Lord Byron, Alfred Lord Tennyson, Winston Churchill, and Albert Einstein are among the success heroes whose personal lives reflected their suffering from cyclothymia. The list of symptoms of cyclothymia constitutes another minitest for toxic success. They include:

1. Periods of feeling on top of the world followed by emotional crashing
2. Projected high self-esteem masking a deep sense of self-doubt and insecurity
3. Abundant energy to the point of edginess and agitation followed by periods of complete fatigue

4. Withdrawal from others and a sense of detachment
5. Excitability and quickness to anger
6. Grandiosity to the point of poor judgment
7. Neglected or chaotic intimate personal relationships
8. Neglect of personal health often accompanied by destructive behaviors such as substance abuse, reckless driving, or neglect of diet and exercise
9. Distrust of compliments and suspicion of others' motives
10. Cynicism to the point of hostility

Unfortunately, the above behaviors have become all too common in our modern world. If everyone who suffered from them was diagnosed and treated, our clinics would be overwhelmed. They have become so common, in fact, that few would seek professional help for these conditions because they have become "used to them." Even if they did seek help, they would likely end up with a therapist unable to acknowledge their own cyclothymic propensities associated with the achievement of their success.

Unhappy Guys with Perfect Lives

"Life just isn't fun anymore. Golf, sex, new cars, big business deals—nothing seems nearly as much fun as it was years ago." These are the words of one of the most successful members of the winners group. Like many of his fellow winners, he was suffering from the persistent downside version of cyclothymia clinicians call "dysthymia." First identified in 1974 but receiving little attention from a society that sees its symptoms as "normal," it is a condition well known to the toxically successful and those who love them. Here is a list of the symptoms:

- At least two years of lingering sadness and depressed mood (everybody gets down sometimes; persistent mild down-ness is the danger sign)
- Poor appetite or overeating or drinking
- Insomnia or oversleeping
- Fatigue not relieved by sleep
- Low self-esteem despite apparent success
- Poor concentration

- Poor short-term memory
- Difficulty making decisions
- Sense of hopelessness
- Withdrawal from spouse/family
- Feeling of being trapped in a rut

Unlike sufferers of cyclothymia who have mood swings from high-level excitement to depression, those experiencing a majority of the above symptoms of dysthymia seldom feel energized, up, or excited. They more often lead lives characterized by the quiet desperation described by author Henry Thoreau. Like many in the winners group, they tend to be educated, affluent, and highly successful yet feel unable to enjoy their accomplishments.

Hearing reports of these failures at success, writer Joe Kita of *Men's Health* magazine posted an ad on the magazine's website.[15] It read, "We are looking for unhappy guys with perfect lives. If you have a great job, a great family, a great house full of great stuff, but you're still feeling unfulfilled and, at times, even miserable, then we'd like to hear from you." Kita told me by phone that the response to the ad was remarkable and drew hundreds of responses. Dysthymia, a chronic sense of sadness and lack of life energy in spite of high-level success and apparent happiness in life, seems to be increasingly "normal."

Poet Edgar Allen Poe, himself a very successful sufferer of cyclothymia and eventually dysthymia, wrote of the cost of the normal ways to success. He asked if the highest success was not really a "disease of thought" that led to personal misery no matter the amount of experienced glory.[16] Whether we suffer from the exaggerated mood swings of cyclothymia or the persistently nagging lack of joy and energy of dysthymia, high-level success seems to have become a major health risk factor for those who experience it and those who love them.

The good news is that we can think smarter and learn to control the mood in which we find ourselves. Our families and we do not have to suffer as the famous cyclothymic succeeders suffered. Nor do we need to allow ourselves to be drained by the dysthymia that tugs at the hearts of so many of the successful people around us. We do not have to allow our success to make us feel like such failures or lead lives void of the joy and contentment that makes it a sweet success. If we are willing to risk being abnormal by paying more attention to what so many others are failing to see, we can survive and even thrive through our success.

On Being Culturally Creative

We do not have to accept the current cultural normality of toxic success. We don't just have to live in a culture, we can be a part of its creation. We do not have to be "outsighters" reacting with monkey minds suited better for primitive personal survival than shared spiritual meaning. We can become "culturally creative" and practice a sweeter success that may help others see a different path to success. Researcher Paul Ray conducted an extensive study of the American culture.[17] He reports that less than one of every four of us are what he calls "cultural creatives," persons who risk going against the accepted values of a given society and try to improve upon them.

In terms of the quantity of material-plane things available and acquired, the speed at which we live our lives, and our ability to use up the planet's resources to serve our own comfort and pleasure, our civilization has achieved the highest level of "success" in history. If we look back at those who had their turns at high-level success, we will see that most highly prospering civilizations have come on hard times; some have even vanished. History teaches that prosperity can come at a high price. The kind of success purchased with the rapacious "normal" behaviors listed in this chapter could lead to big trouble for our civilization.[18]

One of the winners said, "The trouble with being on top of the world is that no one ever falls up." She was describing the feeling of many TSS sufferers that it often seems that when we are most on top of the world, our world tends to fall apart. Just when things finally seem to be going well and our way, something trips us up, sets us back, and reminds us that very little really matters other than love and relishing the present moment. Like the striving celebrities whose inattentive blindness contributed to their cyclothymia, the toxic pursuit of success renders us spiritually blinded to what we need to thrive. We get blindsided when we lead lives that are one sided and focused on *doing* more than *being*. In the final analysis, the downfall of toxically successful heroes and heroines almost always seems related to their failure to pay attention to what really matters in their lives.

One of my fellow cancer patients pointed out the tragedy of high-level success. She said, "I think I believed what they said about me. That was my problem. It was like the old joke. I became a legend in my own mind. They said I was one of the most successful women in the world. They said I was one of best and brightest women in the insurance industry. As recipient of the 'achiever of the year' award for our corporation, I was invited to speak at our industry's largest and most prestigious meeting. My title was 'My Keys to Success.' I felt like Superwoman. When what you called my SIN cost me my marriage, I didn't miss a beat. I'm not sure I was ever really mentally or emotionally married. I had the inattentional blindness you lectured on. I felt stronger than I had ever felt in my life.

"Then it happened: everything fell apart," she revealed. "They called me out of a meeting to tell me that my teenage daughter had killed herself. I was devastated. Her note said she didn't blame me, but I know I caused it. I neglected her terribly. I've never come back from that horrible day. I'm sure my depression contributed to my breast cancer. Now, as I sit here with one breast, no hair, and looking like a skeleton, it doesn't look that I've achieved an awful lot, does it?"

Two Lectures on Success

The warning stamped on the top of your computer screen and engraved on your daily schedule should read, "Pay Attention! Success Kills!" It is not a message that will be easily accepted because some of our most envied modern success heroes preach an opposite point of view.

I recently presented to a large group of successful business people meeting on the island of Maui. I lectured with our *hālau*, a group of Hawaiian dancers, and my *'ohana* who help me illustrate the secrets of *po'okela* success through their hula, songs, and music. I spoke of the power of the family, the sources of sweet success, the importance of attending to matters of the heart, and the lost art of contentment. I spoke of the dangers of the five Ds that result from toxic success: deficiency, doubt, detachment, disappointment, and depression.

We learned later that we had followed a keynote address by success hero Peter Schutz, former CEO of the company that produces one of our most treasured symbols of success—the Porsche automobile. He had given a fascinating lecture about how to get "extraordinary results from ordinary people" and emphasized the point that "people are capable of performing far beyond their capabilities."[19] How it is possible to do something we are not capable of doing was not made clear, but Schutz illustrated his message with the example of an exhausted pit crew being able to disassemble and reassemble a blown-out racing engine in the middle of the night. He said that they were able to accomplish in fifty-two minutes what, under the best of circumstances, should have taken six to eight hours.

The audience had anticipated this motivational message and greeted his talk with a shouting standing ovation. His message seemed normal to them, a reaffirmation of how they were pursuing their own success. It had represented competition, struggle against all odds, and the current athletic shoe philosophy of "just do it." There had been very little mention in his talk of family, marriage, love, caring, or connection. This was a motivational talk, and his audience expected it and its focus on the SIN of conquest and competition as "how to succeed."

Our Hawaiian *po'okela 'aha mele*, our lecture-concert celebrating being content, calming down, and connecting always, was also greeted with a standing ovation, but there was no shouting. Instead, we saw tears flowing and couples holding hands and embracing. No matter how strongly toxic success is entrenched in our society, there still seems to be a lingering sense that we were given our lives to make more of a success of them than we are.

Competing for What?

"We are naturally competitive," said one of my interview subjects, a 52-year-old executive who has divorced twice and has survived a heart attack and one heart-bypass operation. Just a few days after we spoke, he was scheduled for further testing for recurrent chest pains. Speaking like a true toxic succeeder, he added, "We really don't have a choice. You can't resist it. We all have a competitive gene, but some of us just put it to better use than others. It just happens to you. We are natural-born competitors. We thrive on it."

Gesturing around his huge office and out the window at the sprawling factory his hard work had helped to create, he continued, "Take a look at the empire I built from the bottom up. You can't tell me that there's a person on

Earth who wouldn't envy my success, no matter what they say. My competitors drool with envy. Not a single person in his right mind would not want to have what I have."

This toxically successful man is not alone in his assertion that competition and the constant pursuit of success is only "natural." In a self-help manual titled *Competing*, author Harvey Ruben writes, "Competition is an inescapable fact of life."[20] He goes on to say later, "We indeed have a competitive 'code' in our chromosomes."[21] His astonishing claim is not backed up by research and no human behavior has ever been traced or is likely to be traced to a single gene. As you will read in chapter 5, competition is no more natural or adaptive than connection and contentment. Each is a choice and a matter of where and how we will attend to the world. The poet T. S. Eliot warned that, if we are unwilling to try to impose our own terms on our own life, we must helplessly accept the terms life offers us. Sweet success results from making the decision to reclaim our attention to set our own terms for what will constitute our view, pursuit, and experience of success.

Living Inside Out

Toxic success is living from the "outside in," but sweet success is living and loving from the "inside out." It is realizing that we can control our attention and do not have to simply react to the world. Those who suffer lovesickness fail to see their entrapment in a bad or even abusive relationship. They resist and even resent efforts to direct their attention to their situation. In similar fashion, the success-sick externalize the pressure they feel and think that they have no choice but to yield to it.

The late American literary critic Joseph Wood Krutch wrote of what he called "the tragic fallacy" of attributing the outcome of our life to our helpless surrender to outside forces beyond our control. He writes that this fallacy "depends ultimately upon the assumption which man so readily makes that something outside his own being, some 'spirit not himself'—be it God, Nature, or that vaguer thing called a Moral Order—joins him in the emphasis which he places upon this or that and confirms him in his feeling that his passions and his opinions are important." [22]

No matter how accustomed we have become to them and regardless of the degree that our culture has become the breeding ground of TSS, the list of "normal" behaviors on the normalcy test represents a tragic life. The toxic success earned through a life dominated and driven by a nagging sense of deficiency, self-doubt, and compensatory competition is a tragic waste of the greatest opportunity being alive offers—the chance to pay attention to sharing a contented and joyful life with those who matter most.

Before completing this book, I tried to recontact all of the hundred members of the winners group. After months of trying, I could only reach sixty-eight of them. TSS sufferers are constantly on the move; they have so many choices and are busy exploring them. Because of the quick and constant changes characteristic of the lives of the toxically successful, most of the winners group had moved onward to move upward.

However, I did manage to reach a secretary at what used to be the office of the man quoted above who was so insistent on the irresistible nature of the competitive drive to succeed. She reported that he had divorced again and moved to Pennsylvania to take a higher-paying position with a larger company. When I called that company and asked to speak with him, the person who answered said, "Oh, I am so sorry if you didn't know. He died of a heart attack some time ago. He died right here on his first Monday in the office. It was a real tragedy."

I hope this book will help you see the tragic nature of the way we have come to consider success and its attainment. I hope it will encourage you to consider the possibility that we can be "abnormal" and culturally creative enough to pay attention to what many of us know matters most: a contented, calm, and connected daily existence shared with those we love. Perhaps if enough of us change our minds about success, our collective consciousness will change to a sweeter version of success. There is much we can do to rewrite the tragedy of success, but first we must recognize that the world we see depends on how we choose to see it—the meaning we give to every day of our life and the life of our family.

CHAPTER FOUR

The Meaning of Monday

The lack of meaning in life is a soul-sickness whose
full extent and full import our age has not as yet
begun to comprehend.

—*C. G. Jung*

You will probably die on Monday. If you feel relatively successful but not totally pleased with your job and the life you have because of it, your chances of dying on Monday morning are high.[1] Research shows that you are more likely to die from a heart attack or stroke between 9 A.M. and 11 A.M. on Monday morning than any other time of the week. Of course, it's not Monday that kills us but the meaning we attach to this artificial walling off of the time of our life.

Wolves and robins don't know it's Monday. There may be successful and not so successful raccoons, but they don't seem to know it or, if they do, they don't seem to care much about it. They don't take weekends off and divide their time into quality and not-quality time. For them, there is no yesterday or tomorrow. We humans are the species that builds boundaries. We create artificial beginnings and endings in our minds and then allow them to govern our life. As you have read, we are aware of an immense array of information, but awareness becomes attention when we decide to assign meaning to the information coming into our brain. We can be aware that it's Monday, but Monday gets its meaning when we focus our attention on that day and make it a black day.

The science of psychoneuroimmunology (PNI) shows that the meaning we assign to events in our life can influence our physiology: It can either enhance or diminish our immune response. How we attend to our life and the meaning of our living that results from that attention can even lead to unintentional "success suicide," the serious health risk of going to work on Monday with the "bad" attitude associated with TSS. If we consciously or unconsciously divide our lives into longing for Friday's relief from the rat race and anxiously anticipating our return to it, we have toxified the time of our life.

TSS suffers have created a code for the days of their lives. "TGIF" is the cheer of those who feel they have struggled past "hump day" (Wednesday) and are ready to thank God it's Friday. Except perhaps for TSS sufferers who consider the weekend a frustrating delay in their unending pursuit of their success or a few parents who have lost their ability to enjoy their children's demands on their attention, TGIM (Thank God It's Monday) is not yet part of the time vocabulary of the toxically successful.

The Dying Day

If heart attacks and strokes are purely physical in nature, how is it possible that Monday sticks out as a dying day? If these and other disease processes are purely biophysical events, they should be equal-opportunity killers that wreak their havoc at random. Research conducted over more than three decades shows, however, that how we attend to our life directly affects our heart, immune system, and entire body system.[2]

You have read that toxic success results from the meaning we attach to our work, our loving, and the days of our lives. The New Testament teaches, "As a man thinketh, so is he," but the issue is not so much "mind over matter" as "mind *is* matter." PNI shows that we literally "are what we think" and what, where, and how we focus our attention. As pointed out in chapter 1, the toxicity of success is not due to working hard and long hours, failure to put in enough so-called quality time, or being a type A workaholic. It is caused by a frantic mind, not a hectic world. If Monday kills us, it is because—even if we are not consciously aware of it—we have given Monday its lethal power. Pointing out this immense power of our attention, author Norman Cousins, who reported that the power of his beliefs contributed to his recovery from a life-threatening illness, wrote, "Belief becomes biology. The head comes first."[3]

The tendency of the toxically successful to be "outsightful," to interpret the world from an external locus of control, has led to several attempts to attribute outside physical reasons to what researchers call the "Black Monday effect." Delayed effects of overeating and drinking on the weekend, the physical stress of moving from the Sunday afternoon couch to the Monday morning desk or automotive assembly line, and exposure to job-related chemicals or other workplace toxins are among some of the "look what is happening to us" explanations offered, but none of these reasons have been proven to account for our Monday morality.[4]

The key factor seems to be that we begin on Monday to turn ourselves "outside in," literally "embodying" or making a part of our body the stresses of the outside world. We make our Mondays toxic because the stressful meaning we give them is physically internalized. Our body becomes what we think of our Mondays.

Along with our uniquely human gift of attention and our capacity to assign meaning to our life comes an awesome responsibility and serious risk. We can kill ourselves by the toxic ways we choose to think about our life, but we can also enhance our health and emotional well-being by harnessing the power of our attention and using it to make Monday just another day on planet paradise.

The Risk Factor

Despite the current health terrorism and dire warnings about diet and exercise, most persons who have their first heart attack under age fifty have none of the major physical risk factors for coronary artery disease.[5] It is only good common sense to avoid known health risk factors such as smoking, high blood pressure, junk food, and elevated cholesterol, but the TSS constellation of deficiency, doubt, detachment, disappointment, and eventually depression may be *the* health risk we are neglecting the most. The most predictive factor for heart disease may not be the so-called physical risk factors but the mental ones—the chronic delight deficiency that results from toxic success. What is killing us is not just what we eat or weigh or how little we exercise. It is our nagging sense of discontentment and the toxic ways we are attempting to compensate for it that renders us vulnerable to the diseases of civilization.

I suggest that *the* risk factor to our overall well-being is our distracted state of mind. When we aren't paying enough attention to what matters most in our life, we begin to compensate for what feels like an unhappy life. We mistake society's definition of success for a possible source of the contentment that eludes us. We focus our attention on living and working in the ways we are promised will lead to sure success, but we are in for trouble: Society's version of success is toxic and prescriptions for its attainment can have deadly side effects.

Perhaps the first question our doctor should ask us at our next physical exam should be "How do you feel about Mondays?" Maybe he or she should ask what is on our minds when we awaken on Monday morning and what we are thinking Friday night. Are our thoughts characterized by contentedness, calmness, and loving connection with our family and friends? Is Monday just another great day in a series of great days, or does it represent a return to pressure, obligation, and frustration? Perhaps the doctor should ask not just how we are feeling but, more importantly, "What's on our mind most of the time?" Instead of counting cholesterol points, perhaps he or she should ask how many times on Mondays or any day we think delightful thoughts about how contented we feel with our work, how calm we feel in our daily living, and how truly connected we feel with the people and things that matter most in our life.

That Nagging Feeling

Do you feel nagged? If so, recognize it as another feature of the toxic success syndrome. *Webster's New World Dictionary*'s definition of *nagging* serves as a diagnostic description of the feeling experienced by the toxically successful that they are constantly under duress, pressure, stress, and feeling pushed to keep going for more.[6] *Webster's* associates *nag* with feelings of being annoyed by continual scolding, urgings, and worries. To feel nagged is to feel that one is always falling short and in continual discomfort.[7]

These are the same feelings reported by the winners group of highly successful people. Despite their success and apparent independence, the winners still felt socially harassed to do better or more or to be vigilant in protecting whatever level of success they had attained. They felt as if some-thing seemed to be eating away at them, so it makes sense that the word *nag* has its origins from the Swedish word *nagga* and the Danish word *nagge,* both meaning "to nibble or gnaw."

When we feel nagged, we cannot focus our attention where and how we want. If we could "hear ourselves think," we might hear (particularly on Monday mornings), "Get up, get going, keep going" echoing through the corridors of our mind. We feel nagged when our mind is full of images of the irresistible demands of an increasingly intrusive world holding us hostage to its pace and demands. We are allowing ourselves to be outsighters consumed by trying to keep up with the latest health warning or psychological rule of what constitutes a successful life. It's as if the pleasure police are looking over our shoulder to be sure we are enjoying our life the "right" way instead of our own way.

If you feel nagged into being successful, remember who is doing the nagging: you! Instead of saying to ourselves, "Look what the world is mak-ing me do," we should be saying, "Look at the world I'm making for myself and my family." If we allow ourselves to be pushed into what has become the normal view of Monday instead of yielding our attention to the pull of the wonders of being alive to begin the adventure of a new week, we might *be able to keep surviving*. The odds are, however, that neither we nor those who love us will *know the experience of thriving*.

Pleasure Paranoia

Electronic surveillance of our almost every move, being constantly "in touch" no matter where we are, constant health warnings and directions about how we should think about health, and all sorts of demands and intrusions on our privacy and attention have made us into pleasure paranoids. We feel that someone is always looking over our shoulder, trying to reach us, or needing more and more of our time. It is not enough if we "think" we are happy; we have to qualify under the terms of what society considers success to be and the way to achieve it. In the modern world, the "look" of success has become as important as actually being successful. To move ahead in the world we have to look the part, but if we feel we are constantly being watched, we end up acting rather than living our lives.

A $40 billion-a-year diet industry tells us how much we should weigh, and many more billions of dollars in advertisements present the menu for developing the image of success.[8] We are even becoming targets of an atomic voyeurism as geneticists begin to peek into our molecules. Physician Larry Dossey points out, "Not even our atoms and molecules will be private, because our DNA, our personal chemical code, is on the verge of being laid bare for anyone to see."[9] It is no wonder that a common statement in the winners group was "I'm dying for just a little privacy, peace, and quiet." Research in PNI indicates that they are more correct than they know.

In my interviews of the one hundred winners, each person complained in their own individual way of feeling nagged by the intrusiveness of electronic devices and constantly urged on by an overdemanding schedule that they somehow forget they themselves established. They felt pressured to succeed in the terms established by the outside world and to "keep up appearances" to appear successful or at least be a seeker of success.

New York Times columnist Thomas Friedman points out that anything powered by electricity will soon have chips embedded in it. The electronic revolution is turning us into receivers and transmitters while true meaningful connection seems less a part of our daily life. Because of the nagging invasive power of the continuing electronic revolution, Friedman writes, "You will always be able to surf the Web everywhere, but it is also going to mean that the Web will be able to surf you, and know where you are, and what you are consuming, everywhere, all the time."[10]

We only have so much attention. When our attention is constantly being drained and nagged out of us or we are attending to how we look, we have less attention available to attend to those we love. We begin to feel that there is too little time left to assign our own meaning to our life. If we are busy projecting an image, we have difficulty knowing who we really are and what we really need. When we work so hard to play the part of being and looking like a success, Mondays kill us and the other days of the week are its accomplices.

It is our lack of being able to read our own "meaning meter" that exposes us to the Black Monday factor. If we are more alert for the buzz of our beeper or ring of our cellular phone than for the calls from our heart, we eventually miss out on what matters most in life and lose our freedom to electively have and keep on our mind what we really want most to be there. Consider the following misreading of the "meaning meter" by one of the 100 winners group.

"I'm on an electronic leash," said the 39-year-old single mother and owner of her own dress-design business. "I can't think of many parts of my life that are not constantly being bugged by some electronic command. I wake up to my alarm, the coffeemaker beeps to tell me when it's ready for me, my computer tells me I have mail, faxes have overflowed and spilled on the floor, voice mail nags me with dozens of things I should do, my car beeps and buzzes to tell me to buckle up, when to get gas, and when to turn off my lights. The television is telling me that my butt's too saggy and my abdominal muscles lack ripples. Even when I sit down for a minute, it seems that something is going off somewhere annoying me. I feel naked if I don't have my cell phone, pager, and laptop with me. When you ask me what is on my mind most of the time and if I want it to be there, my answer is, 'I'm not sure anymore what is on my mind. Something has to tell me.'"

As this woman spoke with me about her toxic success, we both broke into laughter. Just as she was describing her electronic leash, her watch played a little song reminding her that another hour of her life had just passed.

In working with TSS sufferers, I gave up trying to get them to go, what the woman above called, electronically naked. Like cowboys in a cattle town in the old West, they refused to give up their weapons, the electronic gizmos that they saw as essential to their survival. They were clearly terrified of being left off their electronic leash and often took my criticisms of their devices personally. "You're being ridiculous," said one winner. "These things are essential now. They're part of life. You really bug me when you make fun of them. You use them, too, so it's really disingenuous of you to say we shouldn't use them." I answered, "I didn't say you shouldn't use them. I warned that they are using you."

As a compromise, I try to encourage TSS sufferers to use their cell phones and pagers as ways of getting their attention to things other than their quest for individual success. I suggest that the family page each other once or twice during the day without the need for a response. I suggest that these calls be used as signals to stop, sit down for just a moment, take a deep breath, and pay a little attention to what matters most in our life. I suggest that their computer screen savers show a series of pictures of their families. I ask them to set their cellular phones and pagers to vibrate and that family signal them to pay attention by buzzing them only once without a need for an answer.

I've not had much luck with these suggestions because most TSS sufferers become anxious when they feel they've missed a call or page. I have tried asking them to turn their cell phones off for brief periods of time, but the worse sufferers of TSS either resist that suggestion or agree and then fail to comply. They are firmly in striving mode, and they see their cell phone as a key weapon in their war to win more success. When it comes to their electronic weapons used in their success combat, they are quick on the draw. One buzz, beep, or ring and they whip their phones to their ears.

Two Magic Words

There are two magic words that are a key to detoxifying success: Shut up. I am not referring only to not talking but also to quieting our brain so we can refocus on what our heart needs us to attend to. No one can pay attention when they are talking. Speaking takes up a lot of brain space, so to pay attention, we have to learn to listen much more than we talk. We also have to learn to quiet the incessant chatter going on in our brain that leads to the distraction of our attention.

Albert Einstein had his view of the formula for the silence of sweet success. In 1950, he wrote, "If A is success, then A equals X plus Y plus Z. Work is X; play is Y; and Z is keeping your mouth shut."[11] While Einstein was probably referring to talking less, if you think of his "Z" as not only listening more but also being less mentally busy and reactive, you have another formula for sweet success. Discovering the lost art of silence is an important step in detoxifying success.

Success and the Theory of Relativity

Decades after Einstein offered his equation $E = mc^2$, most of us still have trouble understanding how something invisible like energy is the same thing as matter. It is not easy thinking of the book you are holding as a lump of potential energy, but it is. If you had a "book atom accelerator" capable of jiggling this book's atoms at the speed of light, it would transform to an immense amount of energy that would blast you and everything within miles into oblivion. What ties energy and matter together and makes them interchangeable is what Larry Dossey calls "a third thing"—the speed of light.[12] The same is true with the relationship between mind and matter, and the "third thing" that unites them is "meaning."[13]

Toxic success is reduced by calming down and quieting our mind so that we can pay attention as we wish rather than as we feel we must. Just as Einstein showed, whether something exists as matter or energy is relative to how fast it is going. Slow means matter and fast leads to energy. Whether we experience toxic or sweet success is relative to how fast our mind is going. One of my interviewees described his cerebral speed. "I was like a guy driving down the highway with a red warning light on the dashboard flashing 'overheating,'" said the 42-year-old owner of three hair salons. "My wife could see the warning and I sensed it, too, but I tried to fix it by stopping and taking out the red warning light that was annoying me and then driving on as fast as ever. Turning off my cellular phone and pager did not stop me from listening for them. I guess I had to burn out and crash before I really saw the light. I guess it took my heart attacking me and slamming me right in the chest to get my attention on what really matters in life."

Transitioning from toxic to sweet success is first and foremost a matter of a change of consciousness. It requires slowing our thought processes down and "shutting up" the hyperactive brain long enough to remember what we really want to be the purpose and joy of our life. It's like setting the cruise control on our car and establishing our own speed of life rather than racing to keep up with the ever-accelerating speed that society demands of us. We can continue to work hard and be busybodies, but to detoxify our success, we have to have calmer, more connected minds.

The Pressure of a "Successful" Retirement

PNI's idea that when we change our minds we also change our physiology has been recognized for decades.[14] The further danger is that the deadly effects of how we choose to assign meaning to our life can leave cellular memories that become imprinted in our hearts. Several years after retirement, retirees still tend to die of heart attacks most often during the "Black

Monday threshold" period.[15] Even while they are on the golf course, sitting and reading a newspaper, or bouncing a grandchild on their knee, the brain and body remember and react to the dread of Black Monday.

If you are retired or contemplating doing so, it is important to "erase" any toxic cellular memories left by the toxic success mind-set still lingering within your brain and body. You will have to free yourself of the newly emerging senior version of toxic success that demands a highly active, productive, extraordinary, "successful" retirement life.

"When I retire, I'm not slowing down at all," said a 53-year-old female executive from the one hundred winners group. "I'm going to bungee jump, start up my own dress shop, travel the world, and gut my entire house and completely redo it. I'm going to make up for lost time. I'm going to have the best retirement anyone ever had." While all this may sound exciting, it is another form of the Chinese curse for an interesting life discussed in chapter 1. It reflects the same competitive, comparative, deficiency-based mind-set of toxic success that dominates so much of our working life.

One of the most damaging myths about retirement is that those who slow down and just enjoy life will die. Anecdotes abound about retirees leaving their work and dying soon afterward because they "didn't stay active." The fact is that many people die soon after retirement because they are old. Another factor may be that they are finally paying the price for their long-accumulated toxic success debt. They are not dying of their retirement but of their whole lives, and the memory of Black Monday resonates forever within them.

Many retirees I have seen in my clinic have no idea about how to electively attend to their lives once they have the freedom to do so. They suffer from a kind of "peace panic" when they must assume responsibility for their own attention. Whether one jumps out of airplanes or sits talking with other retirees on the beach during their retirement matters less than whether the choice is made free from the pressure to "succeed at retirement."

Writing for *Newsweek* magazine, Ellen Karsh points out that the fact that more people who are now becoming eligible for retirement are in good health and fit enough to do what they please is leading to the expectation that retirement should be as vigorously active and competitive as their prior work lives. She writes, "When did retirees stop playing golf? When did they stop lining up at 4:45 P.M. for the early-bird special that would leave them plenty of time to catch a 6 o'clock movie and still be in bed by 9?"[16] She laments the fact that so many retirees are starting second careers that are even more stressful and time-consuming than their first. She sees the same "toxic success brainwashing" I am warning about.

The message seems very clear: Never be content. Keep going. It is only "normal" not to be satisfied with just sitting around the house relishing the idea that we no longer "have" to do anything at all and can have anything we want on our mind all day long. We are taught that something is wrong if we are "too content."

You can test society's intolerance of "shutting up" by sitting quietly in a chair and doing nothing for a prolonged period of time. Sooner or later, someone will ask, "What's wrong?" or "Are you OK?" Very seldom are we asked these questions when we are going and doing full steam ahead.

A threat to retirees to encourage them to sustain their toxic success into their later years is the dreaded "boredom." Instead of seeing the opposite of the competitive drive of toxic success as a more gentle and enjoyable contentedness with the simple pleasures of life, our society warns that those who do not continue their pursuit of success will suffer from an overwhelming sense of ennui and dullness. Listen to those talking about anticipating retirement. Instead of hearing about the joy of just sitting and being, you will hear statements such as "I will never retire—I am just going to change careers" and "If you don't keep going in retirement, you will be bored out of your mind."

But boredom is not the negative experience the toxically successful world tells us it is. It can be a calming state of mind temporarily free of the hurried pursuit of success. Being "bored out of your mind" can mean being free of a mind that will not give you the chance to let your attention wander freely instead of react quickly.

A healthy retirement is the same as a healthy working life. Its sweet success depends first and foremost on establishing a restful, loving state of mind that allows us to relish every day of our life. As Karsh writes, "Bored? That's not possible. This boredom thing is a myth started by the folks who created elder hostels and continuing education programs."[17]

It's Spreading

We Westerners are not alone in our acceptance of the lethal "normal" way to succeed ourselves to death. Ten thousand to thirty thousand Japanese die from overwork each year—a condition called *karoshi*.[18] It is Japan's second leading cause of death after cancer and 40 percent of Japanese workers say they are afraid they will work themselves to death. The fact that Japan produces 10 percent of the world's exports while constituting only 2 percent of the world's population indicates that they have good reason to fear for their lives. They are literally "working their hearts out."

Karoshi hotlines have been set up in most major Japanese cities. They ring daily with reports of deaths occurring when a blood vessel in the heart or the brain of a worker explodes while they sit at their desks or commute to and from work.[19] It seems that when we say, "We are ready to explode," we may be more medically accurate than we know.

Pay Attention!

It happens in the wink of an eye. It is the single most important thing human beings do, and, unless you surrender it, no one can take it away from you. The moment you awaken in the morning, you make the most important choice you will make all day: You decide where you will focus your attention.

Our attention is the director of the movies of our mind. If we surrender our directorship, the world will take over the script and the director becomes the directed. We give meaning to our life by what we choose to attend to during the day and, as some researchers suggest, even during the night through what are called "lucid dreams." The tragedy of a toxically successful life is that those who suffer from it have often unknowingly given up their most precious gift. They have given away their choice of where and how to focus their attention and their God-given right to create the content of their consciousness. The result is a consciousness dominated by hurried reactive thoughts, past worries, and future fears.

A Competitive Default Mode

Toxic success also results from the surrender of our attention to the brain's competitive default mode. We set that default mode ourselves, but if we wake up on Mondays and think first about what we have to do, we default to a reactive and stressful state of mind the rest of the day. We have a choice as to how we will pay attention. If we choose to strive, we can immediately focus on getting ready for work. If we choose to thrive, we can first pay attention to getting ready to live more fully.

Most of us wake up alarmed. It is our alarm clock and not our spirit that gets us up on Mondays. It is an annoying buzz that typically starts our day and demands our first attention. After that, our attention is constantly being tugged at by more electronic attention-grabbers. As you have read in the words of the winners, e-mail, voice mail, and faxes are lurking and ready to capture our attention. Another winner said, "Even when I sit quietly, it seems that something is demanding my attention. It's as if my mind is constantly on hold waiting for someone to pick up. I seem to always be reacting, coping, solving, planning, and preparing. I just can't seem to get my own attention."

Try an attention experiment right now. Focus your attention on someone you love. After reading these words, stop for a moment before continuing and attend fully to that person, the memories you have shared, and the good times you have treasured together. By the simple act of refocusing your attention, it is likely that your body responded positively. Unless you felt guilty for neglecting the person who came to your mind, a little smile may have appeared on your face. You may have sighed in fond association to a blissful time you shared with the person to whom you just attended. If you attended fully enough, you might even have shed a tear or two on behalf of a remembered love too often ignored.

Being Present for Your Life

Jane Katra, a spiritual healer, and Russell Targ, a pioneer in the development of the laser and in Stanford Research Institute's investigation in psychic abilities, write, "Enduring peace and happiness, or the more all-encompassing 'bliss,' is an internal condition, so it can't be acquired through objects or circumstances outside ourselves."[20] This is a key lesson to be learned by all of us who choose to avoid the tragedy of toxic success. It is the quality of our inner life that ultimately determines if we feel we are living successfully, and the quality of our inner life is determined by how we attend to our life. As one of the mortals group pointed out, "I wish I would have gotten my own attention before my cancer got it for me. What a life I'm afraid I missed. It could have been a really great life if only I had paid attention to it."

We can reclaim our own attention and retrain it to give the meaning to our life that we choose. We can, as you will read in part 2, awaken in time and come to our senses about what life is for and what a successful life means to us. We can go beyond being normal to being more fully alive. We can free ourselves from the fine madness that has become so highly rewarded in our competition-driven and hurried culture. We can reclaim our greatest freedom and most important choice by taking back control of what is on our mind and in our heart. We can learn to pay attention where, how, and to whom we want rather than where we feel we have to in order to succeed.

Getting into the Flow of Things

For decades, psychology has been negative. It has been looking at mentally ill people for lessons about how to be mentally healthy. It has been looking at the miserable to find clues for persistent joy. In the last several years, psychology has finally begun to look at joyful people for how they seem to have achieved such a content, calm, and connected life. Through this new approach, psychologists have learned that what they call "panoramic attention," or open, peaceful calm-mindedness, has a beneficial effect on our PNI health. They have learned that we do not have to be helpless victims striving to survive in a cruel world. They have learned that the world isn't just "how it is," it is also how we are.

This emerging field of psychology is called positive psychology, and it focuses on what psychologists call "optimal experience."[21] It is another new science contributing to our understanding of sweet success. Psychologist Mihaly Csikszentmihalyi is a pioneer in the study of optimal experience. He describes what I am calling sweet success as a sense of "flow" or personal control of our attention in order to determine the quality of our life.[22] His research indicates that we feel we are flowing through life when we can fully attend to what we are doing at the present moment. He reports that those who "flow" feel so content, calm, and connected in what they are doing that they lose all sense of time. Flow-ers are not dominated by Mondays.

Sweet success or "flowing" through life results in losing all sense of self and being free of SIN. The worries and hassles of the world seem to fade away because our attention is elsewhere. First and foremost, we are sweetly successful and flowing when we pay our full attention to what matters most to us. Toxic success is an attention deficit disorder in which our attention becomes diffused in desultory, random, reactive movements. Sweet success is attending in the here and now to those people, activities, and things we love in the present. When we see the vacant, exhausted eyes of the toxically successful that seem so constantly distracted, we sometimes say that "nobody seems home." If we begin each day intentionally focusing our attention in our own chosen direction, we can feel more fully at home again.

Toxic success is a chronic form of psychological absenteeism. We become "absent" because we are no longer "in attendance" to our life. We are not attending when we fail to give our full attention to where and to whom the nurturing energy of our life resides. We are not "here" because we are mentally "back there in the past" thinking about what we should have done or "out there in the future" thinking about what we still have to do. Mondays can kill us not because they are just Mondays but because we let them represent guilt over what we didn't do or fear about what we will never be able to do. Instead of flowing into our week, we begin it in "fight or flight" brain default mode.

Where Depression and Anxiety Reside

Psychologists know that depression is attending to what we failed to do and anxiety is due to focusing our attention on what we fear we will not be able to do. As simplistic as this definition may seem, my more than thirty years of work with depressed and anxious patients indicate that they have their attentions firmly planted in the past or future. Most of our misery is a time disorder. My interviews of very happy people experiencing sweet success indicate that they, like those who flow, are almost always attending to the here and now.

If you are looking for the happiness and contentment of sweet success, stop and look around you right now. There is a vast potpourri of sweet experience just waiting to be attended to, if you are willing to be in psychological attendance and *attentionally* present to enjoy it. Like the stars hidden by the brightness of the day, the cosmic joys that can soothe our local pain are always there. You will not find the contentment of sweet success in days already lived or yet to be; while there is joy to be found there, much of our sadness and fears lurk in our yesterdays and tomorrows. Once you are fully able to attend to what matters now and overcome the SIN of toxic success, you can begin to create a past more full of joyful shared memories and look to a future with the wonder of what your attention will bring. Then it will be safer looking back and ahead.

Csikszentmihalyi points out, "We create ourselves by how we invest the energy of our attention."[23] The bad news is that we live in a world that is constantly vying for our attention and that expects us to attend to computers, cell phones, stock averages, and choosing among the seemingly endless array of goods constantly paraded before us on television. It is a world that values short sound bytes over meaningful discourse and quick changes over contemplation and thinking things over.

The good news is that what we have come to see as the "real" world can change depending on how we choose to invest our attention. We hear what we listen for, see what we look for, and feel what we open our minds and hearts to. To overcome toxic success, we have to pay attention to the less demanding aspects of life and, like the teacher alert to the quietest and shyest student in the crowded classroom, we have to be sensitive enough not to allow the clatter of our modern culture to drown out the whispers of a more restful, joyful, contented way of living.

What Changed Our Minds?

Somewhere along the line, we changed our minds. We began to think differently about the meaning of life and how a successful life should be led. Stephen Bertman, professor of classical and modern languages, literatures, and civilizations at Canada's University of Windsor, writes, "Our lives cease to be what they once were, not so much because life itself has changed, but *because the way we see it* has."[24] An important question to ask regarding our increasingly toxic success is not *what* changed our minds but why *we* changed our minds.

Attributing meaning to our life takes time. It requires slow, reflective, contemplative thought. The huge success of self-help books and an array of "self-growth" weekend seminars offering brief "retreats" from the real world are testimonies to our brain's preference for quick solutions. We seem to think that a few simple steps, new ways to plan our time, the wisdom of the latest motivation guru, or an intense group experience climbing and swinging through the woods will provide a sufficient dose of delight, feelings of connection, and meaning to get us through another Monday. As you will read in part 2, sweet success and the art of contentment require a much more difficult, deeper, slower, and often disturbing and "abnormal" way of thinking. They require curing our inattentive blindness and awakening to sights unseen, the smiles of children, the tears of our spouse, and the joy of a Monday morning pregnant with the possibilities of a lifetime.

Following is the test I gave to my research group of successful men and women to help them see just how fast and automatically they were thinking. All one hundred took the test to assess the status of their "meaning meter," the speed and nature of how they were attending to their lives. Take the test yourself to see how your meaning meter is operating.

SWIFT OR SWEET? THE ATTENTION INVENTORY

Circle the word in each set that best describes how you think. Select the word that best describes the speed, focus, and nature of how you process events and relate to people in your life.

1. Short-term or long-term?
2. Transience or permanence?
3. Sensation or memories?
4. Impulse or insight?
5. Big or small?
6. On top or underneath?
7. New things or old things?
8. Change or maintenance?
9. Now or then?
10. Me or us?
11. Fast or slow?
12. Harebrained (reactive and quick-witted) or tortoise minded (reflective and contemplative)?[25]

If you are like most of us in this toxically successful world, you probably circled more words in the left side of the column. This is the common "swift" thinking of TSS. My interview group averaged seven words in the left side of the column. The "control" or comparison group of my Hawaiian friends, colleagues, and *'ohana* trying to succeed *po'okela* style circled an average of two items in the left column.

There are times in our life when we must think fast. For example, it is not wise to contemplate and reflect on whether or not we should step out of the way of an oncoming car. However, when our "quick-wittedness" becomes habitual, it eventually depresses the immune system, aggravates the heart, and renders us love blind to those who we say matter most in our life. It is at these times when we become toxically successful.

Because successful thinking is seen as fast thinking, it has come to be highly prized and rewarded in our society. Slow thinkers are seen as nitwits, too dumb and slow to keep "up to speed." Fast thinkers are "quick-wits," who quickly and efficiently solve problems or figure out a fast way to avoid dealing with them. We time our intelligence tests because we value fast answers more than just right answers. Those who are abnormal and enjoy letting their attention wax and wane to explore and play with a question are penalized for wasting valuable intellectual time and may be diagnosed as suffering from an attention deficit disorder.

A Retarded Genius

I remember a 6-year-old boy sent to me for psychological evaluation when I was a graduate student in psychology. His teacher reported that he was doing so poorly in her class that she suspected that he was "retarded." One of the worst things we can be called in our society is "mentally slow," so those who design tests of how well we think reserve their lowest category of mental functioning for the "severely retarded," those who cannot keep up with their quick-witted "normal" peers.

I had been learning to administer one of the most frequently used and highly valued intelligence tests, the Wechsler Intelligence Scale for Children (WISC). One of the tasks presented on this test is to be able to arrange a set of different colored blocks in patterns to match various pictures. The examiner is supposed to say, "Begin," and push the button on the stop clock in plain sight of the test taker, who then usually sets diligently to work. The little boy in this case, however, was not "normal."

"Wow, can I play with that?" he asked when I began timing. He tried to grab my watch, but I insisted that he should "get started on the blocks." The test is based on the premise that "successful" people don't mess around because they understand the value of time. The boy moved the nine red and white blocks around on the table and then looked at the pattern he was supposed to replicate. He said, "I can make a pretty one, too." He proceeded to arrange the blocks in a pattern that did not score points on the test and went well over the time limit. When I looked at what he had made with the blocks, it was a colorful and creative pattern that went far beyond the imposed limits of the test and maybe the imagination of those who had designed the test. Unfortunately, he had taken much too long. He had not been successful in the normal and expected fast way.

The boy continued through the test, playing with various objects. Even though I tried to do my job and kept reminding him he was being timed and should try his best to work as quickly as possible, he seemed unwilling or unable to race against the clock and to think as fast as "a normal 6-year-old" should. Looking at one picture he was supposed to describe, he sat for several minutes staring at it. Long after his "time was up," he said, "That picture makes me think of my sister and how sick she was." He went on to make a medically sophisticated and very sensitive case presentation that again earned him no points on the intelligence test. Too much "insight" and not enough "outsight" can make you appear stupid and slow to the normal world.

As we finished the test and were putting all the pieces back in the case, I knew that I would talk to the teacher and parents about the gifted boy who would have scored "retarded" on the test. Without looking at me, he said, "You know, just because they say I'm retarded doesn't mean I'm not smart. Just because I'm slow doesn't mean I'm stupid."

I will never forget the wisdom of that little boy and often wonder what level and kind of success he has achieved in his life. Sweetly successful people are often "retarded" in that they are characterized by a slower, internal-locus-of-control, tortoise kind of thinking. As renowned inventor, engineer, and philosopher Buckminster Fuller pointed out, "None of us is a genius. Some of us are just less damaged than most."[26] Our current sense of normalcy is stifling to the development of a genius based on a less agitated and discontented mind, one that easily tolerates enjoying the moment and playing with and learning from problems and questions.

Discussing the dangers of the increasing dominance of fast thinking, Bristol University professor Guy Glaxton writes, "My argument is not just that the slow ways of knowing exist, and are useful. It is that our culture has come to ignore and undervalue them, to treat them as marginal or merely recreational, and in so doing has foreclosed on areas of our psychological resources that we need."[27] Toxic success is the squandering of our slow-thinking resourcefulness by surrendering to the modern world's view that anyone caught dwelling too long on a question is self-indulgent or "daydreaming." To be sweetly successful, however, there is no better time to dream than during the day—particularly on Monday mornings.

Just Wait a Minute

One skill required to reclaim our attention is to be able to "just wait." To experience the sweet success of a more contented life full of possibilities, ideas, implications, and symbolism, we have to relearn how to take joy in examining questions and problems rather than always trying to quickly solve them. Being able to say "Hmm, let me think that over a while" must become as automatic as "Give me a minute and I'll solve it." Sometimes there is nothing wrong with answering a question with more questions, particularly when that question leads to the search for more and deeper meaning.

To be sweetly successful, we have to learn to embrace our differences in perception rather than working so hard and fast to resolve them and decide which is "right." We have to be willing to honor intuition as much as logical, linear intelligence and to not only tolerate but also take pleasure in prolonged confusion. We have to be willing to accept long periods of lack of closure and employ a more relaxed cognition, free of the "get to the point" approach of toxic success.

Toxic success is increasing, but it is not new. William Shakespeare described life in his time as "these most brisk and giddy-paced times."[28] Because we so often do not seem to have control of our own attention, we feel we are forced to accept the terms life demands of us. If we see ourselves only as products of our culture rather than as cocreators of it, the meaning of life may forever elude us. We can, however, still have a meaningful life by developing our insight and paying attention to what we ourselves want to have on our mind and in our heart.

Toxic success phenomena such as Black Monday may diminish when we reclaim our right to decide why, for whom, and for what we are living. We will be on the path to sweet success when we cease to imbue this artificial calendar designation with the doubt, deficiency, detachment, and depression we now impose upon it. Perhaps then there will be no more Mondays at all, just days and moments for making memories that will last us a lifetime.

PART TWO

The High Cost of Success

I was never more unhappy
than when I had won five Gold Medals.
It's kind of ironic, isn't it?

—*Matt Biondi*, Olympic swimmer

CHAPTER FIVE

Overcoming Competition Obsession

A competitive culture endures by
tearing people down.

—*Jules Henry*

Nike, one of the most successful corporations in the world, is on a mission. Its written mission statement is "To experience the emotion of competition, winning, and crushing competitors." While not always stated as directly as this, most of the business world is governed by this objective. Our success in Western culture depends upon someone else's failure. In our society, success is comparative. The measure of success is how many people we have defeated and how thoroughly.

Unfortunately for those who have measured up to this kind of success, research from the sciences of sweet success—PNI, energy cardiology, and neurotheology—indicates that competition results in the kind of toxic success that destroys our health and threatens quality of life around the planet. It is based on the SIN (self-interest norm) at the core of TSS, and it comes with the consequences of the five Ds of deficiency, doubt, detachment, disappointment, and depression.

In some ways, we have not come very far: We are failing to use our 2-percent genetic advantage over our ape cousins. Their competitiveness is incidental, an unintended consequence of their need to survive in a world that challenges their well-being every moment of their day. They don't intend to crush other apes, only to stay alive. They don't want to feel the emotion of competing and winning. They only want to feel a full stomach. While

TSS sufferers may either ignore or deny the fact, their dogged determination to win takes a terrible toll on our emotional, physical, and spiritual health.

Living in Glass Caves

Boston University psychiatrist Peter Knapp writes, "When you get a Wall Street broker using the same responses a cave man used to fight the elements, you've got a problem."[1] Toxic success results from our reliance on ways of adjusting to life's challenges that should have long ago become extinct. The stress response referred to as "fight or flight" and our mind-set of being ever on the ready to compete against someone for something have become so automatic that we often do not notice their toll on our body. Working in modern-day versions of caves, the towering glass piles of offices where success hunters go every day, we are either fighting or at least ready to fight most of the day.

The fight-or-flight response was perfectly suited to life millions of years ago. Lacking our higher cortical functions, our primitive ancestors needed an automatic alarm system that spurred their bodies to fight the tiger or an enemy, or run for their lives. Their existence depended on acting, not reflecting. In a form of archetypical agitation, we continue to be unthinkingly driven by our primitive compulsion to compete. This victory-at-all-costs orientation is a waste of our evolutional gift of being able to think, reflect, contemplate, and focus our attention where we want, instead of where we fear we must.

We live at a time when most of us could be relatively content. Nonetheless, we are still living and working much of our day as if our lives are at stake. This aggressive and defensive pursuit of success tortures our bodies and drains the loving energy from our most cherished relationships. To sweeten our success, we have to recognize the aggressively competitive fight-or-flight orientation we bring to almost everything we do and see it as very old and unnecessary baggage.

From a roller coaster ride, a gun to our head, or an argument with our spouse or children to the meaning we assign to Monday morning, the competitive stress response that kicks in is the same primitive reflex our ancestors had to rely upon for their survival. But the truth is that unless we choose to see it that way, we no longer live in the hostile and constantly threatening world of our primitive ancestors. Success for them was spent trying to save their life, not trying to have better ones.

Evolution has seen to it that we now have much more control over our outside world. It seems ironic that the most advanced society in history with more resources and more cognitive skills than any other also seems to be so constantly afraid of failure. We have developed the cognitive skills to be able to assign our own interpretation and meaning to what happens to us, yet we continue to react to daily life as if we are at war.

Our success seems toxic and disappointing because our competitive consumerist society has failed to deliver on its promise of contentment. This is because our basic physiological needs are by their very nature insatiable and constantly renewable. Our wants are socially assigned and ever escalating, but our ultimate sense of contentment lies elsewhere.

The research on human happiness is quite clear.[2] It shows that our contentment depends primarily on the nature of our social relationships, the joyfulness of our leisure time, and a persistent sense of self-worth and peaceful pleasure derived from sharing meaningful and joyful work and daily activities. The stress of our defensive "harebrained" reactive competitiveness can take much of the fun out of being alive, resulting in the condition I call toxic success.

Homo Stressiens

We have become chronic malcontents engaged in various forms and levels of constant combat. An economics professor in the winners group said, "If you want to invest in something with good growth potential, invest in losers. The most successful people in the world need thousands of them." He was referring to the fact that success is often measured in our society by how many people we have defeated to get where we are. As a result, we lead our lives with the kind of competitive excitement that our ancestors knew only at times of battle. Despite our evolved capacity to make our world a pleasant and uncompetitive place in which to live, our civilization seems to be becoming less civil.

One of my winners group, an executive at a cable television station, described society's persistent confrontational style. He said, "Just watch the cable news channels. Every talk show has become a shout show. Talking heads are lined up to scream and yell for attention and to win their point. They argue from the 'I'm right, you're wrong' assault on one another. The more interrupting, arguing, and put-downs there are, the better the producers and hosts seem to like it. The loudest, most rude, and most opinionated are seen as successful. It's a caveman mentality that causes the veins in their heads to bulge and their faces to flush. You can't help but get caught up in it yourself and start arguing with them through the television set. It just poisons your whole evening, but we've gotten used to it. I have it on my station, too, and I know we love it when a real donnybrook breaks out."

This television executive is describing how pervasively stressful our competitiveness has become and how easily we accept it as normal. Regardless of the source of our stress, the response is the same—the entire body system goes on a high-alert status that weakens our immunity, squeezes our arteries, and can pound our heart to death.

Our acceptance as normal of an almost continual state of in-your-face interaction and its associated stress is one of the most telling features of how toxic our view of success has become. As one of my winners group, an anthropology professor, pointed out, "Sapient refers to knowing. A 'Homo sapiens' means a being of knowledge and wisdom. I'm afraid the way we view and seek a successful life is causing us to evolve to be 'Homo stressiens.'"

Curing or Managing Stress

To deal with the chronic pressure of daily mental war, a stress-management industry is flourishing. We seem willing to try almost any stress-reduction technique just so long as we don't have to distract ourselves from combat to address the cause of our stress. We take short vacations from the rat race or purchase relaxation tapes and self-help books designed to calm us down, at least for a little while. We swallow the latest herb or medication that promises to relax us or to reduce the depression caused by failed success. We try to numb our stress response with alcohol or overwhelm it with the surge of adrenalin that comes with risky behaviors such as jumping off bridges tied to elastic bands or having sexual affairs. We fail to ask why there is so much stress in our life in the first place when we have at our disposal the means to cure it rather than just manage it. We have our attention.

If you hope to detoxify your success, you will have to be willing to do more than try to "cope" with stress. You will have to be willing to challenge the degree to which you have allowed it to characterize your living, working, and loving. You will have to stop thinking about fighting for your piece of the pie and start thinking about making a whole new pie made from different mental ingredients than SIN-ful competing, fighting, and confronting.

Toxically successful people are not stressed by the world; they are creating a stressful world for themselves by the competitive meaning they give to their daily living. It's not stress we have to cope with, it's how we attend to our world. TSS sufferers are not stressed "outside in" but from the inside out. They look at other people as contestants and situations as contests. Stress is not out there; it's in here. To steal a phrase from a major toy company, "Stresses R Us!"

To Love or To Win?

To achieve, have power, and affiliate—according to one of the leading researchers in human motivation, these are the three motives that drive our lives and, if attained, lead to feelings of personal success. The late Dr. David McClelland did extensive groundbreaking research on what constitutes a successful life and the associated stress that relates to it.[3] One of the first PNI researchers, McClelland identified achieving, feeling in control, and being able to connect intimately as our major life motivators. His study of these motives revealed an alarming finding: seeking power at the expense of loving relationships not only reduces the quality of our life but the quantity of the immune cells that protect us from disease and the strength of our heart.

McClelland's work showed that a toxic success triad exists. Those who are in a constant mental state of competition for control, feel frustrated in that effort, and value success over affiliation—what McClelland called the "inhibited power motive," or IPM—can suffer dire health consequences. This triad is characteristic of almost every sufferer of TSS. McClelland showed that the stress hormones adrenaline, noradrenalin, and the corticosteroids that are the fuel of the competitive "fight or flight" stress response strain the cardiovascular system and reduce the strength and effectiveness of our immune system.[4] Research shows that the diseases of our civilization result, in large part, from bodies worn out by living in SIN and being driven beyond their adaptive capacity by the need for power and control.

113

McClelland found that more than 60 percent of those who value winning over connecting and feel frustrated with the lack of a match between their level of success and the level they seek are at serious health risk. They develop high blood pressure or die young of heart disease.[5] I use the term *toxic success* because of this lethal connection between our health and McClelland's IPM of a self-interest–based competitive and comparative definition of success.

A Cure for the Common Cold?

"My husband has stress spit," said the wife of one of my winners group. "I heard you describe an immune substance called IgA and how when its level goes down in your saliva, your immunity goes down. You joked that the toxically successful can develop 'stress saliva.' Well, my husband's spit must be bone dry when it comes to IgA."

This woman was referring to the research using immunoglobulin A, one of many different antibodies produced by our immune system's B-lymphocytes (B-cells). It is a first line of defense against biological invaders. You may have felt it in action when you experienced the first vague tingles in your nose and throat causing you to say, "I feel like I might be coming down with something."

Many toxically successful people, and particularly those trying hard to compete to be successful, suffer from repeat colds and flus because their way of seeing the world chronically lowers their IgA level. Those who suffer from IPM and experience an incompatibility between what they feel they must achieve and have been able to achieve and are willing to give up love for the sake of success become immune deficient and prone to serious illness.[6] Acting as stress carriers, the pressure they bring to their families may also weaken their spouses' and children's immune systems. It may not be a cure for the common cold, but learning to pay attention to connecting rather than competing can at least increase our defenses against it.

McClelland also discovered IPM's opposite, the "relaxed affiliation syndrome" (RAS). This syndrome is characterized by a more contented orientation to life with more value placed on intimate connection than high-level success and achievement. Is your life more competition than connection? If so, be very careful to protect your health.

I informed you in the introduction to this book that I would be using letters and codes to help you remember the scientific and cultural concepts related to toxic success. One of the winners group, the chairman of the math department at a university, constantly teased me about my codes and lists. He summed up the many letter codes presented earlier by saying, "I think I've finally learned the toxic success alphabet. I know I suffer from TSS (toxic success syndrome) because I have all the five Ds and not enough of the four Cs. I live in SIN (surrendering to society's self-interest norm of competition). I am controlled by the IPM (inhibited power motive) instead of the RAS (relaxed affiliation syndrome). I have your alphabet taped on the top of my computer monitor with the title "My Secret Codes." As stupid as your codes seemed to me at first, I admit that I just have to look at all those letters and they get my attention. I guess that's your whole point."

Your Primitive Side Is Showing

Imagine yourself or someone you love looking and feeling like this:

- Eyes seeming to bulge
- Pupils enlarged as if in a glowering glare
- Sense of unexplainable agitation and feeling ready to explode
- Feeling highly charged with energy to the point of nervousness and shakiness
- Headaches, stiff back, and muscle and joint pain
- Loss of interest in sex
- Feeling bloated, sore stomach, bowels upset, and nausea
- Rushes of high energy followed by crashing lows, tiredness, and difficulty sleeping
- Dry mouth and bad breath
- Stammering and spitting while trying to speak
- Heart racing with occasional palpitations
- Rapid, short breaths
- Feeling "ready to explode" to the point of wanting to hit something or someone
- Frustrated to the point of feeling like "throwing in the towel" and "running away from it all"

- Skin seems to "crawl" and sweat even though there is no physical exertion or exercise
- Food loses its taste
- Making silly stupid mistakes never made before
- Feeling that others are trying to outdo you, beat you, or take advantage of you or your time

If you look or feel like the above description, you are "normal": You are showing all the signs of the fight-or-flight, competition-based stress response that is the accepted way of living in today's world. Like most TSS sufferers, your primitive side is showing. You are placing yourself in great danger because you are drawing upon ancient responses to deal with modern-day problems. You are following your brain's oldest self-survival imperatives rather than your mind's wisdom of what constitutes a sweeter life.

The Deadly Dozen, Then and Now

The physiological signs of the stress responses described above are complex and can vary in degree and manifestation from person to person. To help you understand more about the fight-or-flight stress response associated with TSS, consider the following list of the body's stress reactions. Notice how the fight-or-flight stress reaction worked fine for fighting, hunting, killing, and outrunning a predator trying to eat us but has now become *what is eating us.*[7]

When we feel competitive and our inhibited power motive is dictating our thoughts and feelings, we fall back on what should have long ago become the extinct fight-or-flight response. As a result, the "deadly dozen" bodily responses kick in. Unlike our ancestors, however, we have designer drugs that help us live with our toxic success, a broad "fighter's pharmacy" of medications that are taken regularly by the toxically successful. I have listed some of these with each of the primitive body responses described below.

1. **Hormonal Surges**. *Primitive benefit:* Essential for quick action to stay alive. *Current liability:* Leads to early death.

    The tiny glands on top of our kidneys called the adrenal glands start squeezing out large amounts of stimulating hormones called glucocorticoids. In small amounts, these hormones are essential to life, but in the doses we give ourselves when we are highly competitive, stressed, or in IPM mode, they weaken our immune system and make us vulnerable to many diseases. When we feel threatened, the brain doesn't care how long we live, only that we live. As a result, it neglects our health in favor of winning. *Fighter's pharmacy*: Hundreds of cold and flu medicines to deal with constant infections resulting, in part, from the lowered immunity of the stress response.

2. **Thyroid Pumping**. *Primitive benefit:* Burned the body's fuel for quick and intense energy for killing and running. *Current liability:* Leads to feeling unexplainably nervous and agitated, tired, and having trouble sleeping.

   The thyroid hormones help maintain the energy level of the body. Big and sudden spurts of energy helped save our ancestors' lives, but now they result in living in constant overdrive in a modern world that is nowhere near as threatening as our brain causes our body to prepare for. *Fighter's pharmacy*: Various thyroid medications for overactive or "tired out" thyroid gland.

3. **Endorphin Pumping**. *Primitive benefit:* Natural painkillers allowed primitive people to continue to fight or flee even when they were injured. *Current liability:* Makes us numb to how much we are overdoing it and leads to migraine headaches, back pain, and arthritic discomfort as we deplete our endorphin supply.

   While endorphins have received very good public relations as emotional uppers, in excess they can act as agitators to the body systems or make us insensitive when we should be alert. Too high a level of endorphins for a prolonged period of time is similar to driving a stick-shift car without using the clutch. *Fighter's pharmacy*: Various psychiatric medications and herbs to deal with vacillations in mood. Increased use of a variety of new and stronger painkillers.

4. **Sex Hormone Dipping**. *Primitive benefit:* Lack of libido and sexual interest allowed more time for fighting and fleeing and put less social pressure on the group because there were fewer mouths to feed.

Current liability: Lack of sexual interest interferes with relationships.

Decrease in sex hormones can lead to sexual dysfunctions such as erectile distress and problems with orgasm and disrupted menstrual periods. Sex hormone disruption's side effects can have negative effects on relationships. Many couples are what are now referred to in the popular media as "DINS." These are dual-income, no-sex couples suffering from lack of sexual interest related to sex hormone depletion. *Fighter's pharmacy*: Viagra and herbs to enhance sexual drive and interest.

5. **Digestive Shutdown**. *Primitive benefit:* Blood used for digestion is diverted to muscles used in killing and running. *Current liability:* Leads to bloating, stomach pain, nausea, or diarrhea. Dry mouth resulting from this shutdown also leads to periodontal disease and other dental problems.[8]

Growling stomach, abdominal cramping, and other digestive symptoms have become commonplace. *Fighter's pharmacy*: The abundance of antacids is reflective of the devastation to our digestive system from the constant agitation of a relic stress response.

6. **Sugar High**. *Primitive benefit:* Glucose in the bloodstream caused insulin increase to metabolize the excess sugar. Spurts of compensatory insulin lead to an energy rush needed to fight or flee. *Current liability:* Continued insulin boosts can lead to hypoglycemia and even diabetes.

The increasing incidence of diabetes reflects not only genetic factors and dietary and obesity problems, it is also a cause of insulin depletion associated with the chronic stress of toxic success. *Fighter's pharmacy*: Increased use of insulin for diabetes and dependence on sugar-filled junk food and snacking.

7. **Cholesterol Flows**. *Primitive benefit:* Cholesterol took over when the sugar high passed, providing prolonged intense energy for fighting and fleeing. *Current liability:* Modern people do not need their ancestors' prolonged intense energy, so the excess cholesterol is stored and packed into our arteries.

It's no coincidence that PNI has shown a rise in accountants' cholesterol levels correlated with tax season. It may be good for our health to view our cholesterol level not just as a dietary or exercise issue but also as a barometer of our overdependence on a primitive stress response. *Fighter's pharmacy*: An array of new medications to lower cholesterol levels.

8. **Heart Races**. *Primitive benefit:* Blood raced to the large muscles and legs for running and the arms for fighting. *Current liability:* High blood pressure, heart attack, and stroke.

While our society relies on heart *bypass*, it may be that what we need is more heart-to-heart *connection*. What might offer a buffer against the stress and strain of the modern world are more relaxed affiliation (RAS) and less striving for achievement and power (IPM). *Fighter's pharmacy*: Several blood pressure medications.

9. **Hyperventilating**. *Primitive benefit:* More oxygen was available for all the blood surging everywhere. *Current liability:* Becoming disoriented, showing impulsive poor judgment, and feeling fearful and rushed; taking in more ambient toxins circulating in the air, such as cigarette smoke.

One distinguishing characteristic of the toxically successful is their breathless way of living. Their upper-chest breathing causes them to be gaspers, who take short breaths located in the upper chest instead of the lower abdomen—the so-called iron chest syndrome. *Fighter's pharmacy*: Anti-anxiety drugs and depressants. Also, the appearance of "oxygen bars," where TSS sufferers can get a quick oxygen fix.

10. **Thickening of the Blood**. *Primitive benefit:* Quicker clotting allowed the fighting to continue. *Current liability:* "Thick" blood clogs as it passes through arteries already narrowed by cholesterol, leading to heart attack and stroke.

The frequency of brain attacks (strokes) may relate in part to toxic success syndrome's hardened heart and thickened blood. *Fighter's pharmacy*: Several new blood-thinning agents and increased use of aspirin.

11. **Goose Bumps and Sweat**. *Primitive benefit:* Made the fighter look bigger as hair stood on end, helped cool overheating muscles, and provided increased sensitivity to dangers and foes that may have been lurking. *Current liability:* Look and feel "stressed," clammy, and edgy.

    Despite the fact that it seems normal and we have become used to it, regularly experiencing what we Hawaiians call "chicken skin" is a sign of a body under siege. *Fighter's pharmacy:* Several "calming" herbs and medications.

12. **All Five Senses Heightened**. *Primitive benefit:* Good for being a successful warrior fighting at full alertness and performance. *Current liability:* Burnout from chronic hypersensitivity, senses become numb, and the world seems less intensely stimulating to the senses.

    As our senses suffer from chronic overalert status, they require more and more intense stimulation. This leads to more competing, striving, or thrill seeking to stimulate numbed senses. A vicious circle results of stress-related sensory burnout followed by attempts to stimulate them through more intense activity. *Fighter's pharmacy:* Increased dependence on various stimulants, hallucinogens, and "high inducing" substances. Some of the increase in substance abuse in our society may relate to attempts to compensate for senses numbed by TSS. Alcohol abuse may relate to trying to escape from the overwhelming amount of stimulation that characterizes modern life.

We can see from the contrasts above that our dependence on an old-world way of dealing with our new world can have wide-ranging and potentially deadly consequences. Our body keeps telling us that we are using the wrong responses, but we keep trying to medicate its symptomatic protests away with our fighter's pharmacy. Sweetening up our pursuit of success requires developing more insight into why we are so stressed instead of automatically trying to manage our stress from the outside in with various substances. It is important to look before we leap and realize that we have a choice of how to give meaning to what is happening to us and how we will deal with the frustrations that are prerequisites for being alive.

As Compared to What?

"She's like a woman obsessed," said the husband of one of my interviewees, an attorney. Like most of the spouses of the winners with whom I spoke, he was very aware of the toxic success that had him and his wife in its grip. "She is in win mode in court, watching Ginny play soccer, on the tennis court, and at the grocery store. She even competes with characters on television and points out what losers they are. She hits the floor in the morning ready to compete, and you don't want to be in her way. You really don't want to be around her if she loses. That stress vein in her forehead starts to stick out and pulsate. It's really very scary."

The competitive orientation of the woman above has become so much a part of the fabric of our lives that its subtle influence dominates almost every aspect of our thinking. Ask someone about how they enjoyed their trip, how their children are doing in school, or about a work of art, and you are likely to get a comparative answer. "This was a much better vacation than last year," "David is at the top of his class," or "It is not this artist's best work or as good as the other artist" are examples of how automatically we see the world from a comparative and competitive perspective.

Competing for Life

In his groundbreaking book challenging the role of competition that is at the root of toxic success in American life, author Alfie Kohn writes, "Life for us has become an endless succession of contests. From the moment the alarm clock rings until sleep overtakes us again, from the time we are toddlers until the day we die, we are busy struggling to outdo others. This is our posture at work and at school, on the playing field and back at home. It is the common denominator of American life."[9]

The toxically successful often behave like predators in pursuit of their prey. It seems that they cannot help or free themselves from the ultimate competition—our competition against our own life now as something to overcome or transcend in order to achieve a better life later. Unless we are willing to change our mind about what life means and who and what it should be for, we will remain deprived of a good life because of our competition to get a better one.

Competition has become so much a part of how we work, live, and love that it is difficult to consider a life not based upon it. We are so immersed in our toxic competition to be successful that those who are not driven by this obsession are seen as "out of it," not fully engaged in the game of life, or even cowardly. Most indigenous cultures like Hawai'i are perplexed by the modern world SIN's competitiveness and seeming blindness to its negative effects.

A *kahuna* (Hawaiian healer and teacher) was talking with me about my more than eight-year struggle to find a publisher willing to help me share my views about toxic success. He said, "The modern world is drowning in a sea of poisonous success. The signs are all around them in their struggling families, poor health, and as they hurry past the meaning and joy of life. They are as fish who do not reflect on the nature of the water they are in. They cannot imagine or comprehend its presence and control of their lives because they cannot imagine its absence in their lives."[10]

We compete to find the "best" job, home, car, friends, lover, sex life, diet, exercise program, or shortest and quickest route through traffic. It is not just the stadium full of fans chanting, "We're number one!" or the little league baseball player crying after striking out that reveals the dominance of competition in modern living. It is the low but nagging hum of "you can do it, keep going, you can win, you can do better" that is raising our blood pressure, lowering our immunity, sending us to the fighter's pharmacy, and taking our attention away from those we say we love and the life we say we would like to have. The victory virus has become pandemic, a widespread cultural insanity that is leading to our experience of the failure of success.

Psychoanalyst Karen Horney described the mental illness of a toxic succeeder as "someone who constantly measures himself against others, even in situations which do not call for it."[11] Such persons are our models of success. They are in positions of power and control and receive the rewards our society doles out to those who have honed their competitive edge. They conduct their life without experiencing the need for psychiatric intervention or psychotherapy and are seldom "diagnosed" by the establishment as "crazy" because it itself has gone mad with need for success. They are generally nice neurotics who have become our cultural role models, modern-day versions of the Greek tragic heroes that most of us wrongly and dangerously aspire to be.

As you have read, many if not most success heroes and heroines suffer from IPM. They seek success in life as exclusively derived through some form of competition or victory over someone else. Author Elliot Aronson writes, "The American mind in particular has been trained to equate success with victory, to equate doing well with beating someone."[12]

The opposite of competition is not just trying harder to be cooperative. It is working mentally harder to resist the temptation to succumb to our ancient ways and to seek a mental contentment that allows cooperation to flow naturally and to happen to us. Sweet success requires recognizing and then resisting the brain's competitive default mode, but in a society that considers competition not only good but essential and natural, changing our mind to an "us" instead of "me" mode is not easy.

Selling the Idea

"Would you be content to be number two on the *New York Times* bestseller list?" asked an editor of a large New York publishing house. Their book-acquisitions committee was discussing with me the possibility of publishing this book, and I was doing the best I could to explain the dangers of toxic success and its related competitiveness that controls our lives. "I can't believe you'd be content with that," she said. "Competition is what drives us to succeed and do well, so who is going to buy a book about not competing? Don't you agree that it is what got this country where it is today? It's almost un-American not to compete."

My answer did little to help me sell my idea to the publishing house. "I do agree that competition is what got us where we are today," I responded. "The question I am asking is if we really feel in our most contemplative moments that we are where we want to be in all aspects of our living, loving, and working. Of course I would be thrilled to have a book that becomes number two or number one in sales, but for me, that would be a side effect and result, not a goal. The comparative number means much less to me than whether or not my book turned out to make a constructive difference in people's lives. I think there is sufficient evidence now to show that how we define success and the me-against-you way we are going after it is going to lead to disaster if we don't relearn what it means to be content. Competition by its very nature is detachment, a way of being against people rather than with them and a way of struggling through life rather than enjoying it."

"Well, good luck then," said the editor, leaning back in her chair and shoving my proposal aside. "We, at this house, are not content with being number two, and we want authors who want to be number one. We could never pitch this to our sales staff. Without comparison to others, life has very little meaning or perspective. Your idea of success is just too unrealistic."

More than ten years later, I finally found a home for my book with a company in Hawai'i that embraces *po 'okela* and its central Polynesian value of being of help over being on top. Whether I succeed in convincing you to take a fresh look at the assumptions about the normal and natural way to succeed is now in your hands.

How Fit Are the Survivors?

The competition compulsion you read about in the words of the editor described above is often defended on the basis of Charles Darwin's theories of evolution and what is mistakenly seen as his emphasis on the principle of "survival of the fittest." This famous statement has become the mantra of the modern world, but, in fact, there is no basis in the theory of natural selection from which this survivalist mentality is said to derive.

Darwin himself never said or wrote the phrase "survival of the fittest." It was naturalist Herbert Spencer, not Charles Darwin, who coined it, but even he did not describe this principle in terms of the dog-eat-dog world we think gave birth to us. He was referring to being strong but not necessarily to defeating others. Being fit was not just defined by victory over others but as possessing highly adaptive skills that ultimately enhanced the common good— in other words, less SIN and more RAS.

If Darwin would have written a five-word phrase regarding his theories of evolution, it would more likely have read "survival of the most cooperative." He believed and wrote that those communities that contain the greatest number of cooperative individuals are the most likely to survive. He wrote that his references to the struggle for existence were meant in a "large and metaphorical sense, including dependence of one being upon another."[13]

Scientist Stephen Jay Gould wrote, "The equation of competition with success in natural selection is merely a cultural prejudice."[14] This prejudice has led to the toxic success I have been describing. It has become so pervasive that feeling insanely overwhelmed, chronically impatient, selfishly striving, and hostilely competitive has become more and more accepted as normal in Euro-American cultures. When we say it seems that the world has gone mad, we are right. A society of millions trying to win must inevitably create millions and millions of losers.

If we wish to use nature as our model, we are better advised to connect, combine, and cooperate than to self-assert, compete, and conquer. One hundred years ago scientist Petr Kropotkin reviewed the habits of hundreds of species, from ants to buffalo. His work clearly showed that cooperation, not competition, was the primary element in those species that survived. He wrote, "Competition . . . is limited among animals to exceptional periods. . . . Better conditions are created by the elimination of competition by means of mutual aid and mutual support. Don't compete! Competition is always injurious to the species, and you have plenty of resources to avoid it. . . . That is the tendency of nature. . . . Therefore combine—practice mutual aid! That is what Nature teaches us."[15] Sweet success, then, may be at least as "natural" as the more competitive brand.

Going Against the Grain

It is difficult to argue successfully against the current assumption of the naturalness of competitiveness. Our current mind-set of assertive and comparative individualism is well established and defended. The toxically successful reading this chapter are probably already engaged in rebuttal, nitpicky cynicism, denial, and even attack in defense of their cherished way of thinking about life. They are the "normal" ones, and the craziness of a sweeter success through a less competitive and more contented way of thinking will not go down easily with them. The possibility that we might consider being less than we can be and not always interested in personal victory or being number one will seem crazy to those who have become successfully normalized. The new sciences of sweet success show that, in this case, adjustment is not good for our health.[16]

The "be all you can be, just do it, go for the gold, personal power, self-assertive" orientation of toxic success has dominated the last several decades. It has been celebrated in hundreds of books and success seminars. Despite this trust in competition as the way to ultimate happiness, there is very little research to support it. For example, researcher and psychiatrist Roderic Gorney writes, "Any objective appraisal of modern man will disclose that, in the overwhelming preponderance of human interactions, cooperation *completely overshadows* competition."[17]

Because many scientists suffer from toxic success themselves and feel they must compete to be first in order to move up the academic ladder and to be "outstanding" in their respective fields, any challenge to this orientation is met with skepticism. Psychologist Marian Radke Yarrow has written about this scientific reluctance to consider a sweeter version of success. She comments, "Aggression, anxiety, guilt, and self-centered motives and behavior have been so much the cloth of theory and research that questions of a 'softer' side of . . . human beings seem almost unscientific."[18]

I am not suggesting that we are necessarily any more naturally selfless and caring than we may be inclined to competitiveness. I am suggesting, however, that the almost total dominance of the SIN, competitive way of thinking about life and the cluster of the toxic success fallout characteristics outlined in the "normalcy test" in chapter 1 are not beyond our control or capacity to modify them. We may not be naturally or unavoidably caring, cooperative, and loving, but research shows that we are not unavoidably anything at all—and, as you have read, least of all naturally competitive.

Professional Nags

There are two additional assumptions related to competitiveness: to be inspired and to remain highly motivated. For those who are slacking off and just enjoying life and what they have instead of trying harder to have what everyone is supposed to want, a set of professional nags have emerged in the form of life competition coaches. They call themselves inspirationalists, motivationalists, or life strategists, and for a fee they will share their secrets of success and help us stay competitive.

Most of these parental surrogates offer little research or data to support their strategies other than their own personal success stories. They are talented talkers capable of moving audiences to tears and cheers with gut-wrenching stories of miraculous personal victories. They sound authoritative, confident, and convincing.

Most of these coaches are sincere and truly want to help others to be as successful as they are, but many of them are themselves severe sufferers from toxic success syndrome. Ask them, "How do you know?" and they will usually answer, "From my own personal experience" or "It's just common sense." These answers are usually followed by a series of well-practiced success stories and anecdotes suggesting that anyone can do anything if they will try hard enough to be a winner.

Despite the fact that there is no evidence to support the assertion that survival depends on tapping into some natural competitive instinct or that our success depends upon the defeat and failure of others, the toxicity of vigorously pursuing being number one has led to the emergence of hundreds of success seminars and books espousing their respective steps to success—for some reason usually seven. Millions of dollars a year are spent by corporations to hire "motivational" speakers to stoke up their employees, and hundreds of "success" and "life planning" seminars are offered by groups such as The Learning Annex, Seminars for Success, and other similar companies. These may even have profit-sharing arrangements with the most well-known self-help authors and gurus who offer their various programs on a regular basis. They often give keynote addresses at corporate incentive meetings attended by persons so highly motivated already that they have all but ruined their health and marriages to qualify to attend the meeting.

Seminars for Success

One example of the "success movement" is "The World's Top Success Seminar," offered repeatedly in several cities in the United States. It promises those who have not yet attained sufficient success in their lives that they, too, can "achieve high-level success," just likes the famous motivationalists and inspirationalists on the program. All the success-deprived have to do is pay $250 to listen to "success-perts" such as Dennis Waitley speaking on "Being the Best," the "world's best motivationalist" Zig Zigler speaking on "See You at the Top," General Norman Schwartzkopf speaking on "From the War Room to the Board Room," the "world's foremost inspirationalist" Dr. Robert Schuler speaking on "Tough Times Never Last but Tough People Do," Olympic champion Mary Lou Retton speaking on "The Competitive Edge," and the "world's number one expert on success" Peter Lowe speaking on "Success Skills for Peak Performance."

Anyone who enjoys sweet success can become tired just reading the titles of these presentations. There were no lectures that offered "How to Be a Little Less Than You Can Be" or "Sitting Down and Shutting Up" or "The Joy of Contentment and the Danger of Competition" or "Living in SIN, the Dangers of the Self-Interest Norm."

Dozens of lecture bureaus now match organizations needing a "powerful motivator" or "inspirationalist" with professional speakers who compete among themselves to be the most requested speaker with a new, different, and better pitch. There has recently been somewhat of a "bliss backlash" among those who have been motivated and inspired by these presenters. They are beginning to question their increasing feeling of being somehow fooled or manipulated by a momentary false high induced by the motivationalist's performance. They complain that they are feeling a postinspirational crash a few weeks after the seminar or lecture that had aroused them to such a fevered pitch. The effects of the emotional pep rally wear off, and there is a feeling of being used or misled. These concerns have resulted in a quick adjustment by many speakers on success. As one speaker told me, "Now, *life* is in, so I'm speaking about that."

A lecture bureau president recently told me, "*Balance* is hot now." The current big seller on the lecture circuit is "How to Find Life Balance." As you will read in chapter 8, the pursuit of the always-elusive balance can become something else for which we must strive. Working hard and competitively in order to qualify to attend an incentive meeting is stressful enough. To then be told by a motivational speaker to cut back, work less, and to try to live in more balance can lead to feelings of angry frustration with a company that requires constant striving. It seems that the organization is giving mixed messages, and rightly so. At the office, the message is "Be a winner. Don't be content with second place. Work until you drop if you have to, or you won't qualify to come to the success meeting next year." Then, in the success reward meeting, the message is "We value living in good balance with plenty of time to pay attention to your family and your physical and spiritual health." The result can be "balance stress."

Nature teaches that no system is ever in balance for long. Trying to achieve balance can lead to frustration and guilt when our attempts to win big and love a lot seem to fail. Trying to cut back, cram in, make schedule changes, or put in a little more quality time sound like good life-balancing strategies, but they seldom work. What is needed is a change of mind, a different view of success based less on SIN and free of McClelland's IPM. However, this mind-set goes against the grain of the current model of success and is a very hard sell to those convinced that they can have it all by giving their all.

When we feel the stress of toxic success, we have a choice. We can revert to our primitive fight-or-flight response or intentionally select another stress response called "Tend and befriend." Life is never in balance for long, but if we elect to react to the stress of trying to be successful by thinking, "tend and befriend," we can feel a little more in control of our own life and suffer fewer negative physiological consequences.

The Forgotten Stress Response

"Fight or flight! That's the only way we cope with stress," said my professor years ago. For more than sixty years, our competitive nature has been assumed to be related to our built-in sympatho-adreno-medulary (SAM) response system. This is our automatic alarm state that pushes our body to the max so we can do something very aggressive to win over a predator or perceived source of severe stress, or to hightail it away as quickly as possible. When we feel challenged, our sympathetic nervous system becomes activated and we become agitated. Hormones are released that signal the middle (medulla) area of the adrenal glands, which, in turn, secrets large amounts of stress hormones to help us confront or run away. As you have read, this SAM system can have a devastating effect on our body by lowering our immune system and overextending our heart and circulatory system. It is a full assault- or retreat-system, and it is at the root of our chronic competitiveness.

Psychologist Walter Cannon conducted the classic research on the SAM-mediated fight-or-flight response. His work and that of others clearly documented the powerful stress characteristics you have read about in this chapter. With laboratory research conducted primarily on male rats, he showed that our body reacts to stress through a sympathetic nervous system surge and associated stress-hormone release sequence described above.[19] Until recently, it was assumed that the fight-or-flight response was our only natural intense reaction to perceived stress, but new research by psychologist Shelly Taylor at the University of California, Los Angeles, and her colleagues suggests that learning from male rats has its serious limitations.[20]

Taylor's research indicates that we do not always have to think of ourselves as in competition against others and the world. No matter how normal the fight-or-flight response has become, we have a choice of another, less toxic way of dealing with stress. She calls it the "tend-and-befriend response," and it is related to McClelland's RAS (relaxed affiliation syndrome).

Taylor's conclusions are based on the discovery that females tend to respond to stressful situations by first thinking about protecting themselves and their children rather than attacking the threat. They do so through nurturing rather than aggressive behaviors—"tending" rather than "competing." They also are more likely to deal with stress by thinking about how to form alliances with an extended social group—"befriending" rather than giving up and fleeing. As wives know, men seem more often to fight or take flight when they feel challenged or confronted, while the women turn to taking care of what matters most and seeking support in doing so. As one wife of a TSS sufferer said, "The more I complain that I don't get enough of his attention, the less attention he seems to pay to me."

Evolution of a "second" kind of response to stress may be related to the way our ancestors spent their days. While their cavemen were busy competing, fighting, and fleeing, cavewomen were home at the cave busy caring, tending, and befriending. They were the primary caretakers of the children, and getting killed fighting or deserting their offspring by running away would not have allowed their children—their genes—to continue.

The sweeter success I am suggesting is based on a more selective stress-survival approach. By using our capacity to attend, we can mentally select the stress response that best matches the situation—reflecting rather than just reacting. Even though both genders suffer from it, toxic success is related to the dominance of the male way of giving meaning to life, love, and working. Being aware that loving and connecting can be as effective a stress mediator as competition or surrender is a helpful step in taking at least some of the toxicity out of success.

Now more than ever, I believe my mother's warning was right. Just because "everyone else is doing it" and trying to be successful in the normal way does not mean *we* have to or should do so. We do not have to be like cartoon characters running off a cliff with legs churning so fast they are a blur. We do not have to be propelled over the leading edge by toxic success's mixture of momentum and ignorance. If we don't pay attention to the toxic nature of success, we can end up taking a terrible fall. When we realize that the hormonal rush of competition can keep us going for only so long, our momentum will eventually slow and the gravity of our situation will drag us back down to the realization that we are not thriving. Instead, we are striving ourselves crazy.

CHAPTER SIX

A Measure of Success

> Got everything done.
> Died anyway.
>
> —*Epitaph of the toxically successful*

While on our morning walk around Oʻahu's Maunalua Bay, I heard the loud humming of a pump. It was coming from a tanker truck draining the septic tank in front of a home. I noticed a logo on the side of the tank that showed a smiling worker holding a hose. Beneath the image was the slogan "We are willing to take your crap." I walked over to the man holding the lever that controlled the pump, whom I'll call "Dave," and we began what Hawaiians call "talking story," chatting about nothing in particular. Suddenly, he stopped our conversation and began impatiently pounding on one of the gauges. "Come on, come," he yelled at the pump, "This is taking all day."

"What do you do?" I asked Dave. "What's your job?"

"I own the company," he grumbled while vigorously shaking the lever of the machine.

Another man, "Fred," was standing on top of the truck's cabin. He yelled down, "I pump crap. That's my job."

I walked over to a third man, who was struggling to hold the heavy hose in the septic tank. "Great morning, isn't it?" "Big Al" said. "Do you want to know what my job is?" he said, puffing happily on his cigar. "I'm saving the planet."

These three men illustrate the importance of the meaning we attach to how we spend our days. As one of the founders of modern medicine, physician Sir William Osler, wrote, "The first step toward success in any occupation is to become interested in it."[1] I would add that sweet success depends on which aspect of what you do for a living you elect to focus your attention and the meaning you give to what you do every day regardless of how simple or seemingly unimportant it may appear to others. Author Dick Sheppard wrote of finding a personal measure of success and meaning in what seems to be the most mundane daily work so important to maintaining and enhancing the quality of life. He stated, "I can more easily see our Lord sweeping the streets of London, than issuing edicts from its cathedral."[2]

The impatient owner of the septic tank company seemed obligated and pressured. He could have been doing any job that would provide income and took little pride in his work other than his status as the owner. The second man seemed cynical and to be going through the motions in his work. But the third man, the self-proclaimed ecologist standing over the septic tank and doing the nastiest of the work was the most sweetly successful. Unlike his colleagues focused on the narrow objective of their work, Big Al was able to focus his attention on the value of his work for the common good—a core value of the *po'okela* view of success.

What Do You Do?

One of the first questions that comes up when people meet each other initially is, "What do you do?" Asking for this information is a way we try to get to know a person and establish social connection, but the answer reflects much more than a simple job description. It suggests the person's degree of contentment, purpose, and pride in living, loving, and working. It indicates perhaps the most important and revealing aspect of a person's character—does this person seem happy?

Author Storm Jackson identified five key components that we might listen for in the answer to this question. He defined happiness as "the capacity to feel deeply, to enjoy simply, to think freely, to risk life, to be needed."[3] Does your answer to the "What do you do?" question indicate that what you are doing most of the day allows you to experience sweet success? Following are five questions that if answered affirmatively indicate that you are leading a sweetly successful life:

1. Do you feel energetically alive every day and share life intensely with those who matter most to you?
2. Do you enjoy a relatively uncomplicated and undemanding daily schedule over which you have full control?
3. Do you feel energized or drained by what you do?
4. Are you doing things that you feel are significant and worth spending the largest part of your lifetime doing?
5. Does what you do make you feel connected with those about whom you care and vitally involved in doing what you want to do?

If the five issues listed above are contained in your answer to the "What do you do?" question, you are sweetly successful. Whether you are a butcher or baker or candlestick maker, whether you are a student or teacher or minister or erotic dancer, the answer to the question provides a look inside the heart and soul of the person we ask, a kind of success survey that indicates the person's personal measure of success.

How do you answer this question? Is your response based primarily on *what* you do or on *why* and *for whom*? Would your answer reflect what you feel you have to do and want to do? Does your answer include purpose as much as task, choice as much as obligation, and *us* more than *me*? Which of the three answers given by the septic-tank workers most closely resembles how you answer the "What do you do" question? Are you more like Dave, Fred, or Big Al?

The full measure of our success is determined less by the tangible rewards we receive for our work than by what we have become by doing it. Sweet success depends less on what is on our schedule, our written job description, or the salary we receive than on our own personal noncomparative and noncompetitive measure of success. It relates less to what we do for a living than for what we are living.

On the Wrong Path to the Right Place

I have been a lifelong collector of definitions of success. Like most children, I learned very early that whatever success was, you were supposed to want it and pursue it. In preparing to write this book, I reread most of the more than one thousand definitions in my collection. It was in part from this reading that I decided to share the Hawaiian *po ʻokela* model of an excellent life as a model of sweet success and to focus on the six-word detoxification of toxic success described in part 3: be content, calm down, connect always.

As I read my definitions, I noticed a paradox emerging: The definitions of what it is like to feel highly successful were almost the exact opposite of the many formulas offered for what it took to "achieve" success. In other words, the destination did not seem to match the proposed journey. To illustrate this point, I have selected from my collection twenty definitions of success as offered by creative people from all walks of life. Well-known persons whom most of the world see as highly successful, they include authors, poets, singers, and comedians and comediennes. I will then present twenty formulas for success. See if you notice a contrast between the success we desire and the ways in which we seek it.

THE NATURE OF SUCCESS

1. "There is only one success—to be able to spend your life in your own way." (Christopher Morley, American writer)
2. "I am done with great things and big plans, great institutions, and big success." (William James, psychologist)
3. "Real joy comes not from ease or riches or from the praise of men, but from doing something worthwhile." (Wilfred T. Grenfell, English medical missionary)
4. "Success happens to the man who takes proper care of his family." (Navaho shaman)
5. "Success is to be measured not so much by the position that one has reached in life as by the obstacles which he has overcome while trying to succeed." (Booker T. Washington, American educator)
6. "Success in running a business carries by itself no promise of success outside business." (Peter Drucker, American business author and lecturer)
7. "To know even one life has breathed easier because you have lived. This is to have succeeded." (Ralph Waldo Emerson, American essayist and poet)
8. "What's money? A man is a success if he gets up in the morning and

gets to bed at night, and in between he does what he wants to." (Bob Dylan, singer)

9. "Success is counted sweetest by those who ne'er succeed." (Emily Dickinson, poet)

10. "The successful man is the one who has lived well, laughed often, and loved a great deal." (Arthur J. Stanley, philosopher and author)

11. "I'd rather be a failure at something I enjoy than a success at something I hate!" (George Burns, comedian)

12. "I am not bound to success, but I am bound to live up to what light I have." (Abraham Lincoln)

13. "We cannot do great things in life; we can only do small things with great love." (Mother Teresa)

14. "Do few things but do them well; simple joys are holy." (Saint Francis of Assisi)

15. "Just to be is a blessing. Just to live is holy." (Rabbi Abraham Herschel)

16. "The minute you begin to do what you really want to do, it's really a different kind of life." (Buckminster Fuller, American inventor and philosopher)

17. "The work will wait while you show your child the rainbow, but the rainbow won't wait while you do the work." (Patricia Clafford, author)

18. "Finding the right work is like discovering your own soul in the world." (Thomas Moore, psychotherapist and writer)

19. "The price of anything is the amount of life you are willing to pay for it." (Henry David Thoreau, American writer)

20. "Success is not something you should pursue for yourself. You must live so that it may happen to you and those you love because of how you have lived." (Hawaiian *kahuna* Kawaikapuokalani Hewett)

You may want to return to these definitions as you read part 3 of this book. Note in each the preference for life values over tangible objectives and references to money, status, and power. One would think that the following paths suggested for reaching sweet success as defined above would contain the same gentle and spiritual orientation of these definitions, but do they?

THE WAY TO SUCCESS

1. "The only way to succeed is to make people hate you." (Josef Von Sternberg, Austrian film director)
2. "The trophy is the truth, the only truth. . . . There is no such thing as second place." (The coach in Jason Miller's *That Championship Season*)
3. "Winning is not the most important thing; it is the only thing." (Vince Lobardi, football coach)
4. "For nothing can seem foul to those that win." (William Shakespeare, *Henry IV*, part 1, act 5, scene 1)
5. "The name of the game is win." (Billy Martin, baseball manager)
6. "First we will be best, and then we will be first." (Grant Tinker, television executive)
7. "Ah, but a man's reach should exceed his grasp—or what's a heave for?" (Robert Browning, poet)
8. "Once you say you're going to settle for second, that's what happens to you in life." (John F. Kennedy, thirty-fifth president of the United States)
9. "The lack of money is the root of all evil." (George Bernard Shaw, Irish dramatist and essayist)
10. "The enemy of the 'best' is the 'good.'" (anonymous)
11. "If you don't win the Super Bowl, the whole season was a waste." (lineman playing in the NFL)
12. "If you're not going for number one, you don't deserve a number." (coach of a Big Ten basketball team)
13. "In life, you are either a winner or a loser. There is no in-between. If you're not trying to be all you can be, you're not trying hard enough." (motivational speaker)
14. "Use your personal power. If you can think it, you can do it." (Tony Robbins, motivationalist)
15. "Just do it!!" (Nike athletic shoe commercial)
16. "If you're not going to give your all, don't even bother." (sign in sixth-grade classroom)

17. "I'm a great believer in luck, and I find the harder I work, the more I have of it." (Thomas Jefferson, third president of the United States)
18. "It is no use saying, 'We're doing our best.' You have got to succeed." (Sir Winston Churchill)
19. "If you dream it, you can do it." (Walt Disney, American film producer)
20. "To do all that one is able to do is to be a man." (Napoleon Bonaparte, emperor of France)

Do you see differences between what is usually described as the desired experience of success and the commonly accepted cultural orientation as to how to achieve success? Can you detect a sense of compensation for self-doubt, deficiency, and detachment in the proposed ways to succeed? Do you see the SIN and IPM factors?

We so easily and automatically react competitively that you may have already looked for flaws in the sets of quotes I have included. You may be thinking that I purposely selected "competitive-sounding" quotes for the second list and the more "life connection" or spiritually oriented quotes for the first list. Space does not allow me to share the hundreds of other quotations from my collection and from the one hundred winners group. Despite the competition default mode that is our current societal normalcy, I hope you will consider the paradox that the kind of advice we are being given about how to become successful contrasts with the kind of life most of us would consider truly successful. This contradiction results in our spending much of the day doing what we do not enjoy in an attempt to have the life we say would be deeply fulfilling.

Toxic success results from giving up the life you would love to have now in a dangerous gamble that you will be able to live the life you desire later. By contrast, sweet success is recognizing that "now's the time" to live, love, and work the way your heart needs you to so you can be content, calm down, and connect always.

To see how the current paths to success are so closely tied to competition, power, and deficiency motives in our society, try the "TV test." Make two columns on a piece of paper. Label one "connect" and the other "compete." Listen to the words used in one hour of television programs and advertisements and count the number of words that seem related to caring, helping, sharing, and accepting as compared to those reflecting winning, defeating, having more, and doing better than someone else. I asked my hundred winners to try the TV test, but all of them gave up after the first half hour because the point became so rapidly clear. Almost every commercial or program emphasized *doing* more than *being* or some way to achieve supremacy over someone else.

The SIN, or self-interest norm, of competitiveness has become so prevalent in our modern society that we even compete against ourselves. We are constantly challenged to compare ourselves not only with how others look but how we used to look. Diet books and advertisements for diet drinks urge us to compete pound for pound, and we are told that our hair could be fuller, our skin less wrinkled, or our teeth whiter if we will only "just do it." "Before" and "after" ads contrasting our former failure self with the promise of a more successful-looking future self dominate commercials that promise the look of success and how to avoid appearing like a loser. The problem with these definitions of personal success is that, by their very nature, they require millions of losers so some of us can feel like winners and lots of failures so we can feel successful.

One sweetly successful woman executive offered her support of my emphasis on noncomparative contentment. She joked, "A waist is a terrible thing to mind. I think more people should do the exercise called 'enjoy your size' every day."

Are You a Success?

Have you bought in to the normalcy of toxic success based on winning? What is your personal definition of success? In one sentence, write it down on an index card. Then use your card as a bookmark as you read the rest of this book. Stop reading now and then to reflect on your original definition. Change it if your thinking about success or how it might be accomplished has changed by reading this far. Check to see if your daily behaviors reflect the nature and perspective of your definition and whether or not the six words of sweet success are a part of your view of success and how it is attained.

I asked the one hundred winners to write a one-sentence definition of success. Space allows me to list only ten of their responses, but they are representative of the other ninety in orientation and emphasis and related to the definitions of success offered by the celebrities:

1. "Success is enjoying life every day." (28-year-old female banking executive)
2. "Success is your family and yourself being and feeling healthy and happy." (43-year-old top insurance industry salesman)
3. "Success is recognizing what you have, sharing it, and enjoying it." (36-year-old female dentist)
4. "Success is being able to laugh hard every day and love hard every night." (male vice president of wireless telephone company)
5. "Success is not worrying about what society says is successful." (35-year-old male CEO of a building contract company)
6. "Success is loving what you do at work, and being able to do what you love with those you love at home." (44-year-old male self-employed house painter)
7. "Success is having just enough that you can enjoy your life without worrying about having enough." (29-year-old professional football player)
8. "I would say success is like love. If you try too hard for it, you never seem to find it." (44-year-old female professor)
9. "Success is a feeling—not money, status, and stuff." (62-year-old retired financial advisor)
10. "You're successful when your wife and kids love you, and you know they feel you are always there for them in every way." (the man I described in the introduction to this book who was immersed in watching his son play soccer)

These definitions indicate that something within us seems to long for what sweet success is as it relates to the several definitions offered by the well-known successful people. We seem to hold a vague sense of what it means to feel content, yet we are being convinced that it is a state that seems too illusive, impractical, or idealistic for modern life. So much of our daily life is lived in what I suggest is the "four D" compensatory competitiveness that bliss is hard to come by. Like someone eating a triple hamburger with french fries while on the way to the gym to work out, we seem to be living one way while longing to be another.

Faded Doves

Toxic success has resulted from the fact that somewhere along the way we made a bad choice. However misguided, overdone, and eventually disillusioned and corrupted, the 1960s saw an interest among many in seeking spiritual contentment and loving connection. "Make love, not war" was not only a political statement. However simplistic and romantic, it was also a hopeful expression of a longing for a return to a more gentle and connected way of living. That phrase is mocked now, and many of the "love children" of the 1960s are busy pursuing their own toxic success. The love children have become the SINers, sold out to the self-interest norm of individual success and happiness. Unable to find love, they seem to have accepted toxic success as a substitute.

A few days ago, I saw a rusted old Volkswagon van at Sandy Beach in East Honolulu. It had a faded bumper sticker with a barely discernible white dove of peace, which said, "Choose Love." Parked next to it was a silver Mercedes convertible with a gold-lettered license plate frame that said, "My other car is a BMW. What's yours?" The contrast reflected the lethal choice we made beginning in the selfish 1970s, extending through the greed-oriented 1980s, and peaking in the "you can have it all" 1990s.

We have chosen to squander the real gift from our hard-earned increased capacity to produce more faster, a productivity that could have allowed us plenty of time to pay attention to those things that bring us the sense of contentment, calmness, and connection we say we want. We could have used our unprecedented productivity to thrive in the essence of the definition of that word. We could have used the time it freed to pay more attention to growing, flourishing, and relishing those aspects of life that bring us closer to our definition of a truly successful life. We could have used our time to pay more attention to the ones we love rather than to ways to strive harder. PNI researcher David McClelland would say we have chosen achievement (i.e., striving) over affiliation (i.e., thriving), and we are paying dearly for that choice in the costs to our health, our relationships, and our planet.

Economist Juliet Schor writes, "Since 1948, the level of productivity of the U.S. worker has more than doubled. . . . We could now produce our 1948 standard of living in less than half the time. Every time productivity increases, we are presented with the possibility of either more free time or more money. We could have chosen the four-hour day. Or a working year of six months. Or every worker in the United States could now be taking every other year off from work—with pay."[4] The choice that led to our toxic success was to work the same or even more hours to earn twice as much money. But are we twice as happy as those who came before us?

We have become toxically successful because we made up our mind to consume rather than be content. The consumption levels from the 1970s until now have been the highest achieved by any civilization in human history. We are almost five times richer than our great-grandparents were at the turn of the century, but are we really five times happier? Researchers Joel and Michelle Levey write, "The number of people who report being 'very happy' peaked in 1957!"[5] Our choice to consume rather than be content has resulted in us having more timesaving devices and less time, distraction from our most important relationships, and more depression and illness not only for ourselves but our children.

Gone Shopping

Our assumption that we can buy the feeling of success has made us into the consummate consumers. In the Hawaiian *po'okela* model, being called a "consumer" is considered the ultimate insult. It suggests that we use and eat up things, but modern Westerners seem proud of the label. We have become a nation of shoppers. As one of the winners group said, "We are being malled to death."

Driven by the self-doubt and sense of deficiency perpetuated by the advertising industry, we seem to be in constant shopping mode. A recent poll indicated that 89 percent of women and 75 percent of men feel that as a nation we have become addicted to shopping. In addition, 75 percent of women and 69 percent of men say that "consuming is a substitute for what is missing in our lives." Americans shop almost four times more than their counterparts in Western Europe.[6] When we are spiritually starving, we will consume almost anything, it seems. We are toxifying our systems by gorging ourselves with more and more stuff. As comedian George Carlin pointed out, "Home has become the place where we store our stuff while we go out shopping for more stuff."[7]

Our shopping mentality is not limited to searching for more stuff. It has become a compulsion that extends to looking for a better job, a new and bigger house, and even a better lover. We so consume our relationships that the divorce rate reveals that our serial marriages have become little more than notarized dating. Our attention is in shopping mode and constantly on the lookout for better, newer, bigger, and faster. As one of my interviewees in the winners group said, "I just want neater stuff, so I'm always shopping around."

Constant shopping is a manifestation of the toxic succeeder's deficiency motive. Going out to find and buy something we really need to live is much different than incessant "window-shopping" for something newer or better. We no longer go out to "get something" but to make ourselves available to be "gotten" by the latest new thing. When we answer, "No, I'm just looking," to a store clerk offering help, we are often admitting that we are in our surveillance mode and scanning for something we do not yet know we want. We seem ever on patrol to be sure no one is getting something we do not have or has gotten a better deal, or that nothing escapes our attention that might make us happier.

Our Deepening Debt

Another feature of toxic success that results from its shopping mentality is that almost all of us are in debt. If our home mortgage is included, nearly 70 percent of our spendable income goes to pay the interest on our debts. This means that we are working from Monday morning until Thursday noon just to pay the interest on the debts for things we have already purchased.[8] And those with the highest scores on the toxic success inventory you will be taking in this chapter often spend much of the money they make between noon on Thursday and the end of the workday Friday, purchasing more stuff to go into even deeper debt.

The debt experienced by the toxically successful is not just monetary. It is also, or perhaps foremost, a long-accumulated and increasing spiritual debt. You have read that toxic success involves a "deficiency" mentality. Even if we cannot seem to put our finger on what it is, and no matter how much money, stuff, and status we have attained, something always seems missing. There seems to be an emptiness inside us that cannot be filled no matter how many sales we find or high rewards we receive. No matter how successful society says we are, we cannot seem to feel and share a sense of contentment. Even the most full bag of bargains found by the most proficient and compulsive shopper will not fill the spiritual emptiness that is toxic success.

As you read in chapter 3 when I described the "mild madness" of cyclothymia associated with toxic success, most of our most revered celebrities and success heroes have experienced this spiritual debt. They were constant shoppers for something they seemed to always be needing but were never able to find. Their high-level toxic success eventually made them tragic heroes who, like the fallen heroes described in chapter 1, were never able to find contentment.

For the successful people I interviewed for this book, their consumption led only to a deceptive short-lived pleasantness, inevitably followed by looking for more. No matter what they had obtained, the contentment, calmness, and connection that characterizes sweet success eluded them. As a *kupuna* (Hawaiian elder) told me, "You can't buy your way out of spiritual debt. You have to stop overspending your spiritual energy and start loving your way out."

Wall Street Journal reporter Sue Shellenberger asked several top executives a provocative question in 1998.[9] She queried them, "If you could change one thing about the way you have balanced your career, personal, family, and community activities over the years, what would it be?" Three of the answers Shellenberger received follow:

- "I wish I'd known sooner that if you miss a child's play or performance or sporting event, you will have forgotten a year later the work emergency that caused you to miss it, but your child will not have forgotten that you weren't there." (Laurel Cutler, vice chairman of Foote, Cone and Belding Corporation)

- "I know now that the most creative thing I've ever done is being a parent." (Ilene Dolins, senior vice president and founding partner, Windham International Relocation Corporation)

- "I can remember some blurry choices when my children were young when I may not have attended a play or a soccer game because I had some conflicting business commitment. It's ironic that twenty-five years later I can remember I didn't go to that event, but I can't remember what business thing I was doing. I wish I had been defined as the father of my children, as someone who made my community a better place." (Randall Tobias, chairman and CEO, Eli Lilly Corporation)

I posed another question about success to the one hundred winners. After they had offered their definition of success, I asked them to write one sentence that described a debt they considered they had incurred in their pursuit of their success. My query was, "To whom or what do you feel you owe a spiritual debt, incurred because of how you have lived, loved, and worked?"

Following are ten examples of the "toxic success debt" incurred by the one hundred winners group. Again, almost all of the remaining ninety responses were similar in content to these answers:

1. "I owe my first wife for how I ignored her." (52-year-old senior partner in law firm)

2. "I owe what I'm afraid is an unrepayable debt to my children and my husband for not being there for them as much as I should have been and really wanted to be." (42-year-old female owner of her own software company)

3. "I owe my unborn children dearly for being too busy to notice in time that I would have loved to have had them." (53-year-old tax attorney)

4. "I owe our marriage a debt I can never repay." (42-year-old research psychologist and university professor)

5. "I owe my parents big time for ignoring them until it was too late to show them I loved them." (62-year-old retired manufacturer's representative)

6. "My debt is to my family for letting my work cause my two heart attacks and for the terrible pressure that put on them." (43-year-old male purchaser for large department store)

7. "I cry when I think that I will never be able to show or tell my wife how much I loved her." (40-year-old CEO of venture capital organization whose wife died of cancer)

8. "I probably owe an emotional debt to everyone who has ever had to work with such a pain in the ass." (60-year-old pharmacist and owner of his own pharmacy)

9. "I owe a huge time debt I can never pay back. I owe it to my prior two wives and three children from those marriages. My marriages didn't fail, I failed them. I gave them everything but what they really needed and wanted—me." (41-year-old owner of three restaurants)

10. "My debt is a Willie Nelson kind of debt to all the people in my life I never loved before." (48-year-old chief financial officer of an asphalt paving company)

In all of the above answers and the other ninety responses from the winners group, the debt they experienced related to family, loving, and lack of taking the time to share contentment with others in their life. The tragedy of toxic success is that too few winners realize how deeply in debt they are falling until they approach spiritual bankruptcy. I hope this book will serve as an urgent notice regarding a possible deficit in your own spiritual account and draw your attention to any debts you have or are incurring while you still have time to begin paying them off.

Forget the Pot, Enjoy the Rainbow

Because the toxically successful function from a deficiency motive, they are constantly striving to make up for the feeling that they don't yet have enough of "what it takes" to be happy. Due to a kind of success superstition, they avoid declaring themselves successful because they feel enough might not really be enough. They are driven by society's false promise that we can work ourselves to the point of feeling we have enough. You have read that all human wants are ultimately insatiable and all feelings, whether sad or happy, are transitory. When *more* is the destination, we are left frustrated and exhausted from the endlessness of our journey.

We have been taught to think that anyone can have it all if he or she wants it badly enough and is willing to try hard enough, but this would mean that anyone who has "failed" just didn't try hard enough. And what is the "it" we are supposed to want so badly? What is the "it" the successful are supposed to have? In the case of toxic success, it's more stuff.

Research shows, however, that you can't buy happiness. Ecopsychologist Alan Thein Durning writes, "Studies on happiness indicate that the main determinants of happiness in life are not related to consumption at all; prominent among them are satisfaction with family life . . . marriage . . . work, the leisure to develop talents and friendships."[10] These are the same elements found in the thirty definitions of success listed earlier in this chapter and the same values of the *po'okela* model of excellence.

Toxic success results in satisfaction being squeezed out of life by the manner in which we pursue what we think will ultimately bring us satisfaction. Psychologist Jeremy Seabrook interviewed dozens of older middle-class workers. Based on these interviews, he wrote, "People aren't satisfied, only they don't seem to know why they're not. The only chance of satisfaction we can imagine is getting more of what we've got now. But it's what we've got now that makes everybody dissatisfied. So what will more of it do—make us more satisfied, or more dissatisfied?"[11]

Toxic success means looking for the pot at the end of the rainbow. Sweet success is ignoring the pot and enjoying the rainbow. We cannot consume or own a rainbow. We can only sense and try to share and remember its mystical beauty and feel wonderful when we see it. The only things we ever really truly own are our memories. Try as we might to follow a rainbow to the pot of gold we think rests at its end, we never find the end of the rainbow or the pot and end up wasting our memory-making time looking for the gold. Like the toxic pursuit of success, when we chase rainbows, they only disappear. Try as we might and no matter how motivated or positive thinking we may be, we will never succeed in owning or consuming our own private rainbow.

Rainbows are offered to us as sustenance for the soul. Like all of the elements of sweet success about which you read in the definitions of success offered in this chapter, they become ours as cherished memories only if we are content to admire and relish them in the precious present. We can appreciate but not have them. If we are willing to take the time to sit down with someone we love and wait for a rainbow, we can experience the sweet success of sharing the essence of its beauty.

The Toxic Success Survey

Based on the current research on the toxicity of our definition and pursuit of success, my clinical work with hundreds of "successful people," and work with patients and persons attending my various seminars and lectures, I designed a "toxic success survey." All one hundred of my interviewees took the survey, and I gave it to more than one thousand patients in my clinic at Sinai Hospital of Detroit in the late 1970s and 1980s. I have since given it to more than two thousand persons attending my lectures and seminars around the world, as well as my Hawaiian "control group" of friends and family. Now that you have learned about the risk of what has become our normal way of viewing and seeking success and how the competitive meaning we so often assign to events and people in our life can exact a serious toll, take the survey yourself. It will provide a baseline for your later efforts in part 3 of this book to enter a success "detox" program.

THE TOXIC SUCCESS SURVEY

Think of the person in your life who knows you the best. Now, answer each of the following questions as you think that person would answer them. Like the alcoholic who often denies the seriousness of a drinking problem, the toxically successful are either unaware of or in deep denial about the seriousness of their condition.

Taking the Toxic Success Survey from another person's perspective accomplishes three things. First, it forces you to step outside yourself and look at how you are behaving. Since most toxically successful people are "outsighters" who tend to attribute their condition to "the way things are" or "the world today," taking the test from another person's perspective can help promote a new look at how we are coming across to those who know us and what it is like to seek a successful life with us. Second, it can help confront the denial of the toxically successful by allowing them to begin to look at their situation from the safer distance of "that's how they see me." Finally, the form of the questions allows you to ask another person to score you and you to score another person. This can lead to fruitful discussions as to whether or not you have found a "competitive codependent" who supports and shares your addiction to toxic success.

Use the following scale to respond to each item from the perspective of the person you have selected to score you. As you take the test, remember on this test that a "low score" is a "better," or less toxic, score and a "1" is better than a "5." Toxically successful people often have trouble with this reverse scoring system because, as you read in chapter 2, they think "more" is better than "less" and big numbers are usually better than smaller ones.

> 5 = Not at all like her/him
> 4 = A little like her/him
> 3 = More than a little like her/him
> 2 = Quite a bit like her/him
> 1 = That's her/him

The person who really knows you would say you

1.____ are a total joy to live and work with.
2.____ are as involved and joyfully absorbed in family life as work life.
3.____ pay close attention when others are speaking no matter who they are.
4.____ are calm, patient, easygoing, and reflective.
5.____ would much sooner cooperate than compete.
6.____ are not at all judgmental, sexist, or prejudiced.
7.____ give more compliments than criticisms.
8.____ forgive easily and don't carry a grudge.
9.____ seem seldom rushed or "too busy" and always seem to "have time."
10.____ don't have much of "a temper" or "lose it" very often.

11._____ are as full of energy at the end of the day as at the beginning.

12._____ seldom frown or smirk, and smile and laugh a lot.

13._____ don't overreact and stay calm when challenged.

14._____ take criticism easily and well.

15._____ are exactly the same in public as at home.

16._____ seldom interrupt, try to hurry others' speaking, or answer questions before they are completed.

17._____ never push elevator buttons that are already lit.

18._____ don't replay "work war stories" at home and are able to totally forget work problems and obligations when on vacation.

19._____ are not at all moody.

20._____ do not take things personally or complain that you are not getting your due credit, attention, or rewards.

_____ TOTAL SCORE

The higher your score, the more likely it is that you are suffering to some degree from toxic success syndrome. A high score on the Toxic Success Survey indicates that, even though you may be unaware of it or deny it as "just being normal," others sense that you are driven by self-doubt and the sense of deficiency. The higher your score, the more likely it is that you are becoming personally detached and disconnected from those who matter most in your life; tend to be more moody than you realize; and are prone to postsuccess depression stemming from a sense of "never having, doing, or being enough" or to feeling disoriented and even depressed when not having to be "on your game."

The average (mean) score of the one hundred successful interviewees was 72. (The mean score of the Hawaiian "control" group was 44.) There was no significant difference between the scores of the men and women, but one item on the test stood out in the difference of male and female scores. On item number 11 (Are you as full of energy at the end of the day as at the beginning?), all of the fifty women scored 4 or 5 while the fifty men scored mostly 3s and a few 4s. This may be an indicator of the "vital exhaustion" experienced by many female toxic succeeders that will be discussed in chapter 7.

I suggest you discuss your score on this test with the person you pretended was scoring you. Set your score aside and look at it again before and after you try the "toxic success detox" program in part 3.

Written All over Your Face

During my one hundred interviews and in my clinical work with highly successful individuals, my staff and I would often comment that these persons seemed to share a common "look of success." "You can see it on their faces," my secretary would say. "I know the really successful ones waiting to see you because they all have the same look on their faces." My clinical staff noted the same thing, and we began to take photographs of our patients. After we had collected more than two hundred pictures of those coming to "detox" their success, we agreed that there did seem to be a facial appearance that reflected a "look of failed success." While attending a presentation by the pioneer in "type A" research, Dr. Meyer Friedman, I learned that he and his clinical team were using videotaped clinical examinations (VCEs) of their patients that included evaluation of facial features and behavioral habits.[12] The "look of failed success" we noted resembled that reported in their research.

As another step in measuring the kind of success you are achieving in your life and what it is doing to you, take the "Look of Success Test" that we used with our patients. Here is how it is done:

THE LOOK OF SUCCESS TEST

- Have someone stand beside you at a mirror and, even though it will feel awkward, ask them to study your face with you. Go ahead and laugh and tease, but then really take a good look.

    Does this look like the face of contentment? Is this the face of a lover or a warrior? Look for the battle scars of the fight-or-flight response in the form of etched frown lines in the forehead and around the eyes and mouth.

    Many toxically successful people may not think they have time to do something as foolish as a facial analysis with someone else and will try to avoid this exercise altogether, but if at all possible "face" the problem with someone whose opinions you trust.

- Look for "tight jaw." Does your face appear tense, as if you were biting down on a pencil, resulting in a bulging or tautness around the jaws just under both ears?

- Look for the "stress squint." Do your eyelids seem narrow and tense as if you are squinting?

- Look for "flared nostrils." Do the nostrils of your nose seem to be flared out as if you were smelling something foul and unpleasant?

- Look for "stress stains." Are there slight brown or brownish-yellow markings just beneath both eyes? This is due to excess stress hormones that cannot be metabolized or "burned up," causing them to deposit under the eyes. On autopsy, we noted in some of our patients that there was often a large area of brown around the orbits of both eyes, a "death mask" left by the chronic pursuit of toxic success.

- Look for the "stress smirk." Smile. Do your the lips pull back and expose a large, toothy grin? Or, do you note a controlled, straight, tight-lipped "almost smile" that seems to be only a thin veneer covering the doubt, deficiency, detachment, disappointment, and depression of toxic success?

- Now ask the person helping you to face you and look into your eyes. It may be uncomfortable at first, but take your time. Have the person look *in,* not *at,* your eyes. Try not to turn this exercise into a staring contest and just allow yourself to be "looked into." Ask the person what they see in you. Do they sense an underlying contentment or does it seem that "no one is home?" Do they sense calmness or fear?

    When we looked deeply into the eyes of our patients, we noticed in our clinic what we called "the vacant look of a dormant spirit." It was a tired look that seemed to reflect that the person had "given their all."

After completing the face test, return the favor to your partner. Examine his or her face and discuss what you see there. You might also want to look for some old pictures and see what is written on your face in various situations. Using your Toxic Success Survey test results and your face test, you should have some idea of whether or not you are suffering from toxic success and, if so, how severe your condition has become.

Now that you have some idea of your own measure of success and how you have chosen to pursue it, there is another component of toxic success that you may feel too tired to consider. But first, I suggest you take a break from your reading, study the definition of success you wrote on the card you are using as your bookmark, listen to some relaxing music, and reflect on what you have read so far. Before trying to deal with the next aspect of toxic success, the condition known as "vital exhaustion," sit back and reflect again on your definition of success. A little rest will do you good and, who knows, a rainbow might come your way.

CHAPTER SEVEN

Too Busy to Love, Too Tired to Care

The highest reward from your working
is not what you get for it but what you become by it.

—*Sydney Harris*

What's on your mind? If the images and thoughts that constitute your consciousness were recorded for one week and then played back on a large screen for your family, friends, and you to review, would you be pleased with what you saw? What would your grandparents and great-grandparents think of what's on your mind most of the time? If you're not happy with the content of your consciousness, chances are you are suffering from toxic success syndrome.

I asked the winners group to take a "mind walk." Many of them resisted this suggestion, saying it seemed silly or a waste of time. With so much of their attention constantly focused outside, turning it inside is not something those suffering from TSS do easily. A deep personal loss or illness is often needed to force them to examine their own consciousness. I urged the winners to do some precrisis soul-searching by imagining what it would be like strolling through the corridors of their own mind. I wanted them to consider how they felt about the way in which they were investing their most precious and limited resource, their attention.

Sweetly successful people report that their mind walk seems like a calm meandering through treasured images of family and friends. While not without personal crises and regrets, they are able to linger wistfully to look at scenes of memories they want to treasure for a lifetime. One of the Hawaiian control group, a 64-year-old taro farmer from the Big Island, said, "I take that walk every day. I see my ancestors, and they are smiling and nodding at me. I see rainbows, and I can smell the *pīkake* [fragrant flower]. My wife says she knows when I'm doing my mind walk because I always have this silly grin on my face."

Toxically successful people's journeys are less inviting. When they're willing to try it, they say they don't like what they see. One winner said, "It was like walking through a corporate headquarters. I saw some nice things, but mostly it was like walking the streets of New York—everything was moving fast and nothing seemed to be connecting."

The scattered reactive attention of TSS sufferers creates a mind cluttered with the flotsam and jetsam of partially attended to mental litter. They bump into missed opportunities and encounter the ghosts of angry conflicts, unexpressed love, and those they have not taken the time to hold and say "I love you" too. As one winner said, "When I do this mind-walk thing, it tires me out. I keep seeing things I forgot to do and have to do. It makes me feel guilty and depressed. I don't want to go there."

Have You Lost Your Mind?

If you are toxically successful, you've "lost your mind." You've surrendered it to the pressures of the unrelenting demands for your attention by the outside world. You suffer from what the Reuters Business Information group called "information fatigue syndrome."[1] Based on a study of 1,300 successful men and women around the world, Reuters issued a report called "Dying for Information." They identified the following symptoms of information fatigue syndrome:

- Inability to make decisions
- Irritability and anger
- Pain in the stomach and muscles
- Frequent feelings of helplessness
- Listlessness and lethargy
- Inability to sleep
- Waking up during the night with a sense of panic
- Loss of energy

• Lack of enthusiasm for hobbies and leisure activities
• Inability to pay attention[2]

Do these symptoms sound familiar? They all reflect various aspects of the five Ds of toxic success. The sense of deficiency, doubt, detachment, disappointment, and depression that characterizes the toxically successful is not caused by the outside world but by how we have chosen to attend to it. We have become attention-lazy by allowing "out there" to determine what will be "in here." Eventually, our mind is no longer our own.

Where Are You Most of the Day?

How do you spend most of your "mental moments?" What are you thinking about the moment you wake up, most of the day, and before you go to sleep at night? Is your attention energetically and selectively focused on the joy of being alive and sharing life with those you love? Is what is on your mind something you want to be there forever? Do you easily sift through the barrage of information to select what you would like to become and who and how you are as a person? With the average worker in the United States spending half of their day responding to messages and almost two hours a day just dealing with e-mail, mental sifting isn't easy. International Data Corporation estimates that 10 billion "non-spam" (not unwanted) messages are sent per day worldwide and will increase to 35 billion by 2005. Talk about an energy crisis! Our attention resources are depleting, and we are becoming mentally fatigued.[3] We use so much attention all day long that by the time we get home, we're out of it. A spouse of one of the winners said, "In a way, he never really comes home from work. *He* does, but not his attention."

TSS is caused by allowing our mind to be held hostage by a world that is so demanding of our attention that it puts us into a trance. We have only so much attention and if we don't manage this natural resource wisely, it will be gone forever. It will be as if we became hypnotized and unthinkingly compliant with whatever commands our schedule imposes. When this happens, we become a very well-adjusted robot.

Like the parents of a hyperactive child, we can become too frustrated and tired to keep trying to discipline our attention. When it keeps going here and there in response to the most immediate temptation, we eventually give in and let it run wild. We begin to respond to whatever seems to be the most immediate and demanding stimulus. The result is a consciousness full of everything except what we know in our heart needs to be there.

One of the winners reported the degree to which he had "lost his mind." He confessed, "When that little hourglass appears on the computer screen, I start tapping my foot and rocking my chair. I need information *now*! I don't want to waste my attention staring at that stupid little thing. My wife says I suffer from 'premature articulation' because I start cussing the hourglass and swearing at the computer. I guess you'd say I'm a computer abuser because I've been known to hit it and shove it around. Computers might be getting faster, but they're nowhere near fast enough. And while I'm on this issue, I'd like to clip that idiotic paper-clip guy [on the computer screen]. He's a total distraction."

The Human Icon

To disguise their attention deficit disorder, the toxically successful often develop a persona, a social image they project to others that masks what is really on their mind and what isn't. They can nod pleasantly and pretend to pay attention, but they usually aren't attending where you think they are. They might automatically respond by saying, "Fine, thank you," when asked by strangers how they are doing, but they really aren't fine at all. They're tired, overwhelmed, and distracted by the pressure to plan ahead for their next challenge. When TSS sufferers answer, "Oh, nothing really," when asked, "What's on your mind?" they are really thinking, "Too much to even begin to talk about."

Those who live with the toxically successful know that they are not "fine." They are frequently victims of the distracted TSS sufferer's brush-off and stonewalling techniques. One winner's spouse said, "He talks *to* me, but not *with* me. He has too much on his mind to really pay attention to me or to even tell me what he's thinking and what he's feeling."

The spouse of the computer abuser said, "I don't think he is ever really fine. There's too much on his mind, and unfortunately that doesn't usually include me. There's no room in there for me. Paying attention to me is not a priority. He considers me a done deal that doesn't require any of his precious attention. He won't admit it, but I know he feels I'm a distraction a lot of times. I think when I ask for his attention, he sees that little hourglass. I feel like an icon waiting for him to click on, but he seldom does. The only time he really pays attention to me is when he says he needs to bounce something off me. That's exactly what he does. He just throws his work problems at me and then responds to them himself. He's like someone practicing tennis against a wall, and I'm the wall."

Dumping Psycho-Toxic Emotional Waste

Another characteristic of the toxically successful is that they often "dump" a kind of psycho-toxic emotional waste on those they love. The calm and confident facade that everyone else sees is dropped, and a discontented, agitated whiner can take its place. The ones dumped on are the same people TSS sufferers so regularly neglect and who tend to be missing from the corridors of their mind. This dumping is not really paying attention to a loved one or friend; it is using them as a source of stress reduction. One spouse of a winner said, "If she treated me with half the attention and kindness she does her employees, things would be much better around the house."

The spouse of one of the winners group described feeling dumped on when she said, "Dayle comes home looking half-dead. He always says he doesn't bring his work problems home, but he does because *he* is the problem. It's not that he's so physically tired as he is mentally exhausted. He has no attention left to give us. He complains that he is wiped out and needs to be left alone for a while so he can gather his thoughts. But the minute the phone rings, the gathering is over. He jumps up, becomes instantly alert, and puts on his public image as mister energetic charmer.

"It's like he is three of the seven dwarfs wrapped into one. We see Sleepy and Grumpy, but the world sees Happy. He spends most of his energy presenting to complete strangers exactly the pleasant and upbeat image we would love to see around the house. We've become his emotional dumping ground, and it's a waste of time because he doesn't listen to us when we tell him he is burning the candle at both ends."

The husband smiled and poked his wife gently. "Oh, come on now, honey," he laughed, giving her a hug. "I'm not burning the candle at both ends. I don't even have a candle left." The wife looked at me, shrugged her shoulders, and shook her head in disgust. "See what I mean? It's not funny, Dayle," she almost yelled at her husband. "You're just giving him your upbeat self, but you know damn well that when we get home you'll complain about how exhausted and overextended you are or what a waste of time therapy is."

The hectic competitive pace of toxic success and the chronic fight-or-flight response that accompanies it can lead to one of the leading causes of early death. It is a telltale sign that you are suffering from toxic success syndrome and that your exhaustion is exhausting to your family. It is the condition researchers call "vital exhaustion."

Being Type A Won't Hurt You

When it comes to psychological causes of heart disease, most of the media attention has been focused on the "type A" concept introduced more than forty years ago by cardiologists Meyer Friedman and Ray Roseman as a "harrying sense of time urgency."[4] Type A has become a kind of folk wisdom, but as you will read in chapter 8, and as author James Gleick puts it, it has become "standard medical knowledge untainted by research."[5] Four decades of research have failed to confirm that a type A personality exists or that time urgency kills. In contrast, fifteen years ago, Dutch researchers identified a significant risk for heart disease that *is* related to TSS. This research has gone essentially unnoticed by many health-care professionals, but it relates to the "information fatigue" identified by psychologists studying human attention. My research and findings from PNI and the other sciences of success you will learn about in chapter 8 corroborate these findings, which indicate that it is what you have on your mind and not *trying to be on time* that can kill you. It is how we attend to our life that can end up exhausting our heart.

Studies reveal that our heart is often not so much stressed out as tired out. "Vital exhaustion" has been defined as "a debilitated emotional and physical state characterized by fatigue, increased irritability, and feelings of demoralization."[6] This cluster of symptoms is similar to the information fatigue mentioned earlier. It is less the image of the businessperson dashing through the airport, laptop computer in hand and cell phone to the ear, than of the business traveler sitting slouched in the airport gate area staring sadly off into space. The Reuters studies mentioned earlier, research from the Netherlands, and my own clinical work and interviews indicate that it is a depletion of the vital energy essential to a joyful life that causes the beats of our heart to run out.

Loss of Vitality

While the Dutch researchers who identified vital exhaustion were referring primarily to feeling physically overextended and tired, my research indicates that living and working in the toxic success mode drains us of something much more significant, our vital energy. Vital energy is the subtle force that has been given names by almost every culture throughout history.[7] The host culture in my home in Hawai'i calls it *mana*, "the force that gives life," and the *po'okela* model of an excellent life focuses on conserving as much of this energy as we can for those we love.

This idea of a vital force is described as *prana* in India and Tibet, *qi* (*chi*) in China, *baraka* by the Sufis, *yesod* in the Jewish cabalistic tradition, *orenda* by the Iroquois, *megbe* by the Ituri pygmies, and the *Holy Spirit* in Christianity. I have counted more than fifty ancient names for the vital force that modern science denies. The persistent and widespread history of the concept of vital life energy seems to make it prudent for us moderns to at least consider its role in our daily life.

The vital exhaustion of toxic success results from an uncontrolled leakage of our vital energy. It leads to an exhausted mind, tired spirit, and vulnerable body. When this happens, we are no longer able to attend fully to what we want to have on our minds. We cease to radiate health, feel and look exhausted to our very core, and often have the "stressed and tired face" described in chapter 6.

Because we constantly tire ourselves out trying to pay attention to too much for too long, we tend to also be exhausting to live with. We can become what my *'ohana* calls "*mana* suckers," people whose own loss of vitality leads them, often unintentionally, to leech the vital energy from those around them. You may have noticed the recent invasion of the *mana* suckers. They are where you work, in your home, at the malls. Just being around them can be tiring as you sense that they are sapping your mental and emotional energy by their selfish nonattention to anyone other than themselves and their feelings.

The young daughter of one of the winners I interviewed said her dad "always has a sourpuss face, and Mommy tells us not to bother him when he looks that way because it means he is tired out. When he's that way, we all have to work harder not to bother him. My mom says Daddy makes her very tired sometimes." This little girl's words show how the effects of TSS can be contagious.

The Eeyore Syndrome

"She looks like Eeyore," said the young son describing his mother, who was an executive at a phone company. "You know, the always sad and gloomy donkey in *Winnie the Pooh*? When she's around other people, she seems more like Tigger, the hyper and happy tiger, but when she is alone with us, she's definitely more Eeyore. She looks droopy like Eeyore does."

"Stress face" manifests itself not only as a sign of reaction to constant pressure and functioning under the toxic hormones of the fight-or-flight response, it is also a sign of someone who has gone past looking stressed to looking very sad. Although men can show it, too, my clinic team noticed it often on the faces of many of the women toxic succeeders who reported that they felt "sick and tired" of having their attention taken by the need to be the resident nurturer and caretaker for almost everyone.

The same facial tension, fixed gaze, straight mouth, and brown discoloration you read about on a "stress face" seems to show itself in the appearance of being defeated. The bulging eyes look more as if they are ready to cry than do battle, and the facial tension looks like the face of a frightened child on the verge of tears. The brown marks under the eyes, called periorbital pigmentation, look like permanent tear stains and the straight, tight lips seem to be an effort to hold back sobbing. One of the winners group who had such a look described her fatigue by saying, "I'm just pooped out, and when I look in the mirror I can see it written all over my face. I run the office at work and have to take care of everyone there. Then I come home and have to take care of everyone there, too. It seems that all I do is care about other people's problems, but it doesn't seem that anyone cares enough for me. I'm to the point now where I just don't want to care anymore and don't have the energy to care. I'm beat, exhausted, and it is really starting to show on my face."

Old Wisdom, Modern Science

Science relies on data and machines, but indigenous peoples have always valued and trusted experience. Shamans have always studied the faces of their patients and looked for the "Eeyore signs" to read the vital energy level of those who come to them in need of healing. They view healing as impossible without reenergizing the spirit and drawing the patient's attention back to connecting with the sacred side of life. They see all illness as stemming from a lack of attention that results in disconnection from our family, the land, and the cosmos. Thousands of years of their unique science of observation has told them that there is indeed a vital force beyond the four that science recognizes (electromagnetism, gravity, and two subatomic forces called strong and weak nuclear energy).

Because shamans and *kahuna* have always known what Sir Isaac Newton proved—that energy couldn't be created or destroyed—they have carefully guided the transition of vital energy at the time of death. Indigenous healers are experienced in observing that mysterious time when the spirit, or life force, seems to leave the physical body.

Those of us who have been near death ourselves have felt that force beginning to slip away. I saw it in the mortals group when, despite the relatively good numbers on the medical charts, we would all sense that one of us was slipping away and losing the vital energy that separates life from death. I have felt my own vital energy leaving my body, and I know the miracle of its return. I have been present during many deaths and noted no difference between the bodies of dead and living people other than the absence of the mysterious animating force that made them who they were.

The most skeptical scientist also knows that the blood, brain, skin, bones, eyes, hair, muscles, and all other organs are essentially unchanged at the time of transition from life to death. It is the spiritual or vital energy that seems to leave the body and render it lifeless, a feeling similar to that experienced by the vitally fatigued. Even the most skeptical physicians who deny the idea of a vital life energy will use terms such as "passed away" or "gone on" to describe the moment of death. When the toxically successful say they feel "dead tired," they may be more accurate than they know.

We may not be able to measure it, but many of us sense that there is a "fifth force" beyond science's accepted four. We sense that there is an energy that makes us feel alive and that can be drained from us to cause us to feel emotionally and spiritually dead. This is the energy that is exhausted when we surrender our attention to striving to do what we think must be done rather than what we sense in our heart will make us feel more like we are thriving.

Vitalism, the idea that some as yet unknown form of energy exists that differentiates living from nonliving things, fell out of favor by the latter half of the nineteenth century. The emergence of the scientific method and its skeptical objectivity turned unmeasurable experiences into delusion, mysticism, or, at best, biomechanical phenomena still awaiting mechanistic explanation. Even today, most scientists reject the idea that some form of subtle life-giving energy exists beyond physiochemical explanation. It lives on, however, in the minds of the general public as the "something more" beyond the purely mechanistic explanation of life as being a chance biochemical phenomenon.[8]

To understand and cure toxic success, you will have to be willing to be a vitalist. At least when it comes to your health and happiness and the welfare of those you care about, you will have to try to keep that energy high by feeding it, by replenishing it, by paying attention to what matters most to you. As I have suggested many times, you will have to risk being seen as "weird" or "abnormal" by considering the idea that we are not just a sack of seven billion cells humming along on biochemical energy until that energy runs out and our cell sack collapses and decays. Although you will stand out as strange in the eyes of the "normal" succeeders all around you, you will have to become comfortable with speaking about the spirit, loving life energy, and the importance of paying less attention to what everyone else seems so attentive to. You live in a world of very busy "outsighters," so becoming a calmer, vitalistic "insighter" will not be easy.

28/7

One of the most common phrases in our toxic successful culture is "24/7." To illustrate its dominance of the quality of our thinking, I asked our patients to put the number 700,000 somewhere where they could easily see it each morning. It represents the total number of hours in a very long lifetime to over age 80. I wanted to help remind them to ask themselves if they really wanted to spend their vital energy "twenty-four sevening" those hours away in the way they were thinking and living every day.

A 47-year-old member of the winners group, an executive with a Toxic Success Survey score of 81 and an obvious sufferer of the Eeyore syndrome, responded to this assignment by saying, "I don't 24/7, I 28/7. By multitasking I can milk more out of the day than there are hours in it." I responded, "So what month of your life are you in?" He answered, "May, of course. It's spring." "That's the planet's month, not yours," I answered. "I'm asking what month of your life you are in due to your 28/7 lifestyle."

As I have done in many of my toxic success seminars, I drew a circle on a sheet of paper and sketched what our clinic team called the "contentment calendar." We used this calendar to get the attention of our most severe cases of TSS. We gave it that name because we were trying to teach the idea that life goes by so terribly fast on its own and it doesn't need our twenty-four sevening or twenty-eight sevening to make it go any faster.

The contentment calendar is divided into months to correspond to the years of our life. A member of the winners group, a highly successful owner of a chain of wholesale jewelry stores, designed and made his own content-ment calendar watch, which he wore on his wrist opposite the one with his regular time clock. Here is how the calendar looks.

THE CONTENTMENT CALENDAR

Birth to 5 years = January
6 to 10 years = February
11 to 15 years = March
16 to 20 years = April
21 to 25 years = May
26 to 35 years = June
36 to 40 years = July
41 to 45 years = August
46 to 55 years = September
56 to 65 years = October
66 to 70 years = November
71 and older = December

I asked the busy 28/7 man to place himself on the above calendar. He responded, "I guess, according to your calendar, I'm in the September of my life." I asked him if he was concerned that what he called his 28/7 approach might not be the way to spend the last four months of his life according to the contentment calendar. "Of course not," he answered, "I'm retiring at age 55; that would be in your October. That is about right and when most people should think about retirement, in the October of their life." He paused briefly as if reflecting on what he had just said. "If I live long enough, that would still give me three months to live the way I really want to live."

I selected the man above as an example of vital exhaustion because he became another toxic success tragic hero. He died early one September Monday morning at age 54. He had been jogging while listening to the stock report. On autopsy, his heart appeared healthy. The pathologist told me, "I see this sometimes. His heart just seemed to finally give out. You won't find it in any medical journal, but these overworked hearts look fatigued and overpressured. The listed cause of death was a fatal arrhythmia, but off the record I would say it was that he died from lack of attention to his life."

Too Tired to Know How Tired We Are

One of the most obvious and dangerous symptoms of toxic success is the fact that we so easily accept the fact that we are becoming an increasingly physically and spiritually exhausted civilization. We know, joke, and even brag that we are mentally driving ourselves too hard and too fast, not getting enough sleep, and have constantly busy brains. We have become accustomed to being overwhelmed, and as a result we have very little vital energy left to be awed and overwhelmed by the simple things and those people our heart cherishes most.

In terms of purely physical exhaustion, it is estimated that the direct annual cost to the nation of tired carpenters, students, teachers, doctors, and pilots is over $16 billion a year. The total cost is closer to $100 billion a year in terms of lost work time and serious accidents.[9] Nearly 70 million people in America say they have either fallen asleep at the wheel of their car or almost did. In terms of the kind of spiritual or vital exhaustion I am discussing as the price of toxic success, the toll in terms of forgotten spouses, neglected children, and missed opportunities to share and make loving memories is immeasurable.

Being physically tired at the end of a happy, productive day feels good. The feeling of having "gotten something done" makes us feel appropriately tired but not drained to our core. We fall asleep easily, rest fully, and awaken refreshed and without an alarm clock to remind us to come back to life. In contrast, being vitally exhausted, as I am using the term, feels terrible. We become too tired to sleep and when we do sleep, we often awaken during the night and cannot get back to sleep, a toxic success symptom researchers call "sleep onset insomnia."

Another prominent symptom of vital exhaustion is being unable to pay attention to those people and experiences we value most. When we do finally sit down to enjoy a little peace and quiet, we doze off. We are psychologically absent, missing out on a good life because we are so very busy competing for a better one. To those who know us best, we just do not seem to be "home." "Hello?" they may joke to awaken us from our stress-induced hypnotic state. "This is Earth calling!"

The Dutch researchers who did the pioneering work on vital exhaustion developed a test called the Maastricht Questionnaire, which measured the degree to which the heart was being pressured by feelings of being emotionally overextended.[10] With our winners group and clinic patients, however, I wanted to use a test that more directly got at toxic success's vital energy leakage and the success fatigue that destroys marriages and families, and takes much of the fun out of living, loving, and working. Following is the test of vital exhaustion that I used with the one hundred winners and patients coming to me seeking to overcome their toxic success syndrome. To avoid confusion with the Dutch test, I called my inventory the Success Fatigue Inventory (SFI).

THE SUCCESS FATIGUE INVENTORY

Using the following scale, score yourself on the items below. The higher your score, the more vital energy you should have available.

5 – Never true
4 – Seldom true

3 – Often true
2 – Very often true
1 – Too often true
0 – Totally true

1._____ I feel tired when I wake up in the morning and would like to stay in bed longer.

2._____ An alarm clock wakes me up.

3._____ People have to repeat things they say to me.

4._____ When I get home at the end of the day, I collapse.

5._____ I have trouble concentrating.

6._____ I count the number of items in the cart of people in the grocery store express lane to be sure they belong in that lane.

7._____ If I sit down and do nothing, I fall asleep.

8._____ Sudden "thought flashes" come to me about what I have forgotten to do or must do soon.

9._____ I feel like crying.

10._____ I feel hassled and overwhelmed.

11._____ I have headaches.

12._____ I feel sleepy when I read for a long time.

13._____ I feel I just do not have my old energy level.

14._____ By feeling mentally tired much of the time, I'm not holding up my "end of the bargain" when it comes to home and parenting obligations.

15._____ I feel resentful when people ask for more of my time.

16._____ I think I am putting my health at risk by "overdoing it."

17._____ I drink coffee or colas several times a day to keep myself going.

18._____ I don't "bounce back" and get reenergized as easily as I used to.

19._____ Sex doesn't interest me like it used to, and when I do have sex, I fall asleep immediately afterward.

20._____ I have an alcoholic drink when I get home as a means of calming me down.

_____ TOTAL SCORE

How does the gauge on your vital energy tank read? As I discussed in the introduction to this book, we used as many gimmicks, tests, letter codes, and fun ways we could think of to try to penetrate the strong defenses and protective cynicism of the toxically successful. To help them understand the risks of success fatigue, we used the following "vital energy gauge" often mocked by the toxically successful but appreciated by those who love them.

VITAL ENERGY GAUGE

90 – 100 = Full
70 – 89 = Three-fourths full
50 – 69 = Half full
40 – 49 = One-fourth full
39 and below = Running near empty

Asleep at the Wheel

A bitterly sad example from my one hundred interviews illustrates the potentially deadly toll of success fatigue and its associated sleep debt. If my gimmicky letter codes and catch phrases teaching about the serious dangers of toxic success do not work or are rejected, I use this true story to emphasize the gravity of the problem.

A retired woman surgeon who had the sad face of success fatigue shared her agony of toxic success and what her vital exhaustion had cost her. Years after the tragic event, she still sobbed through her words and stopped often to stare at a picture of one of her daughters.

"I had worked for years to be able to afford a car like that one. I loved my work and helping patients, but I'm afraid I wasn't mature enough to see it was only the same kind of success symbol as my obnoxiously large home. My car cost more than some houses do, and I was sure it was the envy of everyone at the hospital. All the other doctors had big, expensive cars and I was no exception. When you asked me about what success had done for me and my family and what I thought about the toxicity of success, it brought it all back." At this point, she began to sob. I held her hand and waited.

Drying her eyes, she continued. "I can still hear my daughters laughing. I had just been appointed chief of surgery, a position I had aimed for since my residency—maybe even in medical school. No one outworked me, and I could put in more hours than any man on staff. No matter where I was or what I was doing, my mind was always on my work. As a woman surgeon, you had to constantly prove yourself to the 'good old boy's club.' I earned the reputation of having the best hands and best clinical mind in the department. The doctors and nurses said I lived and breathed my work.

"One night, after hours and hours of surgery that I could have passed on to another surgeon, and after hours of administrative work I could have delegated, completing patient records that could have waited, and a research meeting I could have easily skipped, I took the kids to McDonald's. Like the other people in this group [the winners group], I typically tried to buy my kids off with such activities. It kept them busy and stopped them from distracting me from whatever I was thinking about. I remember them laughing and talking to me from the backseat, but I felt tired and even annoyed by their constant chatter. It seemed that people had been talking to me all day, and I was just too tired to respond to the kids beyond a few words like 'Oh, that's nice.' As usual, my attention was still back at work and planning for the next day. I hated the feeling, but it was like my own kids were bothering me and giving me just something else to have to think about. Can you imagine that? You want to talk about toxic success, tell them about me." At this point, she broke down again and cried bitterly.

After several minutes, I asked if she wanted to continue. "I have to. I really have to and want to," she insisted. She dried her eyes again and went on. "The next thing I remember was waking up in the emergency room at my own hospital with two broken legs, one broken arm, and serious internal injuries. I had shredded my aorta and nearly died. I remember waking up and screaming for my daughters, but I could tell from the nurses' faces that something was terribly wrong. I felt a nauseating dread because I had been with patients in exactly this same situation. You never have to tell them when their family member has died—they know.

"The nurses didn't say anything, but they quickly brought one of my daughters, Gretchen, to my side. Her face was bruised, and she was bandaged almost everywhere, but I could tell she was doing OK. I knew when they did not bring Linda to me, and didn't say anything about her, that Linda had died. I had killed her." At this point and even though she had no tears left, the woman began to sob.

After pausing a few moments and looking off into space, she said, "I remember going to see the car in the police lot. I sat on the ground and cried until my eyes ached and my head throbbed with pain. If it wasn't for wanting to take care of Gretchen, I wish I would have died in that car. That damn success symbol should have been my casket. Now there are only two things on my mind: that terrible crash that took Linda from me and Gretchen, the one thing that makes my life still worth living."

The TSS of daily living like this physician had leaves its sufferers as vulnerable as sleepwalkers crossing a busy street. They are too often "just going through the motions" of living and working and awaken only when a spiritual crisis gets their attention. Despite themselves, they have begun to feel bothered by those they should be cherishing and too tired to really be fully at home in complete mental connection with them. In their attempt to squeeze twenty-eight hours worth of living and working out of a twenty-four-hour day, they become more and more "inattentively blind."

A Life Lesson from John Henry

John Henry is an American folk hero who serves as an example of TSS.[11] He succeeded himself to death. Using only his hammer and a handheld pick, he tried to outperform a steam-powered drill tunneling through a mountain. His single-minded attention to being successful resulted in his victory over the drill, but he fell dead at the moment of his highest success. Fatally exhausted, he died a "winner."

Dr. Sherman James, who coined the phrase "John Henryism," described it as a personality feature of those who cannot say no to a challenge, have a single-minded focus, and try to be never too tired to keep going. They think, "If I make up my mind, I can do it," or "When things get tough, I will just get tougher."

This attitude is an example of where our usually insightful internal locus of control can get us into trouble because we delude ourselves into thinking that we can personally control and accomplish almost anything, no matter how low on vital energy fuel we may be. In fact, the John Henrys of the world seldom stop to check their vital energy gauge. They are too busy going where they are going, and when they run out of gas, it is their heart that finally stalls out.

Despite the popular motivationalists' assertion that we "can move mountains" if we only put our mind to it, I have yet to see a mountain moved. When we come upon one, it is usually better for our health to just say, "What a lovely mountain," sit down a while, and enjoy looking at it with someone we love. While our society applauds and envies those who report the exhilaration of risking their life to reach the highest mountain peak, there seems less attention paid to those who relish the spiritual exhilaration to be had by wondering at the mountain's grandeur from the bottom.

Gazing at mountains does not result in the surge of stress chemicals associated with competing against the mountain and other climbers. It does not lead to the psychochemical buzz that comes with risking our life and possibly putting others' lives at risk in support of our adrenaline addiction. It does, however, afford the opportunity to practice connection with the grandeur of nature given to us not as a challenge to our grit but as a gift to calm and content our soul. TSS is defining success almost exclusively as an exhilarating, competitive, victorious feeling rather than a content, calm, and connected one.

Sweet success is enjoyed by resting a while when we come to the mountains in our life to give our vital energy supply a chance to replenish. Perhaps then we can get up, calmly stroll around them, and look for someone on the other side with whom we can connect.

When I shared my view of dealing with mountains with an audience of top salespeople, one man approached me after my lecture. He had "stress face" and spoke loudly. "You're out of your mind," he said. "You're a dreamer. You've got to go for it or what is life for? Everything good in the world has come from our drive to compete and conquer. What would the world be if we didn't cross the oceans, conquer the mountains, and go to the moon?" I answered, "I guess a world with magnificent oceans and beautiful mountains with a gorgeous moon shining on the water and rising over the hills." The man shook his head in disbelief, waved his hand at me dismissively, and walked away in disgust.

Several minutes later, as I was leaving the lecture hall, a woman tapped my shoulder. "You know what you said about John Henry? You just met him. That was my husband you were talking to a few minutes ago. He sees everything and everyone as a challenge. He's so competitive that even his best friends are starting not to want to play tennis with him. And you really upset him because he just took up mountain climbing. As if he's not gone from home enough already. I'm scared to death he's going to kill himself, but he says he's going to conquer Mount Everest some day. He's a member of the company's motivation group. They call themselves the mountain movers, so that's why you saw so many guys upset with you. I wish he'd be less interested in moving mountains and more interested in moving his butt off the couch to spend some time with me."

Sisyphus, Laurel and Hardy, and Joyless Striving

There is another myth that offers a warning about the failure to say no. Researchers refer to the "Sisyphus reaction," a pattern of a hard-driving, goal-fixated, constantly striving person who, despite these efforts, feels little sense of contentment with life or work.[12] The Sisyphus pattern differs from being type A in that the sufferer feels none of the joy and emotional fulfillment the typical type A experiences from his or her hard and long work.

The chief characteristic of the Sisyphus orientation is one of joyless striving, a good analogy of toxic success. In the Greek myth of Sisyphus, this king of Corinth was condemned forever to push the same stone up the same hill only to have it roll back down. One of the winners group simplified the Sisyphus lesson by saying, "It's SSDD—same stress, different day."

I remember watching a movie in which Laurel and Hardy were pushing a piano up several long and steep flights of stairs, only to have it roll back down and over them each time they reached the top. Lying under the piano at the bottom of the stairs, Oliver Hardy would say to Stan Laurel, "Well, Stanley, this is another fine mess you've gotten me into." Ollie and Stanley might have found more sweet success by just saying no to moving the piano up the stairs and sitting down together to play it. The lack of sufficient vital-energy monitoring to know when enough is enough, and the lack of caring and gentle assertiveness to say no, can contribute to the fine mess of a toxically successful life.

The Power of No

Would you refuse to do a favor for a good friend who has done many favors for you if you felt you were just too tired to do it? Would you turn down a wonderful work opportunity just because you prefer to sit down and do nothing? Could you say no to a chance for a major promotion or new job offering much more money and status because you would sooner be comfortable with and enjoy what you have right now? Can you say no without feeling guilty or that you are letting someone down? Think carefully before you answer these questions because how you answer them reflects to a significant degree whether you will die young or live a long and healthy life.

Physician George F. Solomon is seen as the father of the field known as psychoneuroimmunology (PNI). This is the field that provides much of the data documenting the devastation caused by the prolonged stress of toxic success. Solomon's 1964 research paper titled "Emotions, Immunity, and Disease" helped lay the foundation for mind/body medicine.[13] In studying a group of AIDS patients and comparing long- and short-term survivors, Solomon sampled the vitality of each person's immune system and compared it with the patient's psychological profile.[14] Those patients who said they could answer no to a request for a favor from a good friend were the longest survivors of AIDS.

It is precisely this self-monitoring and capacity to take care of and protect one's vital energy and psychological and physical well-being that is lacking in the toxically successful. Despite their strong assertive seeking of success and apparently powerful personality, they are very reluctant to "just say no." For the toxically successful, *no* becomes a four-letter word. The self-doubt at the core of toxic success causes them to fear rejection or that they will be seen as letting others down. They cherish their hard-earned reputation as "always coming through" and have embraced the popular psychology idea of "just say yes."

"Almost nothing great ever came from the word *no*," said the motivational expert to the large audience of insurance salespersons. "Don't even think no. Stay in the yes mode. Think yes, yes, yes." This is the same John Henryism that constitutes such a serious risk to our health. A careful self-monitoring *no* is actually a gift not only to ourselves but also to anyone who sincerely cares about us. It shows that we care enough about and trust enough in the integrity of our relationship with them that we feel comfortable to check our vital-energy meter and say yes when we can and no when we must.

What Diem Do We Really Want to Carpe?

The Roman poet Horace wrote, *"Carpe diem."* It means to "seize the day," and it has become a modern-day mantra. It is the opposite of saying no, and has many variations in our everyday popular success psychology. "Go for it," "Follow your dreams," "Live for the moment," "Just do it," "Just say yes," and "Gut it out" are some examples of what may have been necessary to survive in Horace's time, but they have become dangerous dictums in the modern world. Psychotherapist and author David Kundtz warns, "Before you seize anything, go for anything, dream, follow, or risk anything, you'd better know what it is you are seizing, going for, or risking."[15] In other words, you had better know not only to what and to whom you want to say yes, but also to what it is essential to say no.

Saying no requires paying more attention to what our most important "yeses" are. The toxically successful pride themselves on saying yes to almost any challenge, but they often lack a clear perspective on when their vital energy no longer allows them to keep seizing every opportunity without depleting their spirit. One spouse of a winner said, "He's the ultimate 'yes' man, but unfortunately he runs out of yeses by the time he comes home to us. I think he says yes in all the wrong places." Kundtz writes, "We had better know what *diem* we want to *carpe* before we *carpe* it, or we are likely to end up with the wrong day. Before you seize the day [say yes], stop for a day. Or even for a minute [say no]."[16]

One difficulty with trying to avoid or at least reduce our success fatigue is that much of the modern popular success psychology telling us how to reduce our stress is actually causing it. We are told to keep going, trying, and saying yes but to also slow down, cut back, and take it easy. Much of the current advice on success and the management of its associated stress is often based more on the personal opinion of a motivationalist, inspirationalist, or life-balance and stress-reduction seminar leader than on sound research or long-tested indigenous cultural wisdom, such as the *po'okela* concept.

Before we can learn to reduce our success fatigue by saying a loving no, we have to learn what of the currently accepted common sense about stress and success should not be so common and may not make sense. Our first practice at saying no should be to the gurus of self-growth and the myths about what constitutes a successful life, and this is the focus of the next chapter.

CHAPTER EIGHT

The Sciences of Sweet Success

To know how to wonder and question
is the first step of the mind toward discovery.

—Louis Pasteur

A popular psychology of success has evolved over the last several decades. Hundreds of books offer advice on how to be successful and reduce the stress associated with its pursuit. While much of this advice has come to be accepted as fact, a closer look at what we are being told about how to motivate ourselves and deal with the consequences of constant competition is seldom based on sound research.

The leading psychologists of success are typically those who are sufferers of various degrees of TSS. They came through an educational system based on competition and SIN, the self-interest norm of outdoing and outscoring other students. They earned their credentials by being harebrained, outsighted, and valuing power over affiliation. The lessons they propose are based upon the acceptance of the toxicity of success as necessary and normal. They see stress as something to be coped with rather than examined and dealt with. Yet the keys to success they offer open the wrong door, one leading to the attention deficit, spiritual emptiness, neglected families, and vital exhaustion about which you have been reading.

Our success advisors have themselves often become blind to the toxic kind of success they continue to seek. They are powerful and convincing in their message, so challenging what seems to be the only right way to seek a successful life meets with strong resistance. Before you enter the toxic success detoxification program offered in part 3 of this book, consider the four examples of the "wrong" keys to success you will find in this chapter. They are psychological principles that are not really principles at all because they do not hold up to scientific scrutiny. They are nice sounding ideas that, like the type A concept, seem to make such good common sense because they have evolved as a part of the accepted nonsense we now consider the normal way to live, love, and work. Here is a summary of some of the wrong keys to success:

- Seek life balance.
- Your personal power is unlimited.
- Practice good time management.
- Don't be a type A.
- Don't be a "workaholic."
- Think positively.
- Time is money.
- Have a mission statement and stick with it.
- Visualizing your goals will help them come true.
- Saying self-affirmations will raise your self-esteem.
- Quality time is more important than quantity of time.
- If you feel pressured, just cut back.
- If you work hard enough, you can have it all.
- It can be so if you will it so.

These myths of success can be summarized as four major fallacies or wrong keys to success. The sciences of sweet success, including PNI, energy cardiology, neurotheology, positive psychology (sometimes called the psychology of optimal human functioning to contrast it with psychology's traditional focus on pathology), and other areas of psychological research you will read about in this chapter and part 3, provide evidence that we are being led over the leading edge by the well-meaning but ill-informed pied pipers of prosperity. With each "wrong key" that follows, I have suggested a "right key" that will lead us down the path of sweet success.

Wrong Key #1

Wrong key: Seek life balance
Right key: Balance is impossible. Relish life's natural chaos.

Balance—I've heard of it.

—Les Kurtz

The New BS (Balance Stress)

"Life sucks. Live with it." I saw this bumper sticker and at first thought how cynical and depressing it was. Upon reflection, I thought the five words were a very concise way of expressing a fundamental truth of life and the cosmos that modern science documents. I might change the word *sucks* to *is chaos* and the word *live* to *love*, but the message is essentially the same. Sweet success is not struggling to maintain balance while we strive for success. It is finding and sharing the joy in one of the most basic facts of life: chaos is our natural state of being. Denying and struggling against this principle lead to endless frustration and, eventually, to toxic success and vital exhaustion.

Sciences that study chaos, including mathematics, meteorology, astronomy, and chemistry, have shown that John Updike was right when he pointed out in a poem, "Human is the music, natural was the static." In other words, life is sweet, but also chaotic.[1] Life's magnificent variety and change are what make it sweet. Nothing in the cosmos from snowflakes to heartbeats exists "in balance." As you read in chapter 4, the current popular psychology of trying to live in balance tends to create a BS, the "balance stress" of trying to live in a way that is just not realistic.

Reflect for a moment on those times in your life when you felt, "At last! I've made it. I'm a success. Everything is in perfect balance and just as it should be." What happened next? Most likely, at least a low-level catastrophe. As someone pointed out, we make plans and God laughs. If we learn to laugh with him and accept that the purpose of life is not to exist in balance but to learn to thrive through the natural, wonderful mess of our daily existence, we open the door to sweet success. If we resist, resent, and fight against life's natural chaos, we are in for disappointment. If we focus our attention in search of balance, we become blind to what researchers know is the ultimate source of happiness: change.

The Joy of Being Wiped Out

As I was sitting on the beach at Waikiki writing these words, I stopped to watch the surfers. They would paddle out and wait for the perfect wave, catch it, stand up on their boards, and move back and forth and side to side, seeking to stay in the wave and on their boards. We Hawaiians consider the ocean a source of infinite *mana* and wisdom, and I thought how the waves these young men and women were trying to ride could represent the ebb and flow of daily life. I thought how the contentment, calmness, and connection of sweet success were reflected in the most joyful of the surfers. Here are some of my observations as I watched them:

- No matter how intently I look out at the horizon, I can't see where the waves begin. It looks so calm out there, but I know there are big waves coming. No matter how peaceful life seems, any balance is merely a transition between states of chaos. Sweet success is being content through the chaos and not seeking relief from it.

- The surfers are watching and trying to pick the perfect wave, but they almost always seem to pick the "wrong" one. Even though they topple over before the wave fully forms or are left paddling on flat water because the wave ended up not being as big and powerful as they thought it would be, they have the calmness of sweet success. They seem to be able to let the waves pick them. They aren't surfing, they're being surfed, and that's a lot like daily life. We may think we have control and pick our problems, but we seldom determine the wave we will have to ride. Sweet success is remaining calm through the chaos.

- I can see dozens of surfers clustering around in excitement—they think they see a big swell coming. Here it comes and there they go. What were dozens ready to ride are now only two or three. The rest wiped out, but they don't seem to mind. They're laughing and looking for another wave. They really aren't competing against each other or anything. They seem to be trying to join with the ocean, not win against it. They are experiencing the sweet success of connection. Even when they seem ready and willing, the waves usually control the situation. If this were a contest, the waves would almost always win. No matter how self-assertive and confident we feel, we are ultimately the pawns in a much larger cosmic game. Good surfers seem to know that and enjoy that part of surfing.

• Some surfers are giving up on a wave far too soon; they are bailing out while others are enjoying a long, fun ride. Others can't seem to make a choice among the waves and end up spending most of the afternoon waiting instead of surfing. The happiest surfers, enjoying the longest and most enjoyable rides, seem to be those who are willing to take the risk, stick it out, and be content with and have faith in their choice of a wave. If we try to free ourselves from making the "perfect" choice, we are more likely to enjoy the choice we've made, and this is the calmness and contentment of sweet success.

• A very few surfers seem upset and even angry. It looks like they are trying too hard or cursing the ocean for giving them bad surf. They seem to be unable to accept the ocean's chaos and dance within it like the surfers having all the fun. They're waiting to get their perfect balance on the perfect wave, and it's frustrating them. If we are frustrated by and struggling against life's chaos, we will never allow ourselves to feel fully alive, and that feeling is the sweetest success of all.

As I watched the surfers, it seemed that those who were the least concerned with "balance" were having the most fun and enjoying the longest rides. Those who were struggling to control their boards, get the perfect wave, and do better than the other surfers seemed to wipe out more often.

As I finished writing the above notes to myself, a white-haired surfer who looked about 60 years old breathlessly dragged his large board to my chair. "Did you see that?" he asked, dripping water on my notes. "Did you see how I wiped out? It was a blast. This was a great day. My only regret is that I waited so long to get out there. I was 60 before I finally tried surfing, and I'm 76 now. You really ought to go surfing." As I shook the water from my notes, I thought to myself, *In a way, we all are.*

The senior surfer jogged back to the water and paddled back out into the fray. He never seemed to find his balance on his board. Nevertheless, he seemed perfectly content. I could see him smiling and waving at me just before he was gleefully knocked head over heels. He would disappear for a few moments and just when I would begin to wonder if he was in trouble, his head would pop to the surface and he would give a yell and a thumbs-up. I thought that I had seldom seen anyone enjoy failing as much as this surfer, but then I recognized that he was not failing at all. To the contrary, he was one of the most successful surfers on the sea.

About an hour later, as I returned to my car and readied to leave, I noticed the senior surfer tying his board to the top of his car. There were red scuffs on his skin from his many falls against the sand, and the lifeguard had placed a cloth bandage on his injured wrist. "*Aloha*," I said as I shut my door. "*Aloha*," he answered, sweeping his hand toward the ocean. "It doesn't get any better than this. The ocean beat the hell out of me today, and I can't wait until tomorrow. My wife is coming with me, and we'll wipe out together. That's the most fun." There, I thought, goes a sweetly successful man.

As simplistic and overromanticized as it may sound, life can be seen as a form of surfing. Those of us who love the thrill of the challenge while still retaining our joy, no matter how many times we wipe out, are the sweetly successful ones. Those of us who are driven to master rather than ride the waves do not know when to accept and even enjoy being wiped out. After being thrown several feet in the air and slammed to the sand by a twenty-five-foot wave, one surfer riding the famous big waves on the north shore of O'ahu told me, "They call it surf riding, but actually we don't ride much. They should probably call it enjoying wiping out. If you don't wipe out, you don't have fun. If you don't enjoy being wiped out, you can't be a really good surfer."

If you want to find balance, surfing is not for you. If you cannot tolerate being out of balance, you will never be able to enjoy wave riding. But if you enjoy life's constant shifts and surprises and can thrive in the natural choppiness of life, you can surf to your heart's content.

The Joy of Living in Perfect Imbalance

My surfing observations revealed the secret of living in imbalance. Those having the most fun and doing the best at staying with a wave had mastered the fine skill of being unbalanced. For just a brief moment, some surfers seemed to have found their balance point and were in just the right spot on their boards. They seemed to be steady, but that moment lasted less than the blink of an eye. Like life, most surfing is struggling, falling, wiping out, and getting back on your board.

Your children will not always do well. You will fail to meet expectations. Your marriage will experience conflict. You will feel guilty about not doing enough with your family. Just when you think you've made it, something will mess up everything. When you finally get a chance to relax, something will call you back to attention. Just when you think you are feeling great, you'll get sick. One of the winners group expressed the joy of imbalance by saying, "If you expect to live in balance, forget it. The best thing I did for myself and my family was to stop being guilty about not living in balance. I thought other families were living in better balance than we were, and I actually started competing to have more balance than they did. Then I realized all families are dysfunctional. They're as messed up and pressured as we are. It's learning to live in imbalance that is the key to a life that feels successful."

Content with Catastrophe

Sweet success is not seeking a state of quiet, blissful balance. Like the surfers dancing on the boards, it is, as psychologist Jon Kabat-Zinn calls it, being able to dance "in the gale of the full catastrophe, to celebrate life, to laugh with it."[2] Kabat-Zinn uses the word *catastrophe* not to refer to disaster but to the full richness of life's inevitable sorrows, crises, and endless series of dilemmas. Sweet success comes with being able to answer yes to the question Einstein said was the one he would ask if given the chance to question the cosmos: "Is the universe a friendly place?" If, despite the chaos of your life, you can answer yes to Einstein's question and see that beneath the catastrophes of life there is always a loving energy that gives life its excitement and meaning, you do not have to go in search of balance.

No matter how hard you are working and how many wipeouts you experience, you can enjoy surfing along with the rest of us, but first you have to accept that the highest-level success is experienced by being able to be content with the catastrophes that are our life. Sir Laurens Van de Post, writing about his discussion with the famous psychologist Carl Jung, discussed the dangers of seeking a perfectly balanced life. He wrote, "No wonder Jung told me with a laugh that he could not imagine a fate more awful, a fate worse than death, than a life lived in perfect harmony and balance."[3]

Like the universe, the ocean's immense destructive power matches its grandeur. If, like the successful surfers, we respect and appreciate that power and maintain our awe even when we are afraid, we can realize that the ocean also gives life. Seeking balance in the infinitely unbalanced ocean of life can lead to a kind of "seasickness." Those who experience seasickness know that the more they try to balance and right themselves with the rise and fall of the ocean, the more seasick they become. Being sick at sea results from an intolerance of imbalance and the persistent but always futile attempt to keep trying to find it. Those who finally get their "sea legs" are in no more balance than the seasick, but they have managed to learn to live in imbalance. Toxic success might be seen as a kind of daily life sickness that comes from the pressure of trying to find balance in a naturally unbalanced world.

Bliss Is Not Balance

Physicists know that all systems exist in a perpetual state of imbalance and are, therefore, forever wearing down and out. They—and we—have an undeniable tendency to wear down. Ecologist Garret Hardin describes this principle by saying, "We're sure to lose."[4] Life does go on, but it is as much downhill as up. Knowing and embracing this fact results in a truly successful life.

Try it for yourself. Try to stand in perfect balance. Put this book down, stand up, look in a mirror, and try to stand perfectly still, straight, and in perfect balance. You will not win. You will see yourself constantly moving and swaying, and the more you try to balance yourself, the more you will move because balance is always a transition state. We are naturally dynamic beings living in a constantly chaotic world. As you read these words, every cell in your body is in a state of imbalance. They are vibrating with the constant changes going on within them. Learning to not only endure but also to enjoy the fact of our dynamic state of being leads to the sense of sweet success, free of too much BS. Suggestions for how to be joyfully unbalanced will be presented in part 3, but the process is begun by the acceptance that bliss is not balance.

Wrong Key #2

Wrong key: Use your personal power to be all you can be.
Right key: Always be a little less than you can be.

> *Be what ya is, not what ya ain't because if ya ain't*
> *what ya is, you is what ya ain't.*
>
> —E. Jean Tracy, director of the
> Salt Lake Convention and Visitors Bureau

Don't Take Power Personally

Just as balance is an illusion and pursuing it leads to toxic success, personal power is also an illusion—a manifestation of the rise of selfishness in America.[5] The idea of the strong individual able to overcome any obstacle and achieve any goal has become an American code of conduct, yet this celebration of the self has not seemed to bring the blissful joy we say we desire or the kind of success we seek.

Ancient cultures have always taught that a successful life derives not from competitive individualism but from the power of "us." We all exist in what physicists view as a "vast porridge of being," and any attempt to separate ourselves from that porridge only results in an energetic backlash from a universe that does not tolerate boundaries. Einstein pointed out that individuality and separateness are the ultimate optical illusion, yet modern psychology has persisted in glorifying the ego at the expense of the "us." Our society has spent the last hundred years living in SIN—governed by the self-interest norm.

Transpersonal psychologist and philosopher Ken Wilber points out, "The ultimate metaphysical secret, if we dare to state it so simply, is that there are no boundaries in the universe."[6] Physicists know that an object that seems to be in balance and at rest to one observer is at the very same time in imbalance and motion to the eyes of a different observer. As Einstein might say, it's all relative. Waves and particles, of which we are but one ever-changing version in the cosmos, are not distinct. They are forever changing from one form to another depending on who's looking, and how and when. Our life becomes what our attention makes it.

Do We Have to Be Warriors?

You have read that we are admiring the wrong heroes. We look up to those who have been big winners, topped others, and exerted their personal agenda to gain control. We have come to embrace a warrior mentality in our daily life. We see the pursuit of success as engaging in constant conflict. The way of the constant competitor has overwhelmed the way of the contented, as there seems to be less and less value placed on closeness, trust, and love as the source of a true and adaptive power. It is as if we believe that extreme psychological well-being and high-level success are unrelated to intimacy.[7]

Rugged competitive individualism is the backbone of the American warrior spirit. As you have read, conquest, victory, the personal power norm of strong individualism, and self-motivation have become accepted as normal, but the toll of this rise of selfishness is the disconnection characteristic of TSS. Those of us who seem too content with the status quo and choose not to compete are suspected of lacking the guts to put our personal power to work. The toxic success warning seems to be, "Don't ever be content with who you are, what you have, or what you have accomplished. Be better, get more, do more, and try harder."

Success guru Tony Robbins's mega-selling book *Unlimited Power* and other personal power gurus' seemingly endless series of self-motivation books and tapes are the guides to toxic success. Omnipresent infomercials continue to preach various programs for individual wealth and self-fulfillment. We are urged to be modern-day John Henrys who can outwork and outdo anyone and anything by exerting our personal power. While millions believe in the personal power key to success, millions are also suffering from the failed marriages, depression, loneliness, and sense of spiritual vacancy described earlier in this book as the toxic waste of the wrong kind of success sought in the wrong way.

Another famous personal success guru, John Bradshaw, urges us to find our inner child and free ourselves to be independent individuals. Codependence has become a clinical diagnosis, and there are many persons who surrender to or enable the abuse of someone in their life. Unfortunately, those who admit to strongly needing others are also often seen as codependent or dysfunctional. Yet ask anyone, as I did of my one hundred winners, where their true power lies, and they are likely to tell you that any power or success they experience has been much more an "us" than an "I" thing. They are also likely to tell you, as the winners group told me, that any degree of disappointment with their success or sadness and failure they have experienced derived primarily from their sense of detachment, isolation, or the missed opportunity to love.

To Lose One's Self

I have referred several times to McClelland's inhibited power motive (IPM), which is a scientific designation for personal power. You read about the damage, documented by the new field of psychoneuroimmunology, that IHP can do to our immune system and general health. IPM's opposite, RAS (relaxed affiliation syndrome), has equally powerful salutary effects, not only on our own health but on the health of those we love. Challenging us to maximize our personal power calls into play the potentially lethal consequences of IPM.

Sweet success is based on the paradoxes that the best way to really find oneself is to lose oneself and the best way to get the attention we crave is to give it. Love is the giving up of the prime objective of the last few decades, what psychologist Abraham Maslow called the peak experience of self-actualization. It is trading that experience for a focus on mutual joy and shared success. As historian James Lincoln Collier writes, "People are frequently at their happiest when they are absorbed in something outside themselves—a task, a child, a game, a lover. . . . Surely the most selfless of occupations is involvement with others."[8] Sweet success is first and foremost a selfless occupation. No amount of personal power will bring the sense of contentment, hardiness, happiness, healing, and hope that shared love can.

Wrong Key #3

Wrong key: Don't be a type A or a workaholic.
Right key: Love as intensely as you work.

The only danger of being a type A is that they can end up killing the type B people who have to live with them.

—Wife of account executive

Hot Heads, Hardened Hearts

Are you a type A? Are you ambitious, hardworking, pressured by time, and highly energetic? If so, stop worrying. Summarizing the current research on being type A or a workaholic, neuroscientist Robert Sapolsky writes, "Being time-pressured, impatient, and overachieving probably has little to do with heart disease risk."[9]

There is a joke cardiologists tell that says, "Type A people die young because they must catch something from pushing the 'CLOSE DOOR' button on elevators." Most people get the joke because they are familiar with the concept of type A and the impatient behavior that is supposed to be associated with it.[10] Based on his review on the research on type A, however, James Gleick writes, "We believe in type A—a triumph for a notion with no particular scientific validity. . . . The claim has turned out to be both obvious and false."[11] Recent research shows that it is not our behavior but what is on our mind that can result in the toxicity that impairs our immune system and tears at our heart.

Working very hard, struggling to meet deadlines, feeling stressed by daily frustrations, and being dedicated to going all out in your job are not only unlikely to kill you but can be very good for your health *if* . . . The "if" that can get you in trouble is the H, or hostility, factor, a SIN-based mind-set of hypervigilance for anything and anyone that seems to be in competition for our time, stuff, or status, which can be lethal to our health.[12] To be less toxically successful, change what you're thinking, not just what you're doing.

Every day of our life is filled with "cardiovascular provocations," things that make us breathe faster, raise our blood pressure, and speed up our heart beat. How we react to these cardiac challenges is up to us. The quality of our life and our health is less an issue of mind over matter than what matters we decide to put on our mind. It is our responsibility to be prudent caretakers of our own heart and to create a soothing and safe ecopsychology in which our heart can flourish and be nourished instead of used to serve the demanding brain.

No matter how type A we are, it is the hostility on our mind that threatens our longevity. If we think "fight or flight" while we are working hard, our heart and health are in danger. If we work equally hard and under the same

amount of stress but think "tend and befriend," we buffer our health against
the strain of our behavior. If we are outsighters who think we have no choice
but to do what cardiologist Dr. Robert Eliot calls burning "a dollar's worth of
energy for a dime's worth of trouble," we end up in big trouble.[13] The arteries
around the heart are literally hardened by our "hot head."

Hot Reactors

"Hot reactor" is a psychological term for people who deal with the world
in the toxic way I have been describing throughout this book. They are driven
by the chronic sense of self-doubt, unrelenting deficiency, and competitive
detachment that constitutes the underlying motives of toxic success; their
primary emotional state, no matter how friendly and congenial they may
appear, is one of inner hostility. Dr. Sapolsky writes, "If each day is filled
with cardiovascular provocations that everyone else responds to as no big
deal, life will slowly hammer away at the hearts of the hostile."[14] It is a hot
head, not hard work that can kill us.[15]

"Hot reactor" is more than just a psychological description. It is a serious medical condition that often accompanies toxic success. It is someone
whose blood pressure seems normal at rest but which shoots up dangerously
high when they encounter what to them is a "cardiovascular provocation." It
is estimated that more than one in five of us, including our children, are hot
reactors.[16] Dr. Eliot has shown that our blood pressure and heart rate can
escalate to dangerous levels just in response to playing a video game or doing subtraction.

Most hot reactors are not even aware that they are stewing their own
hearts in a soup of stress hormones. Some of them are what Dr. Eliot calls
"output hot reactors." I call them "speeders" because their quest for success
causes their hearts to beat faster to pump more blood per beat. They are like
a driver with his foot constantly pushing hard on the accelerator.

Others Dr. Eliot refers to as "combined hot reactors" because they not
only pump more blood faster but also through more vessel resistance. This is
because their blood vessels constrict when they feel stress. I call this group
"brakers," as they drive themselves at top speed with their foot still on the
brake.

Eliot's third group of reactors is called "vessel constrictive hot reactors."

I call this group the "crashers" because their vessels have become chronically constricted and their engines (their hearts) have been become exhausted. They become too weak to push the blood through the tight and often clogged arteries. The crashers usually start out with mild TSS (speeders), progress to more chronic struggling for individual success (brakers), and end up with bodies that can no longer take the struggle for success (crashers).

Hot reactors literally place their hearts in a pressure cooker by making them try to maintain the body in an almost constant fight-or-flight state. They react like hypersensitive machines because they are outsighters who have surrendered their attention to automatically reacting to the outside world.

Driving Ourselves to Contraction

Following is the cycle of a cardiovascular system reacting to its hot head. It can happen to you simply by reflecting with hostility to something that happened years ago. Stress is timeless, so just the hostile thought of someone who aggravated you twenty years ago causes your body to react as if that psycho-toxic event was happening right this minute. When working with the toxically successful, I refer to the hot-reaction series of events as the "recipe for stress soup."

RECIPE FOR STRESS SOUP

- The hot reactor sees a challenge and thinks of it as something that must be competed against—the fight-or flight-response. This causes a quick spike in blood pressure.

- The added blood pressure pummels the body's vessels, causing them to quiver and shake, much as a thin lawn hose under too much water pressure.

- The added pressure eventually weakens the lining of the vessels.

- The body quickly tries to patch the tiny scuffs and tears in the vessels caused by the torrents of pressured blood coursing through the arteries.

- The "patches" come in the form of fatty deposits that form in the arteries.

- As with any wound, blood platelets are also dispatched to the damaged vessels and clotting begins.

- As if sensing the pressure we are putting ourselves under, the tiny platelets huddle and quiver together like tiny frightened groups, which further clog up the arteries.

- The arteries contract, become stiff, and harden.

- If the hot reaction continues, more and increased pressure causes more damage as tiny pieces of fatty deposits (plaque) eventually are torn off and can cause a heart attack or brain attack (stroke) by getting stuck in an artery.

So, the next time you feel yourself getting hot above the collar, try to remember the scenario you have just read. Don't worry about being a type A or how hard you are working. Instead, look to why you are thinking in such a hostile manner. Reclaim your own attention, try to have more insight rather than automatically reacting to the outside world, consider living RAS (relaxed affiliation syndrome) style more than the IPM (inhibited power motive) way, try to react by "tending and befriending" rather than "fleeing or fighting," and, most of all, try to budget your reactions to spend your energy dime for dime and dollar for dollar by matching the degree of your reaction to the true nature of the perceived challenge.

A Special Message for Workaholics

You have read in these pages that there is nothing necessarily dangerous about being a hardworking person, totally and almost constantly committed to your work. In fact, being a workaholic can lead to great joy and a sense of well-being—again, as with being type A, *if* . . . !

Minister Wayne Otis coined the term *workaholic* in 1968.[17] Whether or not one can actually become physiologically addicted to work is still in question. The phenomenon of addiction is complex and often overextended and misused, but there is clearly a large number of people who act as if they are addicts. They may seem addicted to their jobs, but it could also be an addiction to parenting, golfing, or ministering. Workaholics who love their jobs, work long hours, get totally lost in their work, and take work to do when they are on vacation are not necessarily suffering from toxic success and the ravages of prolonged stress. Again, it's what is on their mind that matters. Workaholism is fine *if* . . .

The "if" about workaholism is that the danger rests in a busy, hostile, competitive brain that almost never shuts up or down. The workaholic at risk is the person whose brain is working even when they are not. A wife of one of the winners group described this condition by saying, "I don't mind Fred being a workaholic. What gets to me is that he is a wired workaholic. He just never quits even when he quits. I mean, he has gotten very good at covering up what he is really thinking about, and that is usually his work."

You can be an "unwired workaholic" *if* the following characteristics apply to you:

- You don't feel lost, panicked, or depressed when your work or obligations are done.

- You can sit, be quiet, and reflect without thinking about what must be done or is left to do.

- Those who live with you say and feel that you are not "psychologically absent" but are "mentally with them" when you are physically with them.

- You feel physically exhausted but not vitally exhausted and are able to rest up without feeling guilty or distracted.

- You know when to say no and can do so without feeling guilty.

- You don't compete in all that you do and against yourself to get more and more done.

- You can easily tolerate unfinished work. As one of the winners group said, "I've learned to love my work. I can sit and look at it for hours."

- You don't try to "sneak to do work" because your family is "on to you" about your constantly working mind (a toxic success sneakiness, for example, in the form of sneaking off from a family activity to make a business-related phone call).

- You do not sit at concerts, movies, your children's school activities, or other events while secretly working and planning or running over your work in your mind.[18]

You can see from the above list that the dangerous part of workaholism is not hard, long work but a mental set and way of attending to the world very similar to the toxic success syndrome. But there is another important *if* when it comes to workaholism.

Two persons sharing a life together who both go at life hard and long and become highly absorbed in their work may fit well together with a minimum of conflict and a mutual understanding of how one another sees the world and the rules of their relationship. However, a couple in which one person is a workaholic and the other is much less urgently and totally absorbed in whatever daily life activities he or she engages in often encounters feelings of misunderstanding, neglect, isolation, and mutual impatience with one another's way of approaching life. So, if you are going to be a workaholic, go ahead, but only *if* you are not a "wired" one and you can find another workaholic with whom to live and love.

Wrong Key #4

Wrong key: Be optimistic, be upbeat, and use the power of positive thinking.

Right key: All emotions are essential and life affirming.

> *The only negative emotion is a stuck emotion.*
> —Rachel Naomi Remen, physician

The Opponent Process Theory

Are you feeling great today? Too bad—you might be in for trouble. Are you feeling down and blue? Good news—things are about to get better. Despite the popular psychology dictums of "Be happy," "Don't worry," and "Have a positive attitude," there is a well-established scientific finding about happiness and success: trying to be "up" all the time is not only impossible but also unnecessarily stressful and dangerous to your health. Research on human emotion shows that *both desirable and undesirable states are transitory*, which means it does not benefit us to be attached to either.

Dutch researcher Nico Frijda writes, "Continued pleasure wears off. . . . Pleasure is always contingent upon change and disappears with continuous satisfaction."[19] This is another reason why seeking to maintain life balance is counterproductive. Trying to always "stay up" is humanly impossible. It requires and wastes an immense amount of energy that could be spent enjoying our present emotional situation to the maximum.

Based on his and others' research into human emotions, University of Pennsylvania psychologist Richard Solomon formulated the "opponent process theory."[20] This theory states that every emotion triggers its opposite emotion. No matter how "high" and wonderful we may feel, from the very moment that feeling starts, the opponent, or opposite, emotion is already developing. No matter how hard we try, we cannot remain "positive" for long. Even if we could, it would not be pleasurable because change and imbalance are essential to pleasure. Happiness is a moment-to-moment thing, and no matter how dismayed we may feel, we were made not to stay "down" for long. We are never in true emotional balance and are always going through mood swings, so trying to force ourselves to be "emotionally balanced" goes against our very nature. The secret to sweet success is not positive thinking but a mind open to experiencing all emotions to their fullest.

One of the winners I was treating for depression said, "The trouble with being depressed is that it is so damn depressing." While his statement may sound ridiculous, he makes an important clinical point. Successful therapy for depression takes many forms, but I have found that helping patients accept their depression is part of the healing process. The challenge is to encourage them to embrace just enough of their depression to be realistic about their life while telling them that their sadness is as natural as their joy. It's bad enough feeling down, but when we get down because we feel like failures at thinking positively and being up, we are on the slippery slope to more serious depression.

Despite popular psychology's myth that you can "think yourself happy," the brain doesn't work that way. When we are down or anxious, our brain is busy with those emotions and has very little energy available to give us a mood boost. Fortunately, we are neurologically wired to never stay too down or too up for too long. The only really negative emotion is a stuck emotion. If we accept the fact that change is coming, we may not perk up right away, but we might be able to suffer in just a little more comfort.

The opponent process theory is very good news for pessimists and very bad news for optimists for it means that the sad will become happy and the happy will become sad. We are always "on the way" to another emotional state. Like the BS (balance stress) discussed earlier, the pressure to think only positively and be emotionally high all the time is another form of psychological tyranny. No amount of self-affirmations or positive thinking can change the fact of our dynamic emotional state.

The opponent process theory offers additional comfort for those who feel they have not had a very high moment in a very long time. Research shows that the opposite emotion is always waiting in the background and gaining strength. The more lingering an emotion, the stronger is becoming its opposite emotion. For every kick, there is a kickback. If we are patient with ourselves and avoid seeking to quickly relieve ourselves of our suffering by feigning a positive attitude, the opponent process theory assures us that we will be recompensed.

Plato wrote, "How strange would appear to be this thing that men call pleasure! And how curiously it is related to what is thought to be its opposite, pain! . . . Wherever the one is found, the other follows up behind."[21] A *kahuna* described this same nature of our emotions when he said, "We have been given our suffering as a gift. Without it, we would not recognize joy. We were made to know suffering so we would be able to experience great pleasure. It is the constant changing of life that is the delight of being alive. A successful life is not always a happy one and a sadness does not mean you have failed."

Ralph Waldo Emerson wrote of trying to live in the present above time. By "above time," he meant free of trying to beat the clock and enjoying the present moment. This way of living leads to a sweetly successful life, free of the burden to maintain or seek a constantly positive attitude and comfortable in the knowledge that, even at our bleakest moments, we will bounce back. We do not have to "fake" feelings. If we let them, they will happen to us. Psychologist David G. Myers writes, "This side of heaven, we can never create a paradise of endless joy. . . . Even in the short run, emotions seem attached to elastic bands that snap us back from highs or lows. For many pleasures we pay a price, and for much suffering we receive a reward."[22]

The Weakness of Positive Thinking

There is another point about "positive thinking" that makes it a wrong key to success. Popular success psychology emphasizes the idea that "if you can think it, you can do it." Hundreds of books have stressed this visualization approach to success, but again it is not based on good science. The mind is indeed a powerful thing, but no amount of positive thinking and personal affirmations can make us a superstar or cure cancer. We all have our limitations and, to be sure, some are self-imposed, but the pressure to be anything we want to be by just willing it so adds another burden that toxifies our pursuit of success.

There is evidence to show that "going through the motions can alter the emotions." For example, if we act and speak with respect for someone, we are more likely to come to feel more respect for that person. Or try the following: Hold a pen in your teeth while watching a movie, and it will seem funnier; the placement of the pen causes you to use your smile muscles.[23] Go for a brisk walk, swing your arms, look straight ahead, and whistle or hum, and you are likely to feel happier than walking with short, shuffling steps with your eyes downcast.[24] We can, to some extent, come to feel as we behave, but to assume this means that having a winning attitude and a positive outlook can make a 60-year-old rotund person into a ballerina is worse than fallacy. Such an idea suggests that those of us who have not succeeded in the eyes of society simply failed to think positively enough.

The positive-thinking movement stressed the "power of willpower." The assumption is that we can, like John Henry, accomplish anything we "put our mind to." Willpower pioneer Norman Vincent Peale wrote, "The happiness habit is developed simply by practicing happy thinking."[25] But a lot of happy-thinking people still—and, as you have just read, must—experience misery. Failure, illness, and death are not signs of negative thinking or having the wrong attitude; they are signs that we are mortals living in a chaotic, dynamic world.

Fellow at Radcliffe College and contributing editor at *The Atlantic Monthly* Wendy Kaminer refers to the positive-thinking movement as the "new thought" that preceded the "new age." She describes the willpower approach as "an amorphous collection of beliefs about the power of the mind," and questions the validity and helpfulness of telling everyone that they can do anything, anytime by being "strong willed."[26]

Toxic succeeders often believe in the willpower theory of success and view those who fail as "weak willed" or not "thinking positively enough." This orientation often extends to those struggling with serious disease and can have devastating effects not only on the patient's morale but also on the patient's family. When I had cancer, some other patients asked me, "Why did you get cancer? You're a psychologist, and you know all about positive thinking." I answered, "I got cancer because I'm mortal, not because I didn't have a positive attitude."

There is nothing wrong with positive thinking just as long as we are not too positive about its power. Sometimes we have to sit down, cry, curse, pray, and wait. Sometimes our success at work, at love, or at healing depends on admitting that we do not have the control over our life we wish we did.

A Huge Sign of Relief

The following is a report from one of the winners group that summarizes the differences between the right and wrong keys to success. It comes from a 42-year-old professional decorator, and her words illustrate the toxicity that can come from trying to use the *wrong* keys to success. She said, "I attended three lectures in one year that were sponsored by the home office. Every one of them told us that we had to have more balance in our life. They said we had to realize our personal power, have a positive attitude, and think positively. Everyone would cheer, but later I seemed to crash. I felt that my life was never in balance no matter how hard I tried. Many times, I had a rotten attitude and felt drained of my willpower. I was sure everyone else had more personal power, but I was afraid to tell anyone that I didn't. We were told to not be type A's or workaholics, but I knew we all were or we would not have qualified to even be at the meeting.

"When you told us in your lecture that balance was impossible, that being a type A workaholic was just fine, and that no one can or even should try to be positive and up all the time, I gave a huge sigh of relief. I'm still a type A workaholic and part-time sourpuss, but I know I've detoxified my success because my family is more content with me. They are actually happy to see me come home and really be with them. It's a huge sign of relief from the pressure I had been putting on everyone."

Ha'iloa'a: **The Keys to the Problem**

The right keys to success are the ones that open the hearts of those who matter most to you and cause them to feel that they are the ultimate source of your success. The Hawaiian model of success called *po'okela* is, in many ways, the opposite of the "continental" view. Where the West seeks "balance," the oceanic view emphasizes maintaining alignment with the sacred in life, the family, and the land even while coping with its chaos. While the West values SIN, independence, personal power, and competitiveness, Polynesians have always treasured the value of combination, cooperation, and collectivism. The West seems to have a love/hate relationship with what it calls being type A and a workaholic, but the oceanic view of *po'okela* emphasizes the importance of the match between the intensity of working and the depth and manifestation of one's loving. While the West stresses the power of positive and fast thinking, the oceanic concern is with a slower, more reflective and contemplative consciousness.

Po'okela offers a way to a healthier, happier, shared success. Part 3 gives you the keys to this sweet success. It presents the *ha'iloa'a* (ha-ee-low-ah-ah), Hawaiian for "keys to solving the problem." It offers ways to be free of the toxic success you have read about in parts 1 and 2. Before you enter the success detox program, however, consult your bookmark card where you wrote your definition of success. Reflect on that definition, your scores on the tests you have taken, and the words of the winners and mortals. You have the chance for which all of us mortals have long prayed. By reclaiming your attention and being willing to try a less stressful and toxic way to think about life, you can come back to your life before you die.

PART THREE

Coming Back to Life:
A Detoxification Program
for the Toxically Successful

If there is a sin against life, it consists
perhaps not so much in despairing of life
as in hoping for another life and eluding
the implacable grandeur of this life.

—*Albert Camus*

CHAPTER NINE

Secrets of Success from Paradise

To remove those living in this life from the state of misery
and lead them to the state of felicity. At the beginning it is
horrible and fetid, for it is Hell; and in the end it is
prosperous, desirable, and gracious, for it is Paradise.

—Dante Alighieri

I don't regret what I've done with my life," said one of my fellow cancer patients. "I regret what I *didn't* do. It was a great life, but it seems that I wasn't there for most of it." This 56-year-old woman had been a senior editor at a top New York publishing house. Despite her long work hours and dedication to her work, she had tried to spend quality time at home, take vacations with her family, and see to it that her three children were given every possible educational opportunity. As she faced her impending death from leukemia, she was forced into the kind of attention to her life that those living as if they are immortal would be wise to heed.

The rest of the mortals group had returned to their rooms, but she asked me to stay by her bedside. The morning sun was just peeking in the window, and the hectic activity of a day on the sickest unit in the hospital had not yet begun. I could sense her vital life energy seeping away, but as she held my hand, she continued her confessions of her toxic success. "I can't say I was unhappy, but I just wasn't nearly as attentive to what mattered as I could have been. I know that now. The good memories I have are great, but I could have had so many more of them if I would have only paid more attention to what I had.

"I loved editing, but I started to edit my own life," she explained. "I approached almost everything like a new manuscript by looking for problems to be solved. Like I did with manuscripts, I came at life from the point of resistance and skepticism. I was always looking for what was wrong and thinking how to fix things and make them better. That's fine for editing, but I regret that I edited my life rather than being the author of it. I let so many things distract and bother me. When you asked Jeanie [another member of the mortals group] if she looked back on her life as more pleasured or pestered, I was sad because I let myself feel pestered so much of the time. I always thought that sooner or later I would have the time to pay more attention to what mattered, but what in the hell was I waiting for?"

There is a happy ending to this woman's story. Defying all odds and surprising the doctors who had warned her to say her last good-byes to her family, her cancer inexplicably went into remission. As I wrote this chapter, I spoke with her by phone. I told her I was going to share her words in a book about toxic success. I asked how she was feeling, and she answered, "Things are terrible. I have a horrendous case of the flu, one of my daughters just dropped out of college, and the publishing industry is driving me crazier than ever. Things are lousy right now, but I've never been better. I'm just sitting here wallowing in joy and busy being thankful that I'm here to be a part of this mess."

"Anything you'd like me to put in the book about your life right now?" I asked. "Sure," she laughed. "You were always talking about Dante, so tell your readers that life is hell but also paradise. Tell them to be writers and not editors of their life. Tell them to just write their life story and not to look to make it a bestseller. Tell them to pay attention. Most of all, tell them not to wait."

Pestered People

Are you distracted from your life? Do you feel that you just can't seem to pay attention to what you're doing because there are too many demands on your attention? Does it seem that you are incessantly being pestered by a seemingly endless array of what one winner called his "STDs"—still-to-dos? The toxically successful tend to answer yes to these questions.

TSS often involves a very private internal dialogue of regret and despair with how we are leading our life or, more often, how we think life is leading us. We forget that however our mind imagines the world is how the world tends to become. Attention, our consciousness maker, is our own to invest as we choose. If we elect to attend to our working as what Hamlet described as "to do such bitter business as the day would quake to look on," that is what our world feels like.[1] This negative consciousness remains personal until the disappointment and sadness can no longer be denied or "worked away." When the denial and compensation fails, the despair of toxic success spills out. It may implode into depression and withdrawal or explode into angry short-temperedness with family, rage expressed through tantrums, and angry hypercompetitiveness, or even sexual acting out, reckless driving, or substance abuse.

The following are two examples of patients who came to me suffering from severe TSS. They had felt pestered to the brink of their toleration. By going through the TSS detoxification program, they were able to regain their own attention and come back to life. The first patient is an example of a toxic success "implosion" and the second, of "explosion."

"I got to the point where I just didn't give a damn anymore," said the 43-year-old female buyer for a department store chain. "I felt on the verge of tears almost all the time and would make excuses so I could sneak off somewhere alone and cry. They say everyone wants to be with people, but I began to see people as nuisances. I started to resent customers and colleagues because they took so much of my attention. My mind was not my own because I was allowing everyone and everything to take up all the space in my head. Even when I tried to rest, I was like a computer in sleep mode and ready to flash back to attention. I began to call in sick more and more days, but I wasn't physically ill. I just sat home in my nightgown and stared at the television. My husband thought I might be in menopause, but that wasn't it. I literally felt like I was dying of my own success."

"Screw it—that's what I kept saying to myself. Screw it, screw all of them, screw everything," said the second patient, a 28-year-old male broker in the New York Stock Exchange. "I said to myself, if this is how they want it, then that's how they're going to get it. I'm going to bury the bastards. If they want all of me, they're going to get more than they bargained for. That's when I started to drink more at lunch. I got two DUI [driving under the influence] tickets in one month, and that's the same time I had the affair. I was going full speed ahead and really didn't give a damn if I crashed. The more successful I became, the more suicidal I felt."

The toxicity of success reflected in the above statements may also be due to underlying psychiatric problems unique to both of these persons, but trying to succeed in a toxic world can seriously exacerbate such problems. Imploding by just going through the motions or exploding by being in constant motion both profoundly affect the families and friends of TSS sufferers.

Mental Pleonasm

To begin your own success detoxification program, it is necessary to become more "insightful" about your success and to examine your personal internal dialogue. I call it "pestered person pleonasm" because the word *pleonasm* refers to incessantly redundant and repetitive speaking. Remember, I'm using the Hawaiian *po'okela* model of success throughout part 3, so in its tradition of teasing as a way of teaching and learning, you will be encountering alliterations and other gimmicks to get your attention and encourage you to think differently about success and how it is achieved.

If you are going to detoxify your success, you are going to have to mentally clean out the corridors of your mind and free them of the reactive, quick thoughts and associations scattered there. You are going to have to be willing to "loosen up" and develop a more oceanic, flowing, less reactive way of thinking about life. Instead of thinking in the Euro-American way of "Never be content, keep going, and assert yourself," you're are going to have to consider thinking in the Hawaiian *po'okela* way of "Be content, calm down, and connect always."

The word *pleonasm* is usually used to refer to oral speaking, but for the toxically successful, it is the nature of their *internal* dialogue. They are cognitive chatterboxes whose minds seldom shut up. They ruminate about past problems, as illustrated by one winner who said, "Once something's on my mind, I can't get it off, particularly if it's something I think I could have done better. I keep going over and over it in my mind."

TSS sufferers become adept at mentally "talking a good game" and bragging that they are "doing just fine," "thrive under pressure," and "love this fast pace." At the same time, they are saying to themselves when they get to the breaking point, "Just listen to me—what a hypocrite. I hate what I've become and what it is causing me to miss out on." Because they have long and extensive practice at talking others and themselves into and out of almost anything, they are able to quickly talk themselves back into toxic success mode. They are consummate salespeople, always "making the pitch" so they can easily sell themselves on what they are doing to themselves and those around them as "only natural, necessary, and normal."

After interviewing all one hundred of the winners and many of their spouses, family members, and close friends, I found that one characteristic of the toxically successful stood out above all others. They seemed to be pestered people who, despite their attempts to hide or deny it, were not at all in charge of their own minds. Those who lived with them and were constantly compensating for their absent-mindedness also viewed them as "pestering people." Because they were so mentally demanding of themselves, they were demanding of and insensitive to others.

To illustrate the degree to which my patients and the winners group felt mentally pestered, I used the following inventory. As you have seen from some of the sad stories of the toll of toxic success, the issue is a very serious one. The simple and often silly tests I used were intended to make what the toxically successful consider a very threatening message a little easier to consider.

THE PESTERED PERSON TEST

Use the following scale to score yourself on how "pestered" your internal dialogue has become.

> 5 = I feel like this every day
> 4 = I feel like this most days
> 3 = I feel like this several days a month
> 2 = I feel like this one or two days a month
> 1 = I almost never feel like this
> 0 = I never feel like this

1._____ I've had it! It's not worth it.
2._____ If one more thing goes wrong, I'm going to lose it.
3._____ I'm sick and tired of the hectic pace I'm leading.

4._____ Will this endless series of demands on my time ever end?

5._____ Why can't people just leave me alone?

6._____ The moment I finish one thing, something or someone else needs my attention.

7._____ I feel like I'm drowning in an ocean of waves of electronic e-mail, voice mail, and faxes.

8._____ This can't be all there is.

9._____ The more I do, the more there is to do.

10._____ If somebody asks one more thing from me, I'm going to scream.

11._____ I don't have a moment to myself.

12._____ Can't people see or care that I'm overwhelmed?

13._____ Life is becoming a hell populated by rude, demanding people.

14._____ Real contentment and joy must be somewhere in the future, so I'll work like hell now to find heaven later.

15._____ I'm sick and tired of how my life is going.

16._____ I'm tired of putting on the facade that I'm so very happy while I'm really suffering and sad inside.

17._____ I don't know how much longer I can keep up with this crazy pace.

18._____ Every time the phone rings, someone wants something.

19._____ Why do I have to do everything?

20._____ I would give almost anything for just a few moments of peace and quiet.

_____ TOTAL POINTS

The winners group average score was 72. The average score of my Hawaiian friends and family was 23. How does your score compare with these two groups? Take this test again after completing part 3 of this book. If you accept some of the invitations to sweet success you will read about, your internal dialogue will become less "pestered" and a lot more peaceful.

The Promise of Paradise

A high score on the Pestered Person Test reveals a state of mind that aggravates the body and isolates the soul, a mind willing to endure hell on planet Earth now for the promise of a more heavenly existence later. This promise of paradise is what keeps TSS sufferers going. It is a paradise where life is tranquil and calm with endless time to savor and share all of life's wonders. They are mentally working and waiting for paradise on Earth, but they are deluding themselves. Like someone looking for their eyeglasses while already having them on, TSS sufferers are already in paradise *now*. They just are not paying enough attention to know it.

Imagine that something horrible happened as you were sitting at your desk ruminating on a dialogue reflected in the items on the Pestered Person Test. Pretend that just as these thoughts were running through your mind, you were struck dead mid-grouse by a bolt of lightning. (Remember that you have to be willing to imagine your way out of your toxic success). When you awaken, you see large gates to what you assume to be the entrance to the paradise for which you have longed. As you approach, you are greeted by a hideous-looking being, growling, "Welcome back to hell."

Imagine how you would feel if you suddenly realized while standing at the gates to which you have looked forward for so long that you have just squandered your brief sabbatical leave away from hell. Imagine that you now see clearly that you have just finished your privileged brief visit to "planet paradise," a place called Earth that is full of every possible delight the heart could desire. How would you feel if you discovered that you had spoiled your one chance at paradise and wasted it by succeeding only in creating your own hell on Earth.

As reflected in the words of many members of the mortals group, it is one of the saddest aspects of toxic success that those who suffer from it may fail to fully live before they die. While looking and waiting for their midlife crisis, they fail to realize that they have been in an all-life crisis recognized too late. The toxically successful seldom pay full attention to where they are now because they are too busy looking toward *later* or bemoaning *before*. No matter how divine an afterlife may be, failing to be born to this life causes us to miss out on what is likely to be our one and only chance to savor the opportunity to live in paradise on Earth.

Ironically, when TSS sufferers say in futile desperation, "I've had it," they are being unconsciously nudged by the wisdom of their heart that they did indeed "have it" all along. They have been living in paradise but thinking too often of it as hell, thus poisoning their life with their constant attempt to get and be more. Essayist Oliver Wendell Holmes cautioned, "Alas for those who never sing but die with all their music left in them."[2] This is a fitting epitaph for the toxically successful.

The above example of paradise missed is an updated version of a short story by science fiction writer Harlan Ellison called "Strange Wine."[3] I read this story when I was just beginning my research on toxic success and establishing my clinic at Sinai Hospital in Detroit. That clinic was one of the first preventive psychiatry programs in the world, designed to offer help to people and their families who were suffering from what we came to call toxic success syndrome. It was in this program that we designed the toxic success detoxification program I offer to you now.

All of the tests and exercises used in that clinic and with the winners group are included in this *po'okela* program. I asked our patients to read Ellison's story as a warning about the tragedy of dying before we have ever fully lived, and I suggest you do the same. In Ellison's story, his main character had been given a brief vacation from a hellish planet populated by crablike beings. He was so miserable with his life on Earth that he killed himself. However, instead of going to heaven, he found himself returned to the "crab planet," another tragic hero who became aware too late of his one and only chance at paradise.

Ellison writes that the man had wasted "the gift of a few precious years on a world where anguish was so much less than known everywhere else . . . He remembered the rain, and the sleep, and the feel of beach sand beneath his feet, and the ocean rolling in to whisper its eternal song, and on just such nights as those he had despised on Earth, he slept and dreamed good dreams . . . of life on the pleasure planet."[4]

I often ask the busy executives who come to see me to read Ellison's words out loud. Doing this helps slow them down long enough to pay attention to Ellison's warning. I tell them that they do not have to dream of paradise—they can awaken, look around, and realize that if they will only pay attention, they are already there. Satirist Sydney J. Harris wrote, "When I hear somebody sigh, 'Life is hard,' I am always tempted to ask, 'Compared to what?'"[5] I suggest you ask yourself that same question when, in your struggle to have a successful life, you may be thinking and complaining your way right out of paradise.

Einstein's Lament, Gauguin's Reply

In frustration and disappointment with the increasingly harsh, competitive, selfish, cruel, and shortsighted turn life on planet Earth seemed to be taking, Einstein lamented, "Oh, how I wish there existed an island for those who are wise and of good will."[6] Enamored with the gentle lifestyle and way of thinking about life and work he had found in the beautiful Polynesian islands, Paul Gauguin described his newfound paradise as "a place where one can enter into truth, become one with nature and, after the disease of civilization, life is a return to health."[7]

Hawai'i is often seen as paradise, and it does provide a wonderful ecology that makes it very difficult not to see the blessings of being alive. But as the man you read about in the introduction to this book discovered, paradise is not a place, it is a way of thinking. Whether we enter into truth, become one with nature, and immunize ourselves against what one of the winners group called the "victory virus" is up to us and whether we are willing to make a major change of mind.

I live in Hawai'i, and like the Polynesian islands Gauguin describes, the islands do offer a rich and delightful palette from which one can paint a most wonderful, peaceful, and sweetly successful life. But, as I had pointed out to the recovering toxic success victim described in the introduction, paradise is less a destination than a way of mentally traveling through life. You have been reading about some of the ancient lessons from the host Hawaiian culture that can point the way to a sweeter success, but your challenge is to pay attention to what you're thinking about your life wherever you live. To find your own paradise, the only place you need to travel is deeper into your own mind. If you don't bring a sweeter way of thinking about how you live, you will never be able to find a sweeter place to live.

You have read that the sweet success we can experience is more a matter of insight that outsight and of affiliation more than achievement. It requires overcoming our "inattentive blindness" and hypnotic "tension trance." Like the newborn child amazed by every aspect of living, we must begin to pay attention again to the wonders all around and within us. Reawakening our innocence is the sweetest way to come to life.

Enlightened Discontentment

When was the last time you used the word *divine* to describe the nature of your life? Words like *sweet* and *divine* are not favorites of TSS sufferers. They are, however, key words to sweet success, which is finding the divine in our daily life *now*. It is being totally free of the fear that we might die before we have fully lived and relishing the fact that we are living in a paradise on Earth.

Having an excellent life is being and feeling so content that those who know you best sense it and are made to feel content themselves by just being with you. You have read that the toxically successful are often energy suckers who can drain the joy out of their own and other's lives through their harsh and distant approach to living. Fortunately, contentment seems to be at least as contagious as the chronic discontent of the toxically successful. Those who love you can tell you how content you really are because they sense it in their hearts every day of life with you. As it was in ancient Hawai'i, an excellent life is reawakening to the wonderful, chaotically vital nature of living, not trying to conquer, control, master, or drain more out of it. This is contentment; this is sweet success.

I have described toxic success as a state of being malcontent, where the "mal" of sickness is in the contentment with a pressured and disconnected way of thinking about the world. Sweet success may be experienced not only as a desire to be content but also as a state of "enlightened discontentment," an unwillingness to accept life as usual and the spiritual courage to go against the "pathology of the average." It is avoiding the seduction of success in the terms it is now offered and realizing that we don't have to seek success in the future if we realize that just being alive every day in paradise is success enough.

Coming Home

The toxically successful often feel as spiritually empty as the houses for which they work so hard to pay. Even though they are not often home, my interviews indicate that these people long to go home. Like for every member of the mortals group, "going home" holds the highest value in our hearts, no matter how much we try to busy and distract ourselves from that need. Our increasing fondness for the new satellite technology that can give us our location no matter where we are in the world may symbolize our chronic sense and fear of being "lost." However, our electronic connections are poor substitutes for the energetic loving connection we are lacking in our daily life. One of the winner's spouses said, "When my husband's lost, he just drives faster. He has that new North Star satellite location system in his car, and he is constantly poking away at it even when he thinks he knows where he is. If he would just pull over, relax, and take some time to think, I think he could find his own way. I keep telling him that if he is with me, he can't really be that lost because we are where home is, but he doesn't get that idea."

Your TSS detox program requires that you mentally "pull over" from the fast lane, listen to your internal dialogue crying out that you go home again, and look around for the paradise that surrounds you. The problem with which you are dealing is not that you can't see the forest for the trees but that you are so overwhelmed by the forest that you are inattentively blind to the individual trees—the people in your life that ultimately *are* your life.

Another spouse of one of the winners said, "When my wife is lost, she always says she isn't really lost, she just doesn't know where she is." This same unconscious homelessness is characteristic of most toxically successful people. They lack what we members of the mortals group joked was the "cancer advantage." Through our typical black humor, we were referring to the way in which we were thrust into being more aware of our life by the looming threat of our death. As one of the mortals pointed out, "Cancer gives you a lot of things, and most of them suck. But being so close to death sure does give you a new perspective on life." Having cancer caused most of us to stop worrying about a better life and realize, for some of us too late, that we already had it.

Read Any Great Books Lately?

In part 1, I referred to an important but little known field of study called literary ecology. It is an academic discipline that studies the past and present literature of the world for clues and lessons as to why and how we have created the psychological environment we have made for ourselves. It primarily examines literature that has stood the test of time for why we seem to suffer so in our life and continue to do so much damage to others and our planet. It suggests that we can find survival lessons from our unique human capacity to be literate.[8] The dated ways of expression in the classics have the added advantage of forcing modern readers to slow down and, if they are willing, to pay attention.

Hamlet's avoidance of the true causes of his suffering and the ways in which his own unhappiness becomes fatal to others holds important lessons for TSS sufferers, who often misdirect their disappointment and depression. His combination of a powerful personality, keen intellect, and emotional problems makes him seem to be a case study in TSS. His question "To be or not to be" can be examined from an endless set of perspectives related to the five Ds of TSS. Likewise, Herman Melville's Captain Ahab's compulsive and ultimately destructive drive holds warnings for those who blindly seek their selfish goals. Classic literature and quality twentieth-century works are full of examples of sufferers of TSS and how they did or did not deal with it.

As a part of your success detoxification program, I suggest you practice a little literary ecology by beginning to read more and reflect longer about what you read. But be forwarned: Because of the attention deficit disorder associated with toxic success, it won't be easy to do. We just don't seem to have the attention to spare to read serious and significant books. The publishing industry is seeing a decline in the purchase of such reading material. While many complex reasons may account for the almost 10 percent decline in book buying over the last several years, one of these reasons is our lack of attention. In an ABC television news story about the decline in book sales, one former avid book buyer said, "I still love books. I just don't have the time to pay attention to a book that I used to."

Another challenge in practicing literary ecology is our "chrono-centrism," our focus on seeing things based on our time in history rather than how our ancestors saw them. We often consider ourselves too modern-minded to consider spending time looking back for wisdom. One winner resisted my suggestion of reading classic literature as a means of attention training by saying, "Come on. There are plenty of modern-day authors to choose from. That old stuff is pretty formidable to dig through. I haven't looked at it since college. I'm not sure it's all that relevant to today's world anyway. I'm sure you haven't read any of that stuff for years either."

I answered, "In fact, I have. I make it a point to constantly be reading a classic work. That's the whole point. The classics are old. The challenge is to look within them for lessons for today. The fact that they are often difficult to read because they are written in a language and style that can seem awkward and slow us down is precisely why I recommend them. They are excellent attention-training devices, and they aren't too bad for your soul, either."

Our Increasing National Deficit

Our epidemic of attention deficit is worsening.[9] The editors of *U.S. News and World Report* ask, "With so many tasks being juggled and so much information being processed, maybe it's time to slow down and ask: Is America suffering an ADD epidemic?"[10] To help us answer this question consider how many classic works you have read and contemplated deeply since you left school. If you are toxically successful, your answer is probably "few to none." Who has time to pay attention that long to anything, let alone a long book that requires our deep and full attention?

Consider the pace at which our modern perception is speeding. In less than thirty years, the average news sound byte has gone from forty-two seconds to eight. Television commercials have shrunk from fifty-three seconds to twenty-five in that same period, and the number of three-second ads is increasing. (Unfortunately for our attention resource, we're not getting fewer commercials. We're getting more short ones.) The average scene change in movies and on television takes place every four or five seconds. Turn off the sound on your television, turn off the lights, and notice the constant flickering of images to which we have become accustomed. This is the speed at which our life is passing before our eyes.

As pointed out throughout this book, we clearly don't seem to have much attention to spend. Our adult version of attention deficit often manifests itself though thrill seeking in an attempt to stimulate a quick burst of excitement that brings us into the present moment. It also shows itself through our starting many projects but finishing few, being chronically late or behind time, and despising long lines and heavy traffic because we have no idea what to do with our attention when nothing is demanding it.[11]

A Quick Read

When I suggest that you read more to get your attention back, I'm not talking about the novels and adventure fiction you so often see in the hands of the business traveler. During my last flight from Honolulu to New York, I decided to conduct a book survey. I wrote down the titles of the books my fellow air travelers were reading. Adventure novels were popular with the men. Women flight attendants and passengers were Danielle Steele fans and discussed the latest romance novel they were reading. I also counted several versions of the "Chicken Soup for Almost Everything" series. Thin and brief-case-space-saving works such as *Who Moved My Cheese?* and various short guides to happiness or better bodies were prominent.

During this admittedly unscientific survey, I did not see one classic work of any century or any referenced nonfiction books. The various short and simple guides to success, personal happiness, finding the right man or woman, dieting, easy steps to rescuing your relationship, and strategies for better sex were also common fare. One of the popular reviews of these books shared between passengers was, "It's a quick read." Based on my survey, my advice to any budding author seeking a bestseller is to write a very short book with big print titled *Seven Easy Steps to Success in Life, Having Better Sex, Losing Weight, and Finding Happiness in Less than Sixty Seconds a Day.*

The kind of reading above serves as literary Valium for the mind, a form of distraction from stress but not an opportunity for enlightenment or enhancement of attention span. It serves as a success-trance maintenance device to carry us through the dreaded "downtime" between one success-oriented task and another. It allows us to be soothed without really paying deep attention.

The Fear of Going Offline

Another source of resistance to my literary ecology suggestion is the fear of being offline or out of the current information loop. When I ask those going through detox to unplug from the electronic web by reading a meaningful book slowly, they fear that being unplugged even for a little while will cause them to be shut out of the race to success. They worry about how they can keep up and adapt to what it takes to be successful. As the editors of *U.S.*

News and World Report write, "Being shut out is often unacceptable in an era of digital Darwinism, where executives preach, 'Adapt or die.'"[12]

Some scientists question the existence of ADD in any form, least of all the culturally induced variety I am referring to as a symptom of our toxic success. While the label ADD as true clinical diagnosis may be debatable, I suggest that there seems little doubt that there is a worsening deficit in attention in our society. It seems clear that we need to do something to get our attention back, and reading slowly and carefully from a book of established depth, significance, and importance is one way to help do it.

"Which book?" asked one of the winners group in the typical quick, goal-oriented approach of the toxically successful. "I haven't read a classic since I had to in college, so what do you suggest?" I often recommend as a starting point that those in the success detoxification program begin by reading Herman Melville's *Moby Dick*. It provides sufficient excitement and adventure to appeal to their quick-paced minds, and unless their quick thinking leads them to read only the *Cliff Notes* version, it allows them the opportunity to reflect on the lessons learned and not learned by Captain Ahab. I suggest that they think about the five Ds of toxic success and consider whether Captain Ahab might not have suffered from these toxic success factors himself as he relentlessly pursued the success of slaying the great white whale.[13] I ask them what the "white whale" may be in their own pursuit of success.

Earning Your Wings

I recently met one of the founders of the field of literary ecology. We were serving on Hawaiian student Elizabeth Lindsey's doctoral committee. Her research was a unique literary ecology attempt to learn from and appreciate the wisdom of the words of Hawaiian elders as it may apply to modern life. Since traditional Hawaiian teaching was almost always oral, metaphorical, and full of teasing, tricks, and intellectual traps, her challenge was to seek permission from the *kūpuna,* the Hawaiian elders, to put in writing the sacred lessons that had been orally passed down from their own ancestors for centuries.

Converting old oral wisdom to the written word was a first for the field of literary ecology and one that would eventually lead to Elizabeth's work being nominated for an award. (I sought and received the same permission from my *kūpuna* to share the lessons of *poʻokela*.) Her project was a major undertaking that had resulted in hours and hours of very hard work. As with all doctoral students, she was highly stressed when the time finally came to defend her dissertation.

Dr. Joseph Meeker, the chairperson of the doctoral committee, had come to Hawaiʻi to chair the meeting. A highly successful professor, teacher, researcher, and author, he had a humble, gentle, jocular nature that, for those too rushed to listen and learn, masked a deep wisdom gleaned from personal experience and from years spent in the fertile field he helped found.

Joe told me, "I don't take life too seriously, but I take very seriously what we are doing to our life and our planet. If we will only take the time to study and reflect upon them, there is much to be learned by the words written for us over the years. They provide maps for a more meaningful life, and because we can become more intimately connected with everyone and the planet by following these maps, the result can be a healthier ecology." I recognized immediately that Joe was a model of sweet success.

After the doctoral committee had completed its final interviews with our student, she had tears of relief in her eyes. She had done wonderful work, but she had been under more than a year of intense pressure struggling with the important issue of respecting the *kūpuna* and the culture of Hawaiʻi while trying to share some of its oceanic lessons with a modern world of continental minds—a struggle I, too, have experienced throughout my own career. Everyone was relieved when the meeting was over, but the tension only really ended when Dr. Meeker stood and, with mock seriousness, presented Elizabeth with a large set of white lace angel wings.

"I'm not giving you the traditional mortarboard and cap," he explained, "because literature teaches us that the mortarboard symbolizes the gravity of graduation, scholarly weightiness, and the readiness to take on the challenge of truly heavy thoughts. These wings signify that you are free to fly now, to enjoy your success. Like all of us, no matter where we live, you live in paradise. Feel free now to fly around and enjoy yourself."

At our celebratory lunch with our proud and now more relaxed doctoral student, I had a chance to ask Joe about his view of success and what he had learned about it from his field of literary ecology. Instead of answering that question, however, he offered his definition of paradise, which is very similar to what I am calling a sweetly successful life. He said, "Being in paradise [being free of toxic success] means feeling fully engaged and bent on fulfilling not only ourselves but those we love." I thought how helpful this definition would be for my patients and in my attempts to explain the *po'okela* model of success.

A Poet's Paradise

Joe and I were too involved in sharing Elizabeth's sweet success to talk at length about our mutual interests and research in what might constitute sweet success and a more contented and joyful life ecology. Joe referred me to what he called "a very important source of [his] literary ecological research," Dante's *Divine Comedy*. I had read it in graduate school, but I took Joe's advice and read it again. It took me about a year, but I would read it whenever I had the chance. I know now why he suggested it as helpful for my toxic success research and why it would be another reading source in others' biblio-therapy.

The fourteenth-century poet Dante Alighieri offered a version of what I am calling sweet success, a way to finding paradise on Earth. He titled his epic poem *The Comedy*, but theologians later added the word *Divine*.[14] Dante's paradise, like sweet success, is not a final goal or place, it is a state of mind. It is a way of attending to the world and, as Dr. Meeker points out in his writing, a characteristic of those "freed from their dependence upon particular entities, love that transcends attachment to things, process without active agents, relationships without objects, plurality without singularity, truth without facts, comedy without tragedy, play without games, and pure light perceived directly rather than reflected from surfaces."[15]

Literary ecology's lessons and Joe's wisdom seemed to correspond perfectly with my Hawaiian heritage and what I had been taught about sweet success by several of my Hawaiian *'ohana* (family), Hawaiian *kūpuna* (elders), and a *kahuna* (healer)—the concept called *po'okela* that I am using as the basis of this detox program. *Po'okela* means excellence through values rather than objectives. It is based on cherishing life rather than trying to control it. It is focusing our attention on the values of protecting the land, honoring our family, and seeking meaning in life through faith that there is

217

something more that transcends our limited understanding of why we were given life.

Where Western culture emphasizes competition, *po'okela* values contentment free of comparisons. Where the modern attitude encourages assertive action, *po'okela* treasures calm patience. Where the modern world stresses SIN, the self-interest norm, *po'okela* is first and foremost collectivist in its orientation. Because of its emphasis on these values, it seems a perfect model for a sweeter shared success. It offers a path to the Hawaiian-style success, a way to come back to life, and a call to awaken to our presence in paradise.

Po'okela literally translated means "foremost, best, superior, prime, outstanding, and to excel."[16] It refers to success attained from much the same perspective that Dante offered through his description of paradise, called *paradiso*. It teaches that success in life is a matter of calm, contented, respectful, loving interaction with others and the planet, a mind-set from which one realizes that he or she does not and cannot control life but must learn to acknowledge and appreciate belonging to life. It is thinking, living, working, and loving every day, not to seek paradise but to be able to receive it.

Are You Willing to Take a Third Path?

All authors write from a cultural context. Most books dealing with the nature and quality of life are written from either a Western or Eastern culture bias. Most of us are keenly aware of the remarkable contributions of Western cultural thinking. Its science has changed the world forever by easing the burden of living and dealing with threats to our health and survival.

The Eastern meditative traditions have had a significant positive impact on our toxically successful Western culture. Their spiritual practices and contemplative philosophies have been helpful and often life-altering to those who have paid attention to them. Through their experience with yogic disciplines such as Buddhism and Hinduism, Asians have been studying various ways of paying attention for thousands of years. What they have learned offers some of the longest tested ways of getting our own attention.

The cures I offer for toxic success derive not only from my Western culture training as a scientist and clinician but from my Hawaiian background, the wisdom of my Hawaiian teachers, and my Hawaiian family. Since you are probably used to Western and, more recently, Eastern teachings underlying various philosophies and ideas about living, loving, and working, the oceanic, waterlike logic of Polynesia may seem strange at first. If you use the insight that comes from your tortoise mindedness and take the more relaxed, affiliation-oriented point of view characteristic of sweet success, the uniqueness of the Hawaiian *po'okela* concepts can offer strategies for augmenting the mechanistic power of the West and spiritual enlightenment of the East. Because the Hawaiian concepts are so different from how you are likely to think about what constitutes a successful life, I have a word of warning: You might get upset with what you will read about detoxifying your success.

If you let it, the Hawaiian way of thinking can cause you just enough cognitive dissonance or mental discomfort to get your full attention without leading you to give up on its repetitive style, full of stories and life examples. The Hawaiian cultural lessons of *po'okela* offer a "third path" to a successful life that can augment the wisdom of the West and East, but it requires your full and undivided attention. To give the detoxification program a chance to work, you will have to be willing to tolerate a little mental discomfort and learn a more fluid way of thinking.

These ideas derive from a culture that did not write books, so putting its lessons into words is not easy. Oceanic thought is interactive, and talking back and forth is central to its way of teaching; one person sitting alone reading words on a page is not the Hawaiian way of learning. However, with the permission of my elders, *'ohana*, and *kumu*, I have attempted to put in writing hundreds of years of Hawaiian wisdom about how to lead a successful life.

How you are about to attempt to detoxify your success will not be easy, but the proof of *po'okela*'s power is found in the history of Hawai'i. It is found in ancient Hawaiians' success in being able to navigate thousands of miles of ocean before the Vikings even left their shores. It can be seen in their success at carving a paradise out of a pile of volcanic rock in the middle of the largest ocean in the world. It is revealed in their being able to not only survive but thrive within the confines of the limited resources of island life. It can be seen today in the engineering of their fishponds that still exist as monuments to a successful civilization.

Hawaiian practices of systematic conservation and sharing of resources have sustained them through the worst of times, and the wisdom of their view of success is noted in their consistently hard work, resulting not in exhaustion but singing, dancing, and joyful storytelling. *Po'okela* is to be found in the Hawaiians'unwavering emphasis on and commitment to an extended family that includes anyone willing to share *aloha*. It is to be seen in the joy of spirit, trust in the sacred, and value of prayer as the way the created connect with the Creator. It can be felt in the gentle loving nature and deep spiritual connection with all things that visitors almost unanimously say they experience when coming to the islands.

Of course, Hawai'i and Hawaiians are not innocent noble savages living in blissful joy. They are not always content or without their own struggles, anger, and flashes of the symptoms of toxic success. Particularly today, the toxicity of the Western version of success has found its way to the islands. I offer the *po'okela* model not because it is perfect but because it offers another way to accept not being perfect. To those willing to pay attention, your modern mind may find a sweeter way to be successful by considering lessons from the Hawaiians' hearts and their indigenous souls.

Beware of Misoneism

Another word of caution to the toxically successful: New ideas, even if they are really old ideas revisited, can bring out the hatred and intolerance of those ideas that challenge our way of thinking. *Misos* is the Greek word meaning "hatred," and many TSS sufferers are "misoneists," hating, fearing, or being intolerant of innovation or change. Some sufferers reading about a sweeter Hawaiian way to success might become upset or even have an angry, hot reaction during their detoxification program. I have sometimes encountered resistance and even anger when I offer the oceanic way of thinking about a successful life. At a recent lecture I gave to a small group of highly successful senior citizens who had spent most of their lives in Hawai'i, my proposal of Hawaiian-style thinking met with fierce rejection even here in the birthplace of *po'okela*. "Hawaiians make me very uncomfortable," said one woman. "If they're so smart, why don't they have more? Why are they the ones committing the crimes and doing the drugs? Why do so many of them seem so lazy? Why do they get so militant about their land?" This woman and others at the meeting revealed not only their obvious racism but their falling victim to what psychologists call "cognitive dissonance," the inability to hold in one's mind two opposing ideas.

To benefit from the detoxification program, you will have to be aware of cognitive dissonance. You may have already felt it in the earlier chapters of this book. When we experience the conflict of two different ways of thinking, our tendency is to not only more strongly embrace one way but also do all we can to denigrate the other. If we are deciding between lovers that seem to be equally appealing, we might try to reinforce our acceptance of one of them by telling ourselves how ugly, stupid, and selfish the other one really is after all.

It is not the purpose of this book to address the many very real social and political issues related to the suffering of Hawaiians. From a psychological perspective, however, I suggest that this woman and others like her are encountering a different way of thinking about the world that makes them feel uncomfortable. It challenges the way they have always thought about their lives and what it means.

When we become uncomfortable with a way of thinking alien to us, we experience the frustration-aggression-regression sequence. The toxically successful often experience this sequence whenever they are challenged or asked to change their mind. First, they are *frustrated*. And instead of accepting that frustration and trying to learn more about the challenging idea, they become more entrenched in their old way of thinking. Keep challenging them and frustration turns to *aggression* in the form of angry cynicism and even hostility. Then when anger gets them nowhere (as is usually the case), they *regress* into selfish certainty, prejudicial thinking, and refusal to open their minds. They choose being right over peaceful learning and reflection. If the detoxification program I'm offering is going to be helpful to you, I ask for your patience, open mind, and forgiving and tolerant heart.

I saw a *kupuna* (elder) challenged when she presented on *po'okela*. "That's just plain ridiculous, trite hogwash. It would never work in the real world. That's why you people are so far behind," someone said loudly enough that everyone heard him.

"I only ask that you open your mind," she responded. Beyond the racism in the man's statement, his Western thinking would be expected to begin from a point of resistance, criticism, and self-protectionism. The *kupuna* continued, "If you do not know that you do not know, how can you ever know? Ask yourself why you are so uncomfortable and irritated by what I've said about the Hawaiian way of thinking. I am only asking you to consider another way of thinking about a successful life, not give up your own. Your mind has plenty of room for many ways of thinking. Quiet your self-certain mind for just a while. Ask yourself if I am offering anything worthy of your attention and that could be of help in bringing more peace and connection to your life. I am not competing with you. I am inviting you." The man sat back in his chair, stuck his legs out, and folded his arms to his chest.

The oceanic thinking of Polynesia can seem frustratingly slow, redundant, and banal to the hurried and compartmentalized continental mind. Like water, it knows nothing of the restrictions imposed by the rock-logic view of boundaries. It flows back and forth, so you will notice several times when I have repeated and reviewed concepts. It is slow and ritualistically redundant, so it may seem tedious. The length of the chapters in this book and the many examples and stories may have already stretched your patience and attention.

The "cut to the chase" thinking of the Western mind is different from the "enjoy the journey" way of oceanic thinking. This style can be frustrating to the "say what's on your mind" and "once is enough" cognitive style of the toxically successful mind. Throw in a dose of denial of TSS and the Western mind's comfort level can be pushed to its limit. If you have made it this far in this book, congratulations! Your continued attention means you have endured my Hawaiian style.

The waterlike logic of *po'okela* flows easily back and forth and sees little difference between such seemingly distinct concepts as comedy and tragedy and life and death.[17] It is much more comfortable with "and" than "or" and conceives of everything and everyone as totally, inseparably, and infinitely connected. It does not consider individual success possible, views craving things and status as rude and potentially dangerous to everyone and the planet, and sees self-confidence and seeking personal power as funny at best and at worst impolite, threatening, and sacrilegious.

Hawaiian royalty served only at the pleasure of their subjects. They ruled *for*, not *over,* the common people, and if they became arrogant and selfish, their reign was over. If they ruled in SIN, they were not royalty for long.

Today's model of the self-assured power executive would never have been king and queen in old Hawai'i.

While the Western culture rock-logic values numbers and what science considers "solid" data and whatever is measurable by its mechanical instruments, oceanic thinking is based on thousands of years of experience. I hope you will take that experience into account as you consider detoxifying your own success. If you become impatient or even a little angry, I hope you will consider the words of author Warren McCulloch who wrote, "Do not bite my finger. Look where I am pointing."[18]

Success with *Aloha*

You have been reading about some of the Western research documenting the dangers of toxic success. I invite you in this detox program to consider experiencing as a teaching model the wisdom of one of the most sweetly successful cultures in history, the Hawaiian culture, where success is measured by the degree of *aloha* one feels and shares.

While the word *aloha* has many meanings and most often is used to express greeting, partings, and love in Hawaiian, the sacred ancient principles of a truly and sweetly successful life are represented in each letter of the word. As my *kumu* (teacher) Kawaikapuokalani has stated, "*Aloha* is a single word that manifests the values that perpetuate life." As you begin your detox program by reflecting on your inner dialogue and selecting a classic work such as *Moby Dick* or the *Divine Comedy* for reading throughout this program, consider for a moment the following components of *aloha*. You may also want to reread the definition of success you have written on your bookmark index card. Kawaikapuokalani offers the letters of the word *aloha* as a guide to sweet success:

- *Akahai* (ah-ka-hi), a loving gentleness shown through one's unhurried modesty. It is based on knowing and accepting who you are, the acknowledgment of your capabilities, and the assurance of your purpose without rushed assertiveness, arrogant certainty, or the SIN that leads to toxic success.

- *Lōkahi* (low-ka-he), referring to a harmonious orientation toward life without the striving for independence and the illusion of self-sufficiency of toxic success.

- *'Oia'i'o* (oh-ee-ah-ee-oh), referring to a truth that imparts integrity in all that we say and do, without the guardedness and manipulativeness of toxic success.

- *Ha'aha'a* (ha-ah-ha-ah), referring to a deep humility that imparts respect for God, the environment, and all humankind without the hurried and lonely distance from spiritual meaning that often characterizes toxic success.

- *Ahonui* (ah-ho-new-ee), referring to persistent patience that imparts fortitude, and accepting that in time goodness will prevail, not by hurried, competitive striving but through an open mind and loving heart ready to pay full attention to the goodness of paradise on Earth.

This is *aloha*, the core of *po'okela* and sweetly successful excellence. I hope you will take plenty of time to assess your *aloha* before moving on to the rest of the detox program.

Paradise Awaits You

The Hawaiian culture is still alive and growing, but it has not been without its profoundly deep suffering. The toxically successful Euro-American Western culture that invaded and dominated many indigenous peoples did not understand and appreciate the island version of sweet success, as presented in Kawaikapuokalani's *aloha* and its origins in oceanic thinking. Even today, those with exclusively rock, or continental, logic still fail to take the time or make the effort to understand *po'okela* in the *aloha* style. They persist in their emphasis on conquest over caring, ownership over stewardship, and personal power over connection.

Unless those who live and visit Hawai'i choose to make it so in their minds and hearts, Hawai'i can no more than any other place be paradise.[19] But for those willing to try to work, live, and love with the *po'okela* vision of excellence and the *aloha* that gives it its highly adaptive strength, it is possible to retain the logic of their modern minds and still embrace the gentleness of a Hawaiian heart and the calm contentedness of a Polynesian soul. For those who do, paradise awaits.

Freedom from "Novel-philia"

Po'okela and seeking success *aloha* style are very old concepts. For the toxically successful in love with the new, old ideas are typically not highly valued. They are forever in shopping mode in search of the latest, newest, and most cutting-edge ways to achieve more success, particularly those that do not require much prolonged attention. I call these mental approaches "novel-philia," meaning a love and desire for the new. To detoxify success, we have to fall out of love with "new" and fall back in love with "old." We have to learn to treasure sameness as much as newness and find glory in maintenance as much as in change.

Mark Twain pointed out that it seems as if the ancients have stolen all of our best new ideas. What may seem to be new ways to success are really ancient ways, so if you are looking here for some "brand new" ideas, you will be disappointed. Part 3 presents old ways for a modern world.

Just as when Christopher Columbus referred to his discovery as the "New" World, the Western explorers who stumbled upon Hawai'i described it as "a completely new world." For the Native Americans of North America, the Polynesians of Hawai'i, and other indigenous peoples who already populated the lands "discovered" by the Western explorers and who were about to be made "civilized" by the Euro-American "normal" way of life, their world was certainly not "new" to them. It was very old and successful in its own right and possessed a wisdom and grace that those who came to plunder and stake their claim failed to understand. They thought they took home treasures from paradise, but the real treasure remained untouched—a tried and tested way to excellence.

Describing their conquests of indigenous lands as "new" may have helped explorers justify their attempts to steal paradise, but it was never theirs for the taking. They could have chosen to learn and benefit from the thriving style of successful living they encountered, but instead they attempted to impose their striving path to success on those who already lived in sweet success. Much of the world is still suffering from the lack of awareness of the old and tested indigenous ways to find paradise, and you will not be able to detoxify your own success unless you are willing to avoid the seduction of "totally new and improved" and be open to "really old and the same."

Mākaukau (Ready!)

When hula dancers prepare to dance, the *kumu hula* (teacher) pounds the *pahu* (drum) and asks, "*Mākaukau?*" meaning "Ready?" I am about to ask the same question of you. But first, let's take a look at your own preparation process. You have read about the causes of toxic success and tried to be a little more insightful about the internal dialogue calling you back to a sweeter success. You have reflected back on your original definition of success in the context of the *aloha* concept and have chosen a classic work of literature (or a significant work of any era that will require a lot of your attention) to read during your detox program.

At this point, then, it would be a good time to review again the definition of success you wrote on your index card to see if you might not already be looking at success in a different way. If you're a striver, you will find this next suggestion extremely unrealistic, frustrating, and even somewhat shocking. I recommend that you retake all the tests you have already taken in the prior chapters. Consider again the possibility that you have adjusted to a sick world, are living in SIN, and have become inattentively blind to where the real and true feelings of success are in your life. Ponder again the differences between the IPM and RAS orientations, internal and external loci of control, vital fatigue, and the differences between the wrong and right keys to success. Take plenty of time and give these suggestions your full attention. You cannot detoxify your success without fully remembering and understanding how it became so poisoned.

Then when you are ready, find a quiet place, sit down, put on some relaxing music if you'd like, take a deep breath, and prepare yourself mentally to go deeper into the detox program. I have already asked a lot of you, but a life in paradise is worth it. Like most effective detoxification programs, detoxifying success will take a long time and a continued commitment.

Based on my work with the toxically successful over the last several years, I suggest you dedicate at least a year for the program presented in part 3. Allow a month or so to reflect on each of the three components of sweet success that follow this chapter: contentment, calmness, and connection. Allow at least that long to slowly read the classic work you have selected and, if you can, find a partner who will read the same book and discuss it with you from time to time as it relates to a definition of healthy success and the issues of toxic success—personal deficiency, doubt, detachment, and disappointment.

Remember the Hawaiian phrase *ho'omaka hou* (ho-oh-ma-ka-ho), which means "to begin again." No matter how much society's pressures and your own brain resist and demean the "sweet" approach to success you are about to learn, and no matter how much your attention is demanded to plug back in, get back to "normal," or "get real," do not allow the nagging of the modern world and your power-oriented mind to dissuade you from the opportunity for sweet success. So, with love, with *aloha, ho'omaka hou!*

CHAPTER TEN

Being Content:
Knowing When Enough Is Enough

Life consists of what
a man is thinking of all day.

—*Ralph Waldo Emerson*

"**O**ur milk comes from contented cows." These were the words on a sign I noticed during our visit to dairy-farm country in Michigan. There was a large smiling cow on the billboard. My wife and I stopped a while and watched a large herd of cows sprawled peacefully in the shade of several large trees. From time to time, a few would slowly rise and saunter over to chew some grass. They did, indeed, seem content. I took a picture of the sign and we got back in our car and drove on.

As we continued our drive through miles of green pastures, we came upon another larger and brighter sign than the first one. This one said, "Our cows are not content. They are eager to do better." It had a picture of a cow flexing her muscles and holding up a bottle of milk with a blue ribbon saying "Number One." While the herd itself seemed as content as the first, their owner clearly was not. His sign indicated that he was in competition with his neighbors and wanted to show that the milk he offered came from harder working bovine not content with just average-quality milk.

As we drove back from our trip, I wondered about the signs we saw. I wondered if I would choose the milk from cows pleasantly and contently employed or those who were eager malcontents. I decided that, given the choice, I would prefer to drink the milk of a contented cow. I thought how ingrained the idea had become that we should never be content and should be always anxious to do better. I thought, *We have lost our sense of when enough is enough.*

"Say When"

When we were little, my brother and I each had large drinking glasses with drawings of superheroes painted on their sides. They could hold almost an entire quart of liquid, and it took both of our hands to raise them to our mouths. When our dad poured our milk each morning, he would instruct, "Say when." He delighted in teasing us by ignoring any other word but "when" for our response. It meant "That's enough," and it was Dad's way of teaching us the first challenge in the success detox program, the sense of sufficiency.

I offer the challenge of developing your sense of sufficiency first because it is a prerequisite for being calm and paying attention to connecting fully with life. If we do not feel content, we feel agitated, and restless people are those with whom we will easily connect. Contentment is one of the first things we should have learned as children. Yet left on our own, particularly in a culture of endless temptations and almost unlimited choices, knowing when enough is enough is difficult for adults. It becomes almost impossible for children unless their parents teach and model their own consistent contentment and awareness of when enough is enough. Most children would eat the entire jar of chocolate chip cookies if someone did not stop them by saying, "That's enough." If that someone doesn't show that they know and behave with a sense of "enough," that lesson is more difficult to learn.

My dad's phrase "Say when" was appropriate because sufficiency relates not only to amount but also to having the ability to enjoy what we have already in the present moment. It is living without the monkey mind of getting all I can now because there may be no tomorrow. Unlike our primitive cousins, we can learn to control our appetites and desires. We can learn to pay attention to when we have had enough to live well and no longer have to keep trying to fill our glass. "That's enough" runs counter to the toxic success mantra of "Get as much as you can now and keep going for more later."

Yet, "more is better" is a primitive relic buzzing around in the lower recesses of our brain. Because resources were limited and hard to come by and harsh weather was always on the way, our ancestors had to take all they could when they could get it. Taking "just enough" may have ended up leaving them with not enough, so gluttony was adaptive and good. In a modern world that for most people offers plenty of what they need, the drive for more is, like the primitive fight-or-flight response, a relic that we have to learn to overcome if our planet and we are to remain healthy.

Sweet success is based on a well-developed sense of sufficiency, but society seems stuck in gluttony. Because my father considered milk to be good for us while we craved something much sweeter, such as soda, he would often laugh and keep pouring just a little more after we said "When" as he poured our milk. But when he was pouring soda, he would stop pouring long before we had even thought of saying the magic word. "Did you forget to say 'When'?" he would tease, but we got the message. He was teaching us not only to know when enough is enough, but also when we were seeking too much of those things that might not be so good for us.

Sufficiency Practice

The Hawaiian model of *po'okela* teaches that true success is attained through never taking more than one needs and sharing as much as one can. Most importantly, it is doing so in a regular, ritualistic manner. This Polynesian form of success and the sense of contentment to which it leads are based on the premise that materialistic gains eventually derive from a kind of daily spiritual precision and self-control practiced though shared ritual. It depends on freedom from SIN, the self-interest motive.

In this oceanic view, all rituals such as my father's pouring of the milk, the preparation and eating of *poi*, or the making of a canoe had what Hawaiian researchers and cultural expert George Kanahele called a certain "practicalness."[1] He wrote, "All ritual brings some benefit, directly or indirectly, to material well-being."[2] In this view, rituals that teach sufficiency and collective awareness are not supplementary or parallel to success, they are seen as the only paths to healthy success.

When slow, ritualistic dinnertimes together as a family are disrupted by SIN-based concerns and sacrificed to the pursuit of the individual success of each family member, the rituals that can teach contentment are significantly reduced. If you want to detoxify your own success by learning the art of contentment, you will have to consider building more "sufficiency rituals" into your everyday life. Sitting with family members and watching as "just enough" is meted out, passing dishes from which small amounts are taken, and always leaving plenty for others are ways the sense of sufficiency that characterizes a sweeter success can be learned. Hawaiians considered such practices as pleasing to the gods, who would, in turn, please them by providing the things they needed and wanted. This is the *po'okela* principle that "what goes around comes around" and that, eventually, more always comes from less.

Contentment as a Virtue

"We've won every game this year," said the coach of our basketball team proudly when I was growing up. I played for a small high school in the Midwest and was also proud that we were doing so well, but clearly enough was not enough for our coach. "We will never be content—contentment is our enemy! What do we want?" he would yell, and we knew what to yell back. "More!" we would scream. "When do want it?" he would yell again, and we were trained to respond in unison, "Now!" This approach may lead to a form of athletic success, but as a way of daily living and working, it creates a constantly pressured sense of deficiency.

The "never be content" motto of toxic success has become ingrained in our culture. The materialism of our modern world has overwhelmed and overloaded our sense of sufficiency and displaced any true sense of contentment. We are bombarded with television ads constantly reminding those who already have a lot that they do not yet have enough. In fact, the whole idea of advertising is to convince the "haves" that they are really latent "have nots," lacking some very essential thing or experience. "You don't sell to people who don't have much," said the winner who owned several car dealerships. "You have to convince those who have the most that they must have more. Contentment is the enemy."

Psychiatrist Thomas Szasz wrote, "Happiness is an imaginary condition, formerly attributed by the living to the dead, now usually attributed by adults to children and by children to adults."[3] The first of the five Ds of toxic success syndrome is a **"D**eficiency"-driven mind that thinks happiness must be "out there," somewhere amidst all the fantastic stuff and experiences other people seem to have. Yet while we are busy trying to achieve the degree of success other people seem to have, they are busy trying to have what they think we have. If you let the memories of the wisdom of your parents' or grandparents' words "That's enough" become a part of your thought process and take the time for more shared contentment rituals, you can begin the difficult but crucial task of learning how to be content.

The research on happiness and success shows clearly that objective life circumstances play a negligible role in our ultimate feeling of success.[4] Once we commit this fact to memory and practice being content with what we have, we can begin not only to learn to recognize when enough is enough but also to be much more content with it.

During the writing of this book my 82-year-old mother was in a nursing home. She was suffering from cancer and emphysema and was very weak. In preparing for her entry into the home, we had had to clean out her home, organize her papers, and get rid of more than eight decades of stuff. She was very mentally alert and deeply saddened by the necessity of this period of life transition.

As she sifted through her possessions, she said, "Look at all of this. I have a memory associated with almost every bit of it, but now what do I do? I have no need for it now and I have no room to keep it. You and your brother don't have room for it. I guess you spend the first part of your life getting ready to be able to get all you want, the second part getting it, and the last part getting rid of it. I could have saved a lot of valuable time not getting all this in the first place." Applying my mother's wisdom in my attempts to help the toxically successful, I suggest they look at their possessions and desires from the perspective of the last part of their lives while they are still in the early parts.

Materialistic Madness

You read earlier about the constant state of shopping mode that characterizes toxic success. One indication of the consumer mentality that is numbing our sense of sufficiency is the invasion of our homes by infomercials and the cable shopping networks. We may have hundreds of television channels to choose from, but even the fastest remote-control zapper can not escape the commercials, paid announcements, and one of the most sufficiency-dulling phenomena and contentment-discouraging of all, the new cable consumerism of the video retail business.

The QVC (quality, value, convenience) television program's "buy it now" approach is enforced by a ticking clock and "quantity left" code on the bottom of the screen. The question is not only do you have enough, but also can you act fast enough to know that you don't and remedy the situation by quickly calling in to an operator standing by. In a "charge it or lose it" approach, QVC's major competitor, the Home Shopping Network, only allows purchases while the merchandise is on-screen as "hosts" warn that "quantities and time are running out" and that "we may never offer this item again." Its automated phone system can field more than twenty thousand calls per minute from an audience of eager and often repeat consumers—the "haves" converted to "have nots."[5]

The home shopping programs have become electronic psychological support groups for the sufficiency impaired. Homebound buyers can "join the club" or call in, as if attending church, to give testimony to the glories of the product they have just purchased. During such calls it is not unusual that the caller will talk on a first-name basis with the salespersons and tell them how much they love them. They trade praise for the product for the attention of the seller and tell how it has or will change their lives forever. They talk about their families, a birth of a child, and often intimate details of their illnesses. Closing the deal, the salespeople nod, often saying, "God bless you," and end the call with the now traditional and sugary sweet, "Bye bye!" And that is precisely what one has to do to become a member of this congregation of consumers: buy, buy. The testimonials sanctioned by the "salespeople and surrogate family" provide affirmation for making the right buy and psychological conditioning to keep on buying. We have accepted all of this as entirely normal, but they are side effects of TSS.

So what is the harm in all this? Certainly these programs seem to provide convenience and entertainment to hundreds of thousands of people. It all seems so natural and easy, and therein lies the danger. The commercial caring offered comes at the price of the purchase, a form of programmed prostitution in which "tele-love" is given in exchange for a credit card number. The need to buy a symbol of success reflects just how numb our sense of sufficiency has become and how barren and socially deprived so many in our society seem to feel.

For those struggling to put food in their stomach, it must seem strange to see yet another set of collectible porcelain dolls being offered as something everyone needs. In fact, the whole notion of a "collectible" is not something the true "have nots" can easily understand. It is discomforting and saddening to think about those struggling to meet their most basic needs watching so many others busy consuming so much of what they could not possibly need. As professor Stephen Bertman writes, "As more and more material goods fill up society's intellectual space, they crowd out the significance of non-material concerns. . . . Society reverts to its primitive state [the monkey mind], to a time when meeting physical needs left little occasion for anything else. In this new primitivism, matter reclaims its place as the consummate source of human satisfaction."[6]

We have mistaken the widening of consumption for social progress and high-level success for what professor Lee Burns calls "commoditization," using goods to increase our sense of success.[7] This shopping mentality causes us to lose all sense of "enough" and to be constantly in the "get more while we can or we'll die" mode of our primitive ancestors.

Resensitizing Your Sense of Sufficiency

To reawaken your sense of sufficiency, watch television and other advertising media from the perspective of someone who has almost nothing at all. Imagine you are hungry, cold, and without a roof over your head. Now watch and listen as almost every commercial plays loud and fast music underneath rushed words and images designed to convince you that what you really need is a pair of athletic shoes that can be pumped full of air, a better-structured stock portfolio, or a much faster and sexier car. Notice how you are constantly being nagged and told what you should want with little concern for what you really need. Pay attention to the excitement and almost religious fervor of the salespeople, for they are TSS enablers.

Next, take a sufficiency walk around your house. Take along a pad and pencil and make a "need" and a "want" column. Write down every item you really need to be in your home. You will have to know the difference between what you need and what you want, and therein lies the challenge of this aspect of the detoxification program. As you walk, remember the phrase "Needs sustain my life, wants enhance it." The problem with toxic success is that those who suffer from it often are so focused on self-enhancement that they lose sight of their basic needs. A *kupuna* warned, "If you mistake *sustain* for *obtain*, you end up with a lot of nothing."

Take plenty of time to do your sufficiency walk. Pause at some of the items and reflect on why you have brought them into the most sacred place in your life—the privacy of your home. Do not mistake items that seem to save time as something that is needed. These are "wanted" things that may enhance your life but, if you really reflect about them, may also be controlling your life.

You will have to take your sufficiency walk many times. Like most of us, you have probably "stuffed your home with stuff." Here are some questions to ask yourself during your walk:

- How many televisions do you really need?

- How many computers, phones, and other electronic devices do you really need?

- Is there any place in your home where there are only the "bare essentials" and very little stuff?

- Is there a place in your home that is "your place" and free of other family members' stuff?

- Do you have a "stuff overflow" area such as an attic or basement full of stuff you retain because of the "throw-out phobia" of the toxically successful?

- Are you suffering so severely from a numbed sense of sufficiency that you actually shop through other people's junk at garage sales for stuff to take home to keep your personal junk company?

- Are the many "time-saving devices" you notice around your home adding to the quality of your life or controlling your life?

- Are the things you notice during your walk there because you really want them there or because they might impress guests?

• How many truly beautiful things do you see during your tour?

• How many "mementos" and family pictures have prominent places throughout your home?

After you complete your first preliminary "stuff" tour, take some time to study your list. Reflect on the balance between the needs and wants columns. Does there seem to be a significant imbalance in favor of wants?

On your next sufficiency walk, take along a set of small dot stickers. Place a dot on items that you consider wanted rather than needed. You can come back to reappraise the value of these items again later, after you have considered the art of renunciation discussed below.

What Are You Worth?

"I'm sorry to be pushy, but approximately what are you worth?" asked the cable news reporter. She was interviewing the CEO of a large corporation and attempting to pin him down on his salary and stock holdings. "I'm worth quite a bit," he answered. "Let's just say I'm worth much more now than I was ten years ago." As I listened, I wondered if he really meant what he said.

Because of the dominance of the deficiency motive in the toxically successful, there has been a boom in financial advisors and cable-television money shows. Day traders sit like gambling addicts at slot machines in Las Vegas trying to increase their "worth." We micromanage our finances by watching for every swing and sway in the stock market, and because of the speed with which we can now monitor changes and the electronic connection between the world markets, the likelihood of financial overreaction and its related emotional stress have vastly increased over the last decade. We have come to equate security almost exclusively with money, and worth almost totally with the amount of money we have.

Thomas J. Stanley and William D. Danko are authors of the bestseller *The Millionaire Next Door*. They studied hundreds of millionaires and offer their advice on how to "increase our wealth," but they first ask us to determine our "net worth starting point" before we try to begin to increase our worth. Their formula to determine personal worth is A (age) multiplied by I (income) divided by 10. There you have it: a formula for your worth. There is no specific mention of C (a contentment factor), but they do discuss the fact that the millionaire living next door to you is likely to not be seeking and buying expensive things and personal frills. The assumption is that everyone wants to be a millionaire, and their book is full of charts and numbers showing how to do it. Yet there is no mention of the four concepts that are keys to success *po'okela* style: enough, ordinary, contraction, and renunciation.[8]

Can You End with a Starter House?

Congratulations! You have just won a $53 million home over sixty-six thousand square feet in size with its own Olympic-sized pool, large theater, library, exercise gym, and, of course, the latest in every electronic toy imaginable. What is one of the first things you would do upon moving into your castle? If you are like its current owner, you would immediately apply for a building permit to make your home bigger. This is what Microsoft founder Bill Gates did when his most unordinary home was completed: He complained that he was short on space now that he had a family. His actions are an example of the kind of toxic success thinking that must be reversed if you are to rid yourself of the pressures of toxic success—a "never enough," "don't accept the ordinary," "always expand and extend," and, most of all, "buy, own, and control" kind of thinking. When interviewed by *U.S. News and World Report*, Gates stated, "Everything is in a state of flux, including the status quo."[9]

We buy "starter homes" with the idea that whatever we have is already not really enough. We "expand" and "extend" until we finally decide to try to own a bigger, more extraordinary house that better reflects how successful we have become. Yet the house we buy ends up sitting next to all the other empty monuments waiting for the return of their owners, who are busy working harder for more money to buy an even bigger house. This same toxic success mentality applies to how we think of our cars, our computers, and the other stuff of our modern life.

To experience a sweeter success than the one-way drive for more described above, you will have to practice thinking differently about life. You will have to think contraction rather than expansion, enough rather than more, and ordinary instead of extraordinary. Most of all, you will have to learn the art of renunciation, a dirty word in a consumerist world.

The Art of Renunciation

Renouncing will not come easy to the toxically successful brain. It smacks of monklike sacrifice, self-deprivation, and a stark and joyless life with none of the modern conveniences, but this is not what I mean by renunciation. I am referring to trying to think from a less acquisition-oriented perspective and to looking more often to the joys of what we already have and less to what we think we must have to be happy. In its simplest form, the art of renunciation is giving up the illusion of final ownership and knowing when enough is enough.

The phrase "Want what you have rather than try to have what you want" has been around a long time and is expressed in various ways by many spiritual teachers. Author Henry Van Dyke wrote, "It is better to desire the things we have than to have the things we desire."[10] A much older version of this philosophy is a Hawaiian proverb that states, *"E 'ai I ka mea I loa 'a"* (a-i-e-ka-may-ah-e-low-ah-ah), translated as "Be satisfied with what you have." This teaching is embraced as a key principle of *po 'okela*.

Hawaiians are taught that there are two aspects to this phrase. First is the importance of fully and totally enjoying what we do have. Second, and much more difficult, is renouncing our brain's pressure to keep seeking those things we want but don't have. Relearning our sense of sufficiency is focused on this second challenge. It requires learning to renounce the continental view of humans with unlimited wants in a world of limited resources, with the Hawaiian view of intentionally limited human needs experienced in a universe of unlimited gifts.

To "renounce" can be a way to "re-announce" a new approach to our life, to declare our intention to abandon an emphasis on ownership. The ownership imperative of toxic success is based on the illusion that we can really, totally, and finally "own" anything. We may buy something and use it for a while, but nothing lasts forever. In the overall scheme of things, basic physics teaches us that everything, including us, is in the process of falling apart and changing to something else. Even if things lasted forever, we would get bored with them. You have read about the psychological principle that all of our desires and joys are transitional. We are forever on the alert for newer, faster, or better things. Our TSS culture makes almost everything into a commodity:

Our homes, our relationships, our jobs come to be viewed as negotiable things rather than living, cherished systems that are a part of who we are.

If you adopt a renunciation way of thinking, you do not have to move to a monastery. You only have to realize that you already have most of what you could ever want—a little time on planet paradise. A sense of sufficiency requires being mentally aware in the present and fully attentive to what we have now. This relishing mode takes time, but it also leaves less time for our brain to long for what we don't have.

A woman in the winners group described her success in relearning her sense of contentment. "I really don't have time to think about what I could have because I'm really paying a lot more attention to what I already have. It's very, very time consuming to pay attention to all I have. During my sufficiency walk, I discovered dozens of things that I was ignoring and not appreciating. I rediscovered my mom's old photo album, and I've spent hours looking though it. It was in the drawer in the cabinet under our television. Now I sometimes turn off the TV, sit back, and thumb through the old pictures. And now I know why the first thing people try to save when their house burns is their family pictures and not their television or computer."

Appreciating What You Don't Have

Psychologists know that there is one sure thing about getting what you want: you won't appreciate it for long. As one of the winners group stated, "I think it is sometimes more fun appreciating and enjoying things before you get them than actually getting them." Learning to appreciate and want what you have is one thing, but learning to appreciate what you don't have, without craving something more, is much more difficult.

We are urged to seek high rewards as a sign of our success and source of more happiness, but modern research and ancient wisdom show that high-level extrinsic rewards for performing intrinsically rewarding activities result in those activities becoming less rewarding.[11] This means that sometimes it is more fulfilling to be able to retain our wonder at the quality of things we do not have and not spoil that wonder by actually getting them. Getting what we want can take the fun out of wanting.

One of the winners group described the "value of wanting" when he said, "Sometimes I long for the days when there was so much that I thought

I wanted and could never have. Now I have almost all I want, but I'm not sure I'm really much happier. There was something invigorating, tempting, and very interesting about fantasizing what it would be like to have something. When you have everything, you lose that feeling."

It is our nature to acclimate. We get used to anything, including suffering and joy. We have to meet our needs, but working constantly to fulfill our wants causes us to achieve only a toxic state of success that leaves us feeling bored and defrauded when all we have worked so hard for leaves us with the sense that we have worked hard for nothing and must now work even harder to try again to get what we want. If toxic success is an effort to be free of our wants, sweet success is accepting and even enjoying wanting.

No matter how highly rewarded we become nor how many great things we acquire, we are not likely to ever feel fulfilled. Feeling contentment is knowing and accepting that all emotional states, including misery and great joy, are transitory. Using our rational intelligence to help us get what we want can lead to some immediate, short-lived happiness, but it is using our imagination to remain in wonder and awe at what we may never have that gives life its energy and the joy of anticipation rather than obligation.

A Chinese proverb states, "We are never happy for a thousand days, a flower never blooms for a hundred." It refers to being able to appreciate the ebb and flow of daily life rather than trying to work ourselves into a state of guaranteed and enduring joy. So the phrase "Want what you have and don't try to have what you want" becomes "Enjoy what you have while you have it; don't think that more and new will bring you happiness," and "Love what you don't have without trying to have it" becomes the code for resensitizing your sense of sufficiency.

Now that you have read more about the nature of renunciation, take another sufficiency walk through your home. This time, check out those items on which you placed the dots, those items that you felt you "wanted" more than "needed." Pick one of these items to donate to charity. Every month during this one-year detoxification program, donate one of the dotted "wanted" items. The objective is not only to un-stuff yourself and de-clutter and simplify your home but also to look at life from the perspective of how much you have that you could be giving away.

All You Really Need

Psychologist Timothy Miller points out, "You can resent your bald spot or be glad you have a head."[12] He was referring to renouncing the better in order to embrace the good. To have a good and successful life requires only three things. Nineteenth-century Polish poet Cyprian Norwid summarized them. He wrote, "To be what is called happy, one should have (1) something to live on, (2) something to live for, and (3) something to die for."[13] Ask yourself if you have these three things in your life now. If you answered yes, you are sweetly successful. If you answered no, you are failing to look in the right places and may have lost your ability to "say when" enough is enough.

Most of us have enough to live on, and research shows that even those who barely have enough are not much less happy than those who have more than enough.[14] If we look into our heart and away from the arrogant selfishness of our brain, we all have something and someone to live for. If we look deeply into our soul, we will see there something worth dying for and why death should not frighten us as much as it does. What could be more successful than having a sense of these three elements in our life and on our mind? If you answered, "More of all three," your sense of sufficiency is still numbed by the comparativeness and competitiveness of toxic success.

You read earlier that when it comes to the search for happiness, neither poverty nor wealth seems to be of much help. That money does not buy happiness has been documented several times in the research and in the laboratory of everyday common experience. Paraplegics and lottery winners do not differ significantly in their degree of reported happiness.[15] If you will cease comparing yourself and your success with others and learn to attend more fully to the simple joyful moments of life, you are more likely to feel sweetly successful. Author Jack Kornfield expressed the nature of sufficiency and sweet success when he wrote, "Even the most exalted states are unimportant if we cannot be happy in the most basic and ordinary ways."[16]

Where the Sweetly Successful Are

I found hundreds of sweetly successful people with highly developed senses of sufficiency. Like the mortals group on the bone marrow transplant unit with me, they were patients in the various cancer units at the hospital where I was treated for stage-four lymphoma. We were in pain, weak, and scared to death, but something about being cast into that deprived state seemed to rekindle our sense of sufficiency or, at the very least, lower its threshold. I had never heard the leaf of a tree until I looked outside my window every day for months on the cancer unit. I'd never felt what food tastes like until my taste buds came back to life once the poisonous chemotherapy ended. I'd never smelled sunshine until my first trip outdoors into the fresh morning air.

Along with my fellow sufferers, I learned that sweet success is a life brought alive by our full attention to the joys of the many small moments. It is an enduring sense of sufficiency that allows the most simple of things to soothe and reenergize us.[17] As we lay bedridden for months, most of us practiced our own individual forms of "synesthesia," the unique kind of sensory perception described in the next section. We didn't tell our doctors for fear of psychiatric referral, but we all were able to appreciate the simplest of everyday things by perceiving them across the artificial boundaries of the physical senses. Like for my fellow cancer patients, it seemed that my dying made me more alive than I had even been in my life.

When I say one can learn to be content with the most elemental and basic of life's activities, I am referring to the celebration of the most basic of daily life processes. During my walks through the halls of the dying, and dragging my IV stand and oxygen tank along beside me, I thought how wonderful it would be to walk freely again and not to be tethered to an outside source of life support. I remember passing another cancer patient who, like me, was bald, skinny, pale, bent over, and covered with burns and bruises from chemotherapy on his arms and legs. "Great news," he whispered. "I just passed gas." We laughed together about a simple joy that only those of us who have known serious illness fully understand. When you put this book down and walk freely to your next activity, I hope you will pay attention to finding at least a small measure of contentment in doing so.

Using Your Cross-Sensory Perception

To this point in your success detox program, you have reviewed your definition of success, reflected on your internal dialogue to check for the "pester factor," considered the five factors of *aloha* as guidelines for sweet success, made an attempt to build in more "sufficiency rituals" into your family life, and taken a sufficiency stroll to discriminate between the stuff you have and the stuff that seems to have you. There is yet another invitation to a sweeter success.

If you have seen the Disney film *Fantasia*, you have seen music represented as colors, and colors as various sounds. Do you ever see or hear something so beautiful and meaningful to you that you actually "feel it" in your bones? Hawaiians do. Their music and chants celebrate the sound of the rainbow resonating throughout the body and the gentle brushing feeling of the sound of the ocean on their cheeks when they lie in their beds. This extraordinary sensory-perception condition is called "synesthesia," and psychologists have been studying it for decades.

You may have experienced a piece of music that made your skin crawl and the hair stand up on your body, but synesthesia is much more than an emotional rush. It's seeing units of time as shapes and the months of the year as the cars on a Ferris wheel with July on top.[18] The name comes from the Greek, meaning "to perceive together," and while it is common in indigenous societies, it is a rare but documented condition in Western society in which people (psychologists call them "syn-esthetes") hear, smell, taste, or feel pain or pleasure in color, taste various shapes, and may even see concepts and numbers as shapes dancing around them. Because so many people who do experience synesthesia have been ridiculed for reporting it or fear diagnosis as being mentally disturbed and thus keep quiet about it, the condition is probably not as rare as the research indicates. It seems likely that if any one of us can do it, all of us may be able to if we open our minds to the possibility.

Imagine the contentment of sitting in your chair and listening to a favorite piece of music while seeing it splash colors across your mind. Imagine feeling your body being played by a thunderstorm as you hear the lightning and see the thunder. Imagine that your body represents the strings of a guitar, with one sound vibrating in your toes, another in your thighs, and so on. As strange as it may seem to the rational brain, another way to experience a fuller appreciation of what you already have is to embellish and enhance it by using your sense of synesthesia. "Feel" your child's picture in your heart, smell the memories of Grandma's Thanksgiving turkey, and hear a sun setting.

Scientists have shown that synesthesia is a very real neurological process. As author Siri Carpenter writes, "Studies have confirmed that the phenomenon is biological, automatic, and distinct from both hallucination and metaphor."[19] While only about one in every two thousand persons in Western societies reports synesthesia, scientists studying it estimate the number is probably closer to one in every three hundred. The most common form of synesthesia is "colored hearing" such as that represented in *Fantasia*, and you can try to experience it for yourself by using your imagination to let your brain work "top down."

Neuroscientists tend to see most of our thinking and mental experiences as a "bottom up" process with the higher parts of our brain, the thinking parts, reacting to stimulation of the lower parts, which are receiving stimulation from the outside world. However, it seems possible to "suggest" to the lower parts that receive signals throughout our body to try to "see what it hears and hear what it sees."

Try a synesthesia experiment yourself. Sit quietly and look intensely at a flower or picture of a loved one. Try to "feel what you see." Or when listening to a favorite piece of music, close your eyes and try to see what you hear. Take plenty of time and don't try too hard. As with most of our seldom-used senses, sometimes referred to as "psychic" or "sixth sense" perception, there is a decline effect through which the harder you try, the less the subtle effects occur. (This same principle applies to success: The harder you try, the more the joy diminishes.)

If your score on the Toxic Success Survey was very high, you will likely have trouble understanding and accepting this part of the detoxification program, but give this invitation several months of practice. You might discover that you don't need drugs to have the "psychedelic experience" of seeing sound and hearing sights. If the brain of a junkie can do it, so can yours— and without the danger of the drugs. If you try this experiment in enhanced appreciation, you can begin to appreciate more of what you already have. You may develop your synesthetic sense and discover that a simple song or a favorite picture will be more than enough to make you recognize that you already have at least a lot of what you really want.

This Chance Could Be Your Last Chance

Psychologist Abraham Maslow noted the nature of sufficiency when he wrote, "All you have to do is go to a hospital and hear all the simple blessings that people never before realized were blessings—being able to urinate, to sleep on your side, to be able to swallow, to scratch an itch, etc. Could exercises in deprivation educate us faster about all our blessings?"[20] As a cancer survivor, my answer is yes, but you don't have to wait to suffer to learn the art of contentment. Put this book down, sit back, close your eyes, and think about someone you love. Imagine that this is your last chance to see this person and that you have only this moment left to hold him or her in your mind and heart. That should be sufficient to awaken your sense of contentment and lead to a feeling of sweet success.

Ecologist Alan Thein Durning wrote, "In the final analysis, accepting and living by sufficiency rather than excess offers a return to what is, culturally speaking, the human home: the ancient order of family, community, good work, and good life."[21] An important step in detoxifying success is to remember to "say when."

CHAPTER ELEVEN

Calming Down: Knowing How to Be Still

Teach us to sit still.

—*T. S. Eliot*

H e walked quickly to the elevator and pushed the UP button. It was already lit, but he seemed to think that another poke might bring the elevator a little sooner. He backed up and did his version of the "elevator shuffle." He paced back and forth, looked at his watch, and jingled the change in his pocket. According to my watch, less than fifteen seconds had passed, but he began to act like he had been waiting for several minutes. He raised his head and began to look around. As if trying to will one of the many elevators to come faster, he scanned between the different arrays of numbers over each elevator door. He began to rock back and forth and, using the mirrors strategically placed to distract the chronically impatient, adjusted his tie and returned to his elevator shuffle.

When one set of doors finally opened, he hurried in before they were completely open. He let out a big sigh and nodded his head as he was forced to wait for the doors to close, that frustrating period elevator manufacturers refer to as "door dwell." Dwelling is not something TSS sufferers enjoy. For most elevators, door dwell lasts less than four seconds, but to this man, that seemed an almost unbearable length of time. He began tapping his foot and punched several times at the CLOSE DOOR button, but another time disaster was about to happen. A woman was dashing for his elevator, and he was faced with the dilemma of being polite or making up for lost time.

The man clearly saw the woman coming. Ignoring the OPEN DOOR button, he looked up and away in feigned distraction and restraightened his tie as if oblivious to his fellow TSS sufferer's plight. As the doors began to close, his bad luck continued. Willing to sacrifice her body for the sake of a few saved seconds, the woman stabbed her arm between the closing doors and stuck her briefcase inside the elevator. A battle ensued between woman and machine as the doors banged and shuttered against her arm and the man pretended to look for the OPEN DOOR button. Disgusted, she finally gave up. As the doors closed, she slammed them with the briefcase she had just barely snatched from leaving without her and began her version of the elevator shuffle. "These damn things take forever," she said to her friend who had finally caught up with her.

Antsyness and Short-Range Vertical Transport Systems

Watching people deal with what engineers call short-range vertical transport systems is a study in our increasing impatience and lack of calmness. Otis Elevator Company spends millions of dollars trying to keep pace with what elevator consultant James W. Fortune calls our natural "antsy" nature.[1] While the first elevators traveled at less than a foot per second, modern elevators can climb as fast as many airplanes and quicker than forty feet per second. On average, they arrive in less than fifteen seconds, but that's not fast enough to stop us from beginning our elevator shuffle.

In a futile attempt to deal with our calmness deficiency, elevator companies have installed what they call "psychological waiting-time lanterns."[2] These are lights set to go on automatically when we push the call button.[3] They signal which elevator will arrive first so we can shuffle over to be ready to be first inside. This invention is designed to decrease the often angry elevator roulette that takes place as hurried people gamble on which elevator will come first, stake their territory in front of that door, and then rush to push in front of the lucky winners whose number came up. In yet another attempt to deal with our antsyness, companies have installed numeric countdown panels showing the race between elevators, as well as mirrors intended to distract us a few seconds by the temptation to admire ourselves.

I suggest you try a little elevator-shuffle watching to learn just how impatient we have become. With the equivalent of the entire planet's population now going up and down in faster and faster elevators every nine days, few of us remember the slow-moving elevator and its white-gloved smiling operator announcing the floors and warning us to watch our step. Even on our way up to the health club to increase our aerobic capacity, stairs have become emergency exits only.

So What's the Holdup?

As you have read, it is not so much our fast moving that is the problem, it is our fast thinking. Our minds seem stuck on fast-forward, so waiting for anything, including an elevator, causes us to feel we have been placed on what we experience as a frustrating involuntary pause. The director of advanced technology at the Otis Elevator Company writes, "When they're waiting for an elevator, as well as when they're in an elevator, they don't really feel they can do much productive."[4]

In our capitalistic society, being productive increasingly means getting something done quickly so we can keep moving on to do something else. If doing things faster and faster and being a quick thinker are being productive, calmness comes to be a sign that something is wrong. We feel we have been placed on mental hold and begin to say to ourselves, "This doesn't feel right. What's the holdup? Shouldn't I be doing something? Shouldn't I be more productive?"

One of the winners group, a vice president at a large computer company, protested my assertion that healthy success required a calmer mind and that productivity should be viewed in the broader context of being content and connected. She said, "We have so many choices now. There are so many things we can do, have, and accomplish. There's an ever increasing amount of information to process. If you're going to be productive, you have to think more quickly. We hire at my company based on mind speed. If you're not thinking fast, someone is going to out-think you. You have to be able to scan an infinite amount of choices in a finite amount of time. You might have what you call a calm mind on vacation, but not in your work. Not if you want to be a success."

The Paradox of Freedom

"I've spent my life trying to exhaust every one of my options, and all

I've ended up with is feeling exhausted," said the 42-year-old hotel manager. "I've worked my whole life to give myself more choices, and now I have too many to ever be sure I'm making the right ones." This sufferer of toxic success is expressing the nature of the paradox of freedom and another manifestation of what can become the curse of success: the rushed feeling that we have to consider every choice as quickly as possible in order to be sure we couldn't have made a better choice.

We have become accustomed to celebrating our hard-earned freedom, but too much freedom can also lead to the nagging feeling that we "are never quite sure" about what we have, whom we have chosen to love, where we have elected to work, or if we are receiving the right medical care. No matter how happy we feel, we may ruminate that there may have been a better choice. The result of this chronic uncertainty is a constantly pestered brain urging us to think fast so we can keep all of our options open. This uncertainty results in feeling pressured to work harder, move faster, and get more and more information.

Philosophers refer to the chronic uncertainty of TSS as "the paradox of freedom." They define it as the contradiction between valuing our complete autonomy to select among the widest array of options and the pressured feeling that there are too many choices to deal with. We can't calm down if we feel "up in the air" about how and what we have chosen.[5] The result is an almost perpetual brain scanning of options and the resulting psychological absenteeism experienced by those who love us and crave our overextended attention.

Psychologist Barry Schwartz describes the paradox of our modern freedom as a kind of psychological tyranny. He suggests that, "Modern American society has created an excess of freedom, with resulting increases in people's dissatisfaction with their lives and in clinical depression."[6] This is the kind of discontentment and disappointed sadness that constitutes toxic success, a form of self-assertion and determination to have and get it all, carried to the extreme. It can lead to, as Schwartz writes, "not the freedom of choice but the tyranny of choice."[7]

Being calm is feeling pleased. We can't feel pleased if we allow our brain to keep telling us that we have either made the wrong choice or haven't seen enough choices. Few of us can keep up with the number and range of options with which we are now presented. The feeling of being mentally overwhelmed by options results in agitation, insecurity, and the sensation of being constantly pushed from one choice to another. We can't feel calm about our decisions when we allow ourselves to be harassed rather than entertained by possibilities. We can't calm down and enjoy our choices when we keep worrying that there might have been a better spouse, job, or house to buy. Instead we find ourselves in "status electus," forever looking, shopping, and hurrying on to make another better choice.

Now What?

To illustrate the unsettling nature of the tyranny of choice, here is another invitation in your detoxification program. Imagine you have just been given ten thousand dollars. The only condition for receiving the money is that you must decide what to do with it before the end of the day. What would you choose to do with your bonus dollars? Make a list of your choices and try to include every option you have.

When I asked the winners group to do this, they began with amusement and finally gave up in frustration. One woman tossed her pencil down in disgust, saying, "Are you kidding? I've got more than twenty things on my list already, and I could go on forever. This is making me anxious and even angry. As soon as I made my choices, I thought of other ones. I got so agitated that I thought I'd just put it in the bank, but then I started to think which bank, which kind of account, and that maybe I should buy stock or bonds. Then I thought, I should pay off my credit card, and on and on and on." This is the tyranny of the too-abundant choices seen by the toxically successful brain, and the result is the five Ds of toxic success.[8]

The tyranny of too many choices feeds the "doubt" factor of toxic success. We begin to feel that whatever we have chosen is not as good a choice as others have made and that they are using their freedom better than we are. We begin to feel that we must keep mentally going and not linger or reflect for too long on any one or two options because there are so many more to which we should attend. We feel a sense of "deficiency" that we must be missing something we could have chosen if only we would have shopped a little faster, harder, and longer. We end up feeling "detached" because we are in scan rather than connect mode. We are unable to share whatever choice we have made calmly and confidently with others.

A toxically successful spouse, for example, may feel constantly tempted away from her choice of a husband because of the increasing access to a wider range of potential partners allowed her by her level of success. Months after accepting a new job, an executive might begin to wonder if there isn't a better one. As soon as we drive off the lot in our new car, we begin to wonder if we should have purchased a different model. From toasters to television to trips for vacation, the tyranny of too many choices lurks all around us.

The result of too many choices is ultimately feeling "disappointed" no matter how much we have because there is "just so much more out there" we might have had. Freedom from this selection stress comes from developing a calmer and narrower mind, a consciousness that allows us to attend patiently, comfortably, and fully to just a few choices without the fear that we should constantly be looking for other ones. It requires doing something that the toxically successful dread: giving up a little of their freedom of choice and the SIN associated with it. It requires calming down and paying more attention to what we have chosen than what we may have missed.

Productive Ignorance

Calmness is ignoring. You have read that attention is really a process of being able to filter out and ignore choices. TSS sufferers try not to ignore much of anything. The word *ignore* means "to refuse to take notice." Paradoxically, ignoring is really a form of intense focused attention. As the Eastern meditative traditions have taught for centuries, to be calm is a delightful state of ignorance achieved by a focused attention that excludes distracting external stimulation. The calmness of sweet success involves a little elective inattentive blindness. While paying attention to what matters most in our life is a key to sweet success, not paying attention to so much that really doesn't matter is also important.

To be ignorant is to be unaware of knowledge, but when there is just too much to know and consider, voluntary ignorance is good for our health and the endurance of our relationships. In the *po'okela* model of an excellent life, the Hawaiian phrase *nānā 'ole* means to disregard (*nānā* means "attention" and *'ole* means "without"). It is a value that stresses the importance of intentionally disregarding all we might have so we can more fully attend to what we already possess. It stresses distinguishing what we need from what we want, the core value of sweet success Hawaiian style. It explains the general Polynesian calmness that the toxically successful Western explorers mistook for lethargy, the so-called "paradise paralysis" of being content with the choice of sitting under a palm tree watching the dolphins play without wondering if there was a better tree or more playful dolphins somewhere else.

In my interviews with the winners group, many of them told me that they often longed for the good old days when their choices were much more limited. They said that even though they were not yet successful, they seemed to feel much calmer then. One bank executive told me, "When I was growing up, there was no choice of what car we would own. We were lucky to have a car and bought the only one we could afford from my dad. I bought a great car yesterday, but sitting at a traffic light, I noticed a new car next to me that I had not seen before. I could have chosen that car, and now I wonder if I bought the right one. I went to the only college I could, the community college a few blocks away. Now, my daughters are considering universities all over the country and even the world. Sometimes I long for the good old days."

The Joy of Narrow-Mindedness

Recommended paths to success in the modern world often emphasize the importance of having an open mind that sees all options and seeks total personal control and certainty in one's life. Because we now seek our success in a society where we have control to a degree that would have been unimaginable to our ancestors, an open mind can quickly become overwhelmed. We have unprecedented mobility in our careers and residences, and, as pointed out above, our options for sexual and marital partners are vastly greater than even our parents experienced, giving new meaning to the statement "So many lovers, so little time." Our options for medical intervention can be overwhelming, particularly at the most critical times, and our dietary choices can boggle the mind, the typical mental state of the toxically successful. As you have read, the Home Shopping Network and other electronic choice generators bombard us with options.

Being "mind boggled" is being driven by the need to be ever vigilant and constantly scanning the event horizon for new and better options. How can we feel "still and calm" when we think we have to be constantly on the lookout? How can we retain some sense of control of what is coming into and out of our consciousness when it seems that there is just too much to process? The challenge for this part of your detox program is to learn an enlightened ignorance by intentionally closing your mind, quieting your busy brain, and realizing that well-being is not being well-off by having made all the right choices. It is a consciousness of stillness that the *po'okela* model calls *ahonui*, a persistent patience that derives from *nānā 'ole*, an intentional disregard of many things in order to fully attend to a few things, achieved by attention to a narrower band of stimulation.

The paradox of freedom also refers to the fact that, for the first time in history, an extraordinarily large number of people can pretty much have any life they choose to have, wherever they choose to have it. We now have the control and autonomy we have been told to pursue, yet the data shows that the rate of depression is growing proportionately to the rate of our success.[9] Depression is ten times more likely to afflict someone now than at the turn of the last century, and this increased rate of profound disappointment with life is not due purely to better diagnostic tools or record keeping.[10] The curse of toxic success is that the most autonomous, self-determining, successful people in history have ended up being the saddest and most uncertain and insecure.

In our modern world, we may have more control than ever of aspects of our external environment, but our expectations about how much control we should and must have, have also increased at an even greater rate. As a result, many are experiencing the condition psychologists call "learned help-lessness," the feeling that nothing we do brings us a sense of calm satisfaction.[11]

Six Magic Words

"Own less, do less, say no."[12] When I discovered this quote from author Geoffrey Godbey, I thought how concisely it illustrated the *po'okela* principle of *ahonui* (ah-ho-new-ee), persistent patience. In chapter 10, you began your efforts to own less by learning the art of renunciation. You read about the sweet success of the ordinary and the stress that results from a brain constantly in search of the extraordinary. Consciously calming down requires you to consider the last four of the six magic words, thinking more about "doing less and saying no" in a toxically successful world that keeps tempting us with more and more things to do and think about, and that says we should always say yes to having and doing more.

In chapter 7, you read about the important research documenting the health-enhancing power of the word *no*. *No* slows you down, but in continental thinking to be successful you are supposed to be ready and willing to take on any challenge and stay "up to speed" at all times. We are taught that saying no may result in missing out on a choice. We are under pressure to own more electronic devices that will help us do more in less time and allow us to log on to an almost limitless range of choices. We have become electronically enabled to say yes to anyone, anywhere, anytime.

This toxic pressure has resulted in the age of "info-anxiety," a time in history where we are becoming more proficient at getting information than we are at knowing what to do with it. We seem afraid that we may be missing out on something, not keeping up with the latest information, or being left out of the loop, the ever-broadening circle of those thinking "full speed ahead" and forever broadening their range of options.

Info-Anxious

You have read about information fatigue. Our choices are presented to us through an incessant array of information. There are now an overwhelming number of options as to where we will get our information to make our choices. We are not limited to asking our family doctor or neighborhood pharmacist about a medicine. We can log on to hundreds of websites or watch a parade of pharmacological advertisements on television. We can enter chat rooms and talk with millions of strangers about the choices they've made. This information overload not only mentally tires us out and depletes our attention, it, and the number of choices with which it presents us, can also cause the info-anxiety that we didn't get all the information we needed to make the right choices.

Author Saul Wurman writes that our information anxiety is due to "the ever-widening gap between what we understand and what we think we should understand."[13] There is a worldwide web of expanding information to which we feel we can never fully log on.

Despite their name, there is really nothing personal about our personal computers. They are tools of connection to an anonymous system of people and data, an electronic arena of competition in which we feel we must know what everyone else seems to know. No matter what they may choose, it is assumed that those with the most choices are more likely to be winners. Our top-of-the-line luxury cars now have more computer power than the Apollo series of spacecraft, and the slowest personal computer is now more than two hundred times faster than IBM's original model.[14] In the hum of this lightning-fast computerized world, we seldom ever really feel mentally "offline" and free of the tyranny of choice.

Children of the toxically successful who live at the speed of computer chips have difficulty imagining handwriting letters to friends that are delivered by a real human being or waiting for days in eager anticipation for film from their camera to be developed. As they cluster at school bus stops talking on their cellular phones, they can't imagine waiting until they return home to talk on the one phone shared by everyone else in the family. They can play computer games with friends they have never seen, so sitting for hours talking with a narrow circle of close friends can seem boring. They can't imagine spending hours reading just for the joy of it rather than staring at a television or computer screen, sitting for a long time during a leisurely family dinner that was not prepared by a precoded microwave oven, or reflecting slowly and carefully about a problem without searching the Internet for the instant answer. "Go ask Mom or Dad" was long ago replaced with "Go check the Internet," and Mom or Dad are probably too busy to be of much help anyway.

With their increasing computer literacy, our children have become both more independent because of their parents' psychological and physical absenteeism and more dependent because they are kept on an electronic leash by their beepers and cell phones. Because of what they can do with their computers and what they see done with them on movie screens, they have become computer cynics who yawn at anything that is not "state of the art" electronics. Who has to wait for a simple misty rainbow when you can paint them faster, bigger, clearer, and brighter yourself with just the click of a mouse? One mother of four teenagers told me, "Our house is mice infested. We have six computers in our home and each one has a mouse. My daughter even has a remote-control mouse that can end up being anywhere in the house."

256

Can You Imagine That?

Another electronic fallout factor from the limitless array of choices we have in the modern world is "dis-imagination." We may think we are being imaginative when we create fantastic images on our computer screen, but it is the computer that does the work and provides the choices. When we and our children can watch virtual-reality characters flying through the air and through walls, spaceships hurling at warp speed across several universes, and dinosaurs and hairy mammoths marching right before our eyes, listening to Grandpa tell and retell the same long story or reading a book can seem pretty low-key and even boring. Such activities require imagination, and computers can do a lot of our imagining for us. Our children and we don't have to pretend anymore. All we have to do is select and click.

Imagination and calmness go hand in hand. We can't rush imagination. We have to be still, ignore all the electro-choices swirling around us, and take plenty of time to conjure up (not click) and picture things in our mind. But who needs to do that when we can quickly bring up anything from a distant star to a virtual sex partner by simply logging on?

If you have been reading this book slowly and reflectively, taken the time to take the several tests and reflect on the many letter-coded concepts, written and reflected back on your own definition of success, you are already practicing my first suggestion for reclaiming your sense of calmness. You have decided to ignore many choices to choose to pay attention to this book. Unless you have been "speed-reading" and "scanning" the words on these pages, the very act of contemplative reading has likely been a calming act. You can't read what is on the pages if you can't ignore your pager. One of the reasons we so often fall asleep when we try to read is that quietness overcomes us and we can't help ourselves. At least for a little while, we have made our choice as to where and how we will attend, and, finally, we calm down.

All Fluxed Up

"I'm all fluxed up," laughed the man. He paused a moment to look at his wife and then, like a child caught with his hand in the cookie jar, continued, "I guess it's not really all that funny. My whole life—*our* whole life— seems to be in a constant state of flux. Nothing stays settled and everything seems to be constantly changing. My state-of-the-art computer became an antique almost before I got it out of the box. As soon as I think I'm getting on top of things, I feel swamped again. I feel like I'm swimming upstream in a river rapids. I'm afraid if I stop, I'll drown. If I keep going like this, I'll get too tired to swim and I'll drown anyway. Either way, I can't keep this up."

The river the "fluxed up" man refers to is the unnatural current of modern life. It is not the natural river of time referred to by Greek philosopher Heraclitus in which "everything flows and nothing stays. . . . You can't step twice into the same river."[15] The river rapids we now encounter are more like a human-made thrill-park ride that we do not calmly step into but are sucked into to be dragged away for what we seek as the thrill of our life. However, the sweetly successful know that if we are willing to calm down enough to recognize it, it is life itself that is thrilling.

We seem to increasingly exist in a chronic state of war with time. Author Jeremy Rifkin says we are waging "time wars" between the more serene state our mind, heart, and body crave and the ever-quickening tempo of the technological demands we have placed upon ourselves.[16] I hope your slow reflection regarding these points about our "normal" but pathological pace of life will cause you to slow down your thinking enough to consider the ideas in the remainder of this chapter. As I have throughout this book, I will be suggesting some behavioral gimmicks to get your attention, but what I am really asking you to do is sit back and think about what you are choosing to put on your mind, what you are leaving out of your consciousness, how fast you are thinking, and what pleasure of life you may be mentally rushing right past.

If it is true that we have too many choices, who is to decide where to draw the line? By suggesting that we must narrow our range of choices, I am flying in the face of what psychologist Barry Schwartz called "the liberal individualism that is the official ideology of modern America."[17] Telling people what they "should" want may seem like trying to impose values on others or even smack of fascism, but we can safely discuss what values may be healthier for all of us without imposing those values on others. For example, except vaccination and a few other public health rules, no one compels us to comply with the choices suggested by doctors as "sound health practices." We are told every day that it is healthier to limit our choices of food to low-fat and high-fiber sources and to deny ourselves sweets and baked goods.

However, whether we choose to comply with this more limited range of choices is up to us.

The same is true for suggesting that you consider the values of *po'okela*. You can choose to focus your attention, limit your choices, have and seek less stuff, and compete less. You can choose to ignore much of what the modern world is foisting upon you, but it's up to you.

By offering the *po'okela*-based model of excellence, I am asking you to reflect on the points in this detoxification process. I am trying to describe more than prescribe, but I admit to "prescribing" more than I would like. I am speaking to TSS sufferers who are used to *doing* more than *reflecting*, so I have tried to get their attention by offering behavioral things to try. My hope, however, is that you are carefully considering what I am offering as a different set of values for an excellent life that constitutes a sweeter and healthier form of success, the *aloha* values of patience, harmoniousness, pleasantness, humbleness, and kindness.

Perpetual Mental Motion

The above description of the drowning "fluxed up" man's hurried way of thinking reveals the constant sense of perpetual motion experienced by the toxically successful. You may be able to feel it as you read these words. It's the sense that you have to get going and that, even as you sit reading this sentence, you are thinking in the back of your mind, "I'll just read a little further and then I have a lot of other things to do. While I'm reading, my ought-to list is getting longer by the minute. I've got a lot of things waiting for me to do." Psychologist Kenneth J. Gergen called this over-full life a "saturated self," a self awash in a multitude of societal-generated stimuli and choices.[18]

Consider the new means of acceleration available to us. Cell phone sales grew from 300,000 in 1986 to over 7 million in just a decade.[19] Over 60 million Americans now carry pagers, more than twenty times the number who carried them fifteen years ago.[20] In 1950, less than one in ten Americans owned a television.[21] In contrast, more than 25 million television sets were purchased in the year 2000 alone and more Americans now have televisions than have indoor plumbing.[22] To save the time it takes to walk to these televisions to change to one of three or four channels, we have millions of choice facilitators called remote controls that allow us to surf hundreds of channels.[23]

These numbers should prompt us to ask what one of my Hawaiian elders asked when she saw several women at a child's birthday party grasping for their purses and listening to them to see if it was their own or someone else's cell phone ringing. "You all seem to have so many means now. Are you sure you still remember the ends?"

Henry David Thoreau, writing about his version of the saturated self and its "modern improvements," called these things "but improved means to an unimproved end."[24] Toxic success is an obsession with newer and faster means with insufficient regard for what and whom we hope in our heart we will finally end up with. Sociologist Robert K. Merten refers to our toxically successful society as "a civilization committed to the quest for continually improved means to carelessly examined ends."[25] Calmness requires much more attention to what our life is really for and to what ends our new techno-terrorism is leading us.

Lament for the Psychologically Absent

The lack of calm satisfaction in our lives is due, in large measure, not so much to our dependence on our machines as to the fact that we have become our machines. Turning again to the sweetly successful Thoreau for his take on mentally calming down, we hear, "Men have become the tools of their tools" and "The man whose horse trots a mile in a minute does not carry the most important message."[26] To remain calm in a hectic world, we will have to stop thinking a mile a minute, be comfortable seeking fewer and not more choices, be able to use rather than be used by our machines, and learn to be still at least for a little while a lot more often.

For the toxically successful, calm patience is often viewed more as a vice than a virtue. Anyone who seems too calm must be "out of his or her mind." One of the members of the winners group has a sign over her desk that expresses the TSS sufferer's suspicion of the calm mind. It says, "Those who can keep their head while all those around them are losing theirs clearly are not aware of what is going on."

Toxically successful people see the chronically calm as not following the rules of life engagement, having given up, or too ignorant or lazy to get with the program. They fear that being too patient will cause them to lose their momentum and be overtaken by someone less patient, on the move, and on the way up. For them, a calm mind is a sign that something must be wrong. They carefully negotiate meeting times to gain an advantage and may even lie to be sure that their calendar does not seem more open than their time-war opponent's schedule. They feel they must maintain at least the image of being in perpetual mental motion and always thinking ahead, resulting in the psychological absenteeism of never being mentally present in the present.

The calmness-deficient are harebrained strivers with constantly racing minds that keep going even when they seem at rest. They are good at feigning attention while at the same time secretly "running through things" in their mind or preparing for the next challenge. The result is the lament of the psychologically absent, "I'm sorry, I wasn't paying attention," or for the more hurried, "Huh?"

You have read that psychological absenteeism is being mentally at home when the person should be working and mentally at work when he or she should be focusing on home. A brochure offered by the American Institute of Stress in Yonkers, New York, states that psychological absenteeism results in over $200 billion worth of losses for American business annually.

Manager's Magazine states that the mental stress and ever-racing mind of the psychologically absent result from the modern pace of life in the new electronic sweatshops and that this way of thinking has become the number one debilitator of the American workplace.[27] The spiritual price is even greater as we become so busy going places that we lose our place in life. We feel disoriented and without a sense of meaning and life coherence. We are going everywhere but seldom feeling that we are totally anywhere. As Carl Sandburg wrote, "We don't know where we're going but we're on our way."[28] Our striving has brought us plenty of means. The challenge we face now is to examine if the ends have been worth it and if they have made us feel as if we are thriving.

Einstein's Brain

Despite the toxic success myth that quick thinkers win, the evidence is clear that most of our society's most important contributions have come from tortoise minds. For example, it is said that Charles Darwin, the father of evolutionary theory, considered himself much too slow of a thinker to engage in debates regarding his controversial theory.

Ecclesiastes 38:34 states, "The wisdom of a learned man cometh by opportunity of leisure. And he that hath little business shall become wise." While Albert Einstein's brain is still stored in formaldehyde and scientists continue to slice off tiny bits from time to time to look for the source of his brilliance, they are not likely to find it in its structure or parts. They wrongly assume that he must have been a quick thinker and that somewhere in his brain there rests the neuro-accelerator, but Einstein himself valued the wisdom that derives from slow and reflective thinking and spoke often about the fertile mental and spiritual ground of a calm and contemplative mind. He considered himself an extremely slow thinker, stating, "Imagination is more important than knowledge."[29] My invitation to those suffering from toxic success is, "Imagine that!"

Curing Your Premature Articulation

Author Guy Glaxton, who coined the terms *hare brain* and *tortoise mind*, points out that calm, slow, reflective, serene thinking is vital to the process of creativity. He warns that our tendency to be "premature articulators" who try to think and speak faster can result in less, not more, creative thinking.[30]

One way to slow your brain down is to talk slower. We assume that fast thinkers speak fast because they have so much to say, but more often they use a lot of words quickly because their thoughts are in process and they can't wait for them to form. Hawaiians are taught that they have two ears so they can listen twice as often as they talk. To them, fast talkers are offensive because they are presenting carelessly formed thoughts and the nonsense of the quick-witted. Speaking of the *po'okela* value of calm, receptive thought, my *kumu* (teacher) said, "Only those who are self-interested speak fast. If we are aware of the necessary value of others in our life and our life to them, we speak and think calmly and slowly enough to allow *aloha* to flow between us." A key sign that people have attained *po'okela* success is their quality of listening much more than they talk and, when they do speak, speaking gently with a calming voice.

I conducted "word rate counts" on the winners group and compared them with a "control" group of randomly selected people who worked as cleaners and clerks, as well as at various service jobs within or near the hospital. The average salary of the winners group was in excess of $200,000 a year higher than the control group. The average "WRPM" (word rate per minute) of the winners group was 245; the control group's WRPM was 95. Clearly, fast talking seems to relate to high-level success, but as reflected by high scores on the Toxic Success Survey, it is often the SIN-ful toxic kind of success.

To develop a calmer mind, try to intentionally slow down your speech. It will frustrate your brain and take months of patient practice, but a slower rate of speech not only can lead to a more serene and less psychologically absent orientation to living, loving, and working. It also has been shown to correlate with a lower heart and respiration rate and lower blood pressure.[31] I suggest you randomly tape your speaking during an average day to determine your own WRPM and then try to reduce.

The Danger of Forward Thinking

I noticed a beeping signal from my son's car as he backed out of our driveway last evening. It sounded like the noise large trucks make when they go in reverse, but my son explained that his car was equipped with a sensor that detects objects behind him. I thought how wonderful it would be if we could implant a "forward detector" in the heads of the toxically successful that warned of the hazards that lie ahead as they strive down their road to success.

How many times a day do you walk backward? We don't often do it because our body was made for going forward. If we want to go back, we turn around and make what was behind us "forward." Our eyes and nose are front mounted, and our joints are made for bending to allow forward movement. Even our ears are slanted to catch sounds from the front. As silly as it may sound, I suggest you try to slow down the unidirectional momentum of your life by doing a little backing up every day. Walk into a room backward and notice how it is likely to elicit amusement or the assumption that you have lost your mind. Remember, that is exactly what you are trying to do: lose your hurried state of mind. It is difficult to be aggressive toward someone if you first walk up to him or her backward, do a pirouette, and then speak your mind.

To be successful in your detoxification program, you will have to go out of the mental box within which you have learned to live and work. That is why I am asking you to consider the *po'okela* way to excellence, a different cultural perspective in order to call your attention to a different way of thinking. Behaviors such as talking slowly, strolling backward, and taking the sufficiency walk suggested in chapter 8 are silly prescriptions that I hope will get your attention so you can reflect more on the points made in this detox program. They are intended to get your attention and to help you, as one of the winners group described it, "make another choice, but this time choose to limit your choices."

Cramming

Our automatic reaction to the demands of the toxic pace of our life is either to try to cram more into every moment of our day or to try to cut back on what we feel we have to do.[32] Cramming is trying not only to do more and more in less and less time, but trying to think more and more things at the same time, and faster and faster. Cramming can seem to work for a while because our electronic systems and ever-increasing computer speed help us to become more and more efficient—to a point. Unfortunately, we have reached that point, what author David Kundtz calls "the critical mass of too much." He says it seems as if we are "suitcases stuffed and crammed so full that our . . . seams are ripping and [our] emotional insides are busting out and spilling in the middle of [our] day." He warns, "There is simply too much to fit in."[33]

Cramming won't work because the rules of physics and mathematics show that we cannot keep going faster and faster and doing more and more. We assume that we will just keep going faster and doing and making more forever, and that we will become more efficient at going faster, but we are deadly wrong. The rate of increase in the pace of change and speed of life is progressing and compacting into shorter and shorter intervals. Change that took place in billions of years shrunk to millions of years, then thousands, then hundreds, and currently decades or less. We have become the first generation that can be born into one world, live in another, and leave yet another for our children.

Physicist Peter Russell describes the frightening prospects of the increasingly rapid pace of change in our life. He writes, "If you plot out the curve of this sort of acceleration, you find that the curve soon approaches the vertical. In other words, the rate of change tends toward the infinitely rapid. Mathematicians call such a point a singularity, when their equations break down and cease to have any useful meaning."[34]

If our toxic approach to a successful life continues at its current pace and the rate of change continues to accelerate, we can eventually reach a point of no return. If we can calm down, pay attention, and try a little selective ignorance, we may end up feeling more patient with others and ourselves. A Chinese proverb states, "If you are patient in one moment of anger, you will escape a hundred days of sorrow." Calm patience comes with freedom from trying to keep up with all the choices we could have and making the choice to enjoy what we already have. If we keep going as we are, we will have created for ourselves a world of even more havoc than we already sense. If we keep this up, we will really have fluxed things up.

Cutting

Unless we change how we think and learn to pay much more attention to what matters most in our life, what we often refer to as "cutting back" won't cut it either. If by cutting back we mean trying to do less by temporarily escaping the rat race, we are only avoiding the deeper problem of how we are attending to our life in general. It won't do much good to stay home if we are not really mentally at home.

Research shows that most workers who don't show up at work on short notice are not sick. They are staying home because they just can't take it anymore, feel they deserve a day off, and are "cutting out."[35] The real challenge to becoming sweetly successful is not trying to cut out but to tune in.

A favorite word of the toxically successful is "prioritize." This is a form of trying to cut back by ridding ourselves of some obligations so we can make room for others. Unless we learn to pay fuller attention to whatever it is we say we are giving high priority, we fool ourselves with numbering our options from most to least important. Unless we are able to give our full attention to whatever we have assigned priority, our list-making efforts are wasted. One winner said, "I went to a seminar on making priority lists. Now I have to find a place on my list for making a priority list."

Prioritizing can be similar to unpacking our overstuffed suitcase to get rid of some of the clothes that would not fit in and then stuffing the same amount or even more of different clothes back in. You can sit and jump on the suitcase all you want, but full is full and stuffed is stuffed. If you continue this false cutting, the luggage gets to the point of no return, ruptures, and breaks. When that happens, you aren't going anywhere.

"I cut back a few years ago," said one of the winners. "My number one priority was going to be family. I decided I was going to work a four-day week. Of course, I ended up working not just ten-hour days but twelve-hour days. I ended up actually working more. When I entered your detox program, I learned that the problem I had wasn't how many hours I worked but where my mind was. It wasn't so much my schedule as where my attention was. It was everywhere and nowhere. I didn't have to set priorities—I already had them. What was tough was learning to pay more attention to them."

There comes a point when none of us can cut anymore. Especially in our modern society, we have to work hard and long. Cutting becomes cramming when trying to cut back results in trying to do more in less time. Unfortunately, my clinical experience is that the toxically successful often end up cutting what they need most, such as time with old friends or sitting with the family not doing much of anything. Being home more but still exhausted, distracted, and disconnected doesn't do anyone any good. Cramming or cutting are enablers of toxic success, not cures.

Hold It a Minute

When I was learning to read music, I always had trouble with fermatas. A fermata is a rest mark in a musical score that has a half-circle over it. It looks something like an eye without the lower lid. It tells the musician to rest and pause for an indefinite period of time. You don't count as you would with a rest mark; you just "pause and be still for a little while" until the conductor senses it is time to continue. I now use the fermata, a call to just "be still a minute," as a reminder in my own life and for those I am trying to help detoxify their success.

Renowned poet T. S. Eliot wrote, "Except for the point, the still point, telling musicians to pause, there would be no dance, and there is only the dance."[36] It is the pauses in life that allow us to calm down and get our attention back. The dance of life is made more joyfully serene when we learn to "hold it a moment"—or two or three—so we can pay attention when we return to the dance. One of the mortals group members said, "I think what cancer does is make you take pause. Even though it's a horrendous struggle, it is also a strange kind of a long, reflective rest. You're taken out of the game a while, and you get to watch it from a totally different perspective. It would have been nice if I would have paused more on my own. If I get the chance, I will from now on."

Thomas Jefferson pointed out, "It is neither wealth nor splendor, but tranquility and occupation, which give happiness."[37] We seem to have gotten the occupation part of Jefferson's equation done pretty well; it's the serenity part that is still giving us trouble. If we cannot be content, it is difficult to feel calm. If we cannot calm down, we can't seem to pay enough attention to what makes us content. Success detoxification is an all-or-none proposition.

I used to find plane rides a wonderful opportunity to pause—they afforded some calm time for slow, uninterrupted thinking. Over the last decade, however, the toxicity of success has spilled over to the airlines. Human resources consultant Freada Klein writes, "A plane ride is no longer time to work quietly or read the trashy novel. It's time to be scheduled and invaded."[38] I now hear the clicking of computer keys, dictation into tape recorders, the clatter of business talk, and passengers talking on phones. When I finally am able to find a little peace and quiet, I am rousted from my serenity by a seat back being slammed into my face. Then when the plane does land, the race is on: Luggage is torn from the overhead compartments and passengers stand bent over like sprinters waiting for the starting gun.

Author Stephen Bertman writes, "The power of now replaced the long-term with the short-term, duration with immediacy, permanence with transience, memory with sensation, insight with impulse."[39] It is up to us to pause and be still, but we have to take back control of our hurried brain to do it.

To put fermata in your life, stop whatever you're doing, take a deep breath, and just wait a moment. "How long?" is the first question I'm asked by the toxically successful. "You'll know how long," I always answer. You can try the pause technique right now. At the end of this paragraph, rest this book on your lap, close your eyes, take a deep breath, and just "be" for a moment.

Your brain will resist. It will keep asking, "Just how long is a moment?" and keep sending thoughts racing to your mind, but just ignore them for a while as you would an overdemanding and spoiled child. When you feel ready, pick up the book and begin reading again if you wish. Of course, you may just want to close the book and think a while, so don't miss the chance. Fermatas are indefinite. You will sense when you have paused long enough to let serenity set in and then you can, as we say in Hawai'i, *ho'omakahou* (ho-oh-ma-ka-ho)—begin again.

Ten Life Tenderizers: Cures for Modern Motion Sickness

The perpetual mental motion of toxic success results in a form of motion sickness, the feeling of being constantly mentally buffeted about by the turbulence of daily pressures. While you have read that reducing this motion sickness is primarily a matter of thinking differently about how and why you live and work, my patients and the winners group asked for "behavioral prescriptions" to help get them started and keep their attentions on a calmer way of living. One man in the winners group said, "You can't get me detoxed without giving me something to do. I know I have to think differently, but can't you at least give some more things to try that will help me remember to calm down my thinking? Just a few gimmicks, that's all I ask."

Follwoing are ten "motion sickness cures" that I have offered to patients over the last decades of my clinical work and research on toxic success. In the spirit of *po'okela*, I have given silly names to each of the ten suggestions in an attempt to get your attention away from the brain's dependence on its toxic success mode. Even if you can't really do these silly suggestions, at least discuss them with your spouse, family, or friends to initiate the consideration of why these ideas may have come to seem so silly in the first place. As the patches behind the ears or the magnets around the wrists that people use to reduce seasickness are not really cures for the problem, they do provide a way of thinking that may help reduce it.

1. **Queue down.** See long lines not as aggravations but as invitations to calm down. "Queue down" (get in line) by looking for the longest, slowest-moving line and get in it. Strike up a conversation with one of your line-mates who is likely to be a fellow sufferer of toxic suc-

, cess. Try to actually enjoy the forced delay in your typically rapid forward motion.

2. **Reduce "wrist watching."** Leave your watch in your pocket or purse. This will at least delay the "wrist watching" reflex associated with constant clock watching.

3. **Stop dancing the hurrier's hustle.** Pretend you have a "life stress fracture" that makes it impossible for you to walk fast. Consider replacing the modern dance of the "hurrier's hustle" with strolling, ambling, sauntering, and meandering. To calm it down, take your brain out for a long stroll.

4. **Soak, don't shower.** Replace the quick shower with the long soak. Warm baths can lower your blood pressure, expand the vessels throughout your body and around your heart, and provide a place to get away from it all. Take a leisurely warm bath with the lights out and practice ignoring the pestering of your hyperactive brain.

5. **Have a "detox dinner."** Have at least one "detox dinner" a week. Eat slowly with the rules that no electronic intrusion will be allowed to pester your mealtime, no one leaves the table until everyone is finished eating, everyone helps clean up, no cell phones or pagers are allowed, and no one answers the phone. Whatever it is, it can wait.

6. **Pause many moments.** Experience a life fermata. Pause several times during the day for just a moment, take a deep breath, and sigh out loud as your exhale. If you practice this a while, you will become a habitual pauser and your rushed brain will begin to get the message that it is not always the timekeeper of your life. A good time to practice this is when you are waiting for an elevator.

7. **Call in "well."** Once every month or so when you wake up feeling remarkably good, call work and tell them you are just too well to work today. Sit around, do nothing, and just "be home." Fake a cold by doing what you might do if you really had a very bad cold or flu. Indulge yourself. Lie on the couch, cover up, take the time to read the classic book you have never had time to get to, and snack to your heart's delight.

269

8. **Correspond instead of "electrond."** Once a month, handwrite a long letter to a friend or family member. Take your time, write slowly, and try to remember your elementary school days when penmanship mattered. Stamp and mail it; don't fax or e-mail it.

9. **Drive quietly.** Drive as if there was an egg between your foot and the accelerator and try to keep your engine quiet rather than roaring. Drive the speed limit, stay in the slow lane, and come to a complete stop at all stop signs. Read them as "STOP STRESSING YOUR-SELF" signs or see them as a fermata. (Be careful with this suggestion. You are surrounded by toxic succeeders who are quick to anger when they encounter someone actually following the traffic laws.)

10. **Day pray.** Data shows that even those who call themselves atheists sometimes pray. Don't wait until you feel you need to pray or until bedtime. Stop during the day, bow your head, and try a "receptive prayer." Instead of "saying a prayer" to a higher power, try listening for that power. Relax, take a deep breath, be open to the sacred signals all around you, and ask yourself, "Do I deserve God's faith in me?" and "Are my ancestors, who are always watching, proud of how I am living, what's on my mind, and what's in my heart?" When you "hear" the answer to these two questions, softly say the word *mahalo* (ma-ha-low)—Hawaiian for "thank you." The Hawaiian language's emphasis of saying every syllable and the sound of the syllables can be relaxing in itself. Having this attitude of gratitude is also good for your mind, body, and soul.

Giving Too Much To Gain Too Little

If we fail to calm down, we are in danger of becoming like the tree in poet Shel Silverstein's classic story *The Giving Tree*. We end up feeling as if we are constantly being taken from, until we are left feeling exhausted and—much like the "giving tree's" dead and totally used-up stump—lifeless and used up.[40]

I suggest as a part of your detoxification program that you sit somewhere quiet and read *The Giving Tree* out loud to yourself. Read it slowly and pause after each page to reflect on its lessons as they might apply to living, loving, and working. There is a special message for toxic success sufferers about the dangers of not being able to say no and the risks of giving too much, too fast, and for too long to too many, only to discover, too late, that it has all been for much too little.

CHAPTER TWELVE

Connecting Always: Remembering "And"

> Human life and humanity come into being
> in genuine meetings.
>
> —*Martin Buber*

"I had a feeling of oneness with the universe."

"I experienced the palpable presence of God."

"I lost all awareness of where or who I was."

"It was like I was connected with everyone and everything."

"I lost all sense of who and where I was and just had this profound sense of timelessness and infinity."

"It felt like I was part of the cosmos with no sense of where I ended and it began."

These are not the words of people high on drugs. They are the words of six of the winners I interviewed for this book. They were each describing their feelings when they focused their attention completely and totally on something as simple as a cloud, their child's face, or their own breath. They all said that something miraculous had happened, causing them to feel what one of them described as "the overwhelming peace of total connection."

Perhaps the most damning mistake sufferers of TSS make is to assume that a sense of personal success and of standing out above the crowd will lead to the ultimate feeling of satisfaction. As Olympian Matt Biondi points out in his foreword to this book, the sweetest feeling of leading a successful life results not from distinguishing our self but from replacing *self*-consciousness with *us*-consciousness. A sense of the miraculous overwhelms us when we experience a blurring of the boundaries of the self, lose all sense of our individual concerns and fears, and are freed from the brain's illusion of the boundaries of body, time, and space. It is at these times that we are no longer concerned about what we want because we have all we could ever need, the sense of sacred connection.

Humans have always searched for the feeling of being connected with a higher power. Even the SIN, or self-interest norm, of Western society has not dimmed our longing to connect beyond time and space with something that transcends what we call the real world. No matter how cynical and individually competitive we have become, few of us would consider ourselves to have led a truly successful life unless we have attained some sense of spiritual meaning and connection in our life.

The Neurobiology of Selflessness

The new science of neurotheology demonstrates that it is our neurobiology that compels this urge. We are wired to lose all sense of self and to feel connected with everything and everyone beyond time and space. Something within us doesn't want to be as selfish and disconnected as we behave most of the days of our lives. No matter how self-assured and independent we try to be, our need to feel connected will not go away. Neurotheology shows that it is constantly on our minds.

Neurotheology is the study of the neurobiology of religion and spiritual experiences.[1] It examines how the brain works when it is paying intense attention. When we focus our attention, SPECT (single photon emission computed tomography) shows the front of the brain lighting up and the upper back going dark. When this happens, the part of our brain that tells us where our self ends shuts down. This frees what some researchers call "the God spot" to sense a deeper reality and an inspiringly emotional connection with something profoundly more meaningful and important than the self.

Neurotheology is showing that we are neurologically wired to seek connection with what matters most in our life, a sense of profound one-ness with everyone and everything. As two pioneers in neurotheology, Drs. Andrew Newberg and Eugene D'Aquili, write, "As long as our brains are arranged the way they are, as long as our minds are capable of sens-ing this deeper reality, spirituality will continue to shape the human experience, and God, however we define that majestic, mysterious con-cept, will not go away."[2]

It is beyond the scope of this book to go into details about the findings from neurotheology. In essence, it is proving that when we pay focused and total attention to something simple and calming, we lose our sense of self. We are no longer aware of where our body ends and begins or a boundary between the past and future. Brain scans show when the areas of our brain associated with deep and focused attention are operating, the areas where our sense of self and time fall silent. As a result, we feel we are one with everything and experience a sense of timelessness.

Ask anyone who has fallen in love what it feels like, and they will tell you that the feeling is also one of loss of self and total merging with the other person. When we are with someone we love, time seems to stand still. This happens because someone becomes the "apple of our eye," the focus of our total and undivided attention. I suggest that sweet success is first and fore-most the experience of loss of self and freedom from the constraints of time and self-protection and enhancement. It is the ultimate reward for having come back to life and paid our full attention to some small, simple, but sa-cred part of it.

In addition to neurotheology, there are two other sciences that document our drive to be "us" more than "me." You read earlier about the field called energy cardiology, which shows that our heart can literally think, feel, and connect with other hearts.[3] Careful studies of the energy of the heart show that it is capable of falling into synchronization with other hearts and being calmed by that connection. It shows that our heart energy can be measured several feet from our body and can blend with the energy of another heart to form a heart-to-heart bond. As cardiologist Dean Ornish writes, "The heart is a pump that needs to be addressed on a physical level, but our hearts are more than just pumps. We also have an emotional heart, a psychological heart, and a spiritual heart."[4]

You have already read about the findings from the field of PNI (psychoneuroimmunolgy) that show how living for affiliation more than power leads to a healthier immune system. Combining what scientists are learning about our brain, heart, and immune system, we have plenty of evidence that connection is not just a popular psychology buzzword—whether or not we end up with a sweetly successful and healthy life depends on it.

There are two assumptions embraced by the modern world that violate the principle of connection and render success toxic. One is that unwavering self-confidence is the way to a successful life. The other is that individual happiness is rightly the primary motivating factor in almost every human act. These assumptions have become so ingrained in our view of what constitutes a successful life that to suggest that their opposites are the way to sweeter, healthier, and more lasting success is a difficult proposition for most people to accept.

As you consider the third component of your success detoxification program, the principle of connecting always, you will have to consider changing your mind about these two false assumptions about success. You will have to be open to considering the possibility that the sweetest success comes with the surrender of selfishness and by seeking to make the world a happier place.

When Self-Assurance Kills

I was afraid to tell him, and it almost resulted in someone's death. In my role as a clinical neuropsychologist at Sinai Hospital of Detroit, I was assisting in a very risky neurosurgery. The surgeon was one of the most respected neurosurgeons in the country. Outside the operating room, he was a mild-mannered, kind man; inside it, he was known for his cockiness and certainty but also for his hot temper when that certainty was challenged. As one nurse warned, "Even when he's wrong, you'd better let him think he's right." He had been known to humiliate other doctors and nurses when they dared question his decisions, and I had never known him to admit a mistake. He would say, "This is my patient and my operating room. Get with it or get out."

We all felt tense during his surgeries, and as a result little things always seemed to be going wrong. (Of course, so-called little things would not seem so small to the patient.) Instruments were dropped, machines were bumped, and we behaved like frightened children. He was, after all, certain that he was always right and had the reputation that made challenging him a serious career mistake.

My job was to speak with the patient to help her remain calm and to help the surgeon map the areas of the brain. I had done this dozens of times before, but this time I noticed that the heart monitor seemed to indicate an irregular heartbeat. No one was saying anything, so I looked at the eyes of the anesthesiologist. He raised his eyebrows with a "not me" look. I looked at the resident and the nurses, and they looked at the monitor, then at the surgeon, and back at me again with the "You tell him, we're not" look.

I know very little about cardiology and was not at all sure anything serious was wrong, but I wanted to ask just in case. Yet I was afraid that if I did I risked not only humiliation but might put the patient at risk by upsetting her surgeon. I kept hoping the monitor would settle down, but it did not. Finally, summoning all the courage I could muster, I said softly, "Doctor, I'd like to learn more about this procedure. Could you tell me if that kind of heart rhythm is characteristic of patients at this point in the operation?" The surgeon stopped working, lowered his arms in disgust, and glared at me. "Do I have your permission to go ahead, or do you want to take over?" he asked. Shaking his head in disgust, he went back to work.

A few moments later, I saw him looking intensely at the heart monitor. He peered over his mask, and I could see concern in his eyes. He stopped work and whispered something to the anesthesiologist. He, in turn, whispered something to a nurse, and she moved quickly to the crash cart that held the emergency resuscitation equipment. At that moment, the patient's heart stopped.

After several tries, the woman's heart was finally jolted back to life. The surgery was completed and nothing more was said. The next day, when I visited the patient, she was doing fine—the procedure had been a success. As I walked from her room, one of the nurses called me aside. "You might have saved that woman's life," she said. "I heard about it from the nurses. He was completely missing the problem. If you hadn't called it to his attention, things could have been much worse."

Rather than feeling proud, I felt ashamed. I had allowed myself to be intimidated by the "right man syndrome" orientation of the toxically successful, a self-certainty and independent view of success. My distance from this skilled but arrogant surgeon could have been lethal.

The Right Man

The "right man syndrome" is a way of seeing the world that was first described by science fiction writer A. E. Van Vogt and popularized later by British writer Colin Wilson.[5] It refers to a way of individualistic thinking that includes high-level self-assurance and certainty, to the point of intimidating arrogance and the almost manic need to feel that one's actions are justified, "right," and the only correct way to deal with the world.[6] The masculine pronoun is used with this syndrome because it is almost always found in men, but "right women" can also show this same egocentric confidence.

Confidence in those in positions of leadership and high responsibility is crucial, but the norm of independent self-assurance can also result in a dangerous distancing from those being led and in an intimidation that prevents necessary sharing and input. Right men are so sure they know, that they don't know when they don't. Even though I had had years of training and clinical experience as a neuropsychologist and was chief of the psychiatric outpatient clinic at the same hospital where the always-right surgeon practiced, I had been afraid to speak up. I felt an insurmountable distance from him and was sure I must be wrong because he—and almost everyone else— was so sure he was right.

This independent "self-assurance norm" is not only found in medicine. It has become the norm for achieving and demonstrating one's success in most of American life. From boardrooms to classrooms to the cabinet room in the White House, it is assumed that success is related to showing a supreme self-confidence that can impose a potentially destructive distance between those identified as highly successful and those from whom they might learn.

There are many other examples of the negative impact of the detached, distancing, and intimidating orientation that is too often the expected way to show that we are highly successful. Right men tend to receive most of the money, promotions, status, and praise in today's world. Many of our CEOs, generals, senators, and airline captains have become right men.

In one case, hundreds were killed in the crash of a commercial airliner that ran out of fuel while circling in wait of an opening in the weather to allow landing. The plane had been told to circle the airport, and during the long delay, the cockpit crew noticed the fuel was running dangerously low. Crew that survived reported that they had all heard of the captain's reputation as not dealing gracefully with any hint that he might be wrong. They had assumed he knew what he was doing, that he was aware of the fuel problem, and that he would somehow deal with it. Right men cause fearful deference, and no cockpit crew member would question the captain's judgment because, as one crew member put it, "He always seemed so sure he was right. After all, he was one of the most successful captains in the airline, and he made sure anyone who worked with him knew it." His arrogant self-certainty, and the distance it created between his crew and him, resulted in the tragedy of hundreds of lost lives.

In the *po'okela* model of excellence, uncertainty and selflessness are keys to success. Listening to others, trusting them and how and what they think, and being able to gracefully and without defensiveness reflect on what others have to say and offer are seen as fundamental skills for those who would be successful. Once again the ancient wisdom of a Chinese proverb provides insight into TSS. It says, "To be uncertain is to be uncomfortable, but to be certain is to be ridiculous."

While there is lip service given to "teamwork" in the Western way to success (i.e., "There is no *I* in the word *team*," etc.), total self-confidence is typically seen as a sure sign that someone has achieved a high level of success. In a very apt quote related to overcoming the arrogance of self-certainty, suspense novelist Graham Greene wrote, "When we are not sure, we are alive."[7]

As a part of your detoxification process, I suggest you take the following survey. I used it with my patients and the winners group to help them assess the level to which they had bought into the toxicity of the SIN orientation to success.

THE RIGHT MAN SURVEY

Because it is not easy for right men to see the impact of how they act, I suggest you have someone who knows you very well, lives with you, or works closely with you answer the following questions about you. If you can't find such a person, answer the following questions based on how you think that person would score you.

5 = That's me
4 = A lot like me
3 = Somewhat like me
2 = Not too much like me
1 = Only rarely like me
0 = Not at all like me

1._____People would say that I'm quarrelsome, contrary, and contentious.

2._____I'm smarter than most people.

3._____I feel like a last holdout in a world populated by dopes.

4._____If people would only listen to me, they would see that my view of things is the right view.

5._____I very seldom change my mind because I usually had it right in the first place.

6._____I get bored when other people are sharing their ideas and points of view.

7._____I can get more done faster and more efficiently by working alone. Other people's input only slows me down and distracts me.

8._____I hate the "touchy feely" approach to things and think that most of what they call alternative or complementary approaches to health and healing are New-Age gimmicks with no research to substantiate them.

9._____I pretend to be tolerant, but I really feel that most people do not have much to say or offer that will change my mind about important things.

10._____I can tell if a person is smart just by looking at her or him or hearing them talk for a few minutes.

11._____I feel besieged by hordes of nuts with weird ideas.

12._____I respect and take more seriously those persons in a role of authority, status, and of high rank or prestige than I do those without such status.

13._____I don't think you need a committee. I think you should make up your mind, stop asking others for approval, take personal responsibility, stop talking and thinking, and just do it.

14._____Slow-thinking and slow-talking people drive me nuts.

15._____If I want to, I can easily intimidate others with my intelligence and win any argument.

16._____If people would only listen more to my ideas, they would see that I'm right.

17._____My true genius is unappreciated while other people who don't deserve it seem to get all the credit and respect.

18._____I get frustrated just being around dumb people.

19._____I don't care what they say "the research says." I just use my own common sense.

20._____If more people thought like I do, the world would be a much better place.

_____ TOTAL SCORE

The average winners group score on the Right Man Survey was 79. The average score in my Hawaiian control group was 46. In the *po'okela* value of *ha'aha'a* (ha-ah-ha-ah), modest, vulnerable humbleness is central to success Hawaiian style because this culture, as many indigenous cultures, rejects the SIN of modern society.

How Did Self-Interest Become Normal?

Since the publication of Machiavelli's *The Prince* in 1513 and Thomas Hobbes's *Leviathan* in 1651, self-interest and the pursuit of individual happiness became primary human motives.[8] Success in life has evolved to be almost exclusively associated with self-fulfillment and assertiveness. Euro-American cultures assume that personal happiness is the ultimate state of success, that self-interest is only natural and almost undeniable, and that we are primarily motivated to make ourselves happy. Even charitable work or donations are seen as motivated by self-interest because behaving this way is seen as making the giver happier as an individual.

Psychologist Dale T. Miller suggests that the self-interest norm has become a self-fulfilling prophecy.[9] He points out that we often act and speak from the perspective of the "right man, self-assertive, and self-interest" perspective because we have come to believe that to do otherwise is to "violate a powerful descriptive and prescriptive expectation."[10] The institutions that award the signs of success are based on this "self-righteousness" approach to success, and they end up, as pointed out by psychologist Barry Schwartz, fostering and rewarding the very behavior their structure and core assumption presuppose occurs necessarily and naturally.[11] "I hire people who come across as confident and self-assured," said one of the winners, the owner of several car dealerships. "If you want to join us and move up, you have to come to the table sure of yourself. We don't have time to wait for our people to become confident. We want them to learn, but we want them to reek with confidence."

As you move toward the end of your detox program, you have another important choice to make between toxic or sweet success. Will you follow the norm of materialistic self-interest and personal enhancement or, as in the *po'okela* model, live and work by what might be called your "principles of passion," doing and thinking in terms of what is the good, sharing, cautious, and connected way of living and working?

Psychologist Jerome Kagan writes that "people treat self-interest as a natural law and because they believe they should not violate a natural law, they try to obey it."[12] The late twentieth-century triumph of capitalism and free enterprise predicated on self-interest, a price on everything, and obligation to others as subservient to the bottom line has flourished as a celebration of SIN. But we have a choice: Through our attention we can decide what is on our mind, and we can elect to see the world through less selfish eyes. Doing so is the path to sweet success.

While chronic self-doubt and persistently low self-esteem are not conducive to success and well-being in any situation, the current Euro-American overemphasis on self-interest and confidence has resulted in a sadness and loneliness that often accompany the high-level success attained by these motives. It is difficult to be "with" people when we are busy trying to exert control "over" them. We have been told that self-accomplishment will make us happy and that doing those things that bring us personal happiness is the way to a successful life, but this can be a very toxic assumption.

Is Happiness All It's Cracked Up to Be?

"I don't think I have ever been happier in my life," said a man in the winners group. "And for some reason, happiness has not turned out to be all it's cracked up to be. I was so sure I was on the right track, but there seems to be something missing. I can't really tell you what it is, and I'm not miserable or anything like that, but I still feel one brick short of a full load." The tyranny of choice you read about in chapter 11 is often accompanied by a tyranny of the pursuit of happiness that can, as it seems to have done for this man, rob success of its sweetness.

We not only seem to feel we have a constitutional right to be happy, we feel that we have an obligation to our self to be happy. The United States Constitution does not guarantee a right to happiness, but it does protect the right to pursue it, and most of us are taking full advantage of our constitutional right to go after all the happiness we can. Unfortunately, research shows that happiness has serious limitations as a primary human motive.

Is success defined by the amount of individual happiness we have managed to claim for ourselves? If self- happiness is so natural, why does it seem that we are unhappy at least as often, if not more often, as we feel very happy? Experiencing sweet success requires accepting unhappiness as being as natural and necessary as happiness. As one of my patients joked after completing his success detox program, "I think I've got it now. Sweet success is being as happy with being unhappy as you are happy being happy."

Psychologist Mihaly Csikszentmihalyi suggests that unhappiness serves an important evolutionary survival value.[13] He writes, "By dwelling on unpleasant possibilities, we will be more alert and poised to respond to dangerous events that could happen at any time."[14] This is another reason why the "constantly positive attitude" of the popular psychology of success can be counterproductive. Enlightened pessimism has its place.

Sweet success does not mean always being or feeling individually happy. It derives from the capacity to fully and deeply share all the ups and downs of life with another person. It is doing things not to make oneself happy, but because doing them feels like the right thing to do in the broad context of general well-being.

Our success will always be at least a little toxic if we assume that we

283

must always be out there looking for more and more individual happiness and so afraid of a dose of unhappiness that we seek to rid ourselves of any of it as quickly as we can. If we consider individual happiness the natural law of life, we will do almost anything to rid ourselves of unhappiness. We may try to shop it away or to seek some form of intense stimulation or gratification such as drugs, a loud party, or a violent film that can overwhelm and distract us from it.

We go to counselors or therapists to rid ourselves of any degree of unhappiness or healers who mistakenly think that feeling really good is the only sign of health, but healthy success is not the absence of unhappiness. We need our suffering as much as our joy. If we are addicted to the pursuit of happiness, we lose sight of our built-in and essential sense of unhappiness that gives us our mental resilience and spiritual toughness, and, as there is no day without night, gives our happiest times perspective and meaning.

Not Everyone "Just Wants to Be Happy"

In a form of "bliss bartering," Westerners often assume that we should do things to make us happy, but many other cultures, such as the one that gave birth to *po'okela*, consider happiness only one of many possible and desirable emotions. In some cultures, one marries, works, and loves not to make oneself happy but because these things are considered the right things to do. In the *po'okela* model, the primary motivation is called *pono*—the way things are supposed to be and how things are supposed to be aligned in life as passed down through generations. Instead of asking, "What do I feel like doing?" the *po'okela* question is, "How will what I would like to do make others feel?"

"Happiness is everyone's first priority," said the success seminar leader. "It's simple. We all just want to be happy. All we really want out of our life is to lead the good life, and a good life is a happy life." I was sitting with our *hālau* (dancers) waiting for our turn to present about the *po'okela* model of success, and we were taken aback by the woman's statement. "Happiness isn't my first priority," said Mapu, a Hawaiian *kumu hula* (teacher of *hula*). "My priority is to honor my *'aumakua* [ancestors], the *'āina* [land], the gods, and *ke Akua* [God]. My priority is to make things *pono* [right]." In the *po'okela* model of success modeled by Mapu, calm, giving, respectful behavior toward others and the world is the highest priority and the *pono,* or right, way to live, whether or not it always makes the individual person happy.

The idea that everyone is motivated by the need for self-happiness has become so much a part of the Euro-American mind that it explains away motivations and values such as Mapu's and other indigenous people's by saying that their priority to please their ancestors is only due to the fact that it makes them individually happy to do so. This is not much different from saying that people seek to be happy so they can then better honor their ancestors, but personal happiness and self-interest are simply not *po'okela* values for an excellent life.

Psychologist Aaron Ahuvia wrote, "Personal happiness is just one of many possible goals that may underlie human action."[15] Cross-cultural research shows that valuing personal and individualistic happiness in life is strong in the affluent societies of the West but that honoring parents, elders, and ancestors and being seen as a calm, modest, sharing, contributing member of the social group are strong in collectivist or connection-oriented cultures.[16] Take some time to reflect on what may be, to your Western-biased mind, the accepted normalcy of self-happiness and consider whether it is really the most effective motive for having a joyful and blissful life.

Doing the Right Thing

"It's strange that the worst time in my life was also one of the best," said a man in the winners group. "We were as poor as church mice, my wife was having a terrible pregnancy with all kinds of complications, my father had just died, and my job was hanging by a thread. We cried and were miserable, but when I look back on that time, the unhappiness we shared drew us together in a love that I'm not sure we would have ever really known without the unhappiness. My advice is to go ahead and enjoy being unhappy but just be sure you have someone to be miserable with. When life is horrible, you had better hook up."

If you are going to consider a successful life as one of a sense of almost constant self-happiness, you are in for disappointment. The contentment of sweet success is marked by the degree to which one shares all aspects of living and not just the high and happy times. It comes with the sense that one is doing what's right and is able to share that feeling with those who matter most.

285

Doing "the right thing" in order to make oneself happy is different from doing the right thing because it is the right thing to do.[17] The right thing to do is usually the thing that makes everyone feel successful, and this last of the three chapters on detoxifying your success asks you to consider the idea that unshared success is always toxic. If you think, "I've made it," it is time you asked, "And how many people feel they, too, have made it with me?" It is time to ask yourself the most important question of all in your detox program: "Are my most intimate relationships as successful as I am or am I trying to be?" Put more simply, is your life a monologue or in dialogue?

Are You Monological or Dialogical?

Toxic success is a "me" thing, but sweet success is a matter of "us." I am not speaking just of how we act toward others but of how we think about our interactions with them—the first and foremost thing on our mind and our primary way of processing what happens to us in our daily living.

As you read above, the Western model of success tends toward individualism and an instrumental or "using" orientation toward people, things, and events. This is what psychologists call a "monological" way of thinking, a "me first" and almost automatic thought process that begins with the pronoun *I*.[18] Eastern and Polynesian cultures emphasize a more collectivist orientation and a more formative, dynamic, and sensitive view of the "person-other" boundary, what psychologist Ian Choi describes as "rather porous and ill-defined."[19] To find the contentment of sweet success, you have to make sure your brain is speaking not in monologue but dialogue.

As in the case of the right man complex, monological thinking tends to distance persons from the situations they are in by emphasizing what psychologist Edward E. Sampson describes as "sharply drawn person-other boundaries and producing a person-other relationship . . . referred to as independent."[20] Euro-American cultures define their most successful people as being "sharp" and well-defined individualists able to master and manage the distinct outside world of tools, machines, and people. They are "stand outs," not "stand withs," who are able to manipulate the world and other people to their own advantage.

Two timelines seem to have been converging for decades: Our machines seem to be becoming more and more human, and we humans seem to be becoming more and more like machines. Computers can respond to our voices, talk to us, and invite us into their virtual but artificial world with amazing similarities to the real one. At the same time, the machines we are creating are making up our minds for us. They are influencing more and more how we think, live, work, and love. We digitalize almost everything, and even people become events to be managed or data to be processed. As one winner pointed out, "You can't sit in front of a computer for hours a day and not start to think like one. You start to think in short spurts of enter, select, save, delete, cut, paste, send, and on and on. You become a fast thinker getting data, deciding, and acting."

In contrast to the increasingly mechanized Western mind, the more settled agricultural cultures, such as the Eastern and Polynesian, embrace strong and established roots to living systems rather than to mechanical things. This systemic mind-set is related to their interactive and interpersonal cognition. They think like gardeners rather than mechanics, and because cooperation is stressed over competition and combination over self-interest, they not only devalue but also distrust and even fear the SIN-ing, distinct individualist intent on getting whatever he or she needs to be successful.

To be sweetly successful, I suggest you consider mentally looking deeply within yourself to find your indigenous mind, where "us" is much more valued than "me" and humble uncertainty replaces self-righteousness. Sweet success is dialogical and begins with the assumption that, as philosopher Martin Oppenheim wrote, "the deepest things in life are gifts from others."[21] It is awakening in the morning with the thought "How are we today?" rather than "What do I have to do today?"

Philosopher Martin Buber wrote, "What is peculiarly characteristic of the human world is, above all, that something takes place between one being and another. . . . I call this sphere . . . the sphere of between. . . . It is a primal category of human reality."[22] This is the sphere of life lacking in many toxically successful people. Count the personal pronouns they use daily, and you will see how they are thinking about life, a "self sphere" that neglects the "and."

Unlike the toxic success mind-set, which stresses quick categorization to facilitate fast problem solving, sweet success is much more contemplative. It involves taking plenty of time to think and reflect about the particular uniqueness of the person and events we encounter. It is time-consuming to think in dialogue because it involves patience, consideration, and mentally messing things up a bit and slowing things down by always wondering, "What about us?" No intelligence test asks, "How would the two of you solve this problem?" The emphasis is on an "I" quotient, an IQ based on having the skills, quick thinking, and knowledge to be self-sufficient, assertive, and personally happy.

"Self-sphere," or selfish, thinking is often an unconscious process. The toxically successful are not usually obnoxious people always pushing themselves on others and intentionally dominating their lives. They can come across as kind, bright, and very nice people. They are not aware that they are thinking almost always in monologue or, as Buber describes, "living the life of the monologue . . . never aware of the other as something that is absolutely not himself."[23]

Looking into the Minds of Successful People

Readers of autobiographies may notice that they often seem to be written in a "first person" orientation that reflects that the author is in full command and control of his or her life. They tend to be "I" and not "us" oriented, thus neglecting the points of view of the hundreds or perhaps thousands who have been coauthors of the story of their life. When I watch highly successful people being honored at business meetings, I hear their individual accomplishments listed in great detail. When they come to the podium to accept their award, their spouse and family often trail them. They say that, first and foremost, they owe their success to their family, and everyone applauds, but the message is still in monologue. The family appears to be another instrument used as a means to their personal success. They may share the tangible fruits of that success with their family, but seldom what every spouse and family member of every winner I interviewed said they wanted most: their full and undivided daily attention.

A recent national survey asked people if they agreed or disagreed with the statement "I believe it is possible in America to pretty much be who you want to be."[24] Eighty-five percent agreed. Less than half of those surveyed thought that their parents' income, race, and education played any significant role in whether or not one becomes successful.

Clearly, the monologue of toxic success and its John Henry–like mantra that the powerful, competitive, self-assertive, self-confident individual can do almost anything he or she sets her mind to continues to be on the minds of most Americans. The "land of opportunity" that attracted and still attracts so many to its shores has become the land of individualistic pursuit of more and more. Being whom we want to be as individuals and becoming all we can be takes precedence over all of us working together for a purpose greater than the individual self. In the world of toxic success, the word *and* is used more to join together a list of many things to do in order to become successful than it is to refer to a lovingly connective, dialogical way of thinking about living and working.

As you work your way through this success detoxification program, it is not necessary to choose between being a strong, independent, well-bounded person and surrendering to the role of a faceless person merged with the crowd. The challenge is to change your mind to instinctively think, "What about us?" rather than, "What's in this for me?" and to become more aware of the role of relationship and interdependence in all facets of your life. To paraphrase president John Kennedy, sweet success happens when we think not what's in it for us but what we're putting into life for all of us. Anthropologist Michael Carrithers writes that people do not just live in their relations but create and are created by their relationships in order to live.[25] The norm of self-interest neglects this fact.

The Giggle Factor

One of the most profound experiences of the sense of connection that is so much a part of sweet success is to have the capacity to easily share a hardy, spontaneous laugh. Laughter is an undeniably social phenomenon and no matter how much you try to force yourself to laugh, it still sounds "forced." Researchers are still trying to explain why we laugh, and they have learned that it seems to be associated with a combination of surprise and connection.[26] Because the toxically successful are in too much control to be surprised very often and value their independence more than interdependence, they suffer from giggle deficiency. Reporting on the current research on laughter, *Newsweek* magazine's Sharon Begley writes, "Laughter seems to signal an attempt to ingratiate oneself. . . . People in power seldom giggle."[27]

289

In his analysis of "right men," physician Larry Dossey writes that one of their most striking features is their "truculent, irascible attitude. . . . If there is a gene for jocularity, they are missing it."[28] Over the several years I have been meeting with the very highly successful, I have noted this same characteristic. While they may laugh, they usually do so more socially and as a gesture or announcement than what seems to be a genuine, hardy, and helpless guffaw in a sudden realization that, in the final analysis, almost nothing is as ever as serious and as important as it seems. We laugh the hardest when we realize that everyone we deal with is a fool and so are we.

Now, laughter does not always indicate something funny. The Columbine High School killers laughed as they slaughtered their classmates, and we laugh nervously when we are frightened or embarrassed. But when we allow ourselves to admit a common frailty or shared silliness, our heartfelt, humble, and sincere laughter becomes contagious and helps us connect with others.

Sweet success requires not taking success or ourselves too seriously. No matter how much tofu we eat or how far or fast we jog, we can't under-eat or outrun the fact that life is a sexually transmitted terminal condition.[29] When we laugh hard with someone else, we are acknowledging that, in the overall scheme of things, most things are no big deal.

Psychologist Waleed Salameh writes, "There is, in fact, a powerful potential for self-liberation in 'it doesn't matter.' The psychological bonbons associated with it are feelings of energy, reduced oppressiveness, lifting of burdens, and a more humorous life."[30] Adopting an "it doesn't matter" attitude may, at first, seem like apathy or cynicism, but if placed in the context of what matters most in our life, most things really are nowhere near as important as we make them.

So What?

"I've made my ulcer act up, my migraines are back, and my husband and I are ready to kill each other," said the 57-year-old insurance executive. "We have our housewarming party coming up, and we're nowhere near ready. The previous owners left a mess. The closets need to be cleaned out, the floors cleaned and repaired, and I don't see how we can possibly be ready by next month. I really don't know . . ." I stopped her at that point and asked, "So what?" She looked at me angrily and said, "This is what I come to therapy for, to be asked, 'So what?'"

I answered, "That is precisely why you come to therapy—to learn to ask yourself, 'So what?' So what if you're not ready? Most of what you complain about in here doesn't really matter much. You are the one who attaches significance to the events in your life, so if you want to be the world's most efficient closet cleaner and known for your outstanding housewarming parties, that is completely up to you. I just thought there were more important things in your life."

She laughed and said, "Well, I guess you have a point. But these massive closets in the family room are jammed with junk." I asked again, "So what?" She paused, laughed, and said, "I suppose I could just be sure the closet doors stay shut." "Exactly," I answered.

This person who was so concerned about her closets was one of the first members of the winners group and also one of the first highly successful women in the insurance industry. She was bright, attractive, and had a loving husband and family. She had come to therapy because she said, "I'm just not as happy as I think I should be, considering all I've done and have." Almost everything for her had become an obligation and assignment to be accomplished in order to become happy, and she worked tirelessly every day to protect her image as someone who was always right and knew it. In the process, she had forgotten that her relationships with her husband and family were the source of immense joy and pride for her, a source of great pleasure crowded out by the motive of being in full control and constantly "on top of things."

The evil laughter of someone enjoying harming another person is monologic laughing, but healthy laughter is a delightful dialogue that acknowledges that, whatever it is, we are all in this together. To laugh long and hard, one must give up the self-interest motive and join freely in the gleeful fray of the daily disasters to which not even the most successful are immune.

To detoxify your own success, I suggest asking yourself, "So what?" when you feel yourself getting upset or feeling pressured by having to defend your self-righteous SIN-ing. Sometimes the issue you are dealing with may indeed be important, but by asking yourself, "So what?" you can put your distress in a more collective perspective and learn that most of the emotional stress of the hassles you confront on your road to success are self-inflicted by the meaning you attribute to them.

The "ELMMSEH" Diet and Workout Program

You have now read about the three key components for detoxifying your success, made up of the six key words of sweet success: being content, calming down, connecting always. But there is one more connection you have to maintain to detoxify your success: the vital connection with and protection of your body.

You have probably tried several diets. As someone pointed out, diets are for those who are "thick and tired of it." You may have read books that offer dietary and other health suggestions for staying well and dealing with the pressures of the modern world. The *po'okela* model of healthy success offers a slightly different approach. It asserts that wellness is maintaining connection not only with one's ancestors and the land but a loving and tender connection with one's own body systems. "Connecting always" involves treating and respecting your body as a sacred gift, loaned to you for your brief physical experience as a spirit visiting planet paradise, a way to respectfully recycle the vital energy of your ancestors.

The "health" program I provide to my patients is very brief and simple. The current health terrorism has taken all the fun out of staying healthy and causes us to feel we must deny ourselves the simple pleasures of life. It seems that we are expected not only to be highly successful in our work but also in our dieting and exercise. Our health success level is measured in cholesterol points and body poundage, and the "self-interest" motive of being individually healthy is emphasized over a more collectivist view of health that includes a daily life of enjoyable meals with those we love or a leisurely walk with our spouse at sunset. We are taught we will be happier if we are healthy, but the *po'okela* model suggests that nurturing and caring for our body is the *pono,* or right, thing to do in and of itself. It is a way of honoring the physical gift for which we are responsible, not just another set of must-dos to have the look of success, be more self-fulfilled, and live longer.

I called our simple health program for sweet success the "ELMMSEH" program. The winners group used this phrase when they discussed the three suggestions for healthy living that enhance the experience of sweet success. The ELMMSEH program is guaranteed to cause you to lose weight, feel more energetic, and be much more of a joy to live with, the ultimate criterion of the sweetly successful. It worked wonders for my patients and the winners group, and I hope you will give it a try.

ELMMSEH stands for "eat less, move more, and sleep eight hours." There are dozens of diets, but the most current research shows that by eating less and moving more, you are sure to weigh less. You read in part 1 of this book that we have become a sleep-deprived nation, so go to bed as soon after dark as you can, allowing yourself eight hours a night of sleep in the dark without the television humming. While you're at it, cut way down on your television watching; it is one of the most attention-depleting and numbing things you can do and is a barrier to intimate connection.

Novelist Andre Dubus III noticed the hypnotic pale blue glow of television screens he saw coming from American homes. He writes, "And I am told that many family meals are eaten in front of that screen, as well. And perhaps this explains the face of Americans, the eyes that never appear satisfied, at peace with their work or the day God has given them; these people have the eyes of very small children who are forever looking for their next source of distraction, entertainment, or a sweet taste in the mouth."[31] This is not the look of profound attention focused on simple natural beauty that leads to the selfless merging described at the beginning of this chapter. It is the gaze of the unsatisfied looking for more. It is the look of the toxically successful.

That's it—the ELMMSEH health program for sweet success. In addition to avoiding those things you know are deadly, such as smoking, excessive drinking, eating too much of anything, and not wearing a seat belt, ELMMSEH can help you not only feel and look much better but also have more time to pay attention to enjoying and sharing your life.

"Jocularcizing" Your Way to Success

You have read that the cluster of problems associated with what I have called toxic success is a very serious matter, but becoming free of toxic factors is enhanced more by a sense of humor than by a sense of urgency. In *po'okela* style, then, this next opportunity is the silliest idea of all.

Life is difficult or impossible, but if we laugh, it is only difficult. By opening our heart and mind to the funny and often ludicrous nature of life, we can giggle at what we have come to accept as the natural and normal way to think about the world.

To help you detoxify even further, following is the "jocularcize" exercise I use with those coming for help to cope with their success. To enhance the giggle factor in your own life and detoxify your success, sit with someone you enjoy being with, face each other, and "jocularcize." These are some of the stages of laughter modified from the work of physician Clifford C. Kuhn.[32] Go through them, one to the next, and see if you can't learn to "die laughing," to kill off your self-interest motive and overly personal orientation to success.

1. **Smirk:** Gently and slightly turn up the corners of your mouth.

2. **Smile:** Raise the corners of your mouth a little more.

3. **Repeat** the smirk/smile sequence, back and forth, several times. Toxic succeeders tend to frown a lot, so you may have to recondition your smile muscles.

4. **Grin:** Broaden your smile to expose your front teeth. Make sure your jocularcizing partner can see them. (Think of the Jimmy Carter grin.)

5. **Snicker:** Now it is OK to let out a little sound. Just a few short upper-throat exhalations of air are acceptable. Remember, holding back a snicker may result in the retention of gas, so let it go.

6. **Giggle:** Let more short bursts of air come barking out of you. Caution! Giggling is very contagious, so once you start it, others around you may join in, and efforts to suppress your giggling will become more difficult and only lead to more giggling.

7. **Chuckle:** Let your chest become involved now and lower your voice to a more base-sound quality.

8. **Chortle:** Let your whole body become involved and move your torso rhythmically back and forth.

9. **Laugh:** Bark more and out loud. If you tend to be a silent laugher who doesn't make much noise, go ahead and snort when you inhale and make a snoring sound.

10. **Cackle:** Let the pitch of the sound of your laughter go up and tilt your head back and forth.

11. **Guffaw:** Let your arms and legs become involved. Wave them about while continuing to rock back and forth. Caution! A good guffaw can feel so good and relaxing that some of the body's sphincters may let go, causing tears and fluids from other sphincters to be released involuntarily. Do not be alarmed. This is normal "laughter leakage."

12. **Howl, shriek, roar, and convulse:** Caution! These stages are for the advanced laugher only. The volume and frequency of your laughter barking will greatly increase, and you may lose control of your body, fall down laughing, and seem to be having a fit to the laugh-deprived who may be watching you.

13. **Die laughing:** This is a morbid-sounding way of saying that the skilled jocularcizer will "kill off the self" and lose all sense of arrogant certainty and self-assurance. He or she will no longer cling to any sense of dignity and will succumb totally to a feeling of "So what?" and the profound sense of life's innate ridiculousness.

14. **Be reborn:** Allow yourself to fall to the floor, catch your breath, dry your eyes or whatever else may be wet, and be "reborn" to a fresh, less selfish, more joyful view of what constitutes a sweetly success-ful life.

In Hawaiian, the word *ho'omakahou* (ho-o-ma-ka-ho) means to begin fresh again. You can have all you ever really want without giving up what you need most—a content, calm, connected life shared with those you love. If you learn to think in terms of the *po'okela* model of excellence and the values you have been learning about in this book, you may be amazed how it feels to come back to life and how sweetly successful you will feel you have become.

A BEGINNING

It's Just a Matter of Time

Fear not that life shall come to an end but rather
that it shall never have a beginning.

—*John Henry Cardinal Newman*

Do you have a moment? The word *moment* is defined as a vague unit of time stretching from a minute to about an hour. It refers more to the way we experience time than being an actual measure of it. *Moment* is also defined as "of importance" and indicating motion, as in its place in the word *momentum*.[1] I ask that you consider the meaning of the moments in your life and the importance you will attach to them by how you are paying attention to them. I hope you will take a few more moments to consider these last pages not as an ending to a book but the prelude to the rest of your life. I ask that you feel not that you are finishing your reading but that you are trying to sense momentum in beginning your daily effort to reclaim your attention.

As anything important in life, sweet success is only a matter of time. You have read about the factors that can make success toxic and the six words of sweet success: being content, calming down, connecting always. Reclaiming your attention to define and pursue success differently will not happen quickly. your attention may already be wandering off to the next thing you have to do, and you may be suffering from information fatigue because of all the concepts I have presented to you. You have spent years trying to be successful by the modern rules of the game, so it will take time to learn to seek success *po'okela* style—time trying to pay more attention to your life.

Your brain is used to not paying attention to anything for very long. It is convinced that your success depends on fast thinking and multitasking. It may suffer what one of the winners called "pause panic," a disorientation and reactive resistance to trying any of the suggestions presented in the success detox program. It may rebel when it is asked to be content, calm down, and take the time to attend to more important things than e-mail, faxes, and have-to-dos. When this happens, be patient with your brain. Take a moment and let your attention come back to you. As pointed out earlier, it is this constant coming back to life that trains our attention so that it becomes ours again.

Be patient with yourself as you try to incorporate some of the concepts of this book into your own life. You don't need the added pressure of feeling you have to try harder not to feel pressured. Don't expect yourself to make major life changes, only gradual changes of your point of view as to what constitutes a successful life.

Even though I have based most of the detoxification program on the Hawaiian *po'okela* model, I am not suggesting that sweet success in living, loving, and working is a docile, dreamlike mental state enjoyed by working less. As you have read, it is a matter of mentally calming down to feel still even while you must keep going. It's learning the art of attention management but forgivingly allowing your attention to come back whenever it is not going where you choose. Sweet success is not trying to cram more into less time in order to live in more balance. It is not building an entirely new life of constant meditation and carefree disregard for obligations. It is as simple and difficult as learning to pay more attention so that you make the moments of your life count. Rather than trying to make a whole new life, it is awakening to the one you have and realizing that it is truly momentous.

Your Attention, Please

The Hawaiian *po'okela* model is often misunderstood as encouraging less hard work, sitting wistfully on the beach, and being "laid-back," but the opposite is true. It asks that we do more hard and long mental and spiritual work in order to become more aware of the glory of our gift of life. For more than two thousand years, the *po'okela* model of excellence has seen hard work, high productivity, and efficiency as crucial to the collective good. It shares the modern world's concern with the "bottom line" and sees productivity more as a moral obligation and payback of a spiritual and ancestral debt to those who came before us than as a profit-and-loss statement. Dropping out, retreating into a self-meditative state, or disregarding one's obligations are viewed as the most toxic behaviors in which one can engage.

In the ancient *po'okela* view of an excellent life, the feeling of success is like applause. You can't do it with your fists closed or with only one hand—you have to open your hands and clap them together. *Po'okela* success is attending to being open for connection and seeking applause not for yourself but from your ancestors and those who feel you have truly enhanced their lives.

Sweet success requires taking back more of your mental time so that no matter how busy your body is, you can still pay more attention to finding simple, peaceful delight in the most mundane and ordinary of daily life activities. It is the quality of the thoughts going through our mind when we are mowing the lawn, talking to our spouse, talking to a parent or grandparent on the phone, and eating dinner with our kids that determines whether we are toxically or sweetly successful. If we are mentally present for the moments of our life rather than thinking ahead to what is left to do, or back to what we feel we failed to achieve, we are enjoying the sweet success of practical pleasure.

A Zen saying instructs, "After ecstasy, the laundry." Practical pleasure derives from being fully mentally present when we're doing our wash by appreciating the various colors, thinking about those who wear the clothes, feeling the warmth of the water, and enjoying the cyclical process of even this most mundane task of daily life.

You Do Have an Eternity

Thomas Carlyle wrote, "Eternity looks grander and kind if Time grow meaner and more hostile."[2] If we allow ourselves to succumb to the new normality of toxic success, the time of our life can come to be measured in spurts of hard work, frustrations that we cannot work hard or fast enough, and the feeling that we never have enough time. You have read that when we think we don't have enough time, we are really admitting that we are not paying sufficient attention to the time we have.

When we allow our attention to be directed by the SIN of toxic success, something within us seems to tell us that being free of time would be heaven on Earth. Because time is purely a matter of mind, we always have an eternity if we choose to awaken to it.

Po'okela teaches that because we are connected with everything and everyone, everywhere, and are governed by the same universal principles that guide the oceans and the stars, we have a built-in sense of and longing for eternity. This is the same sense that neurotheology shows is wired in to our brain. Sweet success depends on realizing that we all have all the time we will ever have or need if we will only pay attention to the place in time where eternity rests: now.

"Come on, honey," said the man to his wife as they were checking into a hotel on the island of O'ahu. "We don't have an eternity." The man was coming to see me for "detox" for his success and didn't realize that I was sitting in the lobby as he arrived. I thought, *I hope he realizes soon how wrong he is. If he would only pay attention, he would realize that he does have an eternity, if he is not too mentally rushed to know it.*

Spending Your Time

Toxic success is based on the commonly accepted formula that time-management experts call "time allocations." As if time is a quantity that must be controlled, these efficiency experts assume that success and happiness in life depend on working hard and fast to get the maximum individual satisfaction (S) in the shortest amount of time (T). They tell us to maximize the S/T, the ratio of satisfaction received to time required, the new IQ of the toxically successful.[3] The idea of this commonly used formula is that the less T you put into your S, the more successful you are assumed to be.

Time management author and professor Lee Burns of the Department of Human Planning at the University of California writes, "I call the S/T ratio a 'gazinta' (that's quick for T goes into S). Whether it's sleeping, shopping, cooking, working, helping others—whatever it is—each activity has its own gazinta that tells us how much satisfaction the activity yields compared to the time required."[4] Again, the premise of the self-interest motive as the primary motive is accepted as the norm.

The S/T formula also implies that the less time we put into something, the more likely it is that we might be satisfied with that activity as "time well spent." This idea suggests that it might be good time management to spend as little time as possible doing as many things as possible, which is the increasingly popular concept of multitasking. By investing a little time here and a little time there, we think we might hit on some satisfaction somewhere without wasting too much time.

You read earlier that sweet success is less a matter of time management than attention management. While there are many ways of trying to measure attention, such as observing eye movements, studying brain waves, or simply asking people if they are paying attention, attention is invisible. As authors Thomas Davenport and John C. Beck write, "In the absence of precise attention currency, we often use the proxy of time."[5] Many of the winners I interviewed were masters of time management. They had their day planners, palm pilots, and all sorts of alarms to remind them of appointments. Before they came to learn that it is a clear symptom of TSS and attention deficit, they prided themselves on their multitasking as good time management. They did a lot but paid little attention to much of what they were doing.

When I ask you to take a moment, I mean really possess it. Pay full attention to what you are doing and, more importantly, to the people you are with and where you are. If you want to be sweetly successful, be more concerned with managing your attention than your time. In terms of contentment, calmness, and connection, one moment of your full attention is worth hours of mentally multitasking.

The Time Line Illusion

The *po'okela* model of time is based on the seasonal calendar more than the clock. Hawaiian *po'okela* expert George Hu'eu Sanford Kanahele writes that Hawaiian time "is a continuous unfolding of an endless happening. Indeed, the Hawaiian word for time, *manawa*, may convey not the ticking, fleeting intervals measured out by the clock, but the lingering, gentle ebb and flow of water across a tranquil bay."[6]

You have read that the Hawaiian word *mana* refers to sacred, invisible, infinite energy. The word *wa* refers to a unit of measurement. The word *manawa*, then, expresses a sense of time as immeasurable, sacred, and most fully experienced in full awareness of the eternity of the present moment. It also implies putting our *mana,* or our energy, in the form of our attention into the time of our life.

Toxic success is caused, in part, by the Western view of time as linear and moving from past to future—a time line or even a deadline that if missed could be fatal in terms of our potential for success. *Po'okela* time is circular and based on what mystics from many other indigenous cultures refer to as the perpetual reality of the *now*, the endless or everlasting present, and the eternity that can only be represented as a circle and not a straight line. While these descriptions of time may sound mystical, they are entirely in keeping with what quantum physicists have discovered about the nature of what we call time. They know that it is a multidimensional and endless back-and-forth process, profoundly affected by how we invest our attention.

Someone once said that time is what prevents everything from happening at once, but, in fact, everything is happening at once. The continental Western mind soothes itself with the illusion that things exist and events always happen in a forward-moving series. This works well enough to allow us to have some form or order in our daily life, but we must remember that time is our own invention and not real. As we all must do in the modern world in order to keep things synchronized and organized in daily life, ancient Hawaiians lived and worked in linear time, but their mental and spiritual time, the metronome of their minds, was attuned to the cosmic view of everlasting timelessness.

It is the emphasis on time as a quantity running out somewhere in the future rather than being fully in the precious present that contributes to the lethal acceleration of toxic success. To experience sweet success and practice the six words of the detox program you have just read, you don't have to work slower; all you have to do is learn to think a little slower by paying more attention to where you are now, with whom, and why. This is how we find the time for our life.

Two Timing

Sweet success can be experienced by altering the S/T formula to comply with the Hawaiian view of infinite, unhurried, and interdependent time. To find the peaceful contentment and blissful pleasure that comes with paying full attention to the present moment, we need a fellow timekeeper. Sharing our time with a spouse, family member, or close friend can have the effect of slowing time down enough that we are able to pay more attention. Paying attention to and with someone else about whom we care can have the effect of making time seem to stand still.

Sweet success can be experienced by altering the S/T formula. We can double the T and focus our attention on "time together," TT. Slowing down one's thinking by trying to synchronize our pace of thought with someone else can help our brain calm down so it can pay more attention. Not just sharing time but sharing a sense of time with those you love can lead to a different kind of S, the SS, or "shared satisfaction," of a timeless connection, contentment, and calmness that constitutes sweet success. As one *kahuna* put it, "If you pay attention with someone else, you slow down together and allow yourselves to be brought more into the now. There you might experience the grandeur of eternity."

For the toxically successful, risking putting in a lot of mental T and trying to pace one's thinking with another person's will be a hard pill to swallow, especially if their criterion of satisfaction is SIN-ful. If you are willing to go off your own clock and work and love on shared time, you will discover that life offers much more S than the little mental T we are investing in it.

Time Is Not Money

You have read that TSS sufferers wrongly equate time with money. They make it into a currency in which seconds seem like pennies, minutes like dollars, and days like thousands of dollars, and weeks are worth a fortune. "Time is money" is a mantra of the toxically successful. They feel they have a limited chrono-currency account and, as a result, any time spent that is not making money is seen as a waste of time. This places immense pressure on the toxically successful because they live day to day as if every second was going by at a dollar a minute. Sweet success requires that we heed the words of U.S. Chief Justice William Rehnquist when he warned, "When you are young and impecunious, society conditions you to exchange time for money. But as you become more affluent, it is somehow very, very difficult to reverse that process by trading money for time."[7]

Don't Let Time Tell You

We may think we have learned to tell time, but actually we are allowing what we have made of time to tell us how to lead our lives. The next time someone asks you, "Do you have the time?" consider it a profoundly important question. Don't look at your wrist. Look into your heart and mind and wonder about the time of your life. Translate the question to "Are you paying attention to your life?"

To help you be more aware of the time issue in detoxifying your success, here are some "time stopping" (not time saving) suggestions related to each of the three components of your success detoxification program:

- **Being content:** Try standing and staring. Just look out to nowhere in particular and gaze quietly. Try to "just be" rather than "being vigilant" and to be content just staring. Author William Henry Davies described the simple joy of staring when he wrote, "What is this life, if full of care, we have no time to stand and stare?"[8]

- **Calming down:** Find an egg timer or small hourglass that measures two or three minutes. Sit down, close your eyes, turn it over, and open your eyes when you think the sand has passed through the hourglass. If you are like many sufferers of toxic success, you will be peeking before the two minutes are up. If you practice, however, you will eventually calm your brain down sufficiently so that you can enjoy "being late" when you open your eyes and not fear "wasting your time" by thinking things over a while as the sand passes. English scholar and poet A.E. Housman warned of our harebrained pace when he wrote, "Three minutes' thought would suffice to find this out, but thought is irksome and three minutes is a long time."[9]

- **Connecting always:** Take a few minutes to sit and hold hands with someone about whom you care. Don't talk about daily life problems or plan for the future. Lie in bed and cuddle for a long time, or rock yourself or your child for what feels like a "nice" time, a comfortable and calm few meaningful moments. Even in the sensual aspects of our life, we seem too rushed to connect. English poet and critic Stephen Spender pointed out the hurried nature of our intimate contacts by writing, "Americans are better at having a love affair that lasts ten minutes than any other people in the world."[10]

Walking the Labyrinth of Life

To teach the importance of slowing our thought processes and the circular model of time, I often suggest an ancient practice that promotes the contemplative thought that is often lacking in the toxically successful: the lessons of the labyrinth. The labyrinth is an ancient symbol that conveys the wholeness and interconnectedness of life. It combines the imagery of a circle and spiral formed into a meandering circular yet purposeful path.[11] The walking of labyrinths has been used since ancient times as a method of teaching, meditation, and prayer. It can be one of the most powerful ways of experiencing a profound and intense investment of attention.

Figure 1. Sketch of the labyrinth at Grace Cathedral in San Francisco, California

My wife and I recently walked the labyrinth at the Grace Cathedral in San Francisco. It is a majestic building that seems to quiet the soul from the moment you enter. We commented after our walk that our experience seemed to elicit the feelings of contentment, calmness, and connection that characterize sweet success.

As we walked, we noticed that it was difficult at first to keep our balance. Something within us seemed to be hurrying us along in search of a straight and direct line to a final destination or goal, the same motivation that underlies toxic success. As you can see from the drawing of the labyrinth (figure 1), the paths are narrow and winding. You have to give your full but calm attention to your movements, a kind of "effortless trying" through which you make progress by being unconcerned with proceeding.

I saw a little boy walking the labyrinth. He was smiling and humming as he moved, and he entered and left the labyrinth with much more ease and joy than the adults who were trying to "solve it" or move through it quickly. "You seem so good at it," said his mother. "How do you do it?" The boy answered, "Oh, I'm just messing around."

Therein lies a secret of sweet success. This wise child was playing, enjoying, and "going with the flow." Unlike the hurried adults trying to succeed by getting quickly to the middle of the labyrinth, he was "just messing around" within it, having fun, and allowing it to guide him through.

Trying to rush along only makes the journey more difficult and less enjoyable than if you meander and stroll free of any time limit. To enjoy the labyrinth, you have to gracefully accept your wavering and teetering, but you soon become used to it and it feels comfortable. If you rush yourself and focus on getting to the center as quickly as possible, the trip becomes almost impossible. If you calm down and try to forget about successfully "getting to the end" and instead focus your attention on enjoying the trip, you begin to meander along rhythmically as if you are being drawn into the center. If you are self-conscious and alert to how you appear to others or try, as some did, to do better than the rest, the labyrinth becomes a challenge instead of an opportunity, stressful rather than delightful.

Labyrinths are not mazes. Unless you "toxify" them by making them into a challenge to be met or problem to be solved, they offer a way to a peaceful journey of insight and blissful experience in getting your attention.

A maze is a puzzle to be solved and contains many confusing twists, turns, and deadends. In contrast, a labyrinth has only one unicursal path for one point to move along, and the way in is the way out. The only choice to make is whether or not to enter, but once you do, trying hard does not work. All the personal power in the world is of no use in a labyrinth. What is required is the calm, tortoiselike mind and the gentle grace of feeling that you are going to your center and back out again and accepting the constant flow of life rather than striving for a goal.[12]

Reverend Steven Sturm, a friend of ours from the north shore of the island of Oʻahu, also recently walked the labyrinth at the cathedral. His description of his experience illustrates my point about the importance of being able to find a contented kind of success using the right keys to success. He said, "I really had trouble keeping my balance at first," he said. "You can't rush it—you have to go with the flow. You have to calm down and willingly accept the various turns and returns and realize that, as in life, you are always progressing even if you feel temporarily lost. I experienced it as a metaphor for the journey to the center of my spirit and back out again to the world. You come to accept your shakiness and imbalance as natural, and when I reached the center, it was a holy experience."

All the personal striving in the world is of no use in a labyrinth. That approach will ultimately lead to confusion, frustration, lonely disorientation, disappointment, and a sense of empty victory even if you make it through the path. To successfully transverse a labyrinth, you must not challenge the labyrinth but instead allow yourself to thrive your way through it and to become peacefully drawn in by the challenges it offers you. The path's twists and turns must become not puzzles or tests but invitations to grow and become enlightened. Those who seem to have experienced the spiritual joy of traveling the labyrinth do not report success at completing a task. There is no cheering, celebration, or sense of relief. Instead, there is a gentle contentment, quiet calmness, and a profound feeling of being deeply connected and more awakened to something much more important and powerful than one's self. Those who have been in the labyrinth the longest seem to exit the path with a smile on their face and tears in their eyes. There is no "high-fiving" or shouting. They usually find a quiet place to sit and reflect on their experience. Many pray. When asked about their experience, they say that somewhere along the path, they felt that they had become one with it and lost all sense of self, time, and place.

What seems required to enjoy the labyrinth is also required to experience sweet success. What is needed is a calm tortoiselike mind, forgiving contentment with whatever turns and choices you make, and an openness to being connected with the path rather than trying to conquer it. The reward is the gentle grace of feeling that you have been to your center and back out again. It is feeling that you have, for at least this moment in time, stopped fighting and gone flowing. Any success you feel will not be due to having strived and won but to having thrived and become more alive.

Following is the labyrinth opportunity I provided to my clinic patients and to the winners group when they completed their interviews. I hope you will try it as a part of your success detoxification program.

A Mental Labyrinth

As you reflect on the points about success made throughout this book, the labyrinth in figure 1 may be of help in slowing your thinking to allow more contemplation of the suggestions offered to help sweeten your success. Here is one way to use the labyrinth without actually going to one and walking within it.

Sit with this book in your lap and open to the page with the drawing of the labyrinth. Try to find a quiet place and put on some relaxing music that you can listen to through earphones so that extraneous noise and distractions do not disturb you. Make sure the music will last a long time and that it makes you feel calm. Take a pencil and place it at the entrance to the labyrinth. Pause, reflect on your developing definition of success, and when you feel ready, slowly trace through the labyrinth to its center.

As your pencil moves slowly, breathe deeply and rhythmically. If your brain keeps pestering and rushing you, try to reflect on the six words of sweet success: being content, calming down, connecting forever. You may want to repeat the six words slowly and softly out loud. You might notice that just when a path seems to be taking you to the center, you will be led back away to keep circling. When you feel furthest away from the center, you may actually be closer than ever. There are no dead ends or tricks, and you are not trying to solve a puzzle. Let the labyrinth draw you in and guide you to its center. Try not to anticipate and plan ahead or exert your personal will, for those are the ways of toxic success.

Be content to move slowly, be calm and free of trying to "finish the job," and be fully connected with the labyrinth as a metaphor for the journey of your living, working, and loving. Imagine all the thousands of people, thousands of years ago, who moved within the labyrinth just as you are now and how unimportant whatever personal and local problems they were experiencing ended up being in the overall cosmic joy of life.

Once you arrive at the center, pause and reflect again on your definition of success, for once arrived, you have only just begun. When you feel ready, begin to trace your pencil back through the labyrinth to its exit. Pause at the exit to again consider your definition of success, and this time write your current definition on your card. Keep that card with you every day as you try to make yourself more available to allow sweet success to happen to you. Like moving through the labyrinth, it is within the journey and not the goal that joy is found. Sweet success comes to those who live, work, and love with calm minds, contented hearts, and profoundly connected souls. It comes from coming back to life.

NOTES

Introduction
The Most Successful Person in the World

1. John de Graaf. *Affluenza: The All-Consuming Epidemic* (San Francisco: Berrett-Koehler, 2001).

2. So-called "push technologies" emerged in the late 1990s. They were based on the idea that if customers once showed interest in a product, further information should be "pushed" to them whether they requested it or not. "Pull technologies" are based on requiring the customers "logging on" to the Internet to decide what they might be interested in, search for it, click on it, and consider it. When we feel pushed, we feel overwhelmed and stressed. When we feel "pulled," we feel that our attention is our own. This may explain why "push-based" companies have generally failed. Most Web push technologies are either in trouble or going out of business.

3. As reported by David G. Myers, *The American Paradox* (New Haven and London: Yale University Press, 2000), 5–6.

Chapter 1
The Curse of Success

1. I review the research on the relationship between emotions and the immune system in my book *Superimmunity: Master Your Emotions and Improve Your Health*. (New York: McGraw Hill, 1987).

2. Ken Hubbard, as quoted in D. G. Myers, *The Pursuit of Happiness: Who Is Happy and Why* (New York: William Morrow and Company, 1992), 31.

3. This data is thoroughly reviewed by psychologist David Myers in *Pursuit of Happiness,* 31–46.

4. This phrase was used by psychologist Barry Schwartz in his article "Self-Determination: The Tyranny of Freedom," *American Psychologist* (January 2000): 79-88.

5. This point is also documented by the research review of David Myers in *Pursuit of Happiness,* 51–55.

6. Ibid., 54.

7. Recent research continues to document the serious drawbacks and long-term consequences for children placed in daycare. For a summary of the research on the lack of the financial practicality and true necessity for most parents to use daycare and the economic misassumptions associated with daycare use, see J. L. Collier, *The Rise of Selfishness in America* (New York: Oxford University Press, 1991).

8. M. Blum, *The Day-Care Dilemma* (Lexington, MA: Heath, 1983), 84.

Chapter 2
Coming to Your Attention

1. Drug Enforcement Administration testimony before the Committee on Education and the Workplace, Subcommittee on Early Childhood, Youth and Families. 106th Congress, second session, 16 May 2000.

2. Ellen J. Langer, *Mindfulness* (Reading, MA: Addison Wesley, 1989).

3. I strongly recommend the book *The Attention Economy*. In the context of business and management, it clearly presents the psychobiology of attention, discusses meditation and mindfulness as it applies to the workplace, and is a groundbreaking work in the integration of science, psychology, and the concept of attention. For one of the most complete and well-documented discussions of the issue of attention and a description of the overwhelming amount of material competing for our attention in the modern economy, see Thomas H. Davenport and John C. Beck, *The Attention Economy* (Boston: Harvard Business School Press, 2001).

4. Ibid.

5. R. Benson, "Further Notes on the Relationship Between Productivity of Machines Requiring Attention at Random Intervals," *Journal of the Royal Statistical Society* 14, no. 2 (1952): 200–210.

6. Herbert Simon, "Designing Organizations for an Information-Rich World," in *The Economics of Communication and Information,* ed. D. M. Lamberton (Cheltenham, England: Edward Elgar, 1997).

7. From the author's personal collection of quotations.

8. Joel Levey and Michelle Levey develop the point of "attention precedes control" in their excellent book *Living in Balance* (Berkeley, CA: Conari Press, 1998).

9. Research in "inattentional blindness" began in earnest in 1998 when psychologists Arien Mack and Irvan Rock published their book *Inattentional Blindness* (Cambridge, MA: MIT Press, 1998).

10. This research is summarized in Siri Carpenter, "Sights Unseen," *Monitor on Psychology* (April 2001): 54–57.

11. Ibid., 55.

12. H. M. Lefcourt, *Locus of Control: Current Trends in Theory and Research* (Hillsdale, NJ: Erlbaum, 1976).

13. Phillip L. Rice, *Stress and Health* (Monterey, CA: Brooks/Cole Publishing Company, 1987), 109.

14. Ibid., 109.

15. Blair Justice offers this definition as a summary of the research on "locus of control" in his book *Who Gets Sick: Thinking and Health* (Houston, TX: Peak Press, 1987) 61–62.

16. Alan Thein Durning, "Are We Happy Yet?" in *Ecopsychology: Restoring the Earth, Healing the Mind,* ed. T. Roszak, M. E. Gomes, and A. D. Kanner (San Francisco: Sierra Club Books, 1995), 69.

17. Ibid., 75.

Chapter 3
Being Normal Can Drive You Nuts

1. Erich Fromm, *To Have or To Be* (New York: Bantam, 1982), 5.

2. This data on obesity and lack of exercise is reported by John de Graaf, David Wann, and Thomas H. Naylor in *Affluenza: The All-Consuming Epidemic* (San Francisco: Berrett-Koehler Publishers, 2001), 15. I came upon that book as I was in the final editing process of my manuscript for this one. It is an excellent description of the effects of toxic successful thinking. In their important and well-documented book, the authors discuss the dangers of the cultural "norm" to need and to consume at levels ultimately toxic to us and our planet.

3. Reported in a 1998 pamphlet produced by the New Road Map Foundation and Northwest Environment Watch titled *All-Consuming Passion*, 6.

4. de Graaf et al., *Affluenza,* 13.

5. This data and many of the other statistics reported here were presented in the public television program titled "Affluenza." See also de Graaf et al., *Affluenza.*

6. Ibid., 17.

7. Fromm, *To Have or To Be,* 155.

8. Ellen Goodman, as quoted in D. G. Myers, *The American Paradox* (New Haven and London: Yale University Press, 2000), 58.

9. Historian Arnold Toynbee wrote in detail about the rise and fall of twenty-six civilizations. Some historians criticized his extensive research for its religious overtones that they felt caused his analyses and conclusions to be flawed and biased. However, for an interesting view of at least some of the factors that might contribute to the rise and fall of civilizations, see Arnold J. Toynbee, *A Study of History*, adapted by D. C. Sommerville (London: Oxford University Press, 1987).

10. Charles Derber, *The Pursuit of Attention: Power and Ego in Everyday Life*, 2d ed. (New York: Oxford University Press, 2000).

11. Abraham Maslow, *Religion, Values, and Peak Experience* (New York: Penguin, 1976), 65.

12. As quoted in C. J. Beck, *Nothing Special: Living Zen* (San Francisco: Harper San Francisco, 1993), 41.

13. Referring to the selfish drive for more and more stuff, John de Graaf et al. quote T. S. Eliot's line "We are the hollow men. We are the stuffed men." *Affluenza,* 68.

14. For an example of this research, see K. R. Jamison, "Manic-Depressive Illness and Creativity," *Scientific American* (February 1995): 62–67.

15. Joe Kita called me as I was completing the manuscript for this book. He interviewed me on another of my books, but when I described my research on the winners group and TSS, he told me about his work with "unhappy guys with perfect lives." See his fascinating article "The New Depression," *Men's Health* Magazine (February 2001): 104–109.

16. Edgar Allen Poe, as quoted in K. R. Jamison, "Manic-Depressive Illness and Creativity," *Scientific American* (February 1995): 63.

17. As reported in Joel Levey and Michelle Levey, *Living in Balance* (Berkeley, CA: Conari Press, 1988), 253.

18. R. Leakey and R. Lewin, *The Sixth Extinction: Patterns of Life and the Future of Mankind* (New York: Doubleday, 1995).

19. As quoted from Peter Schutz's address to a large meeting of business executives and reported in "MCAA 2001: An Hawaiian Odyssey," *Convention News,* no. 1 (February 13, 2001): 1.

20. Harvey Ruben, *Competing* (New York: Pinnacle Books, 1981), ix.

21. Ibid., 22.

22. Joseph Wood Krutch, *The Modern Temper: A Study and a Confession* (New York: Harcourt, Brace, and World, 1956), 92.

Chapter 4
The Meaning of Monday

1. C. D. Jenkins, "Psychological and Social Precursors of Coronary Artery Disease," *New England Journal of Medicine* 284 (1971): 244–255.

2. For an excellent summary of this research, see B. Q. Hafen et al., *Mind/Body Health: The Effects of Attitude, Emotions, and Relationships* (Boston: Allyn and Bacon, 1996).

3. Norman Cousins, *Head First: The Biology of Hope* (New York: E. P. Dutton, 1989), 281.

4. Larry Dossey, *Meaning and Medicine* (New York: Bantam Books, 1991), 63.

5. Jenkins, "Coronary Artery Disease."

6. *Webster's New World Dictionary,* 2d ed., s.v. "nag."

7. Dr. Larry Dossey's article titled "The Nag Factor" describes the impact of "medical nagging" and the resulting feelings of guilt and pressure for not being "a success" at the latest health practices. See *Alternative Therapies* 7, no. 1 (January 2001): 12–16, 90–91.

8. For a fascinating discussion of how the joy of living relates to our freedom to assign our own meaning to our own life, see D. Shaw, *The Pleasure Police* (New York: Doubleday, 1996).

9. Dossey, "Nag Factor," 90.

10. Thomas Friedman, "New Age: Politicians Ignore the Issues That Are Changing Our World," *The Dallas Morning News,* 15 May 2000, 11A.

11. Albert Einstein, as quoted in *The Concise Oxford Dictionary of Quotations*, 3d ed., ed. A. Parington (New York: Oxford University Press, 1993), 131.

12. Dr. Dossey develops this point in his book *Meaning and Medicine*, 21.

13. Theoretical physicist David Bohm has developed a theory of the relationship of mind and matter united by meaning. Many consider his theories of "meaning" to be as important as Einstein's work on energy and matter united by the speed of light. See David Bohm, "Meaning and Information," in *The Search for Meaning,* by Paavo Pylkkanen (Wellingborough, Northamptonshire, England: Crucible, 1989).

14. I discuss this research in my book *Superimmunity: Master Your Emotions and Improve Your Health* (New York: McGraw-Hill, 1997).

15. Joel Levey and Michelle Levey, *Living in Balance* (Berkeley, CA: Conari Press, 1998), 230

16. Ellen Karsh, "Bungee Jumping? I'd Rather Watch 'Rosie,'" *Newsweek,* 27 November 2000, 16–17.

17. Ibid., 17.

18. Larry Dossey, "Work and Health: Of Isolation, Sisyphus, and Barbarian Beds," *Alternative Therapies* 3 (January 1997): 8–14.

19. Ibid., 22.

20. Jane Katra and Russell Targ, *The Heart of the Mind* (Novato, CA: New World Library, 1999), 160.

21. Mahaly Csikszentmihalyi, *Flow: The Psychology of Optimal Experience* (New York: HarperCollins, 1991), 20.

22. Ibid., 22.

23. Ibid., 22.

24. Stephen Bertman, *Hyperculture: The Human Cost of Speed* (Westport, CT: Praeger, 1998), 2.

25. These descriptions of reactive versus reflective thinking were coined and developed by author Guy Glaxton in his book *Hare Brain, Tortoise Mind* (Hopewell, NJ: Ecco Press, 1997).

26. From the author's personal collection of quotations.

27. Glaxton, *Hare Brain*, p. 4.

28. From the author's personal collection of quotations.

Chapter 5
Overcoming Competition Obsession

1. Peter Knapp, cited in P. G. Hanson, *The Joy of Stress*, (Kansas City: Andrews, McMeel, and Parker, 1986), 78.

2. For one of the most complete summaries of the research on human happiness, see David G. Myers, *The Pursuit of Happiness* (New York: William Morrow and Company, 1992).

3. David C. McClelland, *The Achieving Society* (Princeton, NJ: Van Nostrand, 1961).

4. David C. McClelland et al., "Stressed Power Motivation, Sympathetic Activation, Immune Function, and Illness," *Journal of Human Stress* 6, no. 2 (1980): 11–19.

5. David C. McClelland, "Inhibited Power Motivation and High Blood Pressure in Men," Journal of Abnormal Psychology 88 (1979): 182–190.

6. J. B. Jemmott et al., "Motivational Syndromes Associated with Natural Killer Cell Activity," *Journal of Behavioral Medicine* 13, no. 1 (1990): 53–73.

7. For an excellent and complete discussion of the stress response and how it fails to serve our needs in the modern world as contrasted to our primitive ancestors' world, see Peter G. Hanson, *Joy of Stress* (Kansas City, MO: Andrews McMeel,1986).

8. "Dry mouth" is such a clear and reliable symptom of stress that the Chinese use it as a lie detector test.

9. For one of the most complete and carefully researched arguments against competition as a central personal and social motive, see Alfie Kohn, *No Contest: The Case Against Competition* (Boston: Houghton Mifflin Company, 1986). This quote is on page 1.

10. This same analogy was drawn by linguist Walker Percy writing about the nature of language and its usages. He wrote, "A fish does not reflect on the nature of water. He cannot imagine its absence, so he cannot consider its presence." In "Questions They Never Asked Me," reprinted in *Conversations with Walker Percy*, ed. L. A. Lawson and V. A. Jackson (Jackson, MS: University of Mississippi Press, 1985), 178.

11. Karen Horney, *The Neurotic Personality of Our Time* (New York: Norton, 1937), 160.

12. Elliot Aronson. *The Sacred Animal*, 2d ed. (San Francisco: W. H. Freeman, 1976), 152.

13. Charles Darwin, *On the Origin of Species by Means of Natural Selection*, chap. 3 (London: John Murray, 1859).

14. Stephen Jay Gould, as quoted in personal communication to Alfie Kohn, *No Contest,* 21.

15. Petr Kropotkin, *Mutual Aid: A Factor in Evolution* (1902; reprint, Boston: Extending Horizons Books, 1955), 74–75.

16. It is beyond the scope of this book to elaborate on the science of evolution and ecopsychology. For one example of the support for ceasing our competitive approach and valuing cooperation, see George Gaylord Simpson, *The Meaning of Evolution* (New Haven, CT: Yale University Press, 1949). For an example of the documented health benefits of a less competitive and more connected and mutually caring way of living, see Dean Ornish, *Love and Survival: The Scientific Basis for the Healing Power of Intimacy* (New York: HarperCollins, 1997).

17. Roderic Gorney, *The Human Agenda* (New York: Simon and Schuster, 1972), 101–102.

18. Marian Radke Yarrow et al., "Learning Concern for Others," *Developmental Psychology* 8 (1973): 240.

19. Walter B. Cannon, *The Wisdom of the Body* (New York: Norton, 1942).

20. As reported by Beth Azar, "A New Stress Paradigm for Women," *Monitor on Psychology* 31, no. 7 (July/August 2000): 42–43.

Chapter 6
A Measure of Success

1. From the author's personal collection of quotations.

2. From the author's personal collection of quotations.

3. As quoted in David G. Myers, *The Pursuit of Happiness* (New York: William Morrow, 1992), 118.

4. As quoted in Alan Thein Durning, "Are We Happy Yet?" in *Ecopsychology: Restoring the Earth, Healing the Mind,* ed. T. Roszak, M. E. Gomes, and A. D. Kanner (San Francisco: Sierra Club Books, 1995), 73.

5. Joel Levey and Michelle Levey, *Living in Balance: A Dynamic Approach for Creating Harmony and Wholeness in a Chaotic World* (Berkeley, CA: Conari Press, 1998), 244–245.

6. Reported in Levey and Levey, *Living in Balance,* 246.

7. From the author's personal collection of quotations.

8. Levey and Levey, *Living in Balance*, 245.

9. Sue Shellenberger, *Wall Street Journal,* 5 January 1998.

10. Alan Thein Durning, "Are We Happy Yet?" in *Ecopsychology: Restoring the Earth, Healing the Mind,* ed. T. Roszak, M. E. Gomes, and A. D. Kanner (San Francisco: Sierra Club Books, 1995), 69.

11. Jeremy Seabrook, as quoted in Alan Thein Durning, 71.

12. For an example of this work, see Meyer Friedman, N. Fleishmann, and V. A. Price, "Diagnosis of Type A Behavior Pattern," in *Heart and Mind: The Practice of Cardiac*

Psychology, ed. R. Allan and S. Scheidt (Washington, D.C.: American Psychological Association, 1996), 179–193.

Chapter 7
Too Busy to Love, Too Tired to Care

1. This research is reported in Thomas H. Davenport and John C. Beck, *The Attention Economy* (Boston, MA: Harvard Business School Press, 2001), 191–192.

2. For more about this research, see E. Vulliamy, "If You Don't Have Time to Take in All the Information in This Report, You Could Be Suffering from a Bout of Information Fatigue Syndrome," *Guardian,* 15 October 1996.

3. This data comes from studies conducted by Ferris Research and Lotus Research unpublished as of this book's publication date.

4. Meyer Friedman and Ray Roseman, *Type A Behavior and Your Heart* (New York: Knopf, 1974), 4.

5. James Gleick, *Faster: The Acceleration of Just About Everything.* (New York: Pantheon Books, 1999), 17.

6. Vital exhaustion as a cardiovascular disease risk factor, particularly for women, was first described in detail in A. Appels, P. Hoppener, and P. Muldur, "A Questionnaire To Assess Premonitory Symptoms of Myocardial Infarction." *International Journal of Cardiology* 15 (1987): 15–24.

7. For a discussion of the cultural aspects of "vitality" and subtle energy, see J. White, *The Meeting of Science and Spirit* (New York: Paragon House, 1990).

8. For an interesting and well-documented discussion of the nature of vital, or "subtle," energy, see W. Collinge, *Subtle Energy: Awakening to the Unseen Forces in Our Lives* (New York: Warner Books, 1998).

9. T. S. Wiley and B. Formby, *Lights Out: Sleep, Sugar, and Survival* (New York: Pocket Books, 2000), 2. Also reported by K. Kelly, "Today's Kids: Overscheduled and Overtired," *U.S. News and World Report*, 16 October 2001, 66.

10. For a copy of their test, see Appels, Hoppener, and Muldur, "A Questionnaire."

11. Dr. Sherman A. James, epidemiologist at the University of Michigan Hospital in Ann Arbor, Michigan, first identified "John Henryism." His work is discussed in R. Sapolsky, "The Price of Propriety," *The Sciences* 36, no. 4 (1996): 14–16.

12. J. G. Bruhn et al., "Psychological Predictors of Sudden Death in Myocardial Infarction," *Journal of Psychosomatic Research* 18 (1974): 187–191.

13. George F. Solomon and R. H. Moos, "Emotions, Immunity, and Disease: A Speculative Theoretical Integration," *Archives of General Psychiatry* 11 (1974) 657–674.

14. George F. Solomon et al., "An Intensive Psychoimmunologic Study of Long-Surviving

Persons with AIDS," *Annals of the New York Academy of Sciences* 496 (1987): 647–655.

15. David Kundtz. *Stopping: How to Be Still When You Have to Keep Going* (Berkeley, CA: Conari Press, 1998), 49. This is one of the most insightful, practical, and helpful books available on learning to "stop" rather than "go" and calming down rather than firing up.

16. Ibid., 49–50.

Chapter 8
The Sciences of Sweet Success

1. For the clearest discussion of chaos theory, see James Gleick, *Chaos: The Making of a New Science* (New York: Penguin Books, 1987).

2. Jon Kabat-Zinn, *Full Catastrophe Living* (New York: Delta Books, 1990), 5.

3. Sir Laurens Van de Post, *Jung and the Story of Our Time* (New York: Random House/ Vintage, 1977), 76–77.

4. Garret Hardin, as quoted in J. E. Lovelock, *Gaia* (New York: Oxford University Press, 1987), 124.

5. James Lincoln Collier presents a thorough and well-documented description of this rise of selfishness and places it in historical perspective in *The Rise of Selfishness in America* (New York: Oxford University Press, 1991).

6. Ken Wilber, *No Boundaries* (Boston: New Science Library, 1979), 31.

7. For a discussion of the point that our heroes and gurus have almost always been individualists, see R. Walsh and D. Shapiro, "Well Being and Relationship," in *Beyond Health and Normality*, ed. R. Walsh and D. Shapiro (New York: Van Nostrand Reinhold Company, 1983).

8. Collier, *Rise of Selfishness,* 26.

9. Robert M. Sapolsky, *Why Zebras Don't Get Ulcers* (New York: W. H. Freeman and Company, 1994), 55.

10. Author Douglas Couple writes, "Type-A personalities have a whole subset of diseases that they, and only they, share, and the transmission vector for these diseases is the DOOR CLOSE button on elevators that only gets pushed by impatient, Type-A people," in *Microserfs* (New York: HarperCollins, 1995), 276–277.

11. James Gleick, *Faster* (New York: Pantheon, 1999), 17.

12. Research supporting this mental state as the real culprit in our toxic success was conducted by V. A. Price. See his book *Hypervigilance: Type A Behavior Pattern* (New York: Academic Press, 1982).

13. Robert S. Eliot and D. L. Breo. "Are You a Hot Reactor? Is It Worth Dying For?" *Executive Health* 20, no. 10 (1984) 1–4.

14. Sapolsky, *Why Zebras Don't Get Ulcers,* 57.

15. B. T. Lohrer et al., "A Meta-Analysis of the Relation of Job Characteristics to Job Satisfaction," *Journal of Applied Psychology* 70 (1985): 280–289.

16. A. G. Goliszek, *Breaking the Stress Habit* (Winston-Salem, NC: Carolina Press, 1987).

17. For a complete description of "workaholism," see Diane Fassel, *Working Ourselves to Death* (San Francisco: Harper San Francisco, 1990).

18. Psychologist Diane Fassel coined the term *closet worker* for those who sneak to do their work because they know their family is "on to them" and has become well aware of their addiction to work and their efforts to pretend to be paying attention while actually "working in their mind." Ibid., 20–23.

19. This point is clarified and documented in Nico H. Frijda, "The Laws of Emotion," *American Psychologist* 43 (1988) 349–358.

20. For a complete description of this theory, see Richard L. Solomon, "The Opponent Process Theory of Acquired Motivation: The Costs of Pleasure and the Benefits of Pain," *American Psychologist* 35 (1980): 691–712.

21. Plato, *Phaedo.*

22. David G. Myers, *The Pursuit of Happiness: Who Is Happy and Why* (New York: William Morrow and Company, 1992), 54.

23. For a description of this phenomenon, see F. Strack et al., "Inhibiting and Facilitating Conditions of the Human Smile: A Nonobtrusive Test of the Facial Feedback Hypothesis," *Journal of Personality and Social Psychology* 54 (1988): 768–777.

24. I heard Sara E. Snodgrass report this "happy walker" effect in a paper titled "The Effects of Walking Behavior on Mood," presented at the 1986 American Psychological Association meeting in Washington, D.C.

25. Norman Vincent Peale, *The Power of Positive Thinking* (New York: Fawcett Books, 1952).

26. Wendy Kaminer, *I'm Dysfunctional, You're Dysfunctional* (Reading, MA: Addison Wesley, 1992).

Chapter 9
Secrets of Success from Paradise

1. From the author's personal collection of quotations.

2. From the author's personal collection of quotations.

3. Harlan Ellison, "Strange Wine," in *Amazing Stories*, 5th ed. (New York: Harper and Row, 1976) 239–256.

4. Ibid., 244.

5. From the author's personal collection of quotations.

6. From the author's personal collection of quotations.

7. From the author's personal collection of quotations.

8. The definition of literary ecology is "the study of biological themes and relationships that appear in literary works." A pioneer in this field is Joseph W. Meeker. For a description of literary ecology, see his book *The Comedy of Survival: Literary Ecology and a Play Ethic,* 3d ed. (Tucson, AZ: The University of Arizona Press, 1997). This definition of literary ecology is on page 7.

9. For a description of this condition, see "Does America Have ADD?" by the editors of *U.S. News and World Report,* 26 March 2001, 14.

10. Ibid.

11. With the average American office worker sending or receiving more than two hundred messages a day and using electronic spurts of communication that produce only a fleeting sense of real interaction, we are left feeling distracted and restless, symptoms associated with the condition referred to as attention deficit disorder. Ibid.

12. Ibid.

13. I describe the "Ahab complex" in detail in my book *Super Joy* (New York: Bantam Books, 1990) 27–30. Psychologist Abraham Maslow referred to the "Ahab complex" as putting all of your emotional eggs in one basket. In the case of the toxically successful, that basket is personal success as defined by modern society.

14. Dante Alighieri, *The Divine Comedy,* trans. Allen Mandelbaum (New York: Bantam Books, 1980).

15. Meeker, *Comedy of Survival,* 97.

16. H. K. Pukui and S. H. Elbert, *Hawaiian Dictionary* (Honolulu: University of Hawai'i Press, 1986), s.v. "po'okela."

17. For a groundbreaking discussion of "rock vs. water" logic and how it applies to our daily living, working, and creative thought, see Edward de Bono, *I Am Right, You Are Wrong: From Rock Logic to Water Logic* (New York: Viking Books, 1991).

18. From the author's personal collection of quotations.

19. It is beyond the scope of this book to deal with the severe and lethal political and economic consequences of Western imperialism and the conquest model of success that invaded Hawai'i. As victims of the toxically successful, the Hawaiian people have suffered greatly due to the competitive and controlling orientation of Euro-American domination and its attempt to impose its view of success and what constitutes an excellent life.

Chapter 10

Being Content: Knowing When Enough Is Enough

1. George Kanahele passed away in 2000. He was one of the most outstanding Hawaiian scholars. Until his untimely death, he continued to write and teach about the application of ancient Hawaiian values to modern living, working, and loving. See his book *Kū Kanaka, Stand Tall: A Search for Hawaiian Values* (Honolulu: University of Hawai'i Press, 1986), 112.

2. Ibid., 112.

3. Thomas Szasz, as quoted in Jon Winokur, *The Portable Curmudgeon* (New York: New American Library, 1987), 25.

4. The most complete summary of the research supporting this point is found in David G. Myers, *The Pursuit of Happiness: Who Is Happy and Why* (New York: William Morrow, 1992).

5. For a description of the home shopping phenomenon, see P. Carlin, "The Jackpot in Television's Future," *New York Times Magazine*, 28 February 1993, 36–41.

6. Stephen Bertman, *Hyperculture* (West Port, CT: Praeger, 1988), 88.

7. Lee Burns, *Busy Bodies* (New York: Norton, 1993), 71.

8. Thomas J. Stanley and William D. Danko, *The Millionaire Next Door* (Atlanta: Longstreet Press, 1996), 13.

9. Bill Gates, *U.S. News and World Report*, 13 January 1997, 68.

10. From the author's personal collection of quotations.

11. E. L. Deci et al., *Journal of Personality and Social Psychology* 3 (1981): 237–249.

12. Timothy Miller, *How to Want What You Have: Discovering the Magic and Grandeur of the Ordinary* (New York: Henry Holt and Company, 1995), 9.

13. Stated by Cyprian Norwid in 1850. As quoted in Wladyslaw Tatarkiewicz, *Analysis of Happiness* (The Hague: Martinus Nijhoff, 1976), 176.

14. Data shows that our buying power has doubled since the 1950s but self-reported happiness has remained unchanged. See R. G. Niemi et al., *Trends in Public Opinion: A Compendium of Survey Data* (New York: Greenwood Press, 1989).

15. See R. Ornstein and D. Sobel, *Healthy Pleasures* (New York: Addison Wesley, 1989), 132.

16. From the author's personal collection of quotations.

17. Psychologist Ed Diener and his colleagues had subjects carry beepers and report over a six-week period those times when they felt happy. It was not how positive but how often they experienced simple positive moments that led to the highest levels of happiness. Many short doses of delight rather than big spurts of excitement seem to be the formula

for happiness. See R. J. Larson, E. Diener, and R. S. Cropanzano, "Cognitive Operations Associated with Individual Differences in Affect Intensity," *Journal of Personality and Social Psychology* 53, no. 4 (October 1987): 767–774.

18. For a description of the process of synesthesia and examples of it, see Siri Carpenter, "Everyday Fantasia: The World of Synesthesia," *Monitor on Psychology* 32, no. 3 (March 2001): 26–29.

19. Ibid., 27.

20. Abraham Maslow and Bertha G. Maslow, *Abraham H. Maslow: A Memorial Volume* (Monterey, CA: Brooks/Cole, 1972), 108.

21. Alan Thein Durning, "Are We Happy Yet?" in *Ecopsychology: Restoring the Earth, Healing the Mind,* ed. T. Roszak, M. E. Gomes, and A. D. Kanner (San Francisco: Sierra Club Books, 1995), 68–76.

Chapter 11
Calming Down: Knowing How to Be Still

1. James W. Fortune, "Mega High-Rise Elevators," *Elevator World* 43, no. 7 (1995).

2. This and others' attempts to deal with our accelerated approach to life are described by James Gleick in *Faster: The Acceleration of Just About Everything* (New York: Pantheon Books, 1999). It was my reading of Gleick's entertaining and insightful book that led me to my observations of elevator behavior as a measure of our calmness deficiency. His informative book is a must-read for anyone willing to slow down enough to reflect on just how rushed they have become.

3. For more information on the elevator shuffle, see G. R. Strakosch, "A New Dimension in Elevator Monitoring," *Elevator World* 42, no. 8 (1994).

4. As quoted in Gleick, *Faster,* 27.

5. K. Popper, *The Open Society and Its Enemies* (London: Routledge and Kegan Paul, 1945).

6. Barry Schwartz, "Self-Determination: The Tyranny of Freedom," *American Psychologist* 55, no. 1 (January 2000): 79.

7. Ibid., 80–81.

8. The tyranny of too many choices may be one reason that so many lottery winners report anxiety and even serious depression when they face the "pressure" of dealing with the rapidly expanded range of new choices with which they are presented.

9. G. L. Klerman et al., "Birth Cohort Trends in Rates of Major Depressive Disorder Among Relatives of Patients with Affective Disorder," *Archives of General Psychiatry* 42 (1985): 689–693.

10. L. N. Robbins et al., "Lifetime Prevalence of Specific Psychiatric Disorders in Three Sites," *Archives of General Psychiatry* 41 (1984): 949–958.

11. For a complete discussion of learned helplessness, see M. E. P. Seligman, *Helplessness: On Depression, Development, and Death* (San Francisco: Freeman, 1975). See also his book *Learned Optimism* (New York: Alfred A. Knopf, 1991).

12. From the author's personal collection of quotations.

13. Saul Wurman, *Information Anxiety* (New York: Doubleday, 1989), 32.

14. For a discussion of the future of computer speed, see G. Kolata, "A Vat of DNA May Become Fast Computer of the Future," *New York Times*, 11 April 1995, B5.

15. *Heraclitus*, fragments 20 and 21.

16. Jeremy Rifkin, *Time Wars: The Primary Conflict in Human History* (New York: Henry Holt, 1987).

17. Schwartz, "Self-Determination," 80.

18. Kenneth J. Gergen, *The Saturated Self: Dilemmas of Identity in Contemporary Life* (New York: Basic Books, 1992).

19. The source for these numbers is the Electronic Industries Association and the Computer Business Equipment Manufacturers Association.

20. The source for this number is the Motorola Corporation, the largest producer of pagers in the United States.

21. This data is from the Nielsen Media Research group.

22. See J. Twitchell, *Carnival Culture: The Trashing of Taste in America* (New York: Columbia University Press, 1992), 43.

23. The source for this number in the Consumer Electronics Manufacturers Association.

24. Henry David Thoreau, "Economy," chap. 1 in *Walden*.

25. Robert K. Merten, in his introduction to *The Technological Society* by Jacques Ellul (New York: Knopf, 1964), vi.

26. Thoreau, "Economy."

27. *Manager's Magazine*, August 1992, 3.

28. Carl Sandburg, "The Sins of Kalamazoo," in *The Complete Poems of Carl Sandburg* (New York: Harcourt Brace Jovanovich, 1970), 172–175.

29. From the author's personal collection of quotations.

30. Guy Glaxton, *Hare Brain, Tortoise Mind* (Hopewell, NJ: The Ecco Press, 1997). See particularly pages 28–47, where he discusses the creativity associated not only with an open mind but with a slow one.

31. N. Friedman, "Cardiovascular Response to Rate of Speech," *Journal of Cardiovascular Nursing* 3 (1994): 111–117.

32. For an inspiring discussion of why cutting and cramming do not work, see D. Kundtz,

Stopping: How to Be Still When You Have to Keep Going (Berkeley, CA: Conari Press 1998).

33. Ibid., 9.

34. Peter Russell, *Waking Up in Time: Finding Inner Peace in Times of Accelerating Change* (Novato, CA: Origin Press, 1998), 10.

35. "Stressed Workers Calling in Sick, Report Says," *Honolulu Advertiser*, 26 September 1999, 3.

36. From the author's personal collection of quotations.

37. From the author's personal collection of quotations.

38. Freada Klein, as quoted in *The Wall Street Journal*, 8 April 1997, B1.

39. Stephen Bertman, *Hyperculture* (Westport, CT: Praeger, 1998), 31. I highly recommend this wonderful book to anyone entering the toxic success detoxification program.

40. Shel Silverstein's classic work *The Giving Tree* can, as all poetry, be interpreted in many different ways and on many different levels. I have suggested it to my patients as a means of illustrating what is left when we give too much and are unable to say no. (New York: Harper and Row, 1964).

Chapter 12
Connecting Always: Remembering "And"

1. For a simple review of this new field of neurotheology, see S. Begley, "Religion and the Brain," *Newsweek,* 7 May 2001, 50–59.

2. This quote is from the groundbreaking book introducing neurotheology by Andrew Newberg and Eugene D'Aquili with V. Rause, titled *Why God Won't Go Away: Brain Science and the Biology of Belief* (New York: Ballantine Books, 2001), 172.

3. I reviewed this field in my book *The Heart's Code: Tapping the Wisdom and Power of Our Heart Energy* (New York: Broadway Books, 1998).

4. Dean Ornish, *Love and Survival: The Scientific Basis for the Healing Power of Intimacy* (New York: HarperCollins, 1997), 11.

5. Dr. Larry Dossey presents a thorough discussion of this syndrome as applied to some of those who often unfairly criticize alternative medicines without knowing the research or being open to a balanced skepticism and fair discussion of the several issues involved. See his "The Right Man Syndrome: Skepticism and Alternative Medicine," *Alternative Therapies* 4, no. 3 (May 1998): 12–19, 108–113.

6. B. Wright, "Here Comes the Backlash," *Fortean Times* 106 (1998), 42.

7. Graham Greene, as quoted in *Pathways* 5, no. 6 (Riverside, CA: Center for Contemplative Christianity, 1996): 22.

8. The origins of the "self-interest motive" are described by Barry Schwartz in *The Battle for Human Nature* (New York: Norton, 1986).

9. Dale T. Miller, "The Norm of Self-Interest," *American Psychologist* 54, no. 12 (December 1999): 1053–1059.

10. Ibid., 1053.

11. Barry Schwartz, "Psychology, Idea Technology, and Ideology," *Psychological Science* 8 (1997): 21–27.

12. Jerome Kagan, *Unstable Ideas: Temperament, Cognition, and Self* (Cambridge, MA: MAL Harvard University Press, 1989), 283.

13. Mahaly Csikszentmihalyi, *The Evolving Self* (New York: HarperCollins, 1993).

14. Ibid., 35–36.

15. Aaron Ahuvia, "Well-Being in Cultures of Choice: A Cross-Cultural Perspective," *American Psychologist* 56, no.1 (January 2001): 77. His comments in this article clarify the danger of assuming that "self-happiness" is the only happiness.

16. H. C. Triadus, C. McCuskee, and H. C. Hui, "Multimethod Probes of Individualism and Collectivism." *Journal of Personality and Social Psychology* 59 (1990): 1006–1020.

17. For a discussion of this idea of "doing the right thing" for self-happiness as compared to doing the right thing because it is the primary and elusive human motive, see philosopher Robert Nozik's book *Anarchy, State, and Utopia* (New York: Basic Books, 1974).

18. For a complete discussion of the origins and nature of individualism and collectivism and the concepts of "monologic" and "dialogic," see Edward E. Sampson, "Reinterpreting Individualism and Collectivism: Their Religious Roots and Monologic Versus Dialogic Person-Other Relationships," *American Psychologist* 55, no. 12 (2000): 1425–1431.

19. Ian Choi et al., "Causal Attribution Across Cultures," *Psychological Bulletin* 125 (1999): 47–63.

20. Sampson, "Reinterpreting Individualism," 1425.

21. Martin Oppenheim, *Speaking/Writing of God: Jewish Philosophical Reflections on the Life with Others* (Albany, New York: State University of New York Press, 1997): 19.

22. Martin Buber, *The Knowledge of Man: Selected Essays* (Atlantic Highland, NJ: Humanities Press International, 1965).

23. Martin Buber, *Between Man and Man* (New York: MacMillan, 1965), 20.

24. R. Powers, "American Dreaming: The Limitless Absurdity of Our Belief in an Infinitely Transformative Future," *New York Times Magazine* 7 May 2000, 66–67.

25. Michael Carrithers, *Why Humans Have Cultures: Explaining Anthropology and Social Diversity* (Oxford, England: Oxford University Press, 1992).

26. For a summary of the latest research on laughter, see Sharon Begley, "The Science of

Laughs," *Newsweek,* 9 October 2000, 75–76.

27. Ibid., 76.

28. Dossey, "Right Man Syndrome," 13.

29. Author Peter McWilliams wrote, "Life is a sexually transmitted terminal disease," but I replaced *disease* with *condition* because I don't consider life a chronic illness. See Peter McWilliams, *Ain't Nobody's Business If You Do: The Absurdity of Consensual Crime in a Free Society* (Los Angeles: Prelude Press, 1993).

30. Waleed A. Salameh, "The Power of 'It Doesn't Matter,'" *Humor and Health Journal* 9, no. 2 (June 2000): p. 1.

31. Andre Dubus III, *House of Sand and Fog* (New York: W. W. Norton Company, 1999), 34.

32. Clifford C. Kuhn. "The Stages of Laughter," *Journal of Nursing Jocularity* 4, no. 2 (1994): 34–35.

A Beginning
It's Just a Matter of Time

1. *Webster's Third New International Dictionary* (Springfield, MA: Merriam-Webster, Inc., 1993), s.v. "moment."

2. From the author's personal collection of quotations.

3. For a description of this formula, see Lee Burns, *Busy Bodies* (New York: W. W. Norton and Company, 1993), 61–62.

4. Ibid., 61.

5. Thomas H. Davenport and John C. Beck, *The Attention Economy* (Boston, MA: Harvard Business School Press, 2001), 11.

6. George Hu'eu Sanford Kanahele, *Kū Kanaka, Stand Tall: The Search for Hawaiian Values* (Honolulu: University of Hawai'i Press, 1986).

7. William Rehnquist, as quoted in "All in the American Family," *Time*, 13 June 1988, 74.

8. From the author's personal collection of quotations.

9. From the author's personal collection of quotations.

10. From the author's personal collection of quotations.

11. For more information on labyrinths, see Lauren Artress, *Walking a Sacred Path: Rediscovering the Labyrinth as a Spiritual Tool* (Berkeley, CA: Berkeley Publishers, 1996).

12. There are dozens of examples of labyrinths all over the world. I selected the version my wife and I experienced, but you can find many other forms. Veriditas, the World-Wide Labyrinth Project, is the creation of Reverend Dr. Lauren Artress. It presents the spiritual enlightenment offered by the experience and understanding of the labyrinth. For information on Veriditas, contact *www.gracecathedral.org/labyrinth/index.shtml*

GLOSSARY

"I ka ʻōlelo no ke ola" (e-ka-oh-lay-low-no-kay-oh-la):
"Words give life."

affluenza: A term coined by authors John de Graaf, David Wann, and Thomas H. Naylor to describe "a painful, contagious, socially transmitted condition of overload, debt, anxiety, and waste resulting from the dogged pursuit of more." This is the "flu" that results from the lowered immunity caused by TSS.

ahonui (ah-ho-new-e): Hawaiian word for persistent, attentive patience, a component of *poʻokela* (Hawaiian excellence).

akahai (ah-ka-high): Hawaiian word for a gentle, kind, tender, unassuming manner, a component of *poʻokela* (Hawaiian excellence).

aloha: Hawaiian word for love, though it has many other meanings. Literally translated, it means to share (*alo*) the sacred breath (*ha*) of life. This deep and profound sharing and connection is fundamental to *poʻokela*.

attention deficit disorder (ADD): The inability to pay or maintain attention. Prescriptions for Ritalin, the primary drug used to stimulate attention, have increased ninefold since 1990. Toxic success syndrome is characterized by a form of cultural ADD that includes being overwhelmed with the amount of information available and an inability to reflect and focus on what matters most in life.

attention management: A term coined by authors Thomas H. Davenport and John C. Beck to emphasize attention as the new currency of modern business and as a contrast to "time management." It refers to learning to give, receive, and maintain attention. Because of our tendency toward the short attention span of our chimpanzee ancestors with whom we share 98 percent of our genetic code, they also define attention management as "the process required to convince a bunch of apes to build a car."

ʻaumakua (ow-ooh-ma-coo-ah): Hawaiian term for family of personal gods—the sacred ancestors forever monitoring our behavior. *Poʻokela* success is based on living, loving, and working so as to impress our *'aumakua.*

Black Monday: The phenomenon of more persons dying on Monday morning between 8 A.M. and 11 A.M. than any other day or time. It is an example of the impact of the toxic meaning we sometimes assign to our working.

continental thinking: The linear, logical way of thinking of the Western mind. It tends to be argumentative, adversarial, competitive, defensive, cynical, and self-enhancing. While effective for quick problem solving, it can become the exclusive consciousness of the toxically successful. It is related to psychologist Edward de Bono's concept of independent, absolute "rock logic."

cyclothymia: A personality characteristic of marked changes of mood from cheerfully energetic to withdrawn, listless, and gloomy. People going through the "up" times of cyclothymia often have highly successful careers but eventually slide into lonely despair, sadness, and even depression. Some researchers have shown an association between cyclothymia and "pyknic," or a stout, hump-shouldered, rounded body build.

dialogical: A word referring to an internal dialogue or consciousness based on "us" rather than "me." It is a collectivist way of thinking common to many indigenous cultures, such as the Hawaiian culture. It is the consciousness essential to sweet success or *po'okela.*

dysthmia: A mood state first identified in 1974, it is a subtle, covert kind of depression sometimes experienced by the toxically successful. Unlike cyclothymia, characterized by mood swings from elation to depression, dysthymia is characterized by a persistent lack of life energy and inability to take joy from an apparently very successful life. While cyclothymia tends to be experienced by the more newly successful, dysthymia seems more common in the long-term toxically successful.

energy cardiology: One of the three new sciences of sweet success. The new research field established at the turn of the millennium by psychologists Gary Schwartz and Linda Russek, it studies the unique energy of the heart and its capacity to think, feel, and connect with other hearts. The brain is associated with toxic success and the heart with sweet success.

flow: The term coined by psychologist Mihaly Csikszentmihalyi referring to a mental state of complete attention so focused and intense that it results in a loss of the sense of self and time, and in a total, joyful absorption in an activity. Sweet success is getting into the flow.

ha'aha'a (ha-a-ha-ah): Hawaiian word meaning humble modesty. *Ha'aha'a* is a key indicator that someone has attained *po'okela* and the opposite of the SIN, or self-interest norm, of the Western version of success.

hare brain: A term used by psychologist Guy Glaxton to describe quick, nonreflective thinking that seeks fast solutions and rapid problem solving. It is the thinking preferred by the toxically successful and the opposite of the tortoise mind of *po'okela,* or sweet success.

ho'omaka hou (ho-oh-ma-ka-ho): Hawaiian phrase meaning to begin again. To be sweetly successful *po'okela* style, one has to be willing to start fresh to try to pay more attention and think in the oceanic style of the tortoise mind.

inattentional blindness: A psychological concept referring to failing to see the most obvious and important things because of failure to pay full attention. Toxic Success Syndrome results from narrow self-sightedness.

inhibited power motive (IPM): A concept developed and researched by the late Harvard psychologist David McClelland. It refers to someone with a high need for power and control, frustration with not having enough power, and a higher need for power than affiliation or intimate connection. It is a common characteristic of TSS and can result in immune-system impairment.

kahuna (ka-who-na): Hawaiian word for healer or an experienced expert with a long lineage of cultural teachers. *Kahuna* were often experts and teachers in *po'okela,* Hawaiian excellence.

karoshi: Japanese word meaning "death from overwork." *Karoshi* has become a leading cause of death in Japan and is their version of TSS.

ke Akua (kay-a-coo-ah): Hawaiian term meaning God, the Higher Power, or the Absolute. Connection with this Higher Power is seen as an essential aspect of *po'okela*.

kūpuna (coo-poo-na): Hawaiian word meaning wise elders. While the modern world tends to focus on seeking more and more new information, *po'okela* is based on keen awareness of the lessons of the past as taught by the *kūpuna*.

labyrinth: An ancient symbol conveying wholeness and the total interconnectedness of life. It is not a maze but a pattern of circular spiral paths to and from a center place. To successfully walk a labyrinth, we must find inner contentment, calmness, and connection with something more than ourselves. This is the same path to *po'okela,* sweet success.

locus (center) of control: A psychological term describing how people attribute the meaning, impact, and manageability of events in their lives. Sufferers of TSS tend to have an external locus of control ("outsighters") and feel they are the helpless victims of undeniable outside forces. Those who attain sweet *po'okela*-style success are more likely to have an internal locus of control ("insighters") and feel that they can impose their own meaning and terms on their lives.

lōkahi (low-ka-he): Hawaiian word meaning living and working in harmonious unity. It is the way of working of *po'okela*.

mākaukau? (mow-u-ka-u-ka-u): Hawaiian word asking, "Are you really ready?" To detoxify success and learn the *po'okela* style of sweet success, persons have to be very ready and willing to change their thinking and take back control of their own attention.

mana (mah-nah): Hawaiian word for supernatural or divine power or energy. In the *po'okela* way of working, it is the vital energy that must be honored, protected, and nurtured in all we do.

manawa (man-ah-va): Hawaiian word for time. *Mana* refers to spiritual energy and *wa* to a unit of measurement. *Manawa* thus refers to measuring one's life work in terms of spiritual rather than physical or mental energy.

mindfulness: A word first used by psychologist Ellen Langer to describe our unique human capacity to choose how, where, and for how long we will pay attention by filtering out what we don't want on our mind. (The opposite of "monkey mindedness." Sweet success requires being mindful.)

monkey mind: A term used in the Buddhist philosophy to denote surrendering our thinking and attention to our primitive encoding for reflexive, automatic, short-term, scattered attention. Toxic success is monkey minded because it involves mental multitasking and switching attention quickly from one thing to another without totally focusing or attending fully to meaning.

monological: A psychological term referring to self-consciousness and internal selfish thinking based on "I, me, mine." This has become a frequent way of thinking of the Western continental mind that can lead to TSS.

nānā 'ole (na-na-oh-lay): Hawaiian term meaning to disregard and not pay sufficient attention to what matters.

neurotheology: One of the three new sciences of sweet success; the field of study that examines the neurobiology of spiritual experience. Using advanced medical technology, it looks at how the brain is wired to allow us to suspend our sense of self, time, and place and to feel totally connected with everything and everyone. It shows how focusing attention can quiet the selfish, time-sensitive areas of the brain and result in an intense transcendent experience.

oceanic thinking: The way of thinking of Polynesia, referring to a boundary-free, collectivist thought process. It is the "water logic" described by psychologist Edward de Bono that flows, takes into consideration the context and circumstance of the discourse, and relates to the ability to find humor in life.

'ohana (oh-ha-na): Hawaiian word meaning family, implying a broad and inclusive view of family as all of those for and with whom we live and work, including those who have passed away.

'oia'i'o (oh-e-ah-e-oh): Hawaiian word meaning to impart integrity in all that we say and do; a key value of *po'okela.*

pono (poh-no): Hawaiian word for working, living, and loving in total and accountable alignment with the land, our family, our ancestors, and the Higher Power. It also means living with goodness and morality, and doing things correctly and in the proper way that benefits all others and the land. It is another key value of *po'okela.*

po'okela (poh-oh-kay-la): Hawaiian word meaning excellence accomplished through shared values rather than personal objectives. It is the hundreds-of-years-old Hawaiian model of leading a life that causes shared success to happen. It is the basis for the success detoxification program.

psychological absenteeism: A form of adult attention deficit disorder, it means being mentally at work when we should be at home and mentally at home when we should be at work. The failure of marriages and families associated with TSS relates to this absenteeism, and researchers estimate that workers who are psychologically absent cause the loss of millions of American business dollars.

psychoneuroimmunology (PNI): One of the three new sciences of sweet success. This field, founded by psychologist George F. Solomon, studies the interaction between how we think and feel and the immune system. Research in this field has documented the immune-depressing effects of toxic success syndrome.

relaxed affiliation syndrome (RAS): The concept developed by psychologist David McClelland that refers to someone who is not primarily concerned with power and control, values intimate connection over personal control, and is calmly contented in their working, living, and loving. It is a characteristic of sweet, or *po'okela,* success. Research in PNI shows that RAS correlates with a balanced immune system.

rock logic: A term coined by physician and psychologist Edward de Bono that refers to rigid, absolute, "I'm right, you're wrong," boundary-based thinking. It is a common way of thinking of the toxically successful. This is the typical logic of continental thinking, and its separatist thinking can lead to the sense of isolation that comes with toxic success.

self-interest norm (SIN): A concept introduced by psychologist Barry

Schwartz to describe the liberal individualism of narcissistic orientation to living, working, and loving that has become the official ideology of the modern American way to succeed. It is based on the continental, individualistic rock logic of the Western mind as opposed to the oceanic, collectivist water logic of Polynesia. A *kupuna* summarized the difference in these ways of thinking by saying, "One rock plus one rock is still two rocks. Water added to water is more water."

spaving: The self-delusion and falsely comforting idea that one can "spend to save," a false belief encouraged by the consumerist culture feeding the ever increasing wants of the toxically successful.

sweet success: A sense of shared contentment, persistent calmness, and loving connection with everyone and everything. Sweet success tends to happen to those willing to work, live, and love by the values of *po'okela.*

synesthesia: A psychological concept referring to a mixing or crossing of the senses. The word derives from Greek, meaning "to perceive together." An example is when someone seems to feel lightning and see thunder, or feels in her bones how a child looks. It is a way of relating to the world with an open mind and heart that allows a full and unique experience of the simplest and most basic aspects of daily life. This is more easily accomplished through water logic than rock logic.

tortoise mind: Psychologist Guy Glaxton's term for the opposite of "hare brain," it refers to a slower, more intuitive, patient thinking that tolerates and even enjoys uncertainty, confusion, and examining rather than answering the question. *Po'okela* requires a tortoise mind, which thinks with oceanic, water logic.

toxic success syndrome (TSS): A chronic sense of being overwhelmed with too much to do, too many choices to make, too much information to process, too fast of a pace to keep up with, and too little attention left to focus on calmly and joyfully sharing the simple but profound things in life.

water logic: A term coined by Dr. Edward de Bono referring to a more fluid, boundary-free, collectivist, unselfish way of thinking. It easily flows back and forth, tolerates dissonance, and is free of quick judgmental decisions and competitive, self-protective discourse. It is the logic of the oceanic thinking that underlies *po'okela.*

BIBLIOGRAPHY

Ahuvia, Aaron. "Well-Being in Cultures of Choice: A Cross-Cultural Perspective." *American Psychologist* 56, no. 1 (January 2001): 77.

Alighieri, Dante. *The Divine Comedy*. Translated by Allen Mandelbaum. New York: Bantam Books, 1980.

"All in the American Family." *Time*, 13 June 1988, 74.

Appels, A., P. Hoppener, and P. Muldur. "A Questionnaire to Assess Premonitory Symptoms of Myocardial Infarction." *International Journal of Cardiology* 15 (1987): 15–24.

Aronson, Elliot. *The Sacred Animal*. 2d ed. San Francisco: W. H. Freeman, 1976.

Artress, Lauren. *Walking a Sacred Path: Rediscovering the Labyrinth as a Spiritual Tool*. Berkeley, CA: Berkeley Publishers, 1996.

Azar, Beth. "A New Stress Paradigm for Women." *Monitor on Psychology* 31, no. 7 (July/August 2000): 42–43.

Beck, C. J. *Nothing Special: Living Zen*. San Francisco: Harper San Francisco, 1993.

Begley, Sharon. "Religion and the Brain." *Newsweek*, 7 May 2001, 50–59.

————. "The Science of Laughs." *Newsweek*, 9 October 2000, 75–76.

Benson, R. "Further Notes on the Relationship Between Productivity of Machines Requiring Attention at Random Intervals." *Journal of the Royal Statistical Society* 14, no. 2 (1952): 200–210.

Bertman, Stephen. *Hyperculture: The Human Cost of Speed*. West Port, CT: Praeger, 1998.

Blum, M. *The Day-Care Dilemma*. Lexington, MA: Heath, 1983.

Bohm, David. "Meaning and Information." In *The Search for Meaning*, by Paavo Pylkkanen Wellingborough, Northamptonshire, England: Crucible, 1989.

Bruhn, J. G., A. Paredes, C. A. Adsett, and S. Worlf. "Psychological Predictors of Sudden Death in Myocardial Infarction." *Journal of Psychosomatic Research* 18 (1974): 187–191.

Buber, Martin. *Between Man and Man*. New York: Macmillan, 1965.

————. *The Knowledge of Man: Selected Essays*. Atlantic Highland, NJ: Humanities Press International, 1965.

Burns, Lee. *Busy Bodies*. New York: W. W. Norton and Company, 1993.

Cannon, Walter B. *The Wisdom of the Body*. New York: W. W. Norton and Company, 1942.

Carlin, P. "The Jackpot in Television's Future." *New York Times Magazine*, 28 February 1993, 36–41.

Carpenter, Siri. "Everyday Fantasia: The World of Synesthesia." *Monitor on Psychology* 32, no. 3 (March 2001): 26–29.

_____. "Sights Unseen." *Monitor on Psychology* (April 2001): 54–57.

Carrithers, Michael. *Why Humans Have Cultures: Explaining Anthropology and Social Diversity*. Oxford, England: Oxford University Press, 1992.

Carson, G. *Corn Flake Crusade*. New York: Rinehart, 1957.

Choi, Ian, et al. "Causal Attribution Across Cultures." *Psychological Bulletin* 125 (1999): 47–63.

Collier, James Lincoln. *The Rise of Selfishness in America*. New York: Oxford University Press, 1991.

Collinge, W. *Subtle Energy: Awakening to the Unseen Forces in Our Lives*. New York: Warner Books, 1998.

Convention News, no. 1, 13 February 2001.

Cousins, Norman. *Head First: The Biology of Hope*. New York: E. Dutton, 1989.

Csikszentmihalyi, Mahaly. *The Evolving Self*. New York: HarperCollins, 1993.

_____. Flow: *The Psychology of Optimal Experience*. New York: HarperCollins, 1991.

Darwin, Charles. *On the Origin of Species by Means of Natural Selection*. Chap. 3. London: John Murray, 1859.

Davenport, Thomas H., and John C. Beck. *The Attention Economy*. Boston, MA: Harvard Business School Press, 2001.

De Bono, Edward. *I Am Right, You Are Wrong: From Rock Logic to Water Logic*. New York: Viking Books, 1991.

Deci, E. L., et al. *Journal of Personality and Social Psychology* 3 (1981): 237–249.

de Graaf, John, David Wann, and Thomas Taylor. *Affluenza: The All-Consuming Epic*. San Francisco: Berrett-Koehler Publishers, 2001.

Dossey, Larry. *Meaning and Medicine*. New York: Bantam Books, 1991.

_____. "The Right Man Syndrome: Skepticism and Alternative Medicine." *Alternative Therapies* 4, no. 3 (May 1998): 12–19.

_____. "Work and Health: Of Isolation, Sisyphus, and Barbarian Beds." *Alternative Therapies* 3 (January 1997): 8–14.

Drug Enforcement Administration testimony before the Committee on Education and the Workplace, Subcommittee on Early Childhood, Youth, and Families. 106th Congress, Second Session, 16 May, 2000.

Durning, Alan Thein. "Are We Happy Yet?" In *Ecopsychology: Restoring the Earth, Healing the Mind*, edited by T. Roszak, M. E. Gomes, and A. D. Kanner. San Francisco: Sierra Club Books, 1995.

Einstein, Albert. As quoted in *The Concise Oxford Dictionary of Quotations*. 3d ed. Edited by A. Parington. New York: Oxford University Press, 1993.

Eliot, Robert S., and Breo, D. L. "Are You a Hot Reactor? Is It Worth Dying For?" *Executive Health* 20, no. 10 (1984): 1–4.

Ellison, Harlan. *Amazing Stories*. 5th ed. New York: Harper and Row, 1976.

Fassel, Diane. *Working Ourselves to Death*. San Francisco: Harper San Francisco, 1990.

Fortune, James W. "Mega High-Rise Elevators." *Elevator World* 43, no. 7 (1995).

Friedman, Meyer, N. Fleishmann, and V. A. Price. "Diagnosis of Type A Behavior Pattern." In *Heart and Mind: The Practice of Cardiac Psychology,* 179–193. Edited by R. Allan and S. Scheidt. Washington, D.C.: American Psychological Association, 1996.

Friedman, N. "Cardiovascular Response to Rate of Speech." *Journal of Cardiovascular Nursing* 3 (1994): 111–117.

Friedman, Thomas. "New Age: Politicians Ignore the Issues That Are Changing Our World." *The Dallas Morning News*, 15 May 2000, 11A.

Frijda, Nico H. "The Laws of Emotion." *American Psychologist* 43 (1988): 349–358.

Fromm, Erich. *To Have or To Be?* New York: Bantam, 1982.

Galloway, J. L. "Loose Ship to Sink Skip?" *U. S. News and World Report*, 2 April 2001, 25.

Gergen, Kenneth J. *The Saturated Self: Dilemmas of Identity in Contemporary Life*. New York: Basic Books, 1992.

Glaxton, Guy. *Hare Brain, Tortoise Mind*. Hopewell, NJ: The Ecco Press, 1997.

Gleick, James. *Chaos: The Making of a New Science*. New York: Penguin Books, 1987.

————. *Faster: The Acceleration of Just About Everything*. New York: Pantheon Books, 1999.

Glisky, et al. "Absorption, Openness to Experience, and Hypnotizability." *Journal of Personality and Social Psychology* 60 (1991): 263–272.

Gorney, Roderic. *The Human Agenda*. New York: Simon and Schuster, 1972.

Hafen, B. Q. et al. *Mind/Body Health: The Effects of Attitudes, Emotions, and Relationships*. Boston: Allyn and Bacon, 1996.

Hanson, G. *The Joy of Stress*. Kansas City: Andrews, McMeel, and Parker, 1986.

Heraclitus. Fragments 20 and 21.

Horney, Karen. *The Neurotic Personality of Our Time*. New York: W. W. Norton and Company, 1937.

Jamison, K. R. "Manic-Depressive Illness and Creativity." *Scientific American* (February 1995): 62–67.

Jemmott, J. B., C. Hellman, D. C. McClelland, et al. "Motivational Syndromes Associated With Natural Killer Cell Activity." *Journal of Behavioral Medicine* 13, no. 1 (1990): 53–73.

Jenkins, C. D. "Psychological and Social Precursors of Coronary Artery Disease." *New England Journal of Medicine* 284 (1971): 244–255.

Jones, J., and W. Wilson. *An Incomplete Education.* New York: Ballantine Books, 1987.

Justice, Blair. *Who Gets Sick: Thinking and Health.* Houston, TX: Peak Press, 1987.

Kabat-Zinn, Jon. *Full Catastrophe Living.* New York: Delta Books, 1990.

Kagan, Jerome. *Unstable Ideas: Temperament, Cognition, and Self.* Cambridge, MA: Harvard University Press, 1989.

Kaminer, Wendy. *I'm Dysfunctional, You're Dysfunctional.* Reading, MA: Addison Wesley, 1992.

Kanahele, George Huʻeu Sanford. *Kū Kanaka, Stand Tall: The Search for Hawaiian Values.* Honolulu: University of Hawaiʻi Press, 1986.

Karsh, Ellen. "Bungee Jumping? I'd Rather Watch 'Rosie.'" *Newsweek,* 27 November 2000, 16–17.

Katra, Jane, and Russell Targ. *The Heart of the Mind.* Novato, CA: New World Library, 1999.

Klerman, G. L., et al. "Birth Cohort Trends in Rates of Major Depressive Disorder Among Relatives of Patients with Affective Disorder." *Archives of General Psychiatry* 42 (1985): 689–693.

Kohn, Alfie. *No Contest: The Case Against Competition.* Boston: Houghton Mifflin Company, 1986.

Kolata, G. "A Vat of DNA May Become Fast Computer of the Future." *New York Times,* 11 April 1995, B5.

Kropotkin, Petr. *Mutual Aid: A Factor in Evolution.* 1902. Reprint, Boston: Extending Horizons Books, 1955.

Krutch, Joseph Wood. *The Modern Temper: A Study and a Confession.* New York: Harcourt, Brace, and World, 1956.

Kuhn, Clifford C. "The Stages of Laughter." *Journal of Nursing Jocularity* 4, no. 2 (1994): 34–35.

Kundtz, D. *Stopping: How to Be Still When You Have to Keep Going.* Berkeley, CA: Conari Press, 1998.

Langer, Ellen J. *Mindfulness.* Reading, MA: Addison Wesley, 1989.

Larson, R. J., E. Diener, and R. S. Cropanzano. "Cognitive Operations Associated with Individual Differences in Affect Intensity." *Journal of Personality and Social Psychology* 53, no. 4 (October 1987): 767–774.

Lawson, L. A., and V. A. Jackson, eds. "Questions They Never Ask Me." 1977. Reprinted in *Conversations with Walker Percy.* Jackson, MS: University Press of Mississippi, 1985.

Leakey, R., and R. Lewin. *The Sixth Extinction: Patterns of Life and the Future of Mankind.* New York: Doubleday, 1995.

Lefcourt, H. M. *Locus of Control: Current Trends in Theory and Research.* Hillsdale, NJ: Earlbaum, 1976.

Levey, Joel, and Michelle Levey. *Living in Balance.* Berkeley, CA: Conari Press, 1998.

Lohrer, B.T., et al. "A Meta-Analysis of the Relation of Job Characteristics to Job Satisfaction." *Journal of Applied Psychology* 70 (1985): 280–289.

Lovelock, J. E. *Gaia.* New York: Oxford University Press, 1987.

Mack, Arien, and Irvan Rock. *Inattentional Blindness.* Cambridge, MA: MIT Press, 1998.

Manager's Magazine, August 1992.

Maslow, Abraham, and B. G. Maslow. *Abraham Maslow: A Memorial Volume.* Monterey, CA: Brooks/Cole, 1972.

McClelland, David C. *The Achieving Society.* Princeton, NJ: Van Nostrand, 1961.

————. "Inhibited Power Motivation and High Blood Pressure in Men." *Journal of Abnormal Psychology* 88 (1979): 182–190.

McClelland, David C., et al. "Stressed Power Motivation, Sympathetic Activation, Immune Function, and Illness." *Journal of Human Stress* 6 no. 2 (1980): 11–19.

McWilliams, Peter. *Ain't Nobody's Business If You Do: The Absurdity of Consensual Crime in a Free Society.* Los Angeles: Prelude Press, 1993.

Meeker, Joseph W. *The Comedy of Survival: Literary Ecology and a Play Ethic.* 3d ed. Tucson, AZ: University of Arizona Press, 1997.

Merten, Robert K. *The Technological Society.* New York: Knopf, 1964.

Miller, Dale T. "The Norm of Self-Interest." *American Psychologist* 54, no. 12 (December 1999): 1053-1059.

Miller, Timothy. *How to Want What You Have: Discovering the Magic and Grandeur of the Ordinary.* New York: Henry Holt and Company, 1995.

Myers, David G. *The American Paradox.* New Haven and London: Yale University Press, 2000.

————. *The Pursuit of Happiness: Who Is Happy and Why.* New York: William Morrow and Company, 1992.

Nakaso, D. "Inquiry Focuses on Style of Leadership." *Honolulu Advertiser*, 14 March 2001, 1.

Newberg, Andrew, and Eugene D'Aquili. *Why God Won't Go Away: Brain Science and the Biology of Belief.* New York: Ballantine Books, 2001.

New World Dictionary. 2d ed. New York: Prentice Hall Press, 1984.

Niemi, R. G., et al. *Trends in Public Opinion: A Compendium of Survey Data.* New York: Greenwood Press, 1989.

Norwid, C. As quoted in *Analysis of Happiness,* by Wladyslaw Tatarkiewicz. The Hague: Maartinus Nijhoff, 1976.

Nozik, Robert. *Anarchy, State, and Utopia.* New York: Basic Books, 1974.

Oppenheim, Martin. *Speaking/Writing of God: Jewish Philosophical Reflections on the Life with Others.* Albany, NY: State University of New York Press, 1997.

Ornish, Dean. *Love and Survival: The Scientific Basis for the Healing Power of Intimacy.* New York: HarperCollins, 1997.

Ornstein, R., and D. Sobel. *Healthy Pleasures.* New York: Addison Wesley, 1989.

Pathways 5, no. 6, 22. Riverside, CA: Center for Contemplative Christianity, 1966.

Peale, Norman Vincent. *The Power of Positive Thinking.* New York: Fawcett Books, 1952.

Pearsall, Paul. *The Heart's Code: Tapping the Wisdom and Power of Our Heart Energy.* New York: Broadway Books, 1998.

————. *Superimmunity: Master Your Emotions and Improve Your Health.* New York: McGraw-Hill, 1997.

————. *Super Joy.* New York: Bantam Books, 1990.

Percy, Walker. "Questions They Never Asked Me." Reprinted in *Conversations with Walker Percy,* edited by L. A. Lawson and V. A. Jackson. Jackson, MS: University of Mississippi Press, 1985.

Plato. *Phaedo.*

Popper, K. *The Open Society and Its Enemies.* London: Routledge and Kegan Paul, 1945.

Powers, R. "American Dreaming: The Limitless Absurdity of Our Belief in an Infinitely Transformative Future." *New York Times Magazine*, 7 May 2000, 66–67.

Prigogine, I., and I. Stengers. *Order Out of Chaos.* New York: Bantam Books, 1984.

Pukui, H. K., and S. H. Elbert. *Hawaiian Dictionary.* Honolulu: University of Hawai'i Press, 1986.

Rice, Phillip L. *Stress and Health.* Monterey, CA: Brooks/Cole Publishing Company, 1987.

Rifkin, Jeremy. *Time Wars: The Primary Conflict in Human History.* New York: Henry Holt, 1987.

Robbins, L. N., et al. "Lifetime Prevalence of Specific Psychiatric Disorders in Three Sites." *Archives of General Psychiatry* 41 (1984): 949–958.

Ruben, Harvey L. *Competing.* New York: Pinnacle Books, 1981.

Russell, Peter. *Waking Up in Time: Finding Inner Peace in Times of Accelerating Change.* Novato, CA: Origin Press, 1998.

Salameh, Waleed A. "The Power of 'It Doesn't Matter.'" *Humor and Health Journal* 9, no. 2 (June 2000).

Sampson, Edward E. "Reinterpreting Individualism and Collectivism: Their Religious Roots and Monologic Versus Dialogic Person-Other Relationships." *American Psychologist* 55 no. 12 (2000): 1425–1431.

Sandburg, Carl. "The Sins of Kalamazoo." In *The Complete Poems of Carl Sandburg.* New York: Harcourt Brace Jovanovich, 1970.

Sapolsky, Robert M. "The Price of Propriety." *The Sciences* 36, no. 4 (1996): 14–16

_____. *Why Zebras Don't Get Ulcers.* New York: W. H. Freeman and Company, 1994.

Schwartz, Barry. *The Battle for Human Nature.* New York: W. W. Norton and Company, 1986.

_____. "Psychology, Idea Technology, and Ideology." *Psychological Science* 8 (1997): 21–27.

_____. "Self-Determination: The Tyranny of Freedom." *American Psychologist* 55, no. 1 (January 2000): 79–88.

Selligman, M. E. P. *Helplessness: On Depression, Development, and Death.* San Francisco: Freeman, 1975.

_____. *Learned Optimism.* New York: Alfred A. Knopf, 1991.

Shellenberger, Sue. *Wall Street Journal,* 5 January 1998.

Simon, Herbert. "Designing Organizations for an Information-Rich World." In *The Economics of Communication and Information,* edited by D. M. Lamberton. Cheltenham, England: Edward Elgar, 1997.

Simpson, George Gaylord. *The Meaning of Evolution.* New Haven, CT: Yale University Press, 1949.

Snodgrass, S. E. "The Effects of Walking Behavior on Mood." Unpublished paper presented at the 1986 meeting of the American Psychological Association in Washington, D.C.

Solomon, George F., and R. H. Moos. "Emotions, Immunity, and Disease: A Speculative Theoretical Integration." *Archives of General Psychiatry* 11 (1974): 657–674.

Solomon, Richard L. "The Opponent Process Theory of Acquired Motivation: The Costs of Pleasure and the Benefits of Pain." *American Psychologist* 35 (1980): 691–712.

Solomon, R. L., et al. "An Intensive Psychoimmunologic Study of Long-Surviving Persons with AIDS." *Annals of the New York Academy of Sciences* 496 (1987): 647–655.

Stanley, Thomas J., and William D. Danko. *The Millionaire Next Door.* Atlanta: Longstreet Press, 1996.

Strack, F., et al. "Inhibiting and Facilitating Conditions of the Human Smile: A Nonobtrusive Test of the Facial Feedback Hypothesis." *Journal of Personality and Social Psychology* 54 (1988): 768–777.

Strakosch, G. R. "A New Dimension in Elevator Monitoring." *Elevator World* 42, no. 8 (1994).

"Stressed Workers Calling in Sick, Report Says." *Honolulu Advertiser*, 26 September 1999, 20.

Thoreau, H. D. "Economy." In *Walden.*

Toynbee, Arnold J. *A Study of History.* Adapted by D. C. Sommerville. London: Oxford University Press, 1987.

Triadus, H. C., C. McCuskee, and H. C. Hui. "Multimethod Probes of Individualism and Collectivism." *Journal of Personality and Social Psychology* 59 (1990): 1006–1020.

Twitchell, J. *Carnival Culture: The Trashing of Taste in America.* New York: Columbia University Press, 1992.

U.S. News and World Report, 18 March 1991, 13 January 1997, 26 March 2001.

Vulliamy, E. "If You Don't Have Time to Take In All the Information in This Report, You Could Be Suffering from a Bout of Information Fatigue Syndrome." *Guardian,* 15 October 1996.

Wall Street Journal, 8 April 1997, B1.

Walsh, R., and D. Shapiro. "Well Being and Relationship." In *Beyond Health and Normality*, edited by R. Walsh and D. Shapiro. New York: Van Nostrand Reinhold Company, 1983.

Webster's Third New International Dictionary. 3rd. ed. Springfield, MA: Merriam-Webster, Inc., 1993

Wheatly, M. I. *Leadership and the New Science.* San Francisco: Berrett-Koehler Publishers, 1994.

White, J. *The Meaning of Science and Spirit.* New York: Paragon House, 1990.

Wilbur, Ken. *No Boundaries.* Boston: New Science Library, 1979.

_____. "Where It Was, There Shall I Become: Human Potential and the Boundaries of the Soul." In *Beyond Health and Normality,* edited by R. Walsh and D. Shapiro. New York: Van Nostrand Reinhold Company, 1983.

Wiley, T. S., and B. Formby. *Lights Out: Sleep, Sugar, and Survival.* New York: Pocket Books, 2000.

Wilson, E. O. "Is Humanity Suicidal?" *New York Times Magazine* 30, May 1993.

Winokur, Jon. *The Portable Curmudgeon*. New York: New American Library, 1987.

Wright, B. "Here Comes the Backlash." *Fortean Times* 106 (1998): 42.

Wurman, Saul. *Information Anxiety*. New York: Doubleday, 1989.

Yarrow, Marian Radke, et al. "Learning Concern for Others." *Developmental Psychology* 8 (1973): 240–260.

INDEX

adaptation, 42
adrenal glands, 116
affluenza, 5, 77
  defined, 329
ahonui, 224, 254, 329
  defined, 329
Ahuvia, Aaron, 285
akahai, 223, 329
alcohol abuse, 120
Alighieri, Dante, 201, 217
aloha, 63, 223–224
  ahonui, 224
  akahai, 223
  defined, 327
  five factors of, 243
  haʻahaʻa, 224
  lōkahi, 223
  ʻoiaʻiʻo, 224
  values of, 259
American Institute of Stress, 261
anxiety, 99–100
appearance, 115–116
attention, 49, 52, 56, 70–74, 90, 98, 101
  altering, 50
attention deficit disorder (ADD), 51, 53, 69,
    71, 99, 158, 212, 213
  defined, 329
attention management, 54–55
  defined, 329
ʻaumakua, 62
  defined, 329
awareness, 50, 51

B-lymphocytes (B-cells), 114
balance, 184
baraka, 161
Beck, John C., 52, 301, 329
Begley, Sharon, 289
Bertman, Stephen, 100, 235, 267
Biondi, Matt, 107
bipolar disorder, 77
Blake, William, 77
blood thickening, 119
Bonaparte, Napoleon, 139
books, 211–213

Boston University, 110
Bradshaw, John, 186
Bristol University, 104
Browning, Robert, 138
Buber, Martin, 273, 287, 288
Buddhism, 51, 218
Burns, George, 137
Burns, Lee, 235, 300
busyness, 55–56
Byron, Lord, 77

calming down, 57, 247–271
  antsyness, 248
  choices, 251–252
  ignorance, 252
  motion sickness cures, 268–270
  satisfaction, 260–261
  short-range vertical transport system,
    248
Camus, Albert, 199
Cannon, Walter, 129
cardiovascular system, 190
Carlin, George, 143
Carlyle, Thomas, 299
Carpe diem, 175
Carpenter, Siri, 245
Carrithers, Michael, 289
catastrophe, 183
chaos, 179
childhood, 40
  attention neglect, 45–48
  self-esteem, 43
  See also parenting
Choi, Ian, 286
cholesterol, 118–119
chrono-centrism, 212
Churchill, Winston, 77, 139
Clafford, Patricia, 137
codependence, 186
cognitive dissonance, 221
Collier, James Lincoln, 187
Columbus, Christopher, 225
commoditization, 235
Competing, 83

competition, 82–83, 109–112, 121, 139–140
  inspirationalists, 126–129
  motivationalists, 126–129
competitive default mode, 96–97
computers, 255–256, 287
  cyber-intimacy, 68
consumerism, 69, 143–144
contentment, 57, 101, 232–233
contentment calendar, 165–166
continental thinking, 330
Cousins, Norman, 86
cramming, 264–265
Csikszentmihalyi, Mihaly, 98, 100, 283, 331
culturally creative, 80–81, 84
Cutler, Laurel, 145
cutting back, 265–266
cyclothymia, 77–79, 145
  defined, 330

Danko, William D., 237
D'Aquili, Dr. Eugene, 275
Darwin, Charles, 124, 261–262
  digital Darwinism, 215
Davenport, Thomas, 52, 301, 329
daycare centers, 46
de Bono, Edward, 333–335
de Graaf , John, 5, 77, 329
debt, 68, 144–147
Department of Human Planning, 300
depression, 87, 99–100, 194
deprivation domino effect, 46
Derber, Charles, 70–71
detoxification program, 204, 263–264, 276
  calming down, 304
  connecting always, 304
  contentment, 304
  motion sickness cures, 268–270
diabetes, 118
dialogical, 286–288
  defined, 330
Dickinson, Emily, 137
diet, 87, 140, 292–293
digestive shutdown, 118
Dillard, Annie, 1
dis-imagination, 257

Disney, Walt, 139
distractions, 202–203
Divine Comedy, 217
Dolins, Ilene, 145
Dossey, Larry, 90, 93, 290
Douglas, Michael, 69–70
Drucker, Peter, 136
Durning, Alan Thein, 64, 148, 246
Dying for Information, 156
Dylan, Bob, 137
dysthymia, 78–79
  defined, 330

Eastern culture, 219, 252, 286, 287
ecopsychology, 64
Eeyore syndrome, 162, 165
Einstein, Albert, 77, 92–93, 185, 262
Eliot, Dr. Robert, 189
Eliot, T.S., 83, 247, 266
Ellis, Tutu Mana, 63
Ellison, Harlan, 208
ELMMSEH program, 292–293
Emerson, Ralph Waldo, 136, 195, 229
Emotions, Immunity, and Disease, 174
endorphins, 117
energy cardiology, 43–44, 50, 57, 275
  defined, 330
evolution, 124
exercise, 67, 87, 292–293
exhaustion, 166–169
external locus of control, 58–60, 87

facial analysis, 152–154
facial appearance, 162
families
  See children; grandparents; parenting
Fantasia, 244
fifth force, 164
fight-or-flight response, 116, 191
finances, 237
flow of things, 98–99, 331
flux, 257–259
Fortune, James W., 248
Francis of Assisi, Saint, 137
freedom, 249–251

Friedman, Dr. Meyer, 152, 160
Friedman, Thomas, 90
Frijda, Nico, 194
Fromm, Erich, 23, 68
Fuller, Buckminster, 103, 137

Gandhi, Mahatma, 54
Gates, Bill, 238
Gauguin, Paul, 209
Gergen, Kenneth J., 259
giggle factor, 289–290
Glaxton, Guy, 104, 262, 329, 335
Gleick, James, 160, 188
glucocorticoids, 117
glucose, 118
Godbey, Geoffrey, 254
gorilla man, 57
Gorney, Roderic, 126
Gould, Stephen Jay, 124
Grace Cathedral, 305–307
grandparents, 60–62
greed, 69–70
Greene, Graham, 279
Grenfell, Wilfred T., 136

ha'aha'a, 224, 331
ha'iloa'a, 198
hālau, 81
Hamlet, 212
hānai, 63
happiness, 283–285
Harden, Garret, 184
Hardy, Oliver, 173
hare brain, 262
    defined, 331
Harris, Sydney J., 155, 208
Hawaiian culture, 62–63, 218–220, 224, 239
    time, 301–302
health, 87–88, 116–120, 292–293
heart, 50, 119
heart disease, 87
Henry, John, 171, 186, 196
Henry, Jules, 109
Herschel, Rabbi Abraham, 137
Hewett, Kawaikapuokalani, 137

Hinduism, 218
Hobbes, Thomas, 281
Holmes, Oliver Wendell, 208
Holy Spirit, 161
home, 68, 210–211
Home Shopping Network, 234, 253
ho'omaka hou, 227, 295
    defined, 331
Horace, 175
hormonal surges, 116–117
Horney, Karen, 122
hostility, 188
hot reactor, 189–191
    brakers, 189
    combined hot reactors, 189
    crashers, 190
    vessel constrictive hot reactors, 189
Hubbard, Ken, 36
hyperventilation, 119

imagination, 257
imbalance, 182
immune system, 86, 114
immunoglobulin A (IgA), 114
inattentional blindness, 57–58
    defined, 329
inattentive blindness, 209
information
    bombardment of, 52, 214–215, 255
    info-anxiety, 255
    information fatigue syndrome, 156–157, 255
inhibited power motive (IPM), 113, 115, 187, 191, 331
insight, 58–60, 164, 209
internal dialogue, 204
internal locus of control, 58–60
International Data Corporation, 157
internet, 68

Jackson, Storm, 134
James, Dr. Sherman, 171
James, William, 136
Japan, 96, 331
Jefferson, Thomas, 139, 267

jobs, 134–135
Jung, Carl, 85, 183

Ka 'ikena, 63
Kabat-Zinn, Jon, 183
Kagan, Jerome, 282
kahuna, 122, 163
   defined, 331
Kalālani, 63
Kaminer, Wendy, 196
Kanahele, George, 231, 301
karoshi, 96
   defined, 331
Karsh, Ellen, 94, 95
Katra, Jane, 49, 97
Kawaikapuokalani, 223
ke Akua, 332
Kennedy, John F., 138, 289
Kita, Joe, 79
Klein, Freada, 267
Knapp, Peter, 110
Kohn, Alfie, 121
Kornfield, Jack, 242
Kropotkin, Petr, 125
Krutch, Joseph Wood, 83
Kundtz, David, 175, 264
kūpuna, 145, 332
Kurtz, Les, 179

labyrinth, 306–308
   defined, 332
Langer, Ellen, 51, 332
laughter, 289–290, 293–295
Laurel, Stan, 173
Levey, Joel, 143
Levey, Michelle, 143
Leviathan, 281
liberal individualism, 258
Lincoln, Abraham, 137
Lindsey, Elizabeth, 215
literary ecology, 211–216
Lobardi, Vince, 138
locus of control, 332
lōkahi, 223, 332
love children, 142

Lowe, Peter, 128
lucid dreams, 96

Maastricht Questionnaire, 167
Machiavelli, 281
Mack, Dr. Arien, 57
mākaukau, 226, 332
mana, 161, 332
Manager's Magazine, 261
manawa, 301
   defined, 332
manic-depression, 77
Martin, Billy, 138
Maslow, Abraham, 71, 187, 245–246
materialism, 69, 233–235
McClelland, Dr. David, 113–115, 129, 130,
   142, 187, 331, 334
meaning meter, 90–91
meditative traditions, 71–72, 218
Meeker, Dr. Joseph, 216, 217
megbe, 161
Melville, Herman, 212, 215
Men's Health, 79
mental moments, 157
Merton, Robert K., 260
Miller, Dale T., 281
Miller, Jason, 138
Miller, Timothy, 241
mind walk, 155
mindfulness, 51, 332
misoneism, 220–222
Moby Dick, 215
Monday, 85–87, 98, 99
   Black Monday effect, 87, 90, 93, 105,
      330
monkey mind, 50–52, 58, 80, 235
   defined, 333
monological, 286–288
   defined, 333
Moore, Thomas, 137
more is better, 230
Morley, Christopher, 136
mortals, 27
motion sickness cures, 268–270
motivational speakers, 127

multitasking, 52–53, 56
Myers, David, 42, 195

nagging feeling, 88–89
nānā 'ole, 252, 254
    defined, 333
narrow-mindedness, 253–254
Naylor, Thomas H., 329
need, 41–42
neurotheology, 44, 274–276
    defined, 333
New York Times, 90
Newberg, Dr. Andrew, 275
Newman, John Henry Cardinal, 297
Newsweek, 94, 289
Newton, Sir Isaac, 163
Nike, 109
normalcy, 65–69
normalcy test, 71, 72–76
Norwid, Cyprian, 242
novel-philia, 225

oceanic thinking, 198, 204, 219, 220, 222,
    231, 333
'ohana, 62–63, 81
    defined, 333
'oia'i'o, 224, 333
Oppenheim, Martin, 287
opponent process theory, 194–195
optimal experience, 98
optimism, 193–197
orenda, 161
Ornish, Dr. Dean, 275
Osler, Sir William, 134
Otis Elevator Company, 248, 249
Otis, Minister Wayne, 191–193
outsight, 58–60, 80, 87, 164, 209

panoramic attention, 98
paradise, 206–208, 224
parenting, 40, 41, 45–46, 67
    attention neglect, 46–48
    praise, 42–43
    See also childhood
Pasteur, Louis, 177

pause panic, 298
Peale, Norman Vincent, 196
pester factor, 243
pestered person pleonasm, 204–206
pestered person test, 205–206
planet riding, 49
Plato, 195
pleonasm, 204
po 'okela, 17–18, 63, 81, 82, 134, 136,
    143–144, 148, 298–299
    characteristics of, 198
    defined, 43, 217–218, 334
    energy and, 161
    eternity and, 300
    four concepts of, 238
    logic of, 222
    pono, 284
    signs of attainment, 262, 264
    success and, 231
    translation, 44
Poe, Edgar Allen, 79
Polynesia, 209, 222, 224, 286, 287
pono, 334
poverty, 36
practicalness, 231
prana, 161
prioritize, 265–266
productivity, 143
psycho-toxic emotional waste, 159–160
psychological absenteeism, 99, 261
    defined, 334
psychologists, 177–178
psychoneuroimmunology (PNI), 43, 50,
    58–60, 174, 187
    defined, 334
    immune system, 86, 275–276
psychopathology of the average, 71
pulled through life, 6
pushed through life, 6

qi (chi), 161
quality time, 55
QVC (quality, value, convenience), 234

Radcliffe College, 196

Ray, Phil, 80
Rehnquist, Chief Justice William, 303
relaxed affiliation syndrome (RAS), 114,
    115, 119, 130, 187, 191
    defined, 334
Remen, Rachel Naomi, 193
renunciation, 239–240
retardation, 102–104
retirement, 93–95
Retton, Mary Lou, 127
Reuters Business Information, 156
Rice, Phillip, 60
Rifkin, Jeremy, 258
right man survey, 279–281
right man syndrome, 278
Ritalin, 329
ritual, 231–232
Robbins, Tony, 138, 186
rock logic, 334
Roseman, Ray, 160
Ruben, Harvey, 83
Russek, Linda, 330
Russell, Peter, 264–265

Salameh, Waleed, 290
Sampson, Edward E., 286
Sandburg, Carl, 261
Sapolsky, Robert, 188, 189
say when, 230
Schor, Juliet, 142–143
Schuler, Dr. Robert, 127
Schutz, Peter, 81–82
Schwartz, Barry, 250, 258, 282, 335
Schwartz, Gary, 330
Schwartzkopf, General Norman, 127
scientific method, 164
Seabrook, Jeremy, 148
self-assurance, 276–277
self-interest norm (SIN), 4, 18, 40, 69, 109,
    115, 281–282
    defined, 334
selfless life, 37
selflessness, 274–276
sex hormone dipping, 117–118
Shakespeare, William, 104, 138

shamans, 163
Shaw, George Bernard, 138
Shellenberger, Sue, 145
Sheppard, Dick, 134
shopping, 67, 68, 143–144, 233–235
silence, 92
Silverstein, Shel, 270
Simon, Herbert, 53
Sinai Hospital, 27, 149, 208
single photon emission computed
    tomography (SPECT), 274
Sisyphus reaction, 173
So what?, 290–292
Solomon, George F., 174, 334
Solomon, Richard, 194
soul-searching, 155
spaving, 68
    defined, 335
Spencer, Herbert, 124
Spock, Dr., 43
Stanford Research Institute, 97
Stanley, Arthur J., 137
Stanley, Thomas J., 237
stress, 112–113
    blood pressure, 190
    facial appearance, 162
    fight-or-flight-response, 190
    physiological signs of, 116–120
    recipe for stress soup, 190–191
stroke, 119, 191
substance abuse, 120
success
    defined, 140–141
    look of success, 152
    nature of, 136–137
    popular definition, 25
    the way to, 138
Success Fatigue Inventory (SFI), 167–169
sudden wealth syndrome, 36
sufficiency, 230–233
    assessment of, 235–237
    impaired, 234
    nature of, 245–246
    rituals, 243
sugar high, 118

surfing, 180–182
survival of the fittest, 124
sweat, 120
sweet success, 42
    calmness, 44
    connection, 44
    consciousness, 44
    contentment, 44
    defined, 4, 335
    formula for, 44
    psychology of, 177
    pull of, 6
    sufficiency and, 242–243
    wrong keys to success, 178–198
sympatho-adreno-medulary (SAM), 129
synesthesia, 244–245
    defined, 335
Szasz, Thomas, 232

Targ, Russell, 49, 97
Taylor, Shelly, 130
tend-and-befriend response, 130, 191
Tennyson, Alfred Lord, 77
tension trance, 209
Teresa, Mother, 137
The Attention Economy, 52
The Giving Tree, 270
The Millionaire Next Door, 237
The Prince, 281
The Problems of Daily Living Clinic, 27
Theory of Relativity, 92–93
thinking, 102
third thing, 93
Thoreau, Henry David, 79, 137, 260
thyroid hormones, 117
time, 301–302
time allocations, 300
time management, 54–55
Tinker, Grant, 138
Tobias, Randall, 146
tortoise mind, 262
    defined, 335
toxic success syndrome (TSS)
    anhedonia, 31
    anxiety, 32–33

characteristics of, 7
chrono-currency, 33
comparative values, 40
competitive values, 40
cynicism, 31
debt, 144–147
deficiency, 38, 81, 109, 157
defined, 4, 25, 335
depression, 32–33, 39, 81, 109, 157
depressive withdrawal, 30–31
detachment, 38, 81, 109, 157
diet, 35
disappointment, 38–39, 81, 109, 157
doubt, 38, 81, 109, 157
exercise, 35
external locus of control, 30
fatigue, 33
five D's of, 81, 109, 157, 215, 232
formula for, 37–39
grouchiness, 31
health, 35
inattentive blindness, 29–30
inhibited power syndrome (IPS), 34–35
ins and outs, 30–31
multitasking, 32
nervous energy, 30–31
normalcy of, 7
pestered feeling, 31–32
polyphasia, 32
power, 34–35
psychological absenteeism, 32–33
relationship exploitation, 33–34
self-interest norm (SIN), 40
self-sightedness, 29–30
sickness, 35–36
sleep patterns, 33
spiritual deficit disorder (SDD), 34–35
stress surrender, 30
survey, 149–152
symptoms of, 28–36
tyranny of freedom, 41
ups and downs, 30–31
weariness, 33
Tracy, E. Jean, 185
TV test, 139

Twain, Mark, 225
twenty-four/seven, 164–166
two-hundred-message-a-day economy, 53
type A personality, 152, 160, 187–189,
    197–198

umbrella woman, 57
University of California, 130, 300
University of Pennsylvania, 194
University of Windsor, 100
Unlimited Power, 186
Updike, John, 179
U.S. News and World Report, 213–215, 238

value of wanting, 240
Van de Post, Sir Laurens, 183
Van Dyke, Henry, 239
Van Vogt, A. E., 278
videotaped clinical examinations (VCE),
    152
vital energy, 161, 169
vital exhaustion, 160–161
vitalism, 164
Von Sternberg, Josef, 138

Wall Street, 69–70
Wall Street Journal, 145
Wann, David, 329

warriors, 186
Washington, Booker T., 136
water logic, 335
wealth, 36
Wechsler Intelligence Scale for Children
    (WISC), 102
Western thinking, 198, 218, 222, 286, 287
Whatley, Dennis, 127
Wilber, Ken, 185
Wilson, Colin, 278
winners, 27
word rate counts, 262–263
workaholic, 187–189, 191–193, 197–198
wrong keys to success, 178–198
    balance, 197
    balance stress, 179–184, 195
    optimism, 193–197
    personal power, 185–187
    positive thinking, 196–197
    type A personality, 187–189
    workaholic, 187–189
Wurman, Saul, 255

Yarrow, Marian Radke, 126
yesod, 161

Zen, 72, 299
Zigler, Zig, 127

ABOUT THE AUTHOR

Dr. Paul Ka'ikena Pearsall is a licensed clinical psychoneuroimmunologist, a specialist in the healing mind. He graduated as Distinguished Scholar from the University of Michigan, and received his master's and doctoral degrees in clinical and educational psychology from Wayne State University. He did postgraduate work at the Albert Einstein and Harvard Schools of Medicine.

He is founder and former director and chief of the Psychiatry Outpatient Problems of Daily Living Clinic at Sinai Hospital of Detroit. He was an adjunct professor in the Department of Psychiatry and Neurosciences at the Wayne State University School of Medicine, and was the director of Professional Education at the Kinsey Institute for Research in Sex, Gender, and Reproduction at Indiana University.

Dr. Pearsall is the author of over two hundred professional articles and fifteen best-selling books, including the *New York Times* No. 1 bestsellers *Super Immunity*, *Super Marital Sex*, and *The Pleasure Prescription*. His most recent book is *Miracle in Maui*, an account of his recovery from Stage IV cancer.

Dr. Pearsall is currently adjunct clinical professor at the University of Hawai'i, and is on the Board of Directors of the Hawai'i State Consortium for Integrative Health Care. He is a member of the heart transplant study team at the University of Arizona School of Medicine.

He has been awarded the *Rush Gold Medal* by the International Psychiatric Association, and has been designated as one of the most influential thousand scientists of the twentieth century by the Oxford University Biographical Society. In Spring 2002, he will be given the Scripps Clinic *Trailblazers Award* in Integrative Medicine. This prestigious award is only periodically given to major medical contributors who have established new approaches and theories in integrative medicine.

Dr. Pearsall is one of the most requested speakers in the world, having addressed AT&T, IBM, EDS, Sprint, Digital Corporation, Paramount Studios, and numerous other Fortune 500 companies. He regularly appears on national television and radio and presents Hawaiian lecture edu-concerts around the world with Kuhai Hālau O Kawaikapuokalani P 'Ōlapa Kahiko. He lives with his wife Celest Kalālani, in Honolulu, Hawai'i.

For further information on Dr. Pearsall's presentations, his e-mail is *kaikena@hawaii.rr.com.*